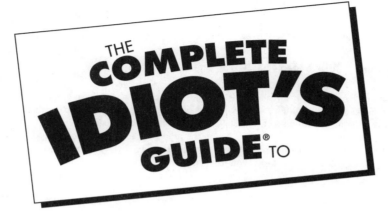

THE COMPLETE IDIOT'S GUIDE® TO

The Reformation & Protestantism

by James S. Bell Jr. and Tracy Macon Sumner

ALPHA

A Pearson Education Company

To my daughter Brigit Bell, predestined for glory as a daughter of the King.

Publisher: *Marie Butler-Knight*
Product Manager: *Phil Kitchel*
Managing Editor: *Jennifer Chisholm*
Senior Acquisitions Editor: *Renee Wilmeth*
Development Editor: *Michael Thomas*
Production Editor: *Billy Fields*
Copy Editor: *Joe Niesen*
Illustrator: *Jody Schaeffer*
Cover/Book Designer: *Trina Wurst*
Indexer: *Ginny Bess*
Layout/Proofreading: *Rebecca Harmon*

Contents at a Glance

Contents

Foreword

C. S. Lewis, the Oxford scholar and literary critic, once observed that nothing in history compared to a shoreline in geography. Historic events never happen in a vacuum and seldom is there a single cause which occasions specific events. History is too complex.

This is true of the Protestant Reformation. Many point to October 31st 1517, when Martin Luther nailed his 95 Theses to the door of the Cathedral Church at Wittenberg as the event that sparked the Reformation. But sparks mean little if there is nothing for them to ignite. The Roman, or Western, Church had produced plenty of its own kindling. The Waldenses had called papal authority into question as early as the 1170s. The schism that produced two popes, one in Avignon as well as Rome, provided more fuel for the fire that was to come. Wycliffe's call for reforms in the Church in England as well as the work of the Lollards who followed him added to the growing discontent. John Huss, the Bohemian, took his lead from Wycliffe and brought reformation interests to the Continent. Savonarola preached moral reform in Florence after that. Both Huss and Savonarola were burned at the stake as heretics but they contributed greatly to circumstances well prepared for Luther.

Economic issues also contributed to the inevitability of reformation. The peasant class was growing weary of exploitation and a growing middle class had an equally growing expectation to be enfranchised with a voice that could speak and would be validated. Politics also contributed to the tinderbox. Nations were beginning to challenge the old structures and traditions that sacrificed regional comforts and concerns to the overarching interests of the Church. Add to this the cultural, sociological, and scientific developments encouraged by the Renaissance. The humanists of the Academy were calling on the Church to consider reforms. This was the powder keg that Luther's spark ignited.

Luther was not interested, at first, in schism. He had offered up his Theses as debating points. He wanted to reform, not splinter, the Church. Some sought to silence him as they had those who preceded him. He was summoned to Worms, in 1521, and told to recant of his views. He refused, and the chasm between the Roman and Protestant could no longer be bridged.

Luther's primary message was that "the just shall live by faith." Those who would have the hope of Heaven did not have to earn God's favor by their works. It was *Sola Fide*, faith alone, that made one right before God; *Sola Gratia*, grace alone, not works. Luther claimed that the Scriptures were his only authority, *Sola Scriptura*; his teaching was based on the Word of God. He translated the Bible into the German vernacular, teaching that everyone should be free to read it and interpret it for himself. In this way Luther democratized the Faith.

History would show that the Reformation itself would splinter into many factions. Perhaps, in its first 1,500 years, the Church sacrificed some degree of truth for the sake of unity. In its last 500 years it could be said that she has sacrificed some of her unity for the pursuit of truth. Which is to be preferred? To say "The reader should decide for himself" owes itself to principles found in the teaching of the Reformation and its continuing influence. The Western world will never be quite the same because of the Reformation, and thinking people would be wise to understand its influence. *The Complete Idiot's Guide to the Reformation and Protestantism* opens a door, for the reader, to an important part of the past and may equally open some doors to understanding the future.

Jerry Root
Professor of Christian Education
Wheaton College

Introduction: What Do You Mean by "Reformation"?

Have you ever wondered why there are so many different kinds of churches in America today, why there seems to be a denomination of the Christian faith for just about any personal taste? Why are there Lutherans, Baptists, Methodists, Mennonites, Presbyterians, and Catholics when all of them basically practice the same faith: Christianity?

And furthermore, why is it that different denominations tend to dominate in different parts of the world? For example, why is the Catholic Church the thing in Italy, while in England Christians tend to worship at the Anglican Church? Why is Lutheranism popular in Germany, while Methodism is big in some parts of the United States?

Well, it isn't because someone simply decided to set up different kinds of churches in different parts of the world—for that matter, in different parts of the United States. It's much more complex than that—not to mention much more interesting.

There was a time when nearly all Christians in the known Christian world of Europe worshiped in the same church (the Roman Catholic Church) and followed its rules and regulations. From about the fourth century on, the Catholic Church wasn't just the dominant church in Europe—it was the *only* church.

During the Middle Ages the Catholic Church held almost absolute power in many areas of the lives of Europeans. The church and the governments of Europe were closely intertwined, and it seemed as if the European people were the ones getting squeezed. In a time and a culture in which we are used to seeing churches as the servants of people, it's hard to imagine a situation where it was the other way around. But that is exactly the way it was in Europe clear into the sixteenth century.

Throughout all those centuries, the Roman Catholic Church grew richer and richer, and more and more powerful. With all that money and power came corruption, materialism, and greed, and in time some people within the church—as well as some who branched off on their own—saw the need for reform. They wanted the church to return to its roots of the first few centuries of the Christian faith.

From about the twelfth century on, there were people who wanted reforms in the Catholic Church, but it wasn't until early in the sixteenth century that all the social, political, and educational pieces needed for a revolutionary religious movement were in place. It was then that a German monk named Martin Luther challenged the religious authorities in a town called Wittenberg to a debate concerning some of the church's practices.

Luther's 95 Theses, which was that written challenge to debate, quickly made their way around Europe, and before long a fire called the Protestant Reformation spread throughout Europe, burning so hot that it couldn't be extinguished.

An Exciting Time, Some Exciting People

We've written this book to give you an overview of the world-changing event that came to be known as the Protestant Reformation. We want to tell the story of the beginnings of the Christian faith, of how the Catholic Church became so dominant in Europe, and how a brave group of people we now call "reformers" gave Christians an option when it came to how they worshiped and where.

The Protestant Reformation—which started early in the sixteenth century and ran through the middle of the seventeenth—is one of the most exciting, fascinating times in the history of Western civilization. It included some of the most intriguing political developments, and some of the most memorable wars in history. There were confrontations and conflicts galore during the Protestant Reformation.

And then there were the people. Some of Western history's most compelling figures earned their fame through the Reformation. There were the Protestant reformers, men such as Luther, Ulrich Zwingli, John Calvin, John Knox, and Thomas Cranmer. Then there were the Catholic reformers—Erasmus, Ignatius Loyola, and Teresa of Avila, just to name a few. Finally, there were those religious and political leaders who opposed Protestantism in all its forms. That included emperors, popes, and monarchs.

There were major players in the Reformation, and there were minor players as well. There were great triumphs and great defeats on both sides. There were men and women who did great things for the cause of reform, and there were those who made mistakes—sometimes big mistakes.

As you make your way through this book, keep in mind that you're reading about fallible human beings living in a different time and place. Because of that, the story of the Reformation wasn't always pretty. The Protestant Reformation wasn't just an argument between Catholics and Protestants. It was far more than a minor disagreement between people of differing religious persuasions. It was a battle for the hearts and minds of the people in Europe, and in many ways it was a battle for control of its political, social, and economic institutions as well.

And when we say "battle," we mean that literally. When opposing sides of the Catholic/Protestant (and sometimes Protestant/Protestant) conflict couldn't settle their differences peacefully, they all too often went to the sword. It's sad but true that during the Protestant Reformation there were a series of religious wars and persecutions that cost the lives of untold millions of Europeans.

That part of the Reformation isn't something that Protestants or Catholics are proud of, but it is part of the history of the movements that made up the Protestant Reformation. And it has been pointed out that these things are further examples of the strength and resiliency of the Christian faith. Through the centuries, historians have marveled at this aspect of Christianity. This "religion" has not only survived persecutions (including some extremely violent ones), divisions, and diversions from its original message, but has thrived and grown in the face of them.

That's our short synopsis of the story we are about to tell you—the story of the Protestant Reformation. It's a story that is exciting, inspirational, mysterious, and violent—and often to the extremes!

But it's a story worth knowing a little about. After all, the Protestant Reformation has made a tremendous difference in the lives of people here in America.

What kinds of differences, you ask? Well, to find that out, you're going to have to read on!

Some Extras

We've included several sidebars per chapter, some of which we hope will help you better understand the material in the text, and some of which we hope will make this book even more interesting. Following are the sidebars we've included, including explanations of each one.

You Can Look It Up

"You Can Look It Up" sidebars define terms and events discussed in the text.

Going Deeper

By taking a look at "Going Deeper" sidebars, you can get a little extra information on different sides of the Reformation.

Protestant Pearls

Think of these sidebars as pearls of wisdom from the mouths or pens of some of history's greatest Protestants. Some are from the Reformation era, and some are from more modern times.

People You Should Know

There were all kinds of major and minor players in the Protestant Reformation. In our "People You Should Know" sidebars, we've furnished some profiles of some of the "lesser lights" who played a part in the movement, either as a proponent or an opponent.

Acknowledgments

The authors wish to thank Joris Heise for helping us achieve a tight deadline with his contribution on the reformed church in early America.

Special Thanks to the Technical Reviewer

The Complete Idiot's Guide to the Reformation and Protestantism was reviewed by an expert who double-checked the accuracy of what you'll learn here, to help us ensure that this book gives you everything you need to know about the Reformation and Protestantism. Special thanks are extended to Joris Heise.

Currently a special education teacher in the Dayton Public Schools and a part-time instructor of Classical Literature and Great Books in the Dayton, Ohio, area, Joris John Heise has been a professor of Biblical Theology in a seminary.

Trademarks

All terms mentioned in this book that are known to be or are suspected of being trademarks or service marks have been appropriately capitalized. Alpha Books and Pearson Education, Inc., cannot attest to the accuracy of this information. Use of a term in this book should not be regarded as affecting the validity of any trademark or service mark.

Part 1

The Christian Faith Before the Reformation

Most great social, political, and religious movements don't just happen on the spur of the moment. It takes preparation to get the world ready for a revolutionary movement. The Protestant Reformation was no exception. For several centuries leading up to the 1600s, the Christian world was being prepared for what would come to be known as the Protestant Reformation.

Almost from the very beginning of the first fifteen centuries of the establishment and spread of the Christian faith, the way was being made for the Reformation. First, there was the decay of the established church in the early Middle Ages, then the initial efforts to reform it during the latter Middle Ages. With that came the changes in politics, thinking, and technology that made the Reformation not just possible, but unavoidable.

Just What Are These Reformers Reforming, Anyway?

In This Chapter

- The Christian church takes root
- The look of the early church
- The growth and expansion of the church
- The apostle Paul's part in the formation—and *Reformation*— of the church

If you're going to have a reformation, the first thing you need is something to reform. And as important as having something to reform is having something to reform it *to*. In the case of the Protestant Reformation of the sixteenth century, the object of reform was the established and dominant church of that time—the Roman Catholic Church—which Martin Luther felt had moved away from the model recorded in the book of Acts in the Bible.

To understand why the Protestant Reformation started by Martin Luther is so important today, we need to define what we mean by "reformation." In this context, the word *reformation*—with a little "r"—means to make something better by changing it, in this case by restoring it to its original state. Luther's goal, and the goal of the many reformers before and after him, was to restore the church—which in the 1520s was almost exclusively Roman Catholic—to what they believed it was set up to look like back in the age of the apostles.

Like the reformers who went before him (and there were many), Martin Luther recognized that something was wrong with the way the church of his day did things. And while Luther didn't initially intend for his movement to cause a split from the church (at first, he wanted to reform the church from the inside), it began what can only be called a revolution in Europe.

We'll talk about the Reformation itself—as well as Martin Luther—in more detail later. But first, let's lay the groundwork for understanding it by describing what the reformers wanted to reform the church *to*: the original church of Christ and its practices and teachings, as described in the New Testament book of Acts.

Against All Odds: How It Started

When you look at the beginnings of Christianity, it seems a miracle that this new religion took hold, expanded, and grew to be the world's most widely practiced religious faith. In fact, it appeared that the faith was all but dead before it had a chance to get started.

Consider this: At the outset, those men and women—and keep in mind that in the beginning there weren't very many of them—who were the key figures in the establishment of that first Christian church were a disillusioned, discouraged, disappointed lot. They were in that condition because their plans and dreams for the future had been cruelly dashed.

In the year 30 C.E., Jesus, the revolutionary teacher who led a core group of twelve disciples as well as hundreds of other followers, was tried by the Roman authorities for what can be described as revolutionary ideas and activities, and then was executed on a cross in Jerusalem. And all of this with the blessings of the Jewish leaders and of the people he had so selflessly served.

This Is NOT What We'd Planned!

The arrest and crucifixion of Jesus wasn't supposed to be a part of the plan—at least as far as his closest friends were concerned. The way they saw it, they were joining a movement that would end in glorious victory over their enemies and in the establishment of a new world order.

Imagine their disappointment when their leader was hauled away.

The original disciples—those closest to Jesus, who believed they had been following the conquering messiah that all of Judaism had expected, but who had seen their master and teacher hauled away like a common criminal—had scattered after Jesus' death, their hearts broken, their hopes shattered.

Obviously, these people weren't in a frame of mind conducive to beginning the greatest religious movement in the history of humankind. They would be doing well just to carry on and return to the lives they'd lived before they ever met Jesus.

 **Protestant Pearls**

> When it is a question of our justification, we have to put away all thinking about the Law and our works, to embrace the mercy of God alone, and to turn our eyes away from ourselves and upon Jesus Christ alone.
>
> —John Calvin (1509–1564), French-born Reformation theologian

The Disciples Are Saying What?

At that time, it must have looked as if this religious movement later dubbed Christianity would never make it. Its leader was dead and buried and his disheartened and frightened followers scattered in every direction. But then something happened in the city of Jerusalem, something that changed the world forever. Within three days of the crucifixion, word began spreading around Jerusalem that Jesus—the same Jesus hundreds had watched die on a cross—was actually *alive*.

The people in and around Jerusalem had heard the rumors that Jesus had been seen alive, but couldn't believe it. Many of them had seen him die with their own eyes. What must have happened, they reasoned, was that someone—probably one of those low-lifes who followed the rabble-rouser Jesus around—had come and stolen the body. Somehow, they had snuck past the armed solider guarding the tomb, rolled that big rock away from the opening, and stolen the body. Not an easy caper to pull off, but you never knew what radicals like that were capable of.

The rumors didn't stop, and word was getting around that some of those closest to Jesus reported seeing him with their own eyes, hearing him speak with their own ears, and talking to him with their own mouths!

This Is Our Story, and We're Sticking to It

At first, even some of the disciples had a hard time buying it. As far as they were concerned, Jesus was dead, and as hard as it was to swallow what had happened to their master, they had to get over it and move on. It wasn't long before all of them were telling the same story.

To the disciples, it now appeared that Jesus was the conquering messiah after all, just not in the way they had expected when they traveled with him for the three years prior to his death, listening to his teachings and watching the way he lived his life.

The first chapter of Acts records how Jesus spoke with the disciples one last time before he ascended to heaven, leaving them with instructions and promising to give them the power they would need to follow through on those instructions. Jesus told them how they would be responsible for taking his message to the regions around Jerusalem, then "to the ends of the earth." The power to do those things, he said, would come in the person of the Holy Spirit, who would soon be sent to them.

Obviously, Jesus was talking of something huge going down in the lives of his followers, something that would change not just their lives, but the world as they knew it.

Happy Birthday, Dear Church

Just ten days after Jesus left came what Christians call the Day of *Pentecost*, that day when God sent his Spirit to those who had put their faith in Christ. The second chapter of the book of Acts tells us that all of Jesus' followers—there were about 120 of them, including the apostles and other disciples, as well as Jesus' mother Mary—had assembled that day to pray when there was the loud sound of rushing wind, and "tongues of fire" appeared and rested on each disciple. Acts also tells us that the disciples, these mostly uneducated and untrained Galileans, began speaking fluently in the various languages spoken by people from all over the world who were in Jerusalem in that day.

You Can Look It Up

Pentecost—the meaning of which is derived from the Greek word for "fiftieth"—was the day of the Jewish "Feast of Weeks," which took place seven weeks after the Passover. Acts records how it was on the day of Pentecost that the first Christians received the Holy Spirit, as Christ had promised in Acts chapter one.

Some witnesses of this event stood in awe at this demonstration of God's power; others insisted that the disciples were drunk. But Peter, the unquestioned leader of the disciples, spoke out and told them that these men and women weren't drunk. After all, it was only nine in the morning, and none of them had touched a drop! (And never mind how mere wine—even the best stuff around—could enable people to speak a language they didn't know!) Rather, Peter told them, they were witnessing what the Old Testament prophet Joel had foretold centuries before—that God would pour out his spirit on all people and that great miracles would accompany that outpouring (see Acts 2:17–21, Joel 2:28–32).

Having said that, Peter, this disciple the Bible tells us had only weeks before denied he knew Jesus, boldly announced that Jesus—the same Jesus who had performed healings and other miracles in their midst, who was betrayed by one of his closest followers, who had been arrested and crucified—was indeed alive and had sent his Holy Spirit as proof.

When those present heard Peter's words, they were cut to the quick and asked the apostles what they should do. Peter was ready with an answer: "Repent and be baptized, every one of you, in the name of Jesus Christ so that your sins may be forgiven" (Acts 2:37–38). The response to Peter's words that day was breathtaking. As a result of that one sermon on the streets of Jerusalem, some 3,000 people became Christians that day.

Not bad for a first-time preacher!

Nothing Can Stop Us Now!

The apostle Peter stepped into the role of leader of the fledgling church. He spoke boldly, bravely, and authoritatively, and he began performing miracles for all to see. Word spread of the goings-on in Jerusalem, and before long Peter and the apostle John, also one of the original twelve, were harassed for what they had been doing. They even spent time in the slammer and were threatened with physical harm if they didn't stop their preaching. Still, the church continued to grow, and the number of believers had soon risen to 5,000.

The known world had witnessed the birth of the Christian church, and from then on, nothing—not even the intense and often violent opposition the church faced—was going to stop this new "religion" from taking its place.

The Early Church: Not What We're Used To

When we in the Western world think of the word *church*, we picture steepeled buildings containing pews, stained-glass windows, altars, and pulpits from which the preacher delivers his sermons. We think of Sunday morning gatherings of people wearing their finest clothes, singing classic hymns, and offering up group prayers to God.

Protestant Pearls

Our clerics neither evangelize like the apostles, nor go to war like the secular lords, nor toil like laborers.

—John Wycliffe (1330–1384), English Reformer

However, the original church—that first-generation congregation of believers in the city of Jerusalem—looked nothing like the church of today. In the New Testament, the word *church* refers to the collection of believers themselves—not to the place where they met. We know that to be fact because the church back then didn't even have a regular meeting place. Believers met in the private homes of individual believers and sometimes in the local synagogues.

The first church was a fairly good-sized and closely knit community of believers who sometimes met and worshiped in the temple. Sometimes they assembled in different members' homes, where they listened intently to the disciples' teachings. Together, they celebrated their faith, met one another's physical and spiritual needs, and welcomed new members daily (see Acts 2:42–47).

When it came to church government, that first church in Jerusalem was a marvel of simplicity. It was a loosely constructed system wherein each believer was to look to the headship of Christ and to the leadership of the apostles, particularly Peter, "who sought the wisdom and direction of the Holy Spirit." It was only as the need arose—as the apostles died off and the church grew so rapidly—that the church developed a more organized system of government that included the offices of bishop, deacon, and other permanent and temporary offices in congregations. Some of those offices have remained a part of church government in one form or another to this day.

The first church didn't have the benefit of what was to become the New Testament, that collection of writings that make up the second part of the Bible. Instead, the believers in Jerusalem heard simple preaching with an emphasis on repentance, the death and *resurrection* of Jesus, and *baptism*. In those days, Luke tells us in the book of Acts, the preaching was often accompanied by demonstrations of the power of the Holy Spirit in the form of signs and wonders. This had the effect of convincing many of the authenticity of the faith, and numerous conversions resulted.

You Can Look It Up

The **Resurrection** is the cornerstone of the Christian faith. Jesus had warned the disciples that he would die at the hands of the authorities, but that he would be raised from the dead (see Matthew 17:22–23). Apparently, they only heard the first half of his promise. They were devastated after his death, but three days later he made good on his promise.

Baptism is the act of being immersed or sprinkled with water as an outward identification with the Christian faith. In the Bible, baptism was first mentioned in the four gospels.

Time to Fan Out—Whether We Want to or Not!

Part of what has made the Christian faith so resilient—not to mention so widespread, even to this day—is its expansive nature. From the beginning, Christians have had an evangelistic or missionary bent, meaning they believe in working to bring others to their faith.

After his resurrection, Jesus charged his followers with the responsibility to "be witnesses to Me in Jerusalem, and all Judea and Samaria, and to the end of the earth" (Acts 1:8 NKJV). This charge was accompanied by the promise of power from God in the form of the Holy Spirit.

Despite the fact that Jesus had commissioned them to preach "to the end of the earth," at first Christ's followers kept their witnessing (meaning spreading the gospel message) confined to preaching to Jews, mostly in the city of Jerusalem. That changed when a group of Jewish leaders stoned to death a disciple named Stephen, who had preached boldly in the city and chided them for their lack of faith. Stephen told the people—including those leaders, who accused him of blasphemy—that the Christian faith was for all people and not for Jews only (Acts 6–7).

Going Deeper

Christians believe that after Christ's resurrection and his appearance to the disciples, he ascended to heaven before their very eyes. That, according to the first chapter of Acts, was followed by the appearance of two angels, who told them that Christ would one day return to earth.

Going Deeper

The account of the Council of Jerusalem (see Acts 15) was a huge turning point in the history of Christianity. The apostles and elders of the first-century church met in Jerusalem to clarify the issue of how non-Jews could convert to Christianity. Some of the early Christians believed that Gentiles should convert to Judaism before turning to the Christian faith. It was decided that non-Jews could convert to Christianity without first observing the laws of Moses.

Up to this time, Christianity had been seen by the religious leaders and by the Roman authorities of the day as more of a sect of the Jewish religion—much like religious leaders of our culture would view a denomination of the Christian church today. It's easy to understand why the Romans saw it that way. After all, the apostles taught that the prophecies from the Old Testament confirmed that the Messiah the Jews had been waiting for was in fact Jesus Christ. But Stephen's words showed the Jewish leaders that what they were dealing with was more than a mere sect of the established religion.

The result of his preaching, and his martyrdom, was the beginning of a period of intense persecution of the Christians in Jerusalem. The eighth chapter of Acts tells us that the Jerusalem believers fled the city in droves because of the oppression they faced for talking openly about Jesus Christ. While this persecution had as its aim stopping the preaching about Christ, it accomplished the opposite. As it turns out, the persecution did for the faith what water does for a grease fire: scattered it with the result that it caused more damage.

People You Should Know

Talk about giving your all for what you believe in! Stephen was the Bible's first recorded martyr (one who loses his life because of his beliefs). Stephen's death was hardly in vain. After he was stoned to death, the church in Jerusalem began suffering incredible persecution (stay with us … it does get better). That persecution caused something of an exodus from Jerusalem, and as the believers spread out, they took the message of Christ with them.

Instead of this new religion being stopped, it expanded dramatically into the areas outside Jerusalem. Instead of shutting Christians up, it caused their words to be heard by more people. Believers who left Jerusalem to escape oppression fanned out to places as far away as Samaria, and as they did, they took their message of salvation through Christ with them.

There is no question that persecution played a huge role in the establishment and growth of the early Christian church. And there is also no question that one of the greatest persecutors of all turned out to be a key figure in the establishment, growth, and expansion of the faith.

The Life of Paul: From Persecutor to Unstoppable Agent of the Faith

Probably the most amazing conversion in either the Old Testament or the New was that experienced by the man known as the apostle Paul.

If early Christians were to have picked someone to be the leading ambassador for their faith, it wouldn't have been Paul. We first read of him when he was called by his Jewish name, Saul of Tarsus. Paul was an intense and committed defender of the Jewish faith, and he was willing to do whatever it took to wipe out this new heresy. When it came to tormenting Christians, Saul was among the worst. His first recorded act of persecution towards a believer was at the stoning of Stephen, where Acts tells us that he held the clothes of those who were stoning Stephen to death.

That was just the beginning for Saul. Immediately after, Saul "laid waste the church, and entering house after house, he dragged off men and women and committed them to prison" (Acts 8:3).

Later, still filled with hatred for this new faith and those who practiced it—"breathing threats and murder against the disciples of the Lord," as Acts describes it—Saul set out to Damascus, where he planned to commit even more violent acts of persecution against Christians. The book of Acts records how it was on his way to Damascus (around 37 C.E.) that Saul had a face-to-face encounter with the same Christ he had blasphemed, the same Christ whose followers he had once imprisoned and put to death.

Going Deeper

One of the key events recorded in the book of Acts is what happened on the road to Damascus. The Bible tells us that it was there that Saul, an intense persecutor of the Christian faith, had a spectacular face-to-face encounter with Jesus Christ. After a time of learning (and after changing his name to Paul), he devoted the rest of his life to one endeavor: preaching the Christian faith.

As Saul approached Damascus, something amazing happened. Acts records that a blinding light from heaven surrounded him, and he was knocked to the ground. Then he heard a voice ask him, "Saul, Saul, why do you persecute me?" The voice then told Paul that it was Jesus he had been persecuting, and instructed him to get up and continue to Damascus, where he would receive further instructions.

After this meeting with Christ, Saul was never the same. Amazingly, he became an even more devoted follower of Christ than he had been persecutor and blasphemer. For the next three decades, Paul would perform works on behalf of the Christian faith that weren't just important to its growth, but vital. It seemed that nothing could stop Paul from spreading the message of the gospel of Christ—not threats, not imprisonment, not physical abuse, not sickness.

The Apostle Paul: The "Gentile" Missionary

Paul's accomplishments as a missionary were nothing short of incredible. The book of Acts records three extensive missionary journeys, during which he established churches throughout Asia Minor, Macedonia, and Greece. In addition, it has been conjectured that Paul spent his first twelve years in the faith—the time before the recorded missionary journeys—performing missionary work in Cicilia and Syria.

Paul was an outspoken champion of spreading the gospel to the Gentiles (non-Jews) in the region and beyond. When the Christian faith began, it was converted Jews who made up the church in Jerusalem, and these people continued to live and worship as Jews, the difference being that they believed that the promised Messiah had come in the person of Jesus Christ. These Jewish believers held that Gentiles had to become Jews—in other words, they must begin observing Jewish laws, including circumcision, the Sabbath, and other matters in the Law of Moses—before they could come to Jesus for salvation.

Paul didn't buy this view of the gospel, holding that Gentiles could be baptized as Gentiles and still be saved (assured of a place in heaven because of their faith in Christ). At the end of Paul's first missionary journey, he arrived in Antioch, where he reported the conversion of some Gentiles, but some of the Christians from Jerusalem came with the teaching that without circumcision according to the Law of Moses, one couldn't be saved (see Acts 15:1).

Obviously, this was a huge issue in the church at that time, and it was discussed at the Council at Jerusalem, where representation included all the apostles and elders and representatives from the whole church. They gathered to consider the vital question of Gentile membership in the body of Christ. While many of the Jewish believers insisted that Gentiles should be bound by the Laws of Moses, Peter stated that Gentiles should be admitted to the church without "putting a yoke upon the neck of the disciples" (Acts 15:5). Paul also argued in favor of dropping the rite of circumcision.

In the end, the leaders concluded that the Mosaic laws were binding upon Jews but not upon Gentile believers. This meant that the church would no longer be a strictly Jewish establishment, but a faith that was open to people of every race and homeland.

This Is Everyone's Faith Now!

Part of Paul's legacy to Christian history was his teaching that in Jesus Christ there was no longer a distinction between Jew and Gentile, that Christ's work was done on behalf of everyone who placed their faith in him. Paul recorded that legacy himself when he wrote, "For there is no difference between Jew and Gentile—the same Lord is Lord of all and richly blesses all who call on him, for, Everyone who calls on the name of the Lord will be saved" (Romans 10:12–13).

Paul's work as a missionary reflected this belief. During his ministry, Paul made three major missionary journeys, each of which resulted in amazing expansion of the faith. He established churches in several major cities in the Roman provinces of Galatia, Asia, Macedonia, and Achaia. By the end of the first century, Christianity had expanded from the Holy Land to Asia Minor, from Macedonia to Greece and Italy, to the islands of the Mediterranean Sea, and to the northern coast of Africa.

Paul also left the Christian faith with volumes of his writings, fourteen of which (counting the book of Hebrews, although the authorship of that letter is still debated) ended up being included in the New Testament. Paul's epistles—that is, letters to some of the different churches and leaders of the day—serve as the basis of doctrine (doctrine means system of beliefs) and teaching throughout the history of Christianity.

While each of Paul's letters is important to the Christian faith, perhaps none of them has had as much of an effect on the history of the church as his letter to the Romans.

Protestant Pearls

Faith alone justifies and fulfills the law; and this because faith brings us the spirit gained by the merits of Christ. The spirit, in turn, gives us the happiness and freedom at which the law aims; and this shows that good works really proceed from faith.

—Martin Luther

Paul's Letter to the Romans: The Seed That Grew into the Reformation

While the four gospels (Matthew, Mark, Luke, and John) recounted the life and works of Jesus—including his teachings, his death on the cross, his resurrection from the dead, and his appearance to the disciples after the resurrection—the letter to the church in Rome clearly and eloquently explained what those events meant. This letter, which has been referred to as "The Gospel According to Paul," systematically lays out the good news of salvation through Christ. It communicates forcefully and with simple eloquence these vital and foundational points of the Christian faith:

◆ Fallen and sinful mankind's need for the righteousness of God

◆ How God has freely provided that righteousness

◆ The life of one whom God has declared righteous

◆ How God empowers believers to live righteous lives

When viewed through the lens of church history, the letter to the Romans can be seen as the seed that many centuries later grew into the movement called the Protestant Reformation. As Martin Luther read this letter, he came to a personal understanding of what grace and the righteousness of God were.

As Luther read Romans 1:16–17—"I am not ashamed of the gospel of Christ: for it is the power of God unto salvation to every one that believeth; to the Jew first, and also to the Greek. For therein is the righteousness of God revealed from faith to faith; as it is written, the just shall live by faith"—which refers to the revelation of God's righteousness as "gospel," or good news, he was troubled. He wondered how the revelation that God's demand for absolute righteousness could be gospel, or good news, to sinful man. After all, if God demanded absolute righteousness as a condition for inclusion into his kingdom, didn't that pretty much doom all of us?

It was during this time in his life that Luther began to believe that the gospel message was simply this: God justifies the sinful—and *all* of us, according to his message, are sinful— through faith and faith alone. In other words, when we embrace in faith what Jesus had done on the cross, God declares us "right" with himself.

When Martin Luther came to the point of seeing the clarity and simplicity of Paul's message to the Romans, he began to realize that some things within the church organization of his day were plainly wrong and needed changing. He believed that the church had complicated the message of salvation through faith.

That was the condition of the heart and mind of the one who would start the greatest movement within the Christian religion of all time.

The Least You Need to Know

- The beginnings of the church can be traced back to the earthly ministry of Christ, whose 120 closest followers at the time of his death were the seeds of the new church.
- In spite of persecution—in many ways *because* of it—the early church grew like wildfire.
- Paul's letter to the Romans would play a huge role in the Reformation begun by Martin Luther many centuries later.

Now This Is a Faith Worth Living For!

In This Chapter

- ◆ The look of this "new religion"
- ◆ The continued expansion of the Christian faith
- ◆ The development of a belief system
- ◆ The church faces obstacles—internal and external—and triumphs

It was a new world—and a new era—for the Christian church at the beginning of the second century C.E. Gone were the days when the church could count on the teaching and preaching of apostles such as Peter and Paul. Both of those great men of the faith had passed on, leaving the church with something of a leadership vacuum.

Just what was the church to do? Here the Christians were, facing incredible opposition—on the part of the Jews *and* the Romans—as well as an infiltration of the kind of teaching Peter and Paul had warned would come into their midst—false teachings such as Ebionism, Gnosticism, and Montanism, which we will cover later. And to top things off, their original leaders were gone and other leaders were growing old.

This was a time of crisis within the church. But this was a group of people—toughened by the world around them and empowered by the Spirit of God within them—that specialized in overcoming whatever calamity came their way. This Christian faith, which at the time was in its infancy, was going to continue.

So What Do We Do Now?

From the time Jesus last spoke in person to the disciples, they had unquestionably become the respected and esteemed leaders of the fledgling church, first in Jerusalem, then in the other areas the faith had spread to. Later, the apostle Paul joined them, working as a church planter, a preacher and teacher, and a leader in the faith.

With all these men having passed on, what would the church do? Who would lead the Christians into the first century and beyond? Who would teach and preach to the believers the truths of Christ?

While the apostles were alive, there was no real need for an "organized" church government. The Christians of the time looked up to them as men with divine inspiration and authority. In the Bible, the apostle Paul as well as St. Luke, the author of the book of Acts, used the terms "bishop" and "elder" almost interchangeably. But when the office of bishop became official and was moved to the top of church government, things began to change.

Bishops, Bishops Everywhere!

It was close to the turn of the first century into the second that the official church office of bishop made its appearance within the structure of the church. Among the first of the bishops was Ignatius, the Bishop of Antioch, who believed in what we could call a monarchical bishop, or one bishop the churches in a certain area submit to.

Going Deeper

Schools of theology arose in Alexandria, in Asia Minor, and in North Africa during the second century. They were originally designed for the instruction of those who were new to the faith. The writings of the scholars who ran these schools are still valued as sources of information on how the church of that time was run.

By around the year 125 C.E. there were bishops all over the known Christian world, each ruling over his own diocese (region), with presbyters (laypeople who were members of a church's governing body) and deacons (subordinate ministers) under his authority. At that time, there was no "Universal Bishop," as the pope in Rome would later be referred to. That position wouldn't be born until centuries later. There were "metropolitan bishops"—or, bishops who became heads of churches in an entire province—in Rome, Constantinople, Alexandria, Antioch, and (after 451 C.E.) Jerusalem.

It wasn't long before this form of church government became the dominant form, and this dominance continued for centuries. And it was a good thing that this church power structure developed, because the church throughout the Roman Empire would face a series of crises that would require someone to stand up and lead.

But there was something else the church needed at that time, and that was a spelled-out, well-defined system of beliefs, known in Christian circles as doctrine.

Going Deeper

During the early years of Christianity, the Romans were polytheists, meaning they worshiped many gods. There were hundreds of "gods" in this belief system and chief among them were Jupiter, Juno, Neptune, and Pluto.

Just What Do We Believe, Anyway?

When the Christian faith first came on the scene, believers practiced a faith that came from their hearts, a faith that was grounded in the teaching and encouragement of the apostles. The faith was more of a personal commitment to Christ, which openly demonstrated itself in many ways, including how believers treated one another.

Early on, there was no Bible as we know it, although many churches possessed letters from the apostles, some of which became part of the New Testament. Some were fanciful versions, some were like fairy tales about Jesus, and others were books that may or may not have come from the apostles. As the church progressed through the first few centuries, there came to be a need among Christians for a system of doctrine to go with that heartfelt faith. They needed to sort out the truth as the church knew it.

Soon, the church's system of beliefs took its place within the church. That system came from some of the writings of the church leaders of the time and from the writings of the apostles. But it was only a matter of time before the church realized that it needed an officially recognized collection of writings that would tell them all they needed to know in order to live as Christians.

How the Church Got "The Book"

Have you ever wondered how the Bible as we know it now came to be? Did a bunch of guys get together one night in a dark, smoke-filled room to decide what to leave in and what to leave out? Did some Christian leader just take it upon himself to compile a list of good reading materials for long trips? Did the church just get together one Sunday afternoon and hold a vote on which books to list?

It might surprise you to know that the way the New Testament came to be is a lot more interesting than any of those scenarios.

All of the books of the New Testament—from the gospel of Matthew to the Revelation of John—had been written by the end of the first century, and in the second century, these books taken together comprised the collection of writings that would become the New Testament. However, it took some time before the books in the list were canonized, or accepted as having been divinely inspired.

There were several reasons the church needed to come up with an official list of readings for its members. First, with the apostles and other eyewitnesses to the life, work, and words of Jesus all gone, the believers wanted something in writing—that is, "Scripture"—to spell out for them the messages of Jesus and of the apostles.

Protestant Pearls

[The five tasks of pastoral care are] to seek and to find all the lost; to bring back those that are scattered; to heal the wounded; to strengthen the sickly; to protect the healthy and to put them to pasture.
—Martin Bucer (1491–1551), Alsace-born Reformation theologian

Also, it was customary at that time for church leaders to read to the congregation. At first, the readings were from the Old Testament, but later they began including "Memoirs of the Apostles." The church leaders wanted to make sure they had readings that reflected the message of God as it came through the apostles and through Christ himself.

Now that we've established the need for this list of books, let's look at how that list was finally compiled.

Loading the Canon

The early church Fathers—those who took the place of the apostles as leaders in the church—needed to figure out which books and letters belonged in their collection, or *canon*. They believed that the only requirement was that the books needed to be inspired—specifically, inspired *by God*. In other words, they wanted to be sure that the words they read were the words God would speak to them.

You Can Look It Up

The **canon** is the collection of writings that together compose the New Testament. All of these writings were finished by the end of the first century. By the end of the second, the church as a whole had pretty much accepted the New Testament books we have today. In 451 C.E., the canon was officially accepted at the Council of Chalcedon.

The problem with that test was figuring out how to know if a book or letter—and there were many of them to choose from—was truly inspired by God. It wasn't long before those in the early church realized that other tests would be needed to decide on the canon of scripture. One of those tests was whether or not the book was written by an apostle or by someone who was close to an apostle. For example, Matthew and John were both apostles, as were Peter and Paul, so their books were automatically included. Luke, who wrote the gospel that bears his name as well as Acts, was not an apostle but he had a very close relationship with Paul, so two of his writings ended up as part of the New Testament.

Gradually, over the course of centuries, the canon developed. It is believed that by about 175 C.E., the canon included pretty much the same books as our present-day New Testament, and by the year 200 the church widely accepted it as canonical. Clement, the Bishop of Alexandria, apparently recognized the books, as did a lot of the church leaders of his time.

This process of canonizing the books of the New Testament was vital to the faith of the early church and is vital to the faith of believers today. But it was also a key for Martin Luther and other reformers, who believed that these Scriptures, and not the church of their time, were the authority for everything related to the Christian faith.

As the second century turned to the third, the church solidified its system of leadership, its system of beliefs, and its official list of readings. It's impressive that a group of people so large (Christians probably numbered in the millions during this time) managed to get its act together like that. But what is even more amazing is that it happened at a time when things weren't so easy for the church.

Nobody Said It Would Be Easy—Or Even Safe!

In its first three centuries, the church proved its resiliency as it survived all kinds of obstacles, most notably periods of intense persecution—including that promoted and carried out by the government of the Roman Empire—and the appearance of some teachings—such as Ebionism, Gnosticism, and Montanism—that didn't threaten just the stability of the church but its very existence.

The church during its first two-plus centuries found itself living in the midst of a fulfillment of one of Jesus' promises: "If the world hates you, keep in mind that it hated me first. If they persecuted me, they will persecute you also" (John 15:18, 20 NIV).

That doesn't sound like a very uplifting or comforting promise, does it? No doubt the disciples would rather have heard Jesus say,

Going Deeper

In the early church, Christians saw all people as equal. This really bothered the ruling classes in Rome, and they saw the Christians as anarchists bent on overturning the social order of the time. This was yet another reason the church was persecuted.

"Look guys, all you need to do is tell people about me and they'll fall at your feet and repent." Who wouldn't want things to be easier—or if not easier, at least safer? Instead what the disciples heard was, "This is going to be anything but easy. The world is going to hate you and persecute you, and all because of me. Some of you might even have to die on account of me!"

Jesus was pointing out what the disciples needed to realize: that their faith and their commitment to him and his teaching would make them oddballs, outcasts, and rejects in a world that had religious, political, and cultural establishments dating back thousands of years. He wanted them to know that the world around them wouldn't just see them as weird, but as real threats to their beliefs and ways of life.

At first, Christians lived and worked in the empire without drawing a lot of attention to themselves. In fact, many of the Romans held the Christians in esteem because of their morals and ways, and because of their respect and love for one another, regardless of race or social class.

But it didn't take long for Jesus' promise of opposition to come true. From the beginning, those who openly embraced the Christian faith were at odds with the world in which it was founded. As we pointed out in Chapter 1, "Just What Are These Reformers Reforming, Anyway?" it wasn't long after the church was born at Pentecost that two of its top leaders—Peter and John—were tossed in jail, followed by others of the apostles. Not long after that, Stephen was stoned to death, James the brother of John was executed, and the apostle Paul was thrown in prison when he refused to stop preaching the Christian message.

The opposition came from both sides: from the Jews, who saw the Christian faith as a threat to and perversion of their own religion; and from the Romans, who saw it as a threat to their political structures and to their own pagan religious practices.

Protestant Pearls

When I read that Christ Jesus came into the world to save sinners, it was as if day suddenly broke on a dark night.

—Thomas Bilney (d. 1537), English martyr

Not in Our Synagogue!

The apostles followed the instructions of Christ to preach to the Jews that he was the fulfillment of the Old Testament prophecies about the coming Savior. Some of the Jews believed their message (remember, thousands believed Peter's sermon and embraced the faith on the Day of Pentecost). But not all the Jews who heard the message received it. In fact, some responded with violent persecution, as when the Jewish religious leaders stoned Stephen to death (see Chapter 1).

When in Rome?

Everything that happened to the church during its first two-plus centuries happened in the presence of sometimes-intense Roman persecution and, later, under an official state ban on the religion (*religio illicita*, or "illegal religion"). While the oppression of Christians wasn't a constant during those early centuries—there were, in fact, times when Christians could live in relative safety—it occurred over periods of years and with sometimes terrible intensity.

At the beginning, the persecution came as a result of the "differentness" of the Christians, whose lives had become radically different from the rest of the Romans. For example, the early Christians lived in a place and time when idol worship was almost as much a part of the people's lives as eating and breathing. In fact, the Romans of that time worshiped literally hundreds, and maybe thousands, of gods. Idols had their place in public and private settings, and there were all kinds of festivals and celebrations just for the purpose of worshiping these idols.

We Won't Bow, and You Can't Make Us!

The laws and customs of the Roman Empire during the first three centuries of Christianity wouldn't allow for an absolute refusal to honor the pagan gods. Some provinces of the empire tried to meet Christians halfway by offering to erect an idol or statue honoring Jesus. But the Christians believed in only one God, and those committed to their faith would have no part of worshiping Christ as just one of many gods. To them, it was Jesus and Jesus alone who was worthy of their worship.

Because the Christians would have no part of this polytheism (the belief in many gods), they were often seen by other Romans as antisocial, people haters, or even atheists.

" " Protestant Pearls

[Parishioners] became exceedingly well learned in the Holy Scriptures, as well women as men, so that a man might have found among them many that had often read the whole Bible through, and that could have said a great sort of St. Paul's epistles by heart, and very well and readily have given a godly learned sentence in any matter of controversy.

—John Foxe (1516–1587), author of *Foxe's Book of Martyrs*

This was also a time and climate in which Roman citizens were expected to hold the emperor himself in the highest regard—to *worship* him as if he were another of their gods. In fact, every city erected a statue of the emperor, and people were expected to worship at the statue by placing incense at its base. Christians refused to offer this kind of worship to the emperor, and it got them in trouble with the empire. To complicate matters, Christians were known to refer in songs to Jesus Christ as their "King," which brought not-so-veiled accusations of revolution and disloyalty to the empire—something that was not tolerated.

The Romans held that the Christians' refusal to worship the gods and the emperor brought the judgment of the gods on the state. In light of that, Christians were seen as haters of humanity and of the empire. And during those first three centuries, Christians were blamed for every imaginable natural disaster that befell the empire.

The Christians were also seen as threats to the security of the Roman government. At the time, the state feared any kind of revolt and distrusted any and all kinds of gatherings of people. As the church became better organized, it was seen as more of a threat to the government.

Christians were also persecuted simply because their ways seemed so "odd." For example, because they often met in secret, rumors began to circulate about them, some of which suggested behaviors such as cannibalism, drunkenness, and gross perversion. These rumors spread because of the nonbelievers' misunderstandings of the way Christians talked to and behaved around one another.

Not in Our Empire!

The persecution of the Christians first took on an "official" feel—in other words, it had the emperor's seal of approval, if not active participation—following the fire of Rome in July of the year 64 C.E., during the reign of Emperor Nero. It was a horrible tragedy that brought tremendous suffering and hardship to the nearly one million Romans living in the city.

People You Should Know

Emperor Nero was the first Roman emperor to officially sanction persecution of Christians. It started when he was looking for someone to blame for a huge fire that broke out in the city of Rome. To him, Christians seemed like the right group to take the fall.

Afterward, some of Nero's political enemies started a rumor that he was responsible for starting the fire. Though that charge was likely not true, Nero felt the need to deflect the blame onto someone else, and that someone else was the Christians. Romans believed Nero's charge, and the resulting persecutions included all sorts of horrible treatment; Christians were burned at the stake and fed to wild animals.

It was during this first Roman persecution (the first state-sanctioned one, that is) that the apostle Paul was martyred. Although it isn't certain, tradition also has it that Peter lost his life during this time, crucified upside down because he claimed he wasn't worthy to be crucified in the same manner as his Lord, Jesus Christ.

The second persecution commenced in the year 95 C.E. under Emperor Domitian. In a way, this persecution was a matter of guilt by association. The opposition was first directed at Jews who refused to pay taxes earmarked to help fund a pagan temple in Rome. Christians, who were in the eyes of the Roman government members of a sect of Judaism, were caught up in the violence.

Domitian also enforced emperor worship, and those Christians who refused to bow were relieved of their property, kicked out of Rome, or killed.

Persecution and Opposition Go "Official"

It was early in the second century before the empire adopted an official policy on Christian persecution. Pliny the Younger, who served as the governor of the Roman provinces of Bithynia and Pontus in Asia Minor in from 111–113 C.E., had a problem in his province: Christians were beginning to outnumber pagans.

Pliny's approach to this "problem" was to begin bringing Christians to trial, where he would ask them (the question was more of a threat) three times if they were Christians. If they answered "yes" all three times, he would have them taken out and executed. Pliny wasn't sure if he was handling the situation correctly, so he asked Emperor Trajan for advice. Trajan replied that the empire wouldn't be in the business of hunting down Christians, but that if they were brought before the authorities, they were to be given a chance to get "straight." They were to be set free if they "repented" and made a sacrifice to the Roman gods.

Thousands of Christians were martyred under this policy, including Ignatius, the Bishop of Antioch, who was fed to wild animals around the year 115.

More Members of the Imperial Persecutors Hall of Shame

Roman persecution of Christians—which included some unspeakable treatment of believers—continued until early in the fourth century, when Emperor Constantine put a stop to it. But before that, there was a long line of emperors under whose rule Christians suffered. Here are the other Roman emperors who made it dangerous to be a Christian:

- *Hadrian* (117–138 C.E.) continued the policies of Emperor Trajan.
- *Marcus Aurelius* (161–180 C.E.). During his reign, Christians were blamed for all sorts of natural disasters. Thousands of Christians were beheaded or fed to wild animals during his reign. The best-known martyr during his reign was Justin Martyr.

◆ *Septimus Severus* (202–211 C.E.). During his reign, conversion to Christianity was forbidden.

◆ *Maximinus the Thracian* (235–236 C.E.). He ordered Christian clergy executed.

◆ *Decius* (249–251 C.E.). Under his reign, the Romans engaged in the first empire-wide persecution. During his first year as emperor, he ordered that everyone in the empire come before special officers and declare their allegiance to the gods.

◆ *Valerian* (257–260 C.E.). He ordered the property of Christians confiscated and prohibited them from assembling.

◆ *Diocletian Galerius* (303–311 C.E.). Diocletian's reign was a case of saving the worst for last. His was the most intense campaign of persecution since the founding of the religion. Churches were destroyed or shut down and Bibles burned during his reign. The civil rights of Christians were suspended.

> **People You Should Know**
>
> There had been persecution of Christians under most of the Roman emperors during the second and third centuries, but Diocletian Galerius was the worst! Under his rule, churches were destroyed or shut down and Bibles burned. If you were a Christian at this time, you could forget about any kind of civil rights.

The Good That Comes from Bad Times

As hard as it may be to believe, there was an upside to the persecution the church faced during those almost 300 years. For one thing, no one joined the church with the wrong motives. People joined for one reason: They wanted to follow Christ. This was a time in history when there was no economic or social advantage in church membership or in having faith in Christ.

In a time when we value the freedom to practice any religion or attend any church or synagogue or mosque we please—or not, if that's what we choose—it's hard to imagine a time when attending a church service could cost you your home, your citizenship, or your life. But prior to the early fourth century, that's what the Christian life under Roman rule was like. For that reason, it took a deep sense of commitment and courage to be a Christian.

The result was what church historians call a "purified" church—a church full of people who, like those during the days of the apostles, were committed to following their master, even to death if necessary. The "weak" in faith left the church, and only those who were willing to risk their property and lives by openly proclaiming faith in him were left behind.

What the Persecution Couldn't Do—Stop the Christian Faith

It has been said that what doesn't kill you makes you stronger. That is certainly true of the early Christian church. While many believers lost their property, their families, and their lives during Roman persecution, the church itself grew bigger and stronger. Evidence—from archaeological examination of burial sites in the area, which include a large number of Christian symbols on the graves—suggests that Christians in the age of Roman domination numbered in the millions.

This church—the one full of people who valued more than anything their faith in and devotion to Christ and to one another, the one who held to sound teaching and to the scriptures they had been given, the one that would stand up to any kind of opposition—this is the church Martin Luther and the rest of the reformers looked to as their model.

Later, things would get easier for the Christians in the Roman Empire. In fact, there would come a time when being a Christian was not only safe, but also advantageous for the believer living in the empire. We'll get to that in Chapter 3, "The Church Goes Imperial," but first let's take a look at another danger the church faced: wrong teaching.

Watch Out for the "Inside Job"

As difficult as the persecution was for the Christians, there was a bigger threat to the faith—what are called heresies, or errors in teaching and doctrine.

While the persecutions took their toll in terms of causing some of the early Christians to abandon their faith and return to the pagan ways of the world around them, this "inner" threat—that of unsound or erroneous teaching—took an even bigger toll.

The apostles Peter and Paul repeatedly and strongly warned believers to be on guard not only for false doctrines but also for the people *within their own church* who would bring those doctrines (for biblical examples of these cautions, take a look at Acts 20:28–31, Colossians 2:8, and 2 Peter 2:1–3).

Errors in teaching within the church are nothing new. Almost from the beginning, the church had to fend off these errors in order to keep the teaching based on Christ and his teachings. But Christianity has shown a remarkable ability to correct itself when errors are introduced or wrong practices develop.

Ebionism, Gnosticism, and Montanism, Oh My!

Ebionism, which appeared on the scene in the second century, was kind of a continuation of the Jews' opposition to the teachings of the apostle Paul. It was a system that stressed salvation through the keeping of the Jewish laws, particularly circumcision and Sabbath-keeping. Some forms of this belief system held to the basics of salvation—namely, that it comes through faith in the work of Christ—but still held to the keeping of Mosaic Law. But most of them denied Christ's deity and the significance of the crucifixion and resurrection. This error in doctrine pretty much died out by the fifth century, and without having much of a lasting effect on the church.

Gnosticism, which many historians see as having been the most insidious threat the church faced, taught that spirit was good and physical matter was evil and that the physical was in opposition to the spiritual. Gnostics believed that salvation came through the knowledge of an invisible spirit world and denial of the physical. They believed that the practice of asceticism (meaning a life of fasting, celibacy, strict moral discipline, and the like) was necessary for salvation and for greater spiritual illumination. Gnosticism, which at first was an entirely pagan religion but later adopted aspects of Christianity, had its roots in the East (India, Babylonia, and Persia) and spread throughout the empire. It contained elements of Christianity, Judaism, Greek philosophy, and Oriental religion.

Montanism, which was named after its leader, Montanus—who taught his followers that the end of the world was at hand and that he was ushering in the Age of the Holy Spirit in preparation—appeared on the scene midway through the second century and involved a strict ascetic life as well as what the mainstream church believed was an overemphasis on certain spiritual gifts.

We've listed just three of the "errors" that made their way into the early church. Over the centuries the church would be challenged by other erroneous belief systems—systems that added to, subtracted from, or bent sound established doctrine, which came from the teachings of Jesus Christ and from those closest to him, the apostles.

Just as the persecutions of the church had a "sifting" effect on its membership—you might say a separating of the wheat from the chaff—the appearance of erroneous or heretical groups gave the church the opportunity to clarify for its membership the correct teachings of the faith.

So the church in the first through the third centuries survived, thrived, grew, and expanded throughout the world as it was known at the time. But as the fourth century began, the faith was on the verge of a new era, an era in which it would not only escape persecution but would become the "official" faith of the Roman Empire.

But would these easier times be a good thing for the faith in the long run? Or would they prove just one more obstacle for the faith as the people in the book of Acts lived it?

Read on and find out!

The Least You Need to Know

◆ The church gathered together a group of leaders to choose inspired books called the "canon" to which church leaders gave absolute authority in terms of Christian faith and practice. The process resulted in our written Bible—the Old and New Testament.

◆ From the start, Christians were persecuted for their beliefs, first by the Jews and then by the Romans. Yet this persecution ironically attracted many more devout followers and eventually the religion took over the Roman Empire.

◆ Various types of erroneous teachings, known as heresies, arose in the church during this time and prompted the church to clarify its teachings. These disputes arose over such topics as salvation, good and evil, and rule-keeping.

The Church Goes Imperial

In This Chapter

- The "legal" church in the Roman Empire
- The centralized (read "Roman") church
- The establishment of the church power structure
- The ups and downs and ins and outs of the papacy in the Middle Ages

As we saw in Chapters 1 and 2, it wasn't easy to be a Christian in the Roman Empire during the first through the third centuries. If Christians weren't dealing with people trying to challenge what they believed from inside the church, they were suffering from life-threatening persecution by those who opposed the new religion.

But the persecutions ended when Constantine the Great, the first Roman ruler to embrace the Christian faith, became emperor.

In the space of less than eight decades, the Christian church in the Roman Empire went from being the object of officially sanctioned persecution to being not just tolerated, but sanctioned as the guardian of the official state religion.

This chapter is the story of how all that happened and how Rome—and in particular the Roman Bishop, who came to be known as the Pope—became the center of power in the Christian world.

Any Friend of Constantine's ...

Constantine was born in 274 C.E. in a place called Nis, in what is now Serbia. He was the son of the Roman commander Constantius Chlorus—later Constantius I—and Helena, who later came to be known as Saint Helena. Constantius became Roman co-emperor in 305, and Constantine joined his father in Britain in 306. Constantine was popular with the Roman soldiers, who named him emperor when Constantius died later that year. But Constantine had to fight off several rivals for the throne, and it wasn't until 324 that he firmly established himself as sole Roman emperor.

Constantine managed to unite the Empire under a single ruler through a series of military successes culminating in the defeat of his western rival Maxentius at the Battle of Milvian Bridge in 312. In 330 he moved his capital to Byzantium (in modern Turkey), which he renamed Constantinople, a name it retained until the twentieth century, when it became Istanbul. As a figure in the history of Christianity, Constantine is best known for the Edict of Milan in 313, which in effect legalized the Christian religion within the Empire and ended nearly three centuries of persecution of the church.

The Religion of Constantine

Early in his life, Constantine—like his father and other third-century emperors—believed that the Roman sun god, Sol, was the visible revelation of an invisible "Highest God," who was believed at the time to accompany the Roman emperor in all he did. But on the day of his battle with Maxentius, Constantine saw a cross in the sky that bore the words "In this sign, conquer." Constantine went on to defeat Maxentius at the Battle of the Milvian Bridge, outside the city of Rome.

Constantine took the victory over Maxentius as an answer to his prayers to the Christian God for help, and although historians have debated whether he converted to Christianity at that time or later in his life, he began a series of reforms that changed radically how the church was treated throughout the later Roman Empire and throughout the Middle Ages.

> **Protestant Pearls**
>
> We ought not to dwell upon the vices of men, but rather contemplate in them the image of God, which by his excellence and dignity can and should move us to love them and forget all their vices which might turn us therefrom.
>
> —John Calvin (1509–1564), French-born Reformation theologian

In January 313 Constantine and his co-emperor, Licinius, issued the Edict of Milan, which lifted the imperial ban on Christianity and made it a legal religion. The church was given new legal rights and large financial donations. In 323, Constantine, who wanted a close relationship between the empire and the church within it, claimed it his right to control the affairs of the church.

Now it was time for the church as it had been known to move into a new era.

The Church Becomes "Official"

From the moment of the Edict of Milan in 313 C.E., the persecution of Christians ended. Not only that, within a period of just a few years, the church as it was known at the time began to benefit from what can only be described as favoritism from Emperor Constantine. Church buildings, which had been seized by authorities and shut down in persecutions under previous emperors, were restored and reopened everywhere. New churches also sprang up throughout the Roman provinces.

But that was only the beginning of easier times for the church.

In 380 C.E., Emperor Theodosius I declared the Christian faith the official religion of the Roman Empire. Public support shifted away from the pagan religions that dominated before to this relatively new religion, Christianity. Government sanctioning of pagan worship and sacrifices ended (although those practices were still tolerated), many of the temples used for them were consecrated as churches, and all public support (read "financial support") shifted from the pagan temples to the churches. In addition, the Christian clergy—once one of the prime targets of mistreatment for nearly three centuries—became a privileged class, even to the point of existing outside the bounds of many of the laws others had to obey.

In a time when we value separation of church and state (although we don't always agree on what it means), it's difficult to imagine an era in which there was such a close bond between a government and one particular religion. Nearly everyone today wants tolerance of the various religious practices (as long as they don't hurt others), but few of us want our government to sanction one religion, denomination, or sect above another.

That, however, is what happened beginning in the fourth century, and it had lasting effects for the relationship between the church and the government of that time.

> **People You Should Know**
>
> In 380, Roman Emperor Theodosius I declared the Christian faith the official religion of the Roman Empire. This made official what had been going on in the Roman Empire since Constantine's Edict of Milan.

The Good, the Bad, and the Ugly: The Church-Government Bond

Constantine's recognition of Christianity as the empire's favored religion, and the later adoption of Christianity as the official state religion, had some positive effects on Roman culture. First was the ending of officially sanctioned persecution of believers. Where before Christians were literally thrown to the lions as entertainment for others, they could now live and work in the empire without fear for their lives or property. Also, some patently barbaric practices of the time—namely the crucifixion of condemned criminals, the killing of infants who weren't accepted by their fathers, the gladiator games, and the near-unregulated practice of slavery—were either modified, repressed, or ended altogether.

There were clearly some positives that came out of the influence of the church on the government, but there were also some negatives. For one thing, this close bond with the outside world and its government allowed for "worldly" and pagan influences to creep into the church, and that caused the church to become very "worldly" in many of its beliefs and practices. In many ways the outside world conformed the church to its image, rather than the other way around—as had happened in the first century church as described in the book of Acts.

The news that Constantine had ended more than two centuries of sometimes-intense persecution against Christians was met with celebration. Who wouldn't be pleased to know they could now worship and live in safety? But it also began a tumultuous period in which there was an uncomfortable union between the church and the government based on mutual needs and concerns.

Bad Company Corrupting Good Morals

Nowadays, when new people come into a church, it is hoped that the church will change them for the better, rather than the new people changing the church for the worse. But the latter is what happened to the Roman church.

With the official sanctioning of the Christian religion came an inflow of membership into the church. In modern parlance, you might say that it was suddenly "in" to be a Christian. On the surface, that may seem like a good thing. After all, what could be wrong with new people coming to church? But this was a time when sincere "seekers" (those who were truly interested in the message of Christianity) were joined at church by those whose membership was motivated by greed and ambition and the desire for social position. This led to a situation wherein the leadership of the church included many people of questionable (and that's being kind!) character and lifestyle.

This worldly influence on the church eventually led to the acceptance of lifestyles and practices that before had been unacceptable. And it also led to the

Protestant Pearls

I hold it for a most infallible rule in the exposition of scriptures, that when a literal construction will stand, the furthest from the literal is commonly the worst.

—Richard Hooker (1554–1600), Anglican theologian

adoption of pagan customs and practices by the church, many of which "mutated" to fit in with church culture. For example, early in the fifth century, the church began to adopt the images of saints and martyrs (people whose lives and deaths did so much to help with the establishment of the faith over the centuries).

Just Whose Church Is This Anyway?

When the Roman Empire adopted Christianity as the official state religion, it not only blurred the distinction between church and state, in a lot of ways it erased it. In many aspects, the church and the state became one! In some regions of the empire, government control of the church robbed it of its energy and ability to change the world around it for the better. In other areas, the church took power over government to the point where the church became mainly a political entity and not a religious or spiritual one.

Emperor Constantine—as well as his successors—had converted to Christianity, and they believed that the emperor was a ruler empowered from above. For that reason, Constantine felt obligated to defend the faith to the point of opposing those who, for their own reasons, stood against it. As a result, the church became answerable and responsible to the emperor, as demonstrated at the Council of Nicaea—which Constantine called in order to settle the Arian conflict, which had to do with disagreements over the nature and person of Christ.

Emperor Constantine was concerned that division within the Christian faith might lead to division within his empire, so he called the Council of Nicaea in 325. This was the first of several key *councils* over the next century and a quarter. Each of these councils had as its goal the promotion of unity within the church, which the emperors knew was vital to the political stability of the empire. The period following these councils—at Nicaea, Constantinople, Ephesus, and Chalcedon— was a time of the church rising within the empire. No longer was the church persecuted, or even looked down on. Instead, it became a dominant force politically and socially as well as spiritually.

You Can Look It Up

Arianism was a heresy founded by Arius, a priest from Alexandria. Arius taught that God created the Son, Jesus Christ, before all things and that Jesus was not equal to the Father or eternal, as was the Father. Arianism held that Jesus was a supernatural creature who wasn't quite human and not quite divine. This contradicted Christian teachings that Jesus was human *and* divine in nature.

> **You Can Look It Up** _____
>
> Historically, when the church has had major issues to settle, it did so using **councils**, which were meetings of the leadership to debate and discuss and settle. The earliest of the councils was the Council at Jerusalem, which is recorded in Acts 15. The General Councils of the early church were called by the Roman emperors of the time. Constantine was the first to call a General Council, the Council at Nicaea in 325 C.E.

Four Guys It's Good to Remember

Before we move on with the story of the ups and downs of the church prior to the Reformation, we need to take a look at some of the important Christian leaders of the time. The four most important are Ambrose of Milan, John Chrysostom, Jerome, and Augustine of Hippo. All four played key roles in the development of the church, and in some ways each of them helped lay the groundwork for the Reformation of the sixteenth century.

Ambrose

Ambrose (340–397 C.E.), who for twenty-five years ruled the church in Milan, was an influential leader and skilled administrator who advocated a church that was free to determine its course apart from outside (in other words, government) influence. He recognized that the church's wealth was increasing largely due to the favor of the emperor and that that favor in many ways cost the church its independence. Ambrose believed that if the church freed itself from its links to the government, it could fulfill its missionary role as commanded by Jesus in Matthew's gospel.

> **Going Deeper** _____
>
> It was at the General Council of Constantinople—in the year 381—that special honor was given to the Bishops of Rome, Alexandria, Constantinople, and Jerusalem. It also stated that the Bishop of Constantinople was second in line behind the Bishop of Rome. It also affirmed the deity of the Holy Spirit.

John Chrysostom

John Chrysostom (345–407 C.E.), a.k.a. "the Golden Mouth," was one of the greatest preachers of his time—maybe of *all* time. In 398, John reluctantly became Bishop of Constantinople, where he preached to huge congregations. His to-the-point preaching, in which he tried to elevate the moral climate in Constantinople, was met with strong opposition—from the emperor and from the local clergy, who didn't like the strict and uncompromising tone of his messages.

Jerome

Jerome (340–420 C.E.), who translated the Bible into the Latin language (this project came to be known as the Vulgate), was one of the critics of the church of the imperial era. Jerome saw the mission of the church as that of diligently preaching the message of Christianity to the world. That, he believed, was the extent of the church's responsibility; the church was not responsible for the failure of others to listen to and act upon that Word.

Aurelius Augustinus

Aurelius Augustinus (354–430 C.E.), or Augustine of Hippo, who lived most of his life in North Africa, was the most important leader of the Imperial-era church. In his younger days, he was a brilliant scholar but very worldly and pleasure-seeking. Upon his conversion (at the age of thirty-three), he became one of the great thinkers of ancient Christianity. Among his many writings was *City of God*, in which he made a plea for Christianity to take the place of what was at the time a falling Roman Empire and to defend the Christian religion from charges that it was the cause of the fall of Rome. Augustine's most important contribution to the ancient church was his writings and teachings on Christian theology, which were to influence Christian leaders for centuries to follow.

Rising to the Top: The Growing Authority of Rome

During the time of Emperor Constantine, church bishops started to be seen as more than officers who cared for the church and their congregations. They began to be seen in much the same light as the emperor himself: as having some kind of sacred character or calling that set them apart from the people they led. They weren't seen as simply representatives of the people or as those who offered prayers on behalf of their parishioners, but rather as actual mediators between God and humans.

This was in contrast to the times of the apostles (the first century) and to the early second century, when bishops were seen as heads of the churches in the different districts of the Roman Empire.

This line of thought was the groundwork for a church well on its way to a deeply established religious power structure. In that respect, Christianity was beginning to look more and more like the Roman Empire itself: more organized and strictly structured, more legalistic, more dependent on a "pecking order" in its leadership.

Protestant Pearls

In youth, in middle age, and now after many battles, I find nothing in me but corruption.
—John Knox (1505–1572 C.E.), Scottish reformer

The Pope Becomes a World Ruler

Under Constantine, the church enjoyed a time free of persecution and a time of increasing power and influence in the world. But it didn't stay that way for long. The situation was reversed during the Dark Ages—the long period following the fall of the Roman Empire and before the Renaissance—when the church began to *control* the kings and empires themselves. Eventually, the pope had great authority over nations and their leaders.

This situation got its start during what could be described as a papal power struggle, which began in the fourth century and continued in one form or another for many centuries.

Rising to the top of the church power structure (and when we say "church" in this context, we mean the church of the entire Roman Empire) was the Bishop of the community of Rome, who—because he saw himself as the successor of Peter, the founder of the church at Rome—came to be seen as the absolute head of the church. This assumption sprang from Jesus' proclamation to the apostle Peter that the church would be built upon his works (see Matthew 16:18).

A Papal Power Struggle

It was Pope Leo I (440–461 C.E.) who made the claim of supreme leadership while holding the position of Bishop of Rome, but his claim was not recognized by the rest of the church. It was through the work of Gregory I (590–604 C.E.), who proclaimed that as Bishop of Rome, he was to fill the role of "servant of servants," that the Roman Bishop received serious recognition as the official head of the church.

In 330, the capital of the Roman Empire was moved to Constantinople. Later, the bishop there began claiming rule over the whole of the Christian world (also known as *Christendom*) and claimed the title of "Universal Bishop." After all, he reasoned, he should rule all of Christendom from the capital city, much as the emperor ruled the entire state from there. It made sense to him, since he worked in the capital of the whole empire! However, Gregory the Great, as Gregory I came to be known, wanted the position of church head to be the Roman Bishop, and he openly ridiculed the position of the Bishop of Constantinople. Other bishops, as well as the rest of the church, agreed with Gregory.

Gregory the Great wasn't interested in supreme rule over the other bishops, even though at one time

You Can Look It Up

Christendom is a big word that means "the Christian world." Christendom prior to the Reformation in Europe meant the Catholic Church, which had been established over several centuries. Now Christendom includes the Catholic world as well as the Protestant world.

Eulogius, the Bishop of Alexandria, referred to him as the "Universal Bishop." But Gregory's successor, Pope Boniface III (606–607), was more than willing to accept the title—as well as the power the one in that position held—for himself.

The superiority of the Roman pope over the other bishops was later affirmed for good when Charlemagne, who was attending a Christmas service at St. Peter's Church in Rome, granted that power to Pope Leo III and recognized him as the head of the church. This followed Leo's crowning of Charlemagne as the Roman Emperor in the year 800, an act that recognized Charlemagne over the "true" Roman Emperor, who happened to be serving and ruling from Constantinople.

This event marked the beginning of what is called the Holy Roman Empire.

Who's Running the Show Now?

This was also the beginning of an arrangement whereby the pope and the Holy Roman Emperor occupied the two top positions of power of the empire. However, there was great disagreement between the pope and the emperor over who had what power over the other, and when he could use that power. Soon, Leo and Charlemagne came to an agreement—came to it reluctantly, we should add—that spelled out what power each had within the empire.

People You Should Know

In 800 C.E., Charlemagne (741–814) was crowned by Pope Leo III as the first emperor of the Holy Roman Empire. As Holy Roman Emperor, Charlemagne (or Charles the Great) ruled with great wisdom. His crowning by Leo set the stage for a great power struggle between the church and the empire.

That agreement became moot in the year 814 C.E., when Charlemagne died. His death left the empire without strong leadership, and the pope emerged as the unquestioned leader of the Holy Roman Empire. In the early 840s, the empire was divided three ways. Although the power of the government was now diluted, the Roman Catholic Church remained unified and strong, giving it the ability to take almost absolute power over the affairs of the empire.

You Can Fool Some of the Papal Some of the Time ...

The superiority of the pope over the emperor was established for good in 850, when a document called the Pseudo-Isidorian Decretals began to circulate. The document contained a list of laws and rules that had supposedly been written and gathered from the time of the apostles (first century) to the present time (mid-ninth century). The Decretals stated, among other things, that the pope was the absolute head of the church and that he alone had specific powers within the church. Though the documents were fakes, the people of the empire accepted them, and that gave the pope authority over the emperor.

With that, the Church of Rome ascended to a place of absolute power over the government of the Holy Roman Empire.

The Pollution of the Papacy

The saying about absolute power corrupting absolutely proved itself absolutely true for the papacy in the Holy Roman Empire. On the eve of the new millennium, the office of pope—which existed at this time in a world of unprecedented luxury, wealth, prestige, and power—became so corrupt that people rebelled against its rule. One pope—John VIII—was so corrupt that he was assassinated while in office. In 955 Pope John XII had become so corrupt that Emperor Otto the Great, a German who was crowned Holy Roman Emperor in 962, demanded that he resign.

Following Otto's death, the battle for the office of pope became quite a spectacle. One pope was murdered, and that was followed by utter corruption in the office and by struggles between popes and "anti-popes" (popes who competed with the one considered the legitimate pope) for power. It got so bad that Pope Benedict IX, who is considered one of the most corrupt popes in history, actually *sold* the office to Gregory VI, then tried to return to the office, stating that he didn't have the right to sell it in the first place. This touched off a papal schism in which three "popes" simultaneously claimed power.

Going Deeper

The Great Schism of the Papacy (1378–1417 C.E.) was a time of great confusion and division in the church. At first two popes—Urban VI and Clement VII—vied for power. Eventually, there would be three competing popes. It ended in 1417 when the Council of Constance deposed all three "popes" and named Martin V the one and only.

The Papacy Makes a Comeback

Things changed—at least for a time—when a man by the name of Hildebrand was elected to the office of pope in 1073. Pope Gregory VII, as he came to be called, made great reforms within the church and within the office of pope. His reforms included cleaning up the greed and corruption that had stained the office in the eyes of the people. He also reestablished the pope's claim of power over the governments. He believed that the church should have control of the state.

Gregory VII used the threat of what is called the interdict—an order from Rome that in a given city or country, priests and bishops and other church leaders were forbidden from performing church services or any other of the rites of the church—to bring national leaders into line. The leaders knew that the people of their cities or nations would be frightened at the prospect of an interdict (since they were not able to take part in those rites, they would worry that their souls would be lost in hell if they died) and rise up and demand that their church be restored. This was, to say the least, a dangerous situation for any emperor!

On Top Again! The Height of Papal Power

Hildebrand's reforms greatly strengthened the power of the medieval papacy. That power reached its high point during the reign of Pope Innocent III (1198–1216 C.E.). Innocent's power was so absolute that he declared the results of an election for a German kingship null and void. Despite the fact that one candidate had the majority of the votes, Innocent stated that his candidate had the "saner" votes.

Innocent is also remembered for calling the Fourth Lateran Council in 1215, in which certain doctrinal matters were settled. The council decided that annual confession to a priest was necessary for all laymen, and it spelled out the doctrine of transubstantiation, which states that the elements of the Lord's Supper (the bread and the cup) literally became the body and blood of Christ. The council also officially sanctioned the seven sacraments and defined them:

> **People You Should Know**
>
> The power of the papacy was at its zenith during Pope Innocent III's reign. Born in 1160, he is remembered for calling the Fourth Lateran Council in 1215, in which the church officially sanctioned the seven sacraments. He died in 1216.

1. Baptism, the sacrament of identification with Christ

2. Confirmation, the sacrament of the receiving of the Holy Spirit

3. Holy Eucharist, the sacrament of the Lord's Supper (communion)

4. Penance, the sacrament of reconciliation (with God and with others)

5. Extreme Unction, the sacrament of anointing the sick

6. Holy Orders, the sacrament of apostolic ministry

7. Matrimony, the sacrament of marriage

The Church Flexes Its Muscle

Innocent III served in the midst of an era of church history known as the Crusades. The Crusades had as their goal liberating the Holy Land from Muslim control. They also demonstrated the power of the church at that time. The first Crusade began in 1096 under Pope Urban II and its goal was to liberate the "Holy Land" (Jerusalem) from the Turks. The last of the seven main Crusades—there were many lesser expeditions undertaken—was in 1248. Although some good came out of the Crusades—for one thing, the power of the church was greatly increased during this time, and for another, it checked Muslim aggression against Europe—they ultimately failed in their original mission of liberating all of the Holy Land from Muslim control.

It's All Downhill from Here: The Decline of the Papacy

After Innocent III, the power of the papacy once again began to decline. Pope Boniface VIII (1294–1303) attempted to restore the power of the Vatican. In his bull—a "bull" is a papal edict, or decree—*Unam Sanctam*, Boniface asserted that all rulers were subject to him and that anyone who wanted to be saved must subject himself to the pope.

Boniface had greatly overreached his authority as pope, which brought him into conflict with France's King Philip. Boniface tried to bring Philip around to his way of thinking by issuing an order forbidding the French government from taxing church property. In turn, Philip issued his own order forbidding the sending of money from the kingdom without his approval. The pope then tried an interdict on France, but that backfired, as the French priests as well as its leading citizens remained loyal to their king. Philip eventually had Boniface arrested and jailed. Boniface died in 1303.

You Can Look It Up

In 1309, the French Pope Clement moved the capital of the church from Rome to Avignon, France, where it remained for seventy years. Catholics came to refer to this period as the **Babylonian Captivity** because they likened it to the seventy years of captivity endured by the Hebrews at the hands of the Babylonians.

Philip then attempted to influence church politics by having a Frenchman elected pope. In the year 1305, that happened, as Clement V took the office of pope. In 1309, Clement made good on a promise he had issued Philip before his election as pope, and moved the capital of the church from Rome to Avignon, France, where it remained for seventy years. This period in church history came to be known as the *"Babylonian Captivity"* of the papacy.

For the next seven decades, Frenchmen occupied the office of pope. That brought about a situation where leaders of other nations believed, in short, that the pope was in the back pocket of the French. During the time of the Babylonian Captivity, the Hundred Years War broke out between France and England, and that greatly reduced the power of the pope in England.

During the war, the pope demanded the surrender of the great reformer John Wycliffe (more on him in Chapter 5, "The Right Message at the Right Time"), but he was protected. To make matters worse for the papacy, it acquired during this time a reputation for corruption, materialism, extravagant spending, and oppressive taxation.

A Papal Fiasco—Uh, Schism

For various reasons—not the least of which was the economic one—Italy wanted the church capital returned to Rome. In 1377, Pope Gregory XI returned to Rome, but died soon after. The following year, Rome elected Urban VI to succeed Gregory XI. Naturally, the French protested that the election of Urban was illegal, and the French clergy elected Clement VII to succeed Gregory. Several councils met to settle the controversy but accomplished little. It was later decided to elect a new pope and demand that the two rivals step down. But after the election of a third pope at the Council of Pisa, neither would step down. All that council succeeded in doing was splitting the papacy in three instead of two. For several years, the church was being "ruled" by three popes who spent a great deal of their time cursing and excommunicating one another.

Christendom was split and confused, and reform movements—notably the Lollards and the Hussites, whom we will discuss in Chapter 4, "Rebels, Rabble-Rousers, and Revolutionaries: The Reformers"—began springing up all over the empire. Finally, Emperor Sigismund, who had grown tired of the mess, demanded that unity be restored within the church. At the 1417 Council of Constance, Pope Martin V was elected to replace the three—by this time, Roman Pope Gregory XII, Avignon Pope Benedict XIII, and John XXIII—who had claimed the position of pope.

Going Deeper

The Great Schism ended on November 11, 1417, when a Roman named Oddone Colonna was elected as pope at the Council of Constance. The news of his election was seen as a relief. He succeeded Gregory XII and served under the title of Martin V. He served as pope until 1431.

The papal schism was ended, but the damage was done. With the election of Martin V, church reformers hoped that the materialism and corruption of the church would be a thing of the past. They were sadly disappointed in Martin, who continued what had become a tradition of papal corruption, materialism, and worldliness.

The Papacy Takes a Beating

During the last part of the fifteenth century and early in the sixteenth, the papacy continued its downward spiral into worldliness, corruption, and paganism. With the spread in Europe of the Renaissance—in which there was a rebirth of interest in classic literature and art—came increasing "secularization" (abandonment of the religious for the temporal) of the church leadership. Popes during that time—Nicholas V (1447–1455), Julius II (1503–1513), and Leo X (1513–1521)—were more preoccupied with the classic literature and arts than they were with leading the Christian world. During the reign of these popes, Rome spent incredible amounts of money on extravagances such as art and architecture.

When you look at the corruption, the materialism, and the preoccupation with things other than protecting and spreading the faith, it's hard to come to any other conclusion than that the office of the pope was a mess. And it wasn't long before the people over whom the papacy ruled saw just how much of a mess it was.

Obviously, it was time for some changes.

The Least You Need to Know

- In 380, Emperor Theodosius I declared Christianity the state religion. Within a space of 80 years, the Christian church went from being severely persecuted to becoming the ruling religious power of the Roman Empire.
- During the Dark Ages the church began to exercise control over the worldly rulers, since the Bishop of Rome now claimed to be the Pope, or supreme ruler of all Christendom. This marked the beginning of the Holy Roman Empire, with Charlemagne as its first king.
- The papacy had its ups and downs in terms of exerting earthly power, culminating in the "Babylonian Captivity" with three competing popes. For seven decades the French controlled the papacy.

Chapter 4

Rebels, Rabble-Rousers, and Revolutionaries: The Reformers

In This Chapter

- ◆ Reformers prior to Martin Luther
- ◆ Reformation movements prior to the Protestant Reformation
- ◆ The church's response to reformers and revolutionaries
- ◆ How earlier reformers influenced the Protestant Reformation

Just about any great historic reformer or revolutionary has forerunners—those who blazed the trails he or she would later follow. Martin Luther was no exception. Before him went countless others who preached, taught, and even gave their lives for the church as they saw it should be.

While these people can be diplomatically referred to as dissidents, in the eyes of the established church of Europe in the *Middle Ages*, they were troublemakers, heretics, and rebels. Clearly, they "rocked the boat" when it came to how they saw and practiced the Christian faith and how they perceived the church of the day.

The actions of some of the *reformers* brought responses from the church membership, from the church authorities, and eventually, from the pope himself. This action included what we have come to know as inquisitions. Inquisitions were proceedings of the church in which "heretics" were sought out, charged, and, if they would not recant, punished for their actions.

There were *heretics* and dissidents in the church during the early Middle Ages, but their movements never spread very far. But from the twelfth century on, there was an increase in dissidents and in their followers—some of whom wanted to try to change the church from within, and others who wanted to break away from the established church completely.

Luther wasn't the first who believed that the church had strayed off course. There were many others who recognized the corruption that had become rampant in the church and in its leadership. There were many who saw that the Christian faith had in many ways been taken captive by a religious system more interested in political and social accomplishment than in following the examples of Christ and of the original church in Jerusalem. They believed that the world—including its political and social orders—had corrupted the mission of the church.

You Can Look It Up

In European history, the **Middle Ages** is the era between the fall of Rome (476 C.E.) to the mid-fifteenth century, or at the dawning of the Renaissance. This period is also known as the Dark Ages.

A **reformer** is someone who through words or actions attempts to improve something by restoring it to its original condition. In the case of religious reformers, it means reforming the established church to the model in the biblical book of Acts.

A **heretic** is someone who holds beliefs that contradict the teachings or doctrine of his or her religion. In the Middle Ages, those who opposed the teachings of the Roman Catholic Church—even on biblical grounds—were branded heretics. Heresy was no small matter in the Middle Ages. Those convicted of heresy were often burned at the stake by mobs.

The things the pre-Reformation reformers preached and taught would lay the ground-work for Luther's world-changing work.

Luther didn't have it easy as he began his movement, and neither did the earlier reformers. In fact, many of them paid dearly for their teaching and preaching—losing their lives. Some of them didn't die in pleasant ways, either—they were oftentimes hanged, burned at the stake, and beheaded.

We'll get to those pre-Reformation reformers in a moment. First, let's talk about a man whose contributions to the cause made Luther's reformation a possibility.

The Apostle Paul, the Trail Blazer for the Reformers

One of the foundational arguments of the reformers was that the revealed word of God, the Bible, was the ultimate authority for all things spiritual. That belief flew in the face of the established church, which had developed over the centuries a power structure with the pope functioning as the head of the church and the ultimate authority over the church as a whole.

In Chapter 1, "Just What Are These Reformers Reforming, Anyway?" we talked about how the apostle Paul, in writing his letter to the church in Rome, planted the seed that not only contributed to the formation of the Christian church, but also played its part in bringing about the Protestant Reformation. Of course, that can be said of all of the New Testament—from the Gospel of Matthew to the Revelation of John. But history shows us that it was Paul's letter to the Roman church that touched something inside Luther.

In his epistle, Paul spelled out simply and eloquently that God's righteousness isn't necessarily the wrath he pours out on sinful mankind in punishment, but the blessing he pours out on those who place their faith in the works of Christ on the cross. Paul was telling the Romans, in other words, that God himself declares us righteous in order that we may have salvation.

In this sense, Paul can be seen as an important forerunner of the church reformers. At the very least, the apostle can be credited with building the foundation that Martin Luther and others later built upon.

Luther is credited with changing the world as we know it by following his courage and convictions in challenging the powerful structure that was the Roman Catholic

> **Protestant Pearls**
>
> I cannot burn. Good people, let me have more fire.
>
> —Nicholas Ridley (1500–1555), Anglican Bishop of London, burnt at the stake

Church. But there were more, and many of them tried to bring about changes within the church itself. Some partially distanced themselves from the church while attempting to do their reforming work. Still others broke from the church and began new religious movements of their own, some of which still have great influence on the church in the twenty-first century.

Here is a look at some of these pre-Reformation reformers.

Where's Peter Waldo?

One of the earliest—and one of the most potent—reformation movements was started by a man named Peter Waldo, a once-wealthy merchant who lived in Lyons, France, during the twelfth century.

One day, Waldo was impressed by the lyrics from a wandering minstrel who sang about God, and he asked a spiritual leader he knew what was "the best way to God." The clergyman replied, paraphrasing Jesus' words to another rich man, in Matthew 19:21: "If thou wouldst be perfect, go, sell that thou hast, and give to the poor, and thou shalt have treasure in heaven; and come, follow Me."

That sounded good to Waldo. He was impressed with the idea of poverty and service to Christ, and he wanted to follow Christ's command to the rich young man absolutely and literally. So in 1176 he sold most of his holdings (he kept aside enough to care for his wife and daughters), gave the proceeds to the poor, and began a life of relative poverty.

Before long, others joined Waldo in a simple life of preaching repentance and eking out a mean existence off of handouts from those who heard their message. These people came to be known as the Waldensians, and by just about any standard you want to apply to them, they were radicals.

And at the time they ministered, they were considered by the Catholic Church to be heretics.

Waldo's Boys: The Waldensians

At first, the Waldensians held no outward hostility toward the Roman Catholic Church, but they rejected a lot of the organization and teaching of the church—for example, the papacy, *purgatory*, the taking of certain oaths, *indulgences*, prayers for the dead, and the necessity of the *Mass*—and proclaimed the Bible their sole source of authority. Their worship services, like their lives, were simple, consisting of readings from the Bible (in their native tongue), the Lord's Prayer, and sermons, which they believed any Christian, as one possessing the Holy Spirit, could preach.

You Can Look It Up

Purgatory is the place souls of the penitent were taken to be made fit for heaven.

Indulgences are the earthly remissions for sins already forgiven. During the Middle Ages, the sale of indulgences for future sins were the church's way of "selling" forgiveness to the church-goers of the time. The abuse of indulgences became a major fundraiser for the church, and were later the issue that moved Martin Luther to write and post the 95 Theses.

Mass is the Catholic Church service in which the various rites and liturgies are performed.

The Waldensians took the teachings and examples set by the apostles and other believers in the book of Acts to extremes. They traveled in pairs, wore the simplest clothing, and preached repentance to anyone who would listen. They did have an organization of bishops, priests, and deacons, but they insisted on the right of laypersons to preach.

At Odds with the Church

The two issues that got the Waldensians in trouble with the church was their unauthorized preaching of the Bible and their rejection of the mediator role of the priest between God and believers. The Waldensians believed that Christians had as their mediator the person of Jesus Christ, and that no further mediation was necessary.

While the Waldensians—or "Poor in Spirit" or "Poor Men of Lyons," as they called themselves—were at odds with the church on many counts, there was a time when they still considered themselves good Roman Catholics, and in 1179 they went to the Third Lateran Council and sought permission from the local clergy to preach. They were denied that permission because they were seen as uneducated, unrefined, and ignorant laymen, and therefore couldn't handle preaching in a way the church would approve.

The Waldensians went to Rome to appeal to Pope Alexander III for permission to preach. Alexander blessed their lives but refused to grant them permission to preach without authorization from the local clergy. But Waldo and his followers—believing that they were living and ministering by the example of the apostle Peter, who proclaimed that he would obey God and not men when it came to preaching the message—rebelled against the authority of the church and continued to preach their unorthodox (by Roman Catholic standards) message.

> **Protestant Pearls**
>
> Be of good comfort Master Ridley, and play the man. We shall this day light such a candle by God's grace in England [the Reformation], as shall never be put out.
> —Hugh Latimer (1485–1555 C.E.), Reformer, Anglican Bishop burned at the stake

The Roman Catholic Church of the time wasn't about to put up with this kind of rebellion, and it wasn't long before the Waldensians would have to pay for what they were doing.

The Waldensians Pay the Price

In 1184, Pope Lucius III excommunicated the Waldensians for their disobedience and formally declared them heretics. In 1211, more than eighty of them were burned as heretics at Strasbourg, beginning several centuries of intense persecution. But just as the persecution of the first church in Jerusalem led to its expansion, Lucius III's actions and the persecution against the Waldensians that followed seemed to have had the opposite of the desired effect. The Pope's actions won the Waldensians a body of sympathizers, and instead of the movement dying, it spread to southern France, Italy, Spain, the Rhine Valley, and Bohemia (which later became the Czech Republic). They were severely persecuted for centuries.

In the fifteenth century, the Waldensians were active in central Europe despite the opposition against them. During this time, there was some connection between the Waldensians and the Hussites (more on them later in this chapter) and the followers of John Wycliffe (more on *him* later in this chapter), and that included a few attempts to unite these groups, which failed mostly because of doctrinal differences among them.

> **People You Should Know**
>
> Pope Lucius III decreed in 1184 that bishops should seek out and prosecute heretics—including the Cathars and the Waldensians, among others. This decree stated that one convicted of heresy should be handed over to secular authorities for punishment.

While the movement Peter Waldo started isn't seen as evangelical in the truest sense of the word, his and his followers' insistence on accepting the Bible and not the centralized Roman Catholic Church as the ultimate authority in all things Christian helped pave the way for the reformers who were to follow.

No Matter How You Spell His Name, John Wycliffe Was Trouble

If there was one man who got under the skin of the fourteenth-century Roman Catholic Church, it was John Wycliffe (about 1320–1384). In the religious sense, Wycliffe (also spelled Wyclif) was truly a man ahead of his time, so much so that many historians have referred to him as "the Morning Star of the Reformation."

Wycliffe not only attacked the place of the church in the government of the fourteenth century, he also severely criticized many of the beliefs and practices of the medieval church, which he considered unscriptural.

Wycliffe lived and worked in England almost 200 years before the Reformation started by Martin Luther. This was a time of increasing and deepening corruption in the Roman Catholic Church, a time when the church owned roughly one-third of all land in England yet claimed exemption from taxation.

Wycliffe was born in Hipswell, Yorkshire, and was educated at Balliol College at the University of Oxford. He received a doctorate in theology in 1372, then taught philosophy at Oxford throughout most of his career, while more or less serving as a priest in a succession of parishes.

Wycliffe believed in the Bible as the ultimate religious authority. He believed in a direct relationship between humanity and God through Christ, that a person didn't need the mediation of a priest to reach God. He believed that Christians could, if they stuck to the teachings of the Bible, govern themselves without the aid of popes or other spiritual leaders.

Wycliffe: A Burr Under the Church's Saddle

John Wycliffe enjoyed the favor of the English government but not of the church. In a 1377 edict, Pope Gregory XI condemned eighteen of Wycliffe's statements. That same year, the English bishops attempted to put Wycliffe on trial for heresy, but John of Gaunt, the Duke of Lancaster and one of the most powerful people in England, intervened and stopped the proceedings from taking place.

Wycliffe's beliefs and teachings were a lot like those of Luther, John Calvin, and other reformers. He condemned the church's beliefs and teachings concerning purgatory, and he also criticized the abuses and false teachings of the church. He was especially hard on the church for its accumulation of wealth and the sale of indulgences, which by that time were basically "advanced pardons from God" people could purchase from the church for sins they were going to commit in the future. Wycliffe also refuted what is called the doctrine of *transubstantiation* (see Chapter 3, "The Church Goes Imperial"), stating instead that Christ was actually spiritually present at the Eucharist, or the Lord's Supper.

Wycliffe interpreted the Bible literally and held that it was the sole authority for the believer. He believed that decrees by the pope were infallible only when they were based in Scripture. That, he taught, is where the infallibility of the pope—or any man—ended. He held that Christ, and not the pope, was the ultimate head of the church.

You Can Look It Up

Transubstantiation is the belief that the elements of the Eucharist—the bread and the wine—physically become the body and blood of Christ.

The Pope versus the Power of the (Poisoned) Pen

Wycliffe, who lived at a time when European Catholicism was ruled by rival popes (see Chapter 3), also downplayed the role of the office of pope. In 1379—while Urban VI and Clement VII claimed rule from Rome and France, respectively—Wycliffe wrote in *The Power of the Papacy* that the office of pope had been instituted by man, not by God, and that the pope's authority extended to the church and not to secular government. He went on to say that the pope's authority depends on his having the moral character of the apostle Peter. He even reached the conclusion that if the pope was too eager for power, then he might be regarded as the Antichrist. Obviously, the church did not greet this position with great enthusiasm! In a time when the power of the pope was considered absolute, even in governmental affairs, Wycliffe's positions were at the very least provocative, and, at worst, dangerous to him.

Wycliffe, with the help of certain Oxford University associates, also bucked church tradition by undertaking an English translation of the *Vulgate*, the Latin Bible, which was used in the Catholic Church. That project resulted in the first translation of the Bible into a European language in more than 1,000 years. (His translation was not actually finished until after he died.)

Lollards Never Fade Away

Wycliffe's preaching and teaching soon attracted a group of energetic followers, who became known as the Lollards. (That name was probably not a compliment to Wycliffe's followers, as it actually meant "mutterer" or "mumbler.") After his death on December 31, 1384, the Lollards spread Wycliffe's teachings far and wide, and distributed his translation of the Bible, which first came on the scene in 1388. By 1395 the Lollards had developed into a fairly well organized group, complete with their own ministers and support systems.

The Lollards stood firm in defense of many of Wycliffe's teachings. Like Wycliffe, they saw the Scriptures as the cornerstone of their faith. They believed the Bible should be available to everyone—in their own language. They believed that the primary role of the priest was to preach the Word of God. They also condemned transubstantiation, the doctrine of purgatory, indulgences, and other aspects of the Catholic religion. They taught the importance of moral, upright living on the part of the clergy—something you may recall was lacking in many of the popes during the Middle Ages.

> **Protestant Pearls**
>
> This must be our ground and anchor-hold, that Christ is our only perfect righteousness.
> —Martin Luther

> **Going Deeper**
>
> The doctrine of justification by faith states that God makes people righteous not because of the good works they do but by the works of Christ on the cross. This doctrine is spelled out in the apostle Paul's letter to the Romans.

And in Conclusion ...

The *Conclusions*, the most complete statement of the Lollards' system of beliefs—which was presented to the English Parliament in 1395—rejected transubstantiation, condemned the use of sacraments and images, and discarded the ideas of prayers for the dead and spoken confession. *Conclusions* spoke out against all war and branded the practices of clerical celibacy and the chastity vows of nuns as unnatural.

"Lollardry," which had broad appeal to most economic classes in England, hit its peak before the turn of the fourteenth century. There were a lot of Lollards around at this time, but their numbers started decreasing during the reign of King Henry IV, as organized persecution took its toll on the movement. They remained a factor in England to the ascension to the throne of Henry V. During the early years of the reign of Henry VI, intense persecution toward the Lollards arose—including a mass hanging and many burnings at the stake—and the Lollard movement became restricted almost exclusively to the poorer classes. But it didn't completely die out until it merged with the Protestant movement of the sixteenth century.

They Couldn't Leave a Good Man Down

Wycliffe's writings also influenced Bohemian reformer John Huss (more on him later in this chapter) in his revolt against the Catholic Church, and Martin Luther acknowledged the influence of Wycliffe's teaching and writing on his own development. Huss was burned at the stake following the Council of Constance in 1415, but his was not the only body to meet that fate. That same council listed forty-five "errors" or "heresies" on Wycliffe's part and the pope decreed that his remains be dug up and burned. This act was carried out in 1428, forty-four years after his death.

While Wycliffe's work took place a century and a half before the Protestant Reformation, he truly helped set the stage for the work of Martin Luther and the other sixteenth century reformers.

John Huss, a Truly Bohemian Reformer

Like the other reformers in this chapter, John Huss (1374–1415) helped pave the way—or at least foretold—the Protestant Reformation. Huss did that by leading a popular reformation movement in his own country, Bohemia. He also gained fame as a martyr for his reformationist ways.

 Going Deeper

On the Church was John Huss's best-known and most important writing. In it, he defined the church as the "body of Christ"—a scriptural term that referred to the believers as a group—and as Christ himself as the only head of the church.

John Huss (or John Hus, or Jan Hus) was born in a town called Husinec, in the southern part of Bohemia. Huss was ordained a priest in 1400 or 1401 C.E., and he also taught at Charles University in Prague and preached at the Bethlehem Chapel, which was close to the university.

In 1360, more than a decade before Huss's birth, the king of Bohemia had invited a man called Conrad of Waldausen to come and preach against church corruption. That was the beginning of a reform movement in Bohemia. Huss's beliefs and writings and teachings were a continuation of that movement, and in time he became the leader of the reform movement that spread throughout his country.

Huss was more conservative in his views than John Wycliffe, but he certainly agreed with many of Wycliffe's points. Huss didn't agree with Wycliffe on transubstantiation, but agreed with him when it came to condemning church abuses and corruption. Both wanted to see the church become an institution of the people, and both held that the Bible, not the church, was the ultimate authority in all religious matters. In Huss's best-known writing, titled *The Church*, he stated that all Christians are members of Christ's church, and that he, not the pope, is the head of that church. Huss stood against "simony" (the sale of church offices) and indulgences.

Someone Try to Put a Muzzle on That Guy!

Because Huss believed in the authority of the Scriptures, he believed preaching should hold an important place in all church services. Like Wycliffe, Huss believed that no one—not priests, not cardinals, not the pope himself—should establish church doctrines that contradicted the Bible, and he believed that no Christian should obey or recognize such a doctrine, as it would be flawed at best.

In 1410, the pope ordered Huss and others to stop preaching in chapels. Huss refused to obey the order, so Archbishop Zbynek of Prague excommunicated him. Huss remained extremely popular in his home country, despite the fact that he had been excommunicated.

Huss stayed at the center of the church controversy in Prague—largely because he continued to defend Wycliffe's doctrines. Later that year, he was summoned to Rome to defend his beliefs. He declined to go in person—wisely, as it might have cost him his life—instead sending legal representation to plead his case.

Huss Gets Burned

Huss lived during the Great Schism (see Chapter 3), and in 1414, he was invited to the Council of Constance, which was convened to resolve a three-way divide of church leadership as well as other church matters. The Holy Roman Emperor Sigismund ordered Huss to attend the council and guaranteed his safety going to and from Constance, no matter what the outcome of his case. Huss decided to attend the council, and within a month followers of Pope John XXII captured and imprisoned him.

With Sigismund doing nothing to interfere—despite his earlier promises of safety—Huss was tried at the council and found guilty of heresy. Some of the charges against him were untrue—for example, the claim that he denied transubstantiation, which he did not—but many of them, especially his teachings on the place of the church, were factual. Huss never got a real chance to explain his views at the council. He was simply told to recant or face the consequences. He refused to recant. He was condemned, then burned at the stake on July 6, 1415.

The reform movement in Bohemia didn't stop at Huss's death. If anything, his execution incited more dissent among the Bohemians. After his death, which was seen by the Bohemian people as an act of heroism, his followers—the "Hussites"—continued as a powerful force in Bohemia and Moravia. In 1420, the Hussites drew up the Four Articles of Prague, which demanded freedom to preach in church services, full communion (both wine and bread) for the laity as well as priests, limitations on church property holdings, and civil punishment of "mortal sin."

Savonarola Turns Up the Heat

Take a classic "fire and brimstone" preacher and place him in fifteenth-century Italy, and what would you have? Girolamo Savonarola!

Savonarola was born in 1452 to a noble family in Ferrara, Italy. He studied humanism (see Chapter 6, "A 'Different' Kind of Reformation") and medicine, but renounced them in 1474 when he joined the Dominicans in Bologna. He made his first appearance as a preacher in 1482 in the Dominican house in Florence. Savonarola's heated sermons and prophesies and predictions—which had a strange habit of coming true—made him a popular preacher among the common people in Florence during the Renaissance, so popular that he was elected city manager.

He severely condemned what he considered the paganism of the times and called for spiritual renewal and a return to moral values. At the 1496 carnival in Florence, Savonarola initiated the "burning of the vanities," in which the people of the city made a huge bonfire of cosmetics, erotic books, and gambling equipment.

Still, Savonarola was extremely popular with the people. He had instituted popular reforms in the government, including those in the tax system and the court system. He also made changes that enabled the city to better aid its poor citizens.

Savonarola's sermons pulled no punches. He preached against the Pope, Alexander VI, and railed against the corruption and immorality in the church leadership. Eventually, the pope offered him a cardinal's position if he would stop preaching from the Bible and, more important, stop exposing the sins of the Vatican. But the fiery preacher refused the "red hat" of a cardinal and replied, "I'll take a red hat of blood."

Lemme Tell You What I Think of Your Excommunication!

In 1495, the Roman Catholic Church called Savonarola to answer charges of heresy. When he failed to appear in Rome, the pope ordered him to stop preaching. As you might expect from a man of Savonarola's personality and temperament, he continued preaching anyway. The situation worsened in 1497 when Alexander VI excommunicated him. Again, Savonarola was defiant to the Vatican, openly declaring that Alexander was not a true pope.

About that time, the citizens of Florence—the same citizenry that had elected Savonarola city manager—rebelled against his rigid demands. (The city was under the threat of a papal interdict, meaning that the priests and other spiritual leaders would have been stopped from doing their priestly duties for the congregations.) In short order, the city arrested him and two of his followers.

In 1498, papal commissioners declared Savonarola guilty of heresy and handed down the death sentence. The records of the proceedings were sent to Rome, and the sentence was confirmed. On May 23, 1498, Savonarola administered the last communion to his two companions and himself, after which the three were hanged and their bodies burned.

While Savonarola retained his Roman Catholic beliefs, he would later be looked at by Protestants as something of a hero, simply because he had the courage to oppose a corrupt and immoral papacy.

Waiting for the Right Time

The history of Christianity is chock-full of reformers and reformation movements—in fact, there are far too many to list in this chapter! Some of these people and movements faded quickly, but others continue to influence the faith to this day. None of these reformers had any idea that his actions were laying the groundwork for what was to come in the sixteenth century—they were just standing up for their beliefs and against what they saw as corruption or unsound teaching on the part of the Roman Catholic Church.

One reformer—Martin Luther—provided what was needed at the right time to usher in what history calls the Protestant Reformation. Some of the reformers prior to Luther advocated the same kinds of changes in the church that Luther did, and many of them started some pretty good-sized religious movements of their own. However, the world and the church as a whole just weren't ready for the "radical" things they preached and taught. But when the 1500s rolled around, Europe was ready for radical, explosive—even revolutionary—changes.

The Least You Need to Know

- There were many reformers who preceded Martin Luther—Peter Waldo, John Wycliffe, John Huss, and Girolamo Savonarola—and many of them had beliefs that mirrored his.

- Many or most of the reformers prior to Luther faced persecution to the point of death when they publicly declared their beliefs or their opposition to the Roman Catholic Church structure.

- While many of the reformers believed as Luther did, that the church needed to return to her "Book of Acts" roots, Luther was the one who came at a time when Europe was ready for his message.

The Right Message at the Right Time

In This Chapter

- ◆ The politics, religion, and thinking of Europeans on the eve of the Reformation
- ◆ The relationship between the Renaissance and the Reformation
- ◆ The importance of print media in spreading the message of the reformers

It would be easy to understand the Protestant Reformation if all it involved was some guy with an ax to grind standing up and starting a new religious movement. But there's a lot more to it than that. And, as you'll see, it's a lot more interesting, too!

There were all kinds of developments within the church that helped prepare the way for the Protestant Reformation. But there were also historic events in the secular world that made this movement not only possible, but also necessary.

As Europe moved into the sixteenth century, Europeans were more than ready for changes within the church system. There had already been huge social, political, intellectual, and educational changes in Europe over the previous few centuries. It was only a matter of time before equally huge changes took place in the religious arena.

In Chapter 4, "Rebels, Rabble-Rousers, and Revolutionaries: The Reformers," we talked about a long list of reformers who came before Martin Luther, and how many of them wrote and taught messages that were similar (sometimes identical) to the message he would later write and speak. For example, a guy named Thomas Bradwardine (1290–1349), an English theologian and mathematician, emphasized the grace of God for salvation. So did Gregory of Rimini (d. 1358), an Italian philosopher turned monk. And John Wycliffe and John Huss emphasized the authority of Scriptures over the authority of the church.

Protestant Pearls

Unless you know why Christ put on flesh and was nailed to the cross, what good will it do you to merely know a history about him?

—Philip Melanchthon (1497–1560), Humanist scholar and Lutheran theologian

Although the earlier reformation movements didn't take off like Martin Luther's, many of these pre-Reformation reformers greatly influenced his thinking and approach. In that respect, we can say that they laid the doctrinal groundwork for what would become the Protestant Reformation.

It's one thing to have the right message; it's another to have the right message at the *right time*. Martin Luther's reformation took off the way it did because 1) Europe was ready for his message, and 2) he was able to get that message to the Europeans in the first place.

Something's Gotta Give!

On the eve of the sixteenth century, Europe stood at the brink of revolution. The ingredients for widespread reformation were present; all it took was a leader ready to add some heat to the pot.

Following are some of the ingredients that led to the Protestant Reformation.

Going Deeper

The decline of the papacy, which began in the fourteenth century and continued into the early sixteenth century, led to growing discontent with the church among all classes of the general population in Europe. Contributing to the decline was the Great Schism, a time in which two, then three, rival popes vied for power.

The Papacy Hits the Skids

You can't talk about Europe's preparation for the Protestant Reformation without talking about the decline of the papacy. After the reign of Pope Innocent III (1198–1216), the papacy lost much of its power and prestige, and starting at the beginning of the fourteenth century, it took a nose-dive.

As we pointed out in Chapter 3, "The Church Goes Imperial," in 1309 the office of pope was moved from Rome to Avignon, at the border of France. It was during this time that the office of pope had become corrupted and materialistic. The papacy eventually returned to Rome, but only after the "Great Schism," a period between 1378–1423 when two and sometimes three men claimed the office of pope.

There were good men who served as pope during the fourteenth and fifteenth century, but not enough of them. The papacy was weighted down with corruption, immorality, materialism, and secularism, so much so that at the close of the fifteenth century, it appeared there was little chance for reformation from within.

Rotten from the Top Down

As went the papacy during these few centuries, so went the "lower" ministers in the church throughout Europe. The corruption and worldliness of the pope found its way through the higher clergy down to the lower offices, which were often filled with men who weren't worthy of their positions. This downhill slide led to a situation in the late fourteenth and early fifteenth centuries in which the existence of the church as it had been known was threatened.

There has been plenty of debate about the depth of the corruption, immorality, and materialism in the Roman Catholic Church on the eve of the Reformation. But there is little doubt that these things existed—from the popes all the way down to the parish priests and beyond. These were the same conditions John Wycliffe and John Huss railed against many years earlier, and the conditions had come to a point of frustrating the common believers in Europe, many of whom believed that, because of the corruption, the church and Europe faced God's judgment.

Too Far from the Bottom to the Top

In hindsight, it looks like the church was doing just about all it could to bring about some kind of rebellion among the people. In addition to the corruption, immorality, and materialism of the papacy, there was an ever-growing distance between the leadership of the church and the laypeople—those who were members of the church. On top of that, the church had long exploited the ignorance among the common people.

The centuries-old practice of paying cash for penance (penance is an act on the part of the churchgoer to atone for sins) had become rampant in the Catholic Church. In Germany, people actually welcomed the chance to pay cash to secure forgiveness for their sins. Church authorities in Germany greedily exploited the people's belief that they could secure forgiveness through money and began selling them what we could call "advanced pardons from God" for sins they were going to commit in the future. These pardons were what came to be known as *indulgences*, and they were what first moved Martin Luther's heart toward reformationist words and actions.

The church at the time was seen by many as having lost its way, and there were calls from within the church for change. Movements such as the Oratory of Divine Love and the Brethren of the Common Life (see Chapter 6, "A 'Different' Kind of Reformation") were examples of the movements that sprang up as a result of the decay of the church.

We Can Take Care of Ourselves, Thank You

During the Middle Ages, the pope held pretty much absolute authority over all the Catholic churches in Europe. But that didn't last forever. Europe at that time was made up of literally hundreds of principalities—smaller territories ruled by princes. But as the era of the Reformation approached, there arose in Europe a new spirit of nationalism.

During medieval times, the papacy depended on this lack of nationalism to maintain its power. There were some countries with royalty "in charge" (France, for example), but in nations where feudalism—a system of political and military relationships among members of the western European nobility—was practiced, there was a lack of central government authority, a lack of national unity, and a lack of national resistance, all of which made it easier for the pope to exercise his power over the churches and over the governments.

The rise of kingdoms throughout Europe—first in France, then in England and Spain—by the beginning of the fifteenth century brought with them a sense of loyalty and patriotism on the part of each nation's countrymen. This was a serious challenge to the power of the pope, which prior to that time had transcended national boundaries or loyalties.

This new brand of patriotism showed itself in many ways in Europe. Nations began asserting their right to self-determination *without* interference from foreign kings or from a foreign pope. People began seeing themselves as citizens of a nation or subjects of a kingdom. No longer were they willing to simply comply with foreign rule—either in their governments or in their churches. They began to resist the pope's appointment—most of the time from a distant land—of leadership for their churches.

> **Protestant Pearls**
>
> We have not a single command in the Scriptures that infants are to be baptized, or that the apostles practiced it, therefore we confess with good sense that infant baptism is nothing but human invention and notion.
>
> —Menno Simons (1496–1561), Anabaptist leader whose followers became known as Mennonites

Show Us the Money!

Throughout the Middle Ages, the church needed a great amount of revenue for its religious and political ventures, and it collected that money from the principalities throughout Europe. That began to change with the rise in Europe of a "middle class" of people, which happened at roughly the same time as the rise of the independent nations.

The people and nations of Europe also began to withhold financial support of the pope and the central church, and the building of garish churches in Rome. This happened as a growing middle class (or *bourgeoisie*) throughout Europe began keeping their own money for their own needs and ventures. Also, the "new" nation states became more and more reluctant to send their revenues to Rome, opting instead to pay for their own military and other government needs.

Obviously, this situation meant major challenges to the papacy and to the church at large. This was pretty much the end of the idea of an entire Europe united under one emperor or one pope.

Bringing Things into the Light

If you considered the teachings of Martin Luther and the reformers who went before him the seeds of the Protestant Reformation and the religious and political climate in Europe as the soil, then you'd have to consider the *Renaissance* the sunlight that caused that seed of reformation to sprout, grow, and bear fruit.

Probably no historic development more effectively paved the way for the Protestant Reformation than the Renaissance. Put in the simplest of terms and in the context of church history, the Renaissance was the time in history when people began thinking, reading, and reasoning for themselves—apart from the Roman Catholic Church.

The transition from the Middle Ages—that era that began with the final stages of the decline of Roman civilization, sometime during the 400's, and lasted around 1,000 years— to the modern era, began in the fifteenth century. This period, which has come to be known as the Renaissance (the word *renaissance* literally means "rebirth"), had its roots in Italy—particularly the cities of Florence, Milan, Rome, and Venice—and spread into northern Europe through commerce and through those who studied in Italy then traveled north to Germany, England, Spain, and other northern European countries.

> **You Can Look It Up**
>
> The **Renaissance**, which sprang up in Italy and spread north into the rest of Europe, marked the end of the Middle Ages. Literally meaning "rebirth," the Renaissance came with the revival of interest in the classic literature of Rome. It also included what we could call the humanist movement, which was vital to the Reformation.

During that time between the fifth and fifteenth centuries—also called the medieval era— darkness, poverty, ignorance, and superstition ruled the common people in Europe. The church was more of a barrier than an encouragement for learning and wisdom, and the leaders in the church did all it could to maintain control over how people thought.

We're Only Human(ists)!

During the time of the Renaissance, Europeans rediscovered the literature, art, and science of the Classic Age of Rome. Those scholars who began studying and learning classic literature, art, and science were called humanists. *Humanism* put less emphasis on the church as an institution and more on man as an individual.

Although they read and valued patently non-Christian authors, humanists weren't necessarily anti-Christian. Rather, they were simply more skeptical and questioning of the teachings and ways of the church as an institution. In fact, many of the early humanists were professing Christians who just happened to begin taking a dimmer view of what the Catholic Church had done with its faith during the "dark ages" of the previous thousand years.

Italian scholar Francesco Petrarca, or Petrarch (1304–1374), who has been called the "Father of Humanism" (although he wasn't the first known humanist—that would be Lovato Lovati, an Italian judge who was born in 1241 and died in 1309), was a poet, writer, and professing Christian (he was a big fan of the writings of Augustine of Hippo) who had an immeasurable effect on literature and on Christianity in Europe. Petrarch left the study of law to concentrate on the study of classic literature, for which he had a great passion. He collected Greek writings, although he couldn't read Greek. He was also the first to refer to the Middle Ages as "the Dark Ages."

You Can Look It Up

Humanism was a system of thought during the Renaissance that stressed the reading and study of classic literature, arts, and science. It was not necessarily an anti-Christian movement, but it stressed individualism and the ability of people to make their world better for themselves. It was also not necessarily Christian in nature, yet it paved the way for the Protestant Reformation.

People You Should Know

Lovato Lovati (1241–1309), a judge in Padua, Italy, was history's first known humanist. He discovered manuscripts of forgotten classic literature in the library of the Benedictine Abbey of Pomposa. This launched a search in Italy for long-forgotten literature, art, and science, which was one of the identifying marks of the Renaissance. The movement called "humanism" later came into its own the following century, through the work of Francesco Petrarca (Petrach), whose writings had an incredible effect on literature in Europe for centuries to come.

What Happens When Reading and Faith Mix

People we now refer to as Christian humanists denounced and made fun of the Catholic Church for its corruption and greed, using irony, sarcasm, and lampoon in their writings and speech. They also promoted learning and education as a way to correct what was wrong with the church. Two fifteenth-century Christian humanists who worked to reform the church were Nicholas of Cusa (d. 1464) and Wessel Gansfort (d. 1489). Sixteenth-century reformers Ulrich Zwingli (d. 1531), Philip Melanchthon (d. 1560), and John Calvin (d. 1564), all of whom we will discuss in later chapters, were considered Christian humanists.

Going Deeper

Christian humanists were some of the key figures in preparing the way for the Protestant Reformation. The object of their criticism, and sometimes mockery, was the established church of the time, and not the Christian faith itself. Ulrich Zwingli and John Calvin, who led reformation movements in Switzerland and France, respectively, were what we call Christian humanists. Christian humanism embraced parts of the Catholic Church and parts of Protestantism, which emerged in the sixteenth century.

During the Middle Ages, scholars—the churchmen of the time—paid a lot of attention to the search for religious truth. However, as Renaissance and humanistic thinking took over, scholars began looking at history, literature, art, and science differently. No longer did they see these things through a Christian or religious lens. Historic events were looked at as simply that—occurrences in history. At the same time, there arose in Europe an interest in classic literature—in Greek and in Latin—that eventually included the Scriptures themselves.

The New Testament of the Bible and the classic literature had something in common: They were written in Greek. And it was only a matter of time before humanists turned their attention from purely secular literature to the sacred. An Italian philosopher by the name of Lorenzo Valla (1405–1457), considered one of the greatest Renaissance minds, was the first to subject Jerome's *Vulgate*—the Bible as it had been translated to Latin—to the same critiques as classic literature. Valla's work influenced the German Reformation, and it was greatly prized by Martin Luther.

This Is Not Our Father's Faith!

While the Renaissance—and the humanist movement—in Italy was mostly a literary or secular event, it had a different look as it spread north to Germany, France, and England. In Germany in particular, it became primarily religious in nature. Instead of focusing only on Greek and Latin literary classics, people became interested in studying Greek and Hebrew scriptures. And as people read the scriptures in their original languages, they saw minor flaws in the Latin *Vulgate*. People of the time were greatly interested in searching the Bible for themselves to find the true roots of their faith. They wanted to know what the original Christian faith looked like in the lives of the early believers—long before the rules, trappings, and authoritarianism of the established church.

In that respect, the Renaissance truly undermined the authority of the Roman Catholic Church, which could no longer keep people from exploring their faith for themselves. It was during this time when more and more people began looking at the Bible and not Rome as the authority for their faith. More than that, as people began reading the Scriptures on their own, many felt that the Catholic Church differed greatly from the church described in the New Testament.

Humanists, Humanists Everywhere!

The humanist movement was vital to the setting of the stage for the Protestant Reformation. History gives us the stories of several key humanists who helped set the stage for religious reformation throughout Europe. Here is an overview of some of them:

◆ In France, the two leading humanists were Jacques Lefèvre d'Étaples (1450–1536) and Guillaume Budé (1468–1540), whose work as scholars prepared the way for reformation in their country.

◆ In Holland, Desiderius Erasmus of Rotterdam (1466–1536) was one of the greatest scholars of the Renaissance and was considered one of the most important humanists of all time. Educated by the Brethren of the Common Life (see Chapter 6), Erasmus trained for the priesthood and was ordained a priest in 1492. He was devoted to literature, and in 1516 he developed the first Greek translation of the New Testament printed, which Martin Luther and Swiss reformer Ulrich Zwingli later used. Erasmus believed in making the Bible available to—and readable by—all: "I wish that the Scriptures might be translated into all languages, so that not only the Scots and the Irish, but also the Turk and the Saracen might read and understand them." Erasmus, who has been referred to by historians as "the journalist of scholarship," was a staunch critic of some of the practices of the Roman Catholic Church, even before the Reformation began. That despite the fact that he remained in the Catholic Church. His writings included *The Praise of Folly*, a scathing satire of the Church and its corruption. In a very real way, Erasmus was an unwitting contributor to the Protestant Reformation. Though he did as much as anyone to prepare the way for the Reformation, he remained a Catholic and was as staunch a critic of the Reformation movement as he was of the church.

People You Should Know

Desiderius Erasmus of Rotterdam (Holland), also known as "the journalist of scholarship," is considered by historians to be the greatest of all the humanists. He is also considered one of the most important forerunners to Martin Luther's Reformation. During a seven-day stay in London, he wrote *The Praise of Folly*, which satirized the practices of the Roman Catholic Church. Erasmus was ordained a priest in 1492, but he left the monastery because he felt unsuited for the life of a monk.

◆ In Germany, Cardinal Nicholas of Cusa (about 1400–1464) and Johann Reuchlin (1455–1522) prepared the way for the Reformation, which later started in their homeland. Cardinal Nicholas was the leading thinker of his time, and Reuchlin was the author of *Rudimenta linguae hebraicae* (1506), which established the study of Hebrew in the West.

◆ In Spain, Cardinal Francisco Ximénez of Cisneros (1436–1517) promoted a humanist project titled the *Complutensian Polygot Bible*. The project included contributions by scholars Elio Antonio de Nebrija (1436–1517).

◆ In England, Christian humanists such as Dean of St. Paul's John Colet (1467–1519) contributed to changes in the church. His Oxford lectures on Paul's epistles were keys in preparing England for reformation.

Thinking, Reading, and Worshiping—As an Individual

One of the reasons the Renaissance helped set the stage for the Reformation was that it included a spirit of individualism. People were now able to—encouraged to—study and think for themselves, apart from the Roman Catholic Church.

This development helped pave the way for Martin Luther's emphasis on the priesthood of the individual believer, as referred to in the New Testament in the apostle Peter's first epistle. It also contributed to the acceptance of Luther's position that each Christian had the right to go directly to God in prayer and to interpret the message of the Scriptures himself. And all of this without the aid or approval of a priest!

As this new atmosphere of individuality spread around Europe, it became more and more difficult for the church to hold sway over the thinking of scholars and teachers, not to mention the average churchgoer. Now, for the first time in ten centuries, people were thinking independently and critically. For that reason, the church could no longer control or exert excessive influence on the thinking of its members.

It was a whole new way of thinking and studying in Europe, and it was aided by one of history's most important inventions.

The Power of the Press

If the pen is mightier than the sword, how much mightier must a printing press be?

The power of the press was demonstrated amply during the Renaissance and during the Protestant Reformation. That's because it was through the advent of the printing press that the messages of Luther and other reformers—as well as the Bible itself—were widely distributed and read throughout Europe.

With one major invention—the printing press that used metal moveable type—Johann Gutenberg revolutionized the history of literature. It is widely believed that Gutenberg invented the printing press, but that is not really accurate. Printing by the use of hand-cut wooden blocks was invented in Asia around the fifth century C.E. You could say that Gutenberg improved on what had been invented already and that he invented a new printing process—one that used individual metal letters that could be placed in a row, then reused.

People You Should Know
Johann Gutenberg was key to the coming of the Protestant Reformation because he made it possible, through his development of reusable metal moveable type (he did not invent the printing press, as is commonly believed), which made it easier for reformers and others to print and distribute their materials.

But you could also say that these developments revolutionized printing, which helped lead Europe to another revolution.

Gutenberg developed his printing press—which has been called Germany's main contribution to the Renaissance—around 1455–1456 at Mainz, Germany, on the Rhine. Because of Gutenberg's work, around the middle of the fifteenth century, people had the ability to print books and other materials in mass quantities. Simply put, what could once be produced and distributed by the dozens or, at best, hundreds, could now be printed and distributed—and quickly, at that—by the tens of thousands and more. People in most social and economic classes now had access to a variety of printed materials.

Gutenberg's new invention was kept pretty much secret until 1462, when Mainz was plundered and Gutenberg's printers dispersed. Within twenty years, printing presses had been set up in Rome, Paris, Cracow, and Westminster. By the time Martin Luther was born in 1483, printing had become well established throughout Europe.

In our day and age, it's hard to imagine a time and place when a copy of the Bible isn't readily available to us. We can walk into any bookstore and purchase a copy of the Bible in any size or color, and in as many translations as we would ever have time to read. But it hasn't always been that way. During the Middle Ages, a Bible cost the equivalent of one year's wages.

The first book printed by Gutenberg's press was the Bible, and it wasn't long before the Scriptures were translated into all European languages. The Scriptures became readily available to many Europeans, and many came to believe that the practices and teachings of the Roman Catholic Church were far from the New Testament model of the church.

In addition to the Bible, the teachings and writings of the first figures of the Protestant Reformation (Luther and Melanchthon) were widely circulated. That included the writings that criticized the Roman Catholic Church for its corruption and preoccupation with material wealth. In short order, Luther's 95 Theses (see Chapter 8, "It All Started Over Indulgences"), as well as his other works, were distributed throughout Germany. For the first time in church history, all classes of society had access to printed reformationist materials.

It was a whole new world in Europe, a world in which the dominant religious establishment would be under an intense public scrutiny like it had never known.

> **Protestant Pearls**
>
> [In an argument with a scholar] If God spares my life, ere many years I will cause a boy who drives the plough to know more of the scriptures than you do.
>
> —William Tyndale (1492–1536), Father of the English Bible

The Time Is Now

Historians look at the events that led to the Protestant Reformation as a fascinating mixture of thinking, reading, and action—all converging to bring about a revolution that would change the whole Western world, including the parts of the world that weren't very well known at the time. Theologians—or just plain Christians, for that matter—see what happened at that time in world history as an example of the sovereignty of God at work, meaning that God himself put the right people with the right message at the right time in the right place to bring about the changes in the church and in society that he wanted made.

The Least You Need to Know

- Corruption and materialism within the Roman Catholic Church helped make the Protestant Reformation both necessary and possible.
- The Renaissance (the "rebirth" that started in Italy and spread north into Europe) was a key factor in preparing Europe for the revolutionary movement known as the Protestant Reformation.
- Humanists—particularly Christian humanists—were key figures in preparing Europe for the Reformation.
- An often overlooked but vital occurrence that helped make the Reformation possible was the invention of the printing press. This made the Bible and printed materials from the reformers widely available to the European population.

Part 2

The Difference the Reformers Made

The history of the Protestant Reformation of the sixteenth century is full of some of the most interesting, inspirational characters the world has ever known. These were people of tremendous faith, commitment, and conviction, people who were willing to stand up and be counted for what they believed in.

In the Middle Ages, standing up to the Catholic Church was no small thing. During that time in history, being seen as a "heretic"—a person who believed in something other than what the established church believed in—could get you excommunicated, banished from your home, or worse.

The sixteenth century is a fascinating time in the history of the Western world, and it was also a time when developments in religion and politics would affect the world for many centuries to come.

A "Different" Kind of Reformation

In This Chapter

- ◆ The decay of "true" spirituality in the Catholic Church
- ◆ The people's desire for something more spiritual and less liturgical
- ◆ Geert Groote, Thomas à Kempis, and the Brethren of the Common Life
- ◆ How these spiritual movements contributed to the coming of the Protestant Reformation

Centuries before Martin Luther launched the Protestant Reformation, there were reformers who wanted to break from the Roman Catholic Church and its teachings, reformers who saw the church and its leadership as so filled with greed and corruption that they felt it would be better to move in a different direction. They recognized that the church was getting richer—at the cost of the common people, who were getting poorer.

But there were also those who, while recognizing the problems within the church, wanted to reform it from within and bring it back to its more spiritual roots. These were the people who considered themselves good Catholics but who wanted their religion to be something they could experience, their God someone they could know *personally*, rather than through sacramental exercises. These people wanted the average church-going Christian—in other words, the laity—to be able to worship God on his or her own.

During the Middle Ages there were protests and movements whose aim was to return the church to the simplicity and devotion to God of the first-century church, and to return to the teachings of the Bible. There were other movements that rejected the Catholic priesthood and sacraments, and there were those who wanted to "clean up" the way the church did things.

This search came to a head at the beginning of the fourteenth century, when a new movement of "mysticism" arose within Christianity, including the established church.

The "Mystical" Side of Christianity

In the context of medieval Christianity, mysticism refers to a life of prayer and contemplation that stresses a personal, experiential knowledge of God apart from any kind of sacramental or religious exercise. Christian mystics believed that God is above humanity and above everything else he created and that God is not just an aspect of reality here on earth.

Going Deeper

Mysticism didn't just suddenly appear on the scene in the few hundred years before the Protestant Reformation. Mysticism, which can be defined as the effort to experience and know God personally, played a huge part in the history of the Christian church, starting with the early bishops and church fathers. The mystics of the fourteenth and fifteenth centuries didn't bring about the Reformation, but they played a part in preparing hearts and minds for it.

The beliefs of mysticism included three major fundamentals of faith: awareness of God and confession to him, a life lived totally under God, and a personal experience of God. In other words, mystics believed that a believer could personally *know* and *experience* the God he or she prayed to.

Going Deeper

A German Theology was what Martin Luther called an important but anonymously written book published by Luther in 1516. This book was a product of the German mystics, and it taught complete abandonment of one's self to the will of God, to the point that one's soul became one with God through Jesus Christ. Luther said of this book: "Next to the Bible and St. Augustine, no book has ever come into my hands from which I have learnt more of God and Christ, and man and all things that are."

The mysticism that arose in the Middle Ages came in an era when Christianity had become too institutionalized and had gotten away from its first-century apostolic roots. But this was hardly the first mysticism to arise within the church.

This Mysticism Is Nothing New!

This "new" mystical movement didn't just suddenly appear on the scene in the fourteenth and fifteenth centuries. Mysticism existed in many forms throughout Christian history. In fact, it wasn't even limited to the Christian faith. There were many examples of mystics and mysticism in Judaism. Christian mysticism had as its roots great teachers of the past, including Thomas Aquinas, Augustine of Hippo, and Bernard of Clairvaux (1090–1153). Also, the Desert Fathers, fourth-century hermits who would go out into the deserts of Syria, Egypt, and Palestine to separate themselves from the material world and ponder the nature of God, are considered forerunners of medieval Christian mysticism.

But these are only a few historical examples of Christian mystics. There are many other mystics throughout church history who greatly influenced the thinking in the church heading into the time of the Protestant Reformation. Early church (pre-Constantine) mystics include Ignatius of Antioch, Polycarp, Justin Martyr, and others. Well-known medieval mystics include Meister Eckhart, Jan van Ruysbroeck, Julian of Norwich, Catherine of Siena, Thomas à Kempis, Nicholas of Cusa, Teresa of Avila, and John of the Cross.

People You Should Know

Jan van Ruysbroeck (1293–1381) was a Flemish Roman Catholic mystic, born in Ruisbroek, near Brussels. His book *The Adornment of Spiritual Marriage* describes spiritual maturity in terms of the preparation of the bride (the human spirit) to receive the bridegroom (Jesus Christ). His books were published in Latin in 1552, in German in 1701, and in English in 1934. Ruysbroeck's work greatly influenced Geert Groote, who was instrumental in the founding of the Brethren of the Common Life, as well as Johannes Tauler (1300–1361), the German mystic.

However, one of the most important of the Middle Ages mystics was a layman who came to be called Francis of Assisi.

What Do You Want to Do with Your Life, Francis?

Francis of Assisi was a layman who won fame and influence in the Christian world by dedicating himself to a life of poverty and service to God and to humankind. Francis was born Giovanni Francesco Bernardone in 1181 in Assisi, a town about midway down the Italian peninsula.

You might say Francis was born with the proverbial silver spoon in his mouth. His father was a wealthy cloth merchant by the name of Pietro de Bernardone. It was after his service in the military in defense of Assisi that Francis began taking his Christian faith and its message seriously and the messages of poverty in the gospels literally. Francis was taken prisoner of war after a battle between Assisi and Perugia. While imprisoned, he became very ill. At that point, he resolved to change his way of life.

After leaving the military, Francis entered a long period of self-doubt and self-examination. In 1205 he went on a pilgrimage to Rome, where he was moved at the sight of the beggars. He then began to personally experience the physical destitution that would later become a huge part of his teaching. Later, Francis is said to have heard the voice of God telling him to rebuild the church of San Damiano. He sold his horse and some of his father's textiles to fund that endeavor. This act angered his father, who saw his son as a do-nothing—or at least an underachiever.

Francis was called to appear before the local bishop, who ordered him to repay his father all Francis owed him. Francis agreed to repay his father, then stripped naked and said "You'd better have my clothes too." Francis, covered with nothing but a tunic the bishop's servants had given him, embarked on a life of simplicity and poverty. He went off to rebuild San Damiano and lived by begging.

If the Disciples Did It, So Should I!

In the winter of 1208 Francis attended Mass, where he heard the account of Christ's sending the disciples out to preach. "Provide yourselves with no gold or silver, not even with a few coppers for your purses, with no haversack for the jouney or spare tunic or footwear or a staff," Christ told the twelve (Matthew 10:9–10), and then sent them on their way.

The message in Christ's words to his disciples touched Francis to the core. He took the call behind those words personally, and he began a life of poverty and preaching, taking with him not so much as a knapsack or a cent.

Protestant Pearls

What is noblest and most to be valued in our souls is not only broken and wounded, but altogether corrupted, whatever of dignity it may reflect.

—John Calvin (1509–1564), French-born Reformation theologian

Francis was later joined in his lifestyle by two men who came to be known as Brother Bernard and Brother Peter. The three of them wondered what the will of God was for their lives, and the story goes that they opened the Bible three times and found three texts, each of which pointed them toward lives of poverty and self-denial.

Others soon joined Francis, Bernard, and Peter. They did everything they could to identify themselves with the poorest of the poor. Francis wrote a set of basic rules, called the *"Regula Primitiva,"* which were probably taken directly from the gospels (Matthew, Mark, Luke, and John). Francis traveled to Rome and submitted the *Regula Primitiva* to Pope Innocent III, who voiced doubt about whether the way of life Francis was suggesting was practical. Innocent gave official church sanction to the movement, on condition that they elect a superior. Francis was elected superior and the group returned to Assisi.

"Lady Poverty" Expands

The movement started by Francis received plenty of attention—as well as new followers. Within less than two decades after embracing "Lady Poverty," Francis had 5,000 followers. By the end of the thirteenth century, there were more than 35,000 "Franciscans." This included the women, who made up a Franciscan order called "Poor Clares," after their founder, Clare Schifi.

Francis of Assisi wasn't trying to reform the church as much as he was trying to follow Christ in the way he saw in the gospels—with simplicity and without any hint of materialism, or even concern for his own earthly existence. In this respect, Francis and his followers, though they were Roman Catholics, were truly forerunners of the Reformation, as they stood as living arguments against the religious power structure and the wealth of the established church.

The Mystics Make a Difference

While the pre-Reformation mystics weren't in complete agreement in all things concerning the faith, their way of practicing that faith remained alive and well. Heading into the fourteenth century, mysticism picked up steam, and that momentum continued through the fifteenth century and into the sixteenth, when the Reformation made its mark on human history.

The Late Middle Ages Church: "We Need Something Different!"

By the end of the Middle Ages, the Catholic Church—particularly the papacy, but also the higher and lower clergy that served under it—was a wreck, and the people knew it. Much, if not most, of the church's "fall from grace" in the eyes of the people was of its own making. The church had been guilty of many evils against its members and against the population in general. The economic and educational oppression, the corruption of the papacy and the clergy, the abuse of indulgences and simony (the sale of church offices) had made the church the target of strong criticism and opposition from within and without.

And if all that weren't enough, the church as an institution had taken on a worldliness at the expense of focusing on the inner spiritual lives of people. This became especially true as the Renaissance swept through Europe. At that time, the popes—we can call them "Renaissance Popes"—seemed more interested in building libraries and adorning the church's headquarters in Rome than in being spiritual leaders of the church.

A Religion the People Could Touch, Feel, Experience

The practices of the church had become in the eyes of many people too "*liturgical.*" This lack of more personal religion practices was one of a growing list of problems for the Catholic Church during the Middle Ages. The church was run using a pretty rigid and legalistic system in which everything flowed from the pope down, through the different levels of clergy, then to the laity.

You Can Look It Up

Liturgy is the catch-all word for all the practices of worship—chants, readings, rituals, sacraments, rites, and so on—in a given church or within a religion or congregation. In the context of the reformers, in some ways liturgy can be seen in opposition to the private, personal devotion to God. Many of the Christian mystics wanted to stress that personal devotion over the **liturgical** practices of the church.

Reformers began to criticize the organization and structure of the church, and many who remained loyal to the church and its practices began to call for a revival of spiritual emphasis. These people wanted to change the church from within, to move it away from its focus on "religious" activities and beliefs and to a focus on practical or "experiential" religion. In the simplest of terms, the people within these movements didn't want a God who was accessible only through their priests or through sacraments and ceremonies and legalisms.

These movements placed value on what is called "personal piety," which means a simple, personal devotion to God himself, rather than to the church as an organization. These movements downplayed "religious" activities and stressed more "spiritual" ones, such as personal prayer and Bible reading, contemplation of God, and individual service to God and people.

The Movers and Shakers in Pre-Reformation Christian Mysticism

There were many "mystical" figures and movements that figured prominantly in preparing Europe spiritually for the Protestant Reformation. Among these was Meister Eckhart (1260–1327), a German mystic who was considered a driving force in the pre-Reformation spiritual world of his country. Johann Tauler (1300–1361), a student of Eckhart, was also a

German mystic. Tauler was a forceful preacher who emphasized the nothingness of mankind before God. These were just two of countless individual mystics who influenced the church toward change.

People You Should Know

Meister Eckhart (1260–1327) was a German mystic and Christian theologian who is considered a driving force in the pre-Reformation spiritual world of Germany. He was Born in Hochheim and studied and taught in Dominican schools, notably in Paris, Strasbourg, and Cologne. He held a series of offices in his order. Eckhart communicated in various ways his burning sense of God's nearness to humanity. Eckhart's mysticism is considered to hold to traditional scriptural teaching.

In addition to the individuals, mystical movements or groups such as the Oratory of Divine Love in Italy, the Observant Franciscans in England, and the Brethren of the Common Life in the Low Countries (the Low Countries are Belgium, Luxembourg, and the Netherlands) began springing up throughout the Christian world in Europe. This desire for a deeper spiritualism made its way to the common Christians of the time, many of whom hungered for devotional books—books that stressed personal dedication to and love for God.

There were mystical movements whose beliefs were—by the standards of both the Catholic Church and the Bible—erroneous (heretical is the word a lot of experts use here). But there were those mystical movements that sought to return the church to its spiritual roots as spelled out in the New Testament. Among the most important of these was the Brethren of the Common Life, a movement that sprang up from an earlier movement called the *Devotio Moderna*.

Serving an Eternal God in a Modern Way

Devotio Moderna literally means "a modern way of serving God." This popular fourteenth-century movement stressed the necessity of becoming more like Christ by following his commands, including loving everyone.

This mystical movement, which got its start in the late fourteenth century in Holland, northern France, and northern Germany—around the same time that the ideas of humanism were taking root in Italy—was like most mystical movements in that it emphasized the more personal form of Christianity. The *Devotio Moderna* stressed the reading of the Scriptures, meditation and prayer, personal reverence for God, and religious education.

While the *Devotio Moderna* was not a reformation movement in the same way Martin Luther's movement—or those of Luther's forerunners, such as John Wycliffe or John Huss—was, it was in its own way a reformation movement. The *Devotio Moderna* was a movement of spiritual revival within the Catholic Church among those who were still loyal to the pope and the church.

The foremost founder of the *Devotio Moderna* was Geert (or Gerard or Gerhard) Groote of Deventer, Holland. Groote was the son of a prominent Deventer merchant, and he studied abroad before settling into a worldly life of self-indulgence and luxury. That all changed in 1374, when Groote was dramatically converted to Christianity. From then on he lived a life of personal devotion and service to God and service of people.

What Did Groote Have to Say?

After his conversion, Groote joined a monastery, where he served for about three years before leaving to begin a traveling mission of preaching and teaching. Groote's preaching had great impact on those who heard him. He taught that true religion was all about loving and worshiping God, and not about taking vows or living by a list of rules.

Groote preached repentance and criticized the clergy of the day for its corruption and materialism. He also wrote tracts criticizing the sale of church offices and the immorality of the Catholic clergy. His criticisms got the attention of the church leadership, which revoked his license to preach in 1383. (Groote, who wanted to stay in the good graces of the Catholic Church, appealed this order to the pope, who gave him permission to preach. However, he died before this permission could reach him.)

Groote's teaching foreshadowed Martin Luther's teachings of justification by faith, which is a fancy, theological way of saying that humans are justified or "made right" with God not on the basis of what they do, but on the basis of faith in the work of Christ on the cross. Groote not only believed in the doctrine of justification by faith, he believed that it was the devil who told people that their good works had anything to do with their salvation.

Groote wanted the common people to be able to read the Bible, and to bring that desire to reality, he began translating parts of the Scriptures into his native language. He believed in a more personal experience with God, based not on taking vows or following rules, but on the love of Christ. He believed in a close personal union with God. He believed that love, faith, and humility were far more important than outward works.

> **Protestant Pearls**
>
> Faith is, then, a lively and steadfast trust in the favor of God, wherewith we commit ourselves altogether unto God. And that trust is so surely grounded and sticks so fast in our hearts, that a man would not once doubt of it, although he should die a thousand times therefore.
>
> —William Tyndale (1492–1536), Father of the English Bible

Groote's teaching and preaching influenced all who heard him. But his greatest legacy may be the part he played in starting a movement that was vital to preparing the way for the Protestant Reformation.

It's a Common Life!

One of Groote's closest associates in the *Devotio Moderna* movement was a man named Florens Radewijns (1350–1400), an ordained priest who had studied in Prague. It was in Radewijns's home and under his leadership that the Brethren of the Common Life, a community made up mostly of laypeople with some clergy—mostly followers of Groote— was formed.

Geert Groote died of the plague in 1384, and Radewijns took over the leadership of the *Devotio Moderna*. In 1387, Radewijns founded the group's most important and influential house, in Windesheim in Holland. It was here that the Brethren of the Common Life were formally recognized by Pope Boniface IX in 1395. The house in Windesheim was combined with already established houses. By about 1500 the movement included about ninety-seven monasteries.

Practical Mystics

The Brethren of the Common Life were a mystical group, and some have referred to them as "practical mystics," meaning that they combined their devotion to God and desire for closeness with him with service to humankind. This movement spread from city to city as houses for men and for women—there was a feminine counterpart of the Brethren of the Common Life called the Sisters of the Common Life—were founded in Germany and in the Netherlands.

The Brethren of the Common Life stressed and practiced the rules of poverty, chastity, and obedience to God. Members dedicated themselves to the spiritual disciplines of Bible reading and prayer. They wanted to get away from the overly complicated rites and theology of the church and replace them with a simpler, more individual and personal devotion to God. They renounced the ways of the world and sought unity with God through prayer and study of the Bible.

Protestant Pearls

Our confidence in Christ does not make us lazy, negligent, or careless, but on the contrary it awakens us, urges us on, and makes us active in living righteous lives and doing good. There is no self-confidence to compare with this.

—Ulrich Zwingli (1484–1531), Founder of Swiss Protestantism

The Brethren of the Common Life supported their community through publishing. They wrote, copied manuscripts, and bound their own volumes. With the advent of moveable type printing (see Chapter 5, "The Right Message at the Right Time"), the Brethren began operating their own presses, which enabled them to spread their message more quickly and effectively.

Learnin' and Lovin' God

The Brethren of the Common Life were also dedicated to the process of education and taught in local schools as well as founding schools of their own in the Netherlands and Germany. These schools were centers where people studied literature as well as learned about personal devotion to God. The Brethren and the schools they operated made huge marks in the history of Christianity. These schools were also key in preparing the way for the Protestant Reformation as they educated several key figures in church history, including Desiderius Erasmus, Martin Luther (he sat under their teaching as a very young boy), and a monk by the name of Thomas à Kempis.

No Doubting Thomas

Thomas à Kempis (about 1380–1471) was one of the best known and most influential students of the Brethren of the Common Life. Thomas, who spent his life clinging to the ways and teachings of the Brethren of the Common Life, wrote or edited *The Imitation of Christ*, the widely circulated and read devotional handbook.

> **Going Deeper**
>
> *The Imitation of Christ* is believed to have been written in 1427. The absence of a reference to its authorship on the most ancient manuscripts have led to questions concerning who wrote it. Various writers such as St. Bernard of Clairvaux, St. Bonaventure, Pope Innocent III, Henry of Kalkar, John à Kempis, Walter Hilton, Jean Charlier de Gerson, and Giovanni Gersen have been thought the author. However, the consensus is that the author was Thomas à Kempis.

Since it began circulating during the second quarter of the fifteenth century, *The Imitation of Christ* has been printed in many languages and literally thousands of editions and has become one of the most-read books ever written. It is believed that outside of the Bible, *The Imitation of Christ* is the most-read spiritual book in the world.

Loving God Means Everything

Thomas à Kempis was born Thomas Hemerken in Kempen, Germany, and schooled in the Netherlands, at the center of the Brethren of the Common Life. He attended the Brethren of the Common Life school at Deventer, where he came under the spiritual teaching and guidance of Florens Radewijns.

People You Should Know

Thomas à Kempis was a German monk who is traditionally considered the author of the book *The Imitation of Christ.* He was born in about 1380 in Kempen, Germany, and schooled at Deventer, in the Netherlands, at the center of the Brethren of the Common Life founded by Geert Groote. A number of his treatises on the monastic life and little devotional essays have been translated into English. Thomas spent 70 of his 90-plus years at the convent of St. Agnes near Zwolle, where he wrote, preached, and counseled.

Thomas à Kempis spent seventy years of his life at the convent of St. Agnes near Zwolle. He was ordained a priest in 1413. Like many members of the Brethren, Thomas worked principally at writing books and copying manuscripts. He also did some teaching and counseling. A number of his writings on the *monastic* life and some of his little devotional essays have been translated into English. He is credited with writing the great devotional book *The Imitation of Christ* in about 1427, although some scholars doubt that he authored it.

The Imitation of Christ, by far the best-known and most influential publication of the *Devotio Moderna,* is a reflection of the ways and ideas of the Brethren of the Common Life. It stresses the abandonment of one's will. It doesn't advocate abandoning outward religious observances and practices, but it minimizes their importance in the life of the believer. It stresses the spiritual disciplines of contemplation and the love of Christ.

The Imitation of Christ was originally written in Latin and was divided into four books, the longest of which is the third:

- ◆ Thoughts Helpful in the Life of the Soul
- ◆ The Interior Life
- ◆ Internal Consolation
- ◆ An Invitation to Holy Communion

You Can Look It Up

Monastic means a life of religious seclusion. In its original language, the root word for monasticism literally means either "dwelling alone" or "celibate and single." In the religious context, monasticism denotes a life of seclusion from the world, under religious vows. The main object of the monastic life is withdrawal from the world and its systems, as they are adopted by most of humankind.

Each of the four books of *The Imitation of Christ* contains anywhere from twelve (book 2) to fifty-two (book 3) chapters, each of which covers a single topic concerning the Christian life. This book is still one of the best loved spiritual books ever printed.

Some Good Words from Thomas à Kempis

The Imitation of Christ contains some of the key beliefs of the Brethren of the Common Life, including the need for a personal, heartfelt love of Christ:

> What can the world offer you, without Jesus? To be without Jesus is hell most grievous; to be with Jesus is to know the sweetness of heaven. If Jesus is with you, no enemy can harm you. Whoever finds Jesus, finds a rich treasure, and a good above every good. He who loses Jesus loses much indeed, and more than the whole world. Poorest of all men is he who lives without Jesus, and richest of all is he who stands in favour with Jesus.

In *The Imitation of Christ*, Thomas à Kempis also wrote of that personal devotion to Christ and the personal experiences that come from that devotion:

> If a man knows what it is to love Jesus, and to disregard himself for the sake of Jesus, then he is really blessed. Keep yourself close to Jesus in life as well as death; commit yourself to his faithfulness, for he can help you when everything else will fail.

The writings of Thomas à Kempis defined the movement known as the *Devotio Moderna*, as well as the movements that sprang from it. These movements, including the Brethren of the Common Life, were responsible—albeit indirectly—for preparing the way for Martin Luther's message. That preparation involved stoking a hunger within the European laity for a more personal kind of spiritualism, a kind they could practice apart from the established church.

Perhaps none of the Brethren's alumni did more to prepare the way for the Protestant Reformation than a man by the name of Desiderius Erasmus.

Erasmus Lays an Egg

In Chapter 5, we discussed Desiderius Erasmus of Rotterdam, Holland, who was considered one of the greatest Renaissance scholars and one of the most important humanists of his time. He was devoted to literature of all kinds and believed that the Bible should be available to people of all social and economic classes.

He also wrote some important literature of his own. In 1503, Erasmus's *The Handbook of the Christian Knight* was published in the Low Countries. This manual reflected Erasmus's educational background with the Brethren of the Common Life in that it stressed the importance of "inwardness" when it came to religion. In this handbook, Erasmus taught that a man's conduct should be determined by personal devotion to God and not traditions and religious practices.

Erasmus is remembered by historians as a committed Catholic, but he is also remembered as an almost unwitting forerunner of the Protestant Reformation—one of the most important. His writings include a scathing satire of the church, the papacy, and the clergy, titled *The Praise of Folly*.

Martin Luther and Erasmus had considerable differences between them. While Erasmus recognized the multitude of problems in the Catholic Church, he didn't have the kind of personality it took to "make waves." But when it comes to talking about the Protestant Reformation, it has still been said that "Erasmus laid the egg and Luther hatched it." Erasmus's writings were widely read during the early sixteenth century, and they set the stage for reformation by exposing and criticizing the shortcomings and corruption of the church.

Erasmus was one of many people in the Middle Ages who wanted to see changes in the church, but whose words and actions didn't lead directly to the revolutionary changes that were to come in the sixteenth century. But at the same time, the words Erasmus spoke and wrote helped get European Christendom ready for what was to come.

By now, the European world was well into the first quarter of the sixteenth century. By that time, Europe had unwittingly become prepared—politically, economically, socially, and spiritually—for the reformation-turned-revolution that was about to sweep the Christian world of the time. It was the eve of the Protestant Reformation, and all the ingredients of a world-changing movement were in place. The time was right for change. Now all that was needed was the right man with the right message to stand up and be heard.

That man, of course, was a monk by the name of Martin Luther.

The Least You Need to Know

- The mystical movement arose to fill in the vacuum of personal spirituality that had developed because the church became too institutionalized and corrupt.
- Geert Groote and Thomas à Kempis foreshadowed the Reformation in their focus on justification by faith, Bible reading, the inner life of the soul, and serving others sacrificially.
- *The Imitation of Christ*, written by Thomas à Kempis, contains key beliefs of the Brethren of the Common Life, fostering a deep relationship with Christ, and has become one of the best-selling books of all time.

Chapter 7

The Making of the Man for the Mission

In This Chapter

- ◆ Martin Luther's youth and education
- ◆ Luther's "call" to the monastery
- ◆ Luther's inner struggles as a monk and as a priest
- ◆ A "time of clarity" for Luther

It's been said that no figure in the Christian faith outside of Jesus Christ himself has been written about as much as Martin Luther. Clearly, Luther is one of the most important figures not just in the Christian faith, but in all of world history. In list after list and survey after survey, historians name Luther in the top five or ten most important figures in Western civilization.

Martin Luther is considered such an important historical figure simply because he is the one who started the Protestant Reformation, a movement—a revolution, in fact—that changed the religious, political, and social culture of Europe, then helped shape the culture of what would later be called the "New World."

What kind of man can have that kind of influence on the whole of a culture? What kind of man can change the course of history, simply by standing up for what he believes in and by issuing challenges when he sees wrongs being done? What kind of man will stand up to the established power structures and tell them they have to change the way they do things, risking his social and religious standing as well as his physical well-being?

Martin Luther, the father of the Protestant Reformation, was just the kind of man it took to lead the revolution. But he was truly a man of humble beginnings.

Martin's Childhood: Hard Work, Hard Discipline, and Lots of Ambition

Martin Luther was born November 10, 1483, in Eisleben, Saxony (today, part of Germany), in the county of Mansfeld. Martin was baptized the next day, St. Martin's Day, after which his parents named him.

Going Deeper

St. Martin's Day, which has been celebrated for centuries on November 11, was the calendar day in 1483 that one-day-old Martin Luther was baptized. The future reformer was also named after the saint, who was the patron saint of beggars. St. Martin's Day was celebrated first in France, and later in Germany, Scandinavia, and the Baltics.

People You Should Know

Hans Luther was the father of the great reformer Martin Luther. He was a miner by trade, and a devoted father and family man and a tough disciplinarian on his eldest son, Martin. Hans Luther was committed to making sure Luther had the best education he could afford, but he didn't approve of Martin's entering the local monastery as a monk or of his being ordained a priest.

Martin's parents were Hans and Margaretha Luther (or "Luder," as it was spelled at the time). Hans Luther was a miner who in time found some financial success as the operator of several mining shafts and smelting furnaces. Margaretha (or "Margaret") is remembered by historians as a deeply religious woman who likely shaped her son's early thinking about the Christian faith.

In search of work, the Luthers had moved to Eisleben from Möhra, where Hans had learned the mining trade. That search for work took the Luthers to Mansfeld when Martin was six months old.

Hans and Margaretha were strict and stern parents, and Luther later recalled in his writings how he was severely punished by both parents when he strayed even slightly off course. The same went for school, where Martin recorded incidents of floggings over grammatical errors in class. These were not pleasant memories for Luther, but many historians say that the treatment Luther received as a child was only slightly more severe than that of most parents in that time and place.

Hans Luther was an energetic and hard-working family man who rose above his peasant background and established for himself a place of respect in the community of Mansfeld. In time, Hans became the owner of at least six mines and two foundries. In addition, he had a seat on the Mansfeld town council.

Hans drove himself hard, and he did the same with his children. He was a severe disciplinarian, but he was also a father who wanted better for his son than what he himself had growing up. Hans did well enough in his business that he was able to provide Martin, his oldest child, with an excellent education.

Martin Hits the Books

Martin Luther received the typical religious education of the time, at home and at the Latin school of Mansfeld. He learned all the beliefs and practices of the Catholic Church, and he was taught how to put them into practice for himself. Martin was taught that God would judge all his actions on judgment day, and he was exposed to the Catholic practice of going to the Virgin Mary and the rest of the saints for mediation between them and God.

The curriculum at Mansfeld was the same as that of other schools of the time. Martin was introduced almost immediately to Latin, and he became familiar with the writings of many classic authors. He was taught religion and music, which helped him to take part in the church's religious services.

At that time in Germany, it was a traditional practice for schoolboys to travel to other cities to study in their schools. At the age of fourteen, Martin was sent to cathedral school at Magdeburg, where he received teaching from members of the Brethren of the Common Life. In 1498, Luther was sent to a town called Eisenach, his mother's hometown, where he finished his preparatory education.

Then, it was time for study at the university.

Hans Luther: "Only the Best for My Son!"

Hans Luther wanted Martin to attend the best university possible. He wanted Martin to be well prepared for a career in the legal field, which Hans himself had chosen for his son. With Hans paying his way, Martin attended the university at Erfurt, which was founded in 1392 and was considered one of the best German universities of the time.

At the university, Martin studied logic, rhetoric, physics, and metaphysics, as well as the ancient classics, such as Cicero, Virgil, Plautus, and Livy. He learned Latin well enough to write it clearly and understandably. Martin also cultivated his love for music. He played the lute and sang well enough to attract the attention of the faculty. He also continued in his religious training. He began each day in prayer and attended mass regularly and observed the daily religious practices of any sincere Catholic.

Luther was a sociable, likable young man at the university, but he was also a hard-working, hard-studying student. He received his liberal arts degree in 1502. This degree allowed him to teach at the university, and he assisted in teaching grammar and logic while he finished his Master's degree, which he received in February of 1505.

What Next for Martin?

After his graduation from the university, Luther wanted to seek God and study the Bible, and he believed the best way to do that was to enter a monastery. But in obedience to his father, who believed young Martin would be more helpful to the family as a lawyer than as a *monk*, he enrolled in law school at the University of Leipzig in May 1505, at the age of twenty-one.

You Can Look It Up

A **monk** is a man who has taken religious vows of poverty, chastity, and obedience in a communal setting, associated with a single location.

Historians record that Luther wasn't happy in law school, that he wanted still more religious education, and that he didn't want to be a lawyer in the first place. Something inside him yearned to know more about God and about the Bible. But Luther wasn't in law school long. The story has it that on July 2, 1505, Luther literally came face to face with death. It was an experience that changed the course of his life and, as it turns out, the course of history.

On the Road to Damascus ... Or Was It Erfurt?

Martin Luther was on his way to Erfurt from Mansfield when he found himself stranded in a terrible thunderstorm that was passing over the village of Stotternheim, just a few miles from home. A bolt of lightning struck so close to him that it knocked Martin to the ground. Fearing for his life—and for his eternal soul, because of the sins of his youth—Martin cried out in terror to the family's patron saint, St. Anna, for help and vowed to become a monk if she would save him from death that day.

Many, many people throughout history have made religious vows during times of trouble or danger, but Martin Luther kept his. He survived the frightening encounter with the storm, and in his mind he was bound by the vow he had made to enter a monastery. On July 16, Martin called his friends and companions to a going-away dinner and announced his decision to become a monk. The next day—against the advice of his friends and against the wishes of his father, who was enraged at his eldest son's decision—Martin entered the Augustinian monastery at Erfurt.

What's a Monk to Do?

As far as Luther was concerned, life as a monk was the highest form of devotion to God. The church had long taught that those who were serious about their faith should enter monasteries and become monks, and Luther fully accepted that teaching.

Going Deeper _____

The Augustinian monastery at Erfurt, which Martin Luther entered in 1505, was known throughout Germany as a place of learning and a place that stressed an exemplary lifestyle. Its seminary was associated with the university at Erfurt. Luther received Bachelor of Theology, Master of the Sentences, and Licentiate degrees and was ordained a priest in 1507.

While in the monastery, Luther studied the Bible and the teachings of the Catholic Church. He learned Greek and Hebrew, and memorized most of the New Testament and much of the Old. Still, in the midst of all the religious learning and practice, something tormented Luther to the depths of his soul.

You would think that a man who led one of the greatest religious movements in the history of mankind would be sure of his own spiritual roots. You would think that from the beginning he would know where he stood with his faith and with his God. But Martin Luther wasn't like that. At least not in his younger days, which history has shown to be a time of uncertainty for him.

During his pre-monastery days at the university at Erfurt, Luther had the opportunity to read a complete Latin Bible in the university library. He was pleased to find that the Bible contained much more than he had been taught at Mass. This Bible was a complete one—containing both Old and New Testaments—and he had never seen one of those before. Not many people at that time had the means to purchase the Scriptures in whole.

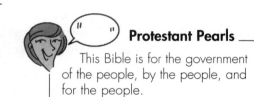

Protestant Pearls _____

This Bible is for the government of the people, by the people, and for the people.
—John Wycliffe (1330–1384), English reformer

But in reading the Bible, Luther saw the righteous God of judgment and not the merciful God of love. Luther, who was keenly aware of his own sinful imperfection, was more troubled than comforted by what he saw. He began to wonder where he stood with God, if he really was doing the things he needed to do in order to make it to heaven.

Luther's frame of mind in this area didn't change for many years. In fact, it was during his time in the monastery that he felt the most doubt and insecurity. Luther's later writings tell us that he was not a happy or secure monk during his three years in the monastery, a time he later called his "martyrdom." Though Martin Luther had entered the monastery believing that taking the vows of a monk would assure him of his standing before God, he was still in turmoil after entering the monastery. He couldn't reconcile his sinfulness with God's requirement for absolute righteousness, or sinlessness.

Martin Luther Tries to Reach God

Luther spent his time in the monastery not just studying, praying, and practicing the sacraments, but examining how he had lived his life. That was standard practice for a monk, but Luther's self-examination led him to deep sadness, fear, and hopelessness over his own sinfulness. In later years, he wrote of great sadness in his heart during this time in his life.

Luther was told to repent of his sins and to do penance, and he did both more than regularly. Luther went to his priest for confession often—so often that he probably wore the man out—and engaged in long periods of prayer, fasting, sleepless nights, and a practice called "flagellation," in which the monk inflicts beatings to himself as punishment for his sins.

Luther did all the things a monk was supposed to do, and he did them almost compulsively. He did all those things because, like most monks, he believed that the practices would bring him closer to God. Later he said, "Could ever a monk have got to heaven by monkhood, I should have attained it."

But no matter how hard he studied, no matter how many religious activities he took part in, no matter how many penances he did, no matter how much he punished himself for his own sinfulness, Luther couldn't shake those nagging thoughts and feelings that something was missing inside him. He couldn't find any kind of inner peace. Luther continued to have doubts about his own standing before God. He began to wonder about his personal salvation and he began to doubt that life in the monastery was a sure path to God.

Martin Luther's feelings of fear and insecurity were made worse by an emphasis within the church at the time on the doing of good works in order to attain the favor of God and on the doing of penances as a way to pay for sins committed.

Luther wanted absolute assurance that he was accepted by God, but it would be a matter of years before that would come.

Martin Luther, the Doubting Priest

Martin Luther was ordained a priest in 1507, but that wasn't the end of his personal spiritual crisis. If anything, his turmoil increased. He later recalled being overwhelmed with fear—almost to the point of fainting away on the spot—and a feeling of unworthiness as he recited the Eucharistic prayer at his first Mass on May 2. For most priests, that first Mass is a great moment. But not for Luther. All he could think about was the great responsibilities involved in being a priest and how weak and unqualified he felt in the face of those responsibilities.

Protestant Pearls _____

Whereas some men think [the Bible] translations make divisions in the faith, that is not so, for it was never better with the congregation of God than when every church almost had a sundry translation. Would to God it had never been left off after the time of St. Augustine, then we should never had come into such blindness and ignorance, such errors and delusions.

—Miles Coverdale (1488–1568), English Bible translator

Luther's "promotion" hadn't done anything to quiet him inside. If anything, he felt worse. The doubt-filled, miserable monk had become a doubt-filled, miserable priest.

Martin was also disturbed by how his father, who had vehemently opposed his son's entry into the monastery, had responded to his entering the priesthood. Hans Luther had appeared at the meal given to honor Martin and had brought a gift to help cover the costs of the proceedings. But he told the dignitaries at the dinner that he still didn't believe his son had been called to the priesthood and that his decision to enter the priesthood represented disobedience to the commandment to honor one's father and mother. "Have you not read in Holy Writ," he said, "that a man must honor father and mother?"

Still, Luther moved forward. The one who had been called "Brother Martin" was now referred to in the monastery as "Father Martin."

The Hardest Working Priest in the Monastery

Luther conscientiously performed the ever-expanding list of duties assigned him at the monastery. He read Mass every morning. Each day, he invoked the names of three of the twenty-one particular saints he had chosen as his helpers. Luther stood out in the monastery for his devotion to his work and to his studies. But he still had serious doubts that the religious activities he took part in did anything in the eyes of God for his eternal soul.

Luther was somewhat comforted in the monastery by his superior, Johannes von Staupitz, who saw in Luther a young man with great intelligence and passion. Staupitz encouraged Luther in his studies and urged him to think of Christ's death on the cross as proof of God's love for sinners, including Martin himself. These words gave Martin only partial and temporary relief from his turmoil.

> **People You Should Know**
>
> Johannes von Staupitz (1460/69–1524) was a Roman Catholic scholar who became professor of Bible at the University of Wittenberg, where he was in close contact with Martin Luther. During Luther's time in the monastery, he encouraged Luther in his studies and tried to comfort Luther in his doubts about his own salvation.

He understood the church's teachings concerning faith, good works, and *grace*, but in his mind those things didn't add up to his being "saved" from eternal damnation. He couldn't believe with any level of assurance that a perfect God could save a sinner like him.

Still, Martin Luther continued to serve and to study, later on in a more high-profile position.

You Can Look It Up

The Christian doctrine of **grace**—one of the key points of the faith Luther struggled to understand early in his life—describes the love of God for sinful mankind as demonstrated in the work of Jesus Christ on the cross. Luther came to the realization that God's grace was truly unmerited and unearned, and that no amount of good works on his part would make him more acceptable to God.

Martin Makes a Move

In the fall of 1508, Martin Luther went to the monastery at Wittenberg to lecture at the new university and to continue his theological studies. Johannes von Staupitz, who had encouraged Luther during his days as a monk in Erfurt, was the first dean of the faculty of theology at the Wittenberg university. Luther was to lecture on Aristotle's *Ethics*, but theology, not philosophy, was his main interest. He received his Bachelor's degree in Bible in the spring of 1509.

In the autumn of 1509, after a year of close contact with Staupitz, Luther was sent to Erfurt, where he spent about two years lecturing on theology. He prepared for the lectures by studying the Bible as well as the works of men of God who had gone before. It was at this time that Luther began to develop his beliefs concerning God and grace.

Luther's uncertainty over his own spiritual condition continued through this time of life, and it wasn't helped by a trip he took to the Holy City, Rome.

Disillusionment in the Holy City

Luther traveled to Rome in autumn of 1510, as a representative of his order. He was eager to see the seat of the government and the headquarters of the Catholic Church and of the Holy Roman Empire. When he arrived, he fell to his knees and cried out, "I greet thee, Holy Rome, thrice holy from the blood of the martyrs that has been shed in thee!" But it didn't take long for Luther's image of Rome as a holy city to be completely shattered.

What he saw instead of the holy place he imagined was a city full of vice and corruption, a papal office that had become steeped in worldliness, and a general population that seemed indifferent to religious matters.

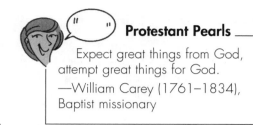

Protestant Pearls

Expect great things from God, attempt great things for God.
—William Carey (1761–1834), Baptist missionary

This was not what he had envisioned when he set out on his journey to Rome. Saddened, appalled, and disillusioned at what he had seen, Luther left Rome with these words: "Let all who would live a holy life depart from Rome. Everything is permitted in Rome except to be an honest man."

Luther returned to Erfurt in the spring of 1511, but Staupitz called him back to Wittenberg, where he preached to the monks in the chapel, and continued his studies. He received his degree of Doctor of Theology on October 18, 1512. He then replaced Johannes von Staupitz on the theological faculty and began lecturing on biblical literature.

Luther became the top man at the university at Wittenberg. He established a reputation as a powerful preacher and lecturer, a reputation he would enjoy until 1517, the year the Protestant Reformation began.

When Luther Turned "Lutheran"

There came a time in Martin Luther's life when all his doubts and insecurities were relieved, a time when he came to a personal understanding of the message of Christ he had spent his life learning to teach.

Beginning in 1513, Luther began lecturing on the Bible at the university at Wittenberg. He lectured on the Psalms from 1513–1515, on Paul's epistle to the Romans from 1515–1516, on Galatians from 1516–1517, on Hebrews from 1517–1518, and again on the Psalms in 1519.

It was during the period of these lectures—a time of intense study of the Bible in preparation for the lectures—that Luther's personal questions concerning salvation and righteousness were answered. It was also during this time that Luther began adopting ideas about theology that would bring him into disagreement with the Catholic Church.

Luther believed that the Bible was the divinely inspired Word of God, and he considered it more important than all other religious writings. Because of this, he concentrated his efforts on the study of the Bible. On the other hand, Luther, as a Catholic priest, was bound by oath to interpret the Bible in light of the tradition and authority of the Catholic Church.

Luther's Time in the Tower

The time of "enlightenment" in Luther's life has come to be known as his "Tower Experience." This is because Luther stated later that it was in the tower of the monastery at Wittenberg that he discovered one of the key Bible passages in his life—Romans 1:16–17, in which the apostle Paul states:

> For I am not ashamed of the Good News: it is the power of God saving all who have faith—Jews first, but Greeks as well—since this is what reveals the justice of God to us: it shows how faith leads to faith, or as the scripture says: The upright man finds life through faith.

Going Deeper

Luther wrote of his Tower Experience, so named because it took place in the tower at the monastery in Wittenberg, in the preface to his Latin Works (1545). This is his account of when he first came to an understanding of the message of the gospel, as it appears in the New Testament. He wrote, "I began to understand that this verse means that the justice of God is revealed through the Gospel ... that by which the merciful God justifies us by faith ..."

Luther had struggled with this passage of the Bible for many years. In fact, he later wrote that he hated the phrase "justice of God," because he had been taught for years that it referred to how God punishes sinners. As he read Paul's words, he wondered how God's demand for absolute righteousness could be good news to sinful man. Luther, who had spent most of his life struggling with this question of righteousness, knew that if God demanded absolute righteousness as a condition for eternal salvation, then everyone—no matter how hard they tried, no matter how many penances they performed—was doomed.

Suddenly, Luther saw what he thought the apostle Paul was really saying: that through what Christ did on the cross, God had declared sinners who have faith in the gospel message righteous in his eyes—that the debt for the sins of those who believe had been declared "paid in full."

Protestant Pearls

I felt myself absolutely born again. The gates of Paradise had been flung open and I had entered. There and then the whole of Scripture took on another look to me.

—Martin Luther

Luther later wrote of this experience using the terms "born again" and "gates of paradise." For him, it was the beginning of a whole new understanding of the Christian faith, the messages in the Bible, and God himself. Previously, he had hated just hearing the words *justice*, *law*, and *righteousness*. To Luther, these words represented a level of holiness and performance he knew he could never reach. But now, he had a new and different view. "I exalted this sweetest word of mine, 'the justice of God,' with as much love as before had hated it with hate," he later wrote.

That "new" discovery of Martin Luther's is the essence of the doctrine of "justification by faith," and it is one of the cornerstone belief systems of the Protestant Reformation.

Amazing Grace!

Martin Luther's new ideas concerning God's justice, forgiveness, and salvation were rooted in what Christians refer to as God's grace. In this context, grace can be defined as the demonstration of God's love through the undeserved giving of good will.

Luther held that this grace was poured out on humans, not through the sacraments of the Catholic Church, but directly on the individual, which gave that person the ability to believe the message of salvation. This grace, Luther believed, was amply and powerfully demonstrated in Christ's death on the cross, which paid the price for the sins of mankind.

Luther believed that God draws people to Him not based on their own merits, but on the basis of his own grace. He believed that the works or merits of people were worthless and it was God alone who chose to bring people to faith in Christ. Luther believed in what is called "the doctrine of *predestination*," which states that God chooses whom to save and when to save them. He believed that people could have the assurance of salvation—something he himself struggled with for many years—when they turned to God and humbly confessed that they were sinners and believed in the gospel. When that happens, he said, people can have personal fellowship with God through Christ and grow in their faith.

You Can Look It Up

The doctrine of **predestination** or election states that God, not people, chooses who will come to faith in Christ and be eternally saved. Luther came to believe in predestination, but he also said that a man or woman's concern over their "election," as it is called, was evidence that they were one of God's "chosen."

What Did Luther Believe and When Did He Believe It?

Historians debate when exactly Luther came to this point of biblical and spiritual enlightenment. His own writings show that he was moving gradually away from certain Catholic teachings as early as 1512. But Luther's own writings—although they were decades after the fact and for that reason could be inaccurate—state that his spiritual "breakthrough" took place in 1518, after he had started the Reformation by posting the 95 Theses on the door of the church at Wittenberg (see Chapter 8, "It All Started over Indulgences").

Whatever the actual timeline of this key event in Luther's life, it is not hard to see that his system of religious beliefs had undergone radical changes from the time of his entering the monastery at Erfurt to the time when the Reformation started, then began picking up steam.

From the time he entered the monastery clear through the time of his reformationist words and actions, Martin Luther's beliefs about God, about salvation, and about Christian doctrine were evolving and coming more in line with the beliefs of the early church and moving away from those of the medieval Catholic Church.

Luther, like many of his predecessors and successors in the various reformation movements, held strongly to principles he saw as being Bible-based. Many of his views—even though they were firmly rooted in the Bible—put him decidedly at odds with the Roman Catholic Church, which saw itself not so much as the source of God's grace and forgiveness, but the dispenser of them.

The beliefs that would eventually get Martin Luther in trouble with the Catholic Church were:

- Sinful humankind was justified by God's grace and God's grace alone.
- The Bible, and not the Roman Catholic Church—not even the pope himself—was the final authority in all things having to do with the Christian faith.
- Church beliefs and practices—even those rooted in centuries of tradition—could not be justified apart from what the Bible said.
- Christ alone was the mediator between God and man.
- Every believer in Christ was a priest, as spelled out in the apostle Peter's second epistle, and as such had the right to go to God directly without the aid of an earthly priest.

Something Is Amiss Here!

Martin Luther knew something was wrong.

As Luther's beliefs took shape and became more rooted in the teachings of Christ, the apostles, and others as they were recorded in the Bible, he began to think that there was something "off" about a lot of the practices and beliefs of the Catholic Church. He couldn't find many of the practices of the Roman Catholic Church in the Scriptures—most notably, the sale of indulgences, which by the time Luther came on the scene had become one of the church's means of fundraising, whereby people could "buy" forgiveness for sin they hadn't even committed yet.

> **People You Should Know**
>
> Catherine von Bora was the wife of Martin Luther. Luther had taught that the clergy should be allowed to marry, and, to the chagrin of many friends and associates, he married Catherine, a nun, on June 13, 1525. It was apparently a happy marriage, as Luther referred to his wife as "My Rib" and "Lord Katie." Martin and Catherine had six children together from 1526–1534.

Luther also believed that the church didn't stress such teachings as justification by faith and the authority of the Scripture in all spiritual matters. In his mind, something had to change. Specifically, he believed that the church had to return to her original roots.

Finally, there came a time in Luther's life when he had to do something about what he saw.

The Least You Need to Know

- Martin Luther's father wanted him to go into the legal profession, but when caught in a violent thunderstorm, Martin pledged to God that if spared, he would become a monk.

- Luther's experience in a tower at the monastery at Wittenberg revealed new meanings of key Bible passages on faith, grace, righteousness, and predestination.

- His final breakthrough in theological insight, which would eventually lead to a break with the Roman Catholic Church, occurred when he posted the 95 Theses on the door of the church at Wittenberg.

Chapter 8

It All Started over Indulgences

In This Chapter

- ◆ The final straw: the Catholic Church's abuse of indulgences
- ◆ The 95 Theses: Luther's challenge to debate
- ◆ The church's and the people's responses to the 95 Theses
- ◆ The consequences of the 95 Theses for Martin Luther

By the time the early sixteenth century rolled around, all the ingredients were in place for the revolutionary religious and political movement that came to be known as the Protestant Reformation. The political and religious world of Europe was in a state of flux—if not disarray in many ways—and changes in the education of Europeans helped set the stage for what was about to take place.

And, of course, there was the man, Martin Luther. He was the right man with the right personality and the right vision to help make the Reformation possible. Many historians agree that without Luther, the Reformation would either have been delayed or had a radically different look.

With everything in place, all that was needed to start a revolution was a catalyst, that "final straw" that brought the world down on the established church. That final straw was the abuse of what were called indulgences.

Just What Was the Argument About?

The Catholic Church of the late Middle Ages took part in all kinds of practices that could have aroused Martin Luther's ire, but it was the practice of the sale of indulgences that first got his attention and moved him to rebel.

In the Catholic Church, an indulgence was a merciful release of the remorseful sinner from penance. The indulgence relieved the sinner of his or her temporal—meaning earthly or "here and now"—punishment for the sins he or she had committed.

The idea behind indulgences dated back as far as Thomas Aquinas—centuries before Luther—and it held that true penance involved not just a pardon from God for the truly repentant sinner, but also some kind of restitution on the part of that person.

In the early centuries of the church, when someone was guilty of a serious sin, he or she was cut off from the church. To get back in the good graces of the congregation, that person had to confess the sin publicly, then perform some kind of "satisfaction," such as fasting, giving to the poor, or other good works.

The practice of paying money as penance has been traced back as far as the seventh century. This was basically the beginning of the church system that came to be known as indulgences, and it became kind of a scandal in the church. It was in the later Middle Ages that the granting of indulgences in return for financial support grew to the point of becoming an abuse. In Germany, Martin Luther's home country, the paying of money in exchange for pardons for sin became very popular. But that didn't stop Luther from taking exception to the practice.

You Can Look It Up

Martin Luther's **95 Theses** were not his way of rebelling against the Catholic Church. They were nothing more than a challenge on the part of Luther to debate relevant issues concerning the church and how it did things—particularly its selling of indulgences in Germany. As was the custom in Wittenberg at the time, he nailed them to the church door to present them for debate.

Get Your Forgiveness Here!

Martin Luther never opposed the use of indulgences themselves, and he stated that in the seventy-first of his *95 Theses*. What he opposed was the additions and conditions that had been placed on indulgences. It was the sale of indulgences, which had become a common practice and a big moneymaker for the Catholic Church, that got his attention.

The scandal of the "holy trade," as the sale of indulgences had come to be called, came to light in the second decade of the sixteenth century, when Martin Luther became aware of the activities of a preacher by the name of Johann Tetzel.

Pope Leo X needed a large amount of money to complete the construction of St. Peter's Church in Rome, and he sent Tetzel on a mission to collect funds by providing indulgences to those who made cash contributions to the cause. Tetzel preached in Jüterbog and Zerbst, which were near Wittenberg. These indulgences, which were actually signed by the pope himself, were certificates that promised pardon of all sins, not just for those who held them, but for the holders' friends and relatives—living or dead—on whose behalf they were purchased. This pardon could come regardless of whether the buyer or the person for whom the certificate was bought confessed, repented, or did any kind of penance.

People You Should Know

Pope Leo X (1475–1521) held the office in Rome from 1513 to 1521 and was known for his extravagance and his love for literature and the arts. He is known more as a patron of the arts than as a spiritual leader. He was one of the best examples of the Renaissance popes. His love of the arts caused him to be indirectly responsible for the Reformation, as it was the church's collection of cash for indulgences that got the attention of Martin Luther, who he excommunicated in 1521.

Historians say that Tetzel was a persuasive speaker, and that he used his gift of gab to persuade many, many people to purchase indulgences. Tetzel played on the people's belief that their financial contributions to the church could, in effect, buy their own remission of sin and punishment in *purgatory*. Indulgences were also supposed to help buy a loved one's way out of purgatory, or at least reduce the amount of time he or she spent there. "As soon as the coin in the coffer rings, the soul from purgatory springs," he is credited with saying. In one sermon, Tetzel went so far as to speak as though he were the deceased relatives of the listeners begging for them to "buy" their way out of the suffering of purgatory. Tetzel made a fortune for the church—and most likely for himself.

You Can Look It Up

In Roman Catholic theology, **purgatory** is a place or condition of punishment for those who have departed this life without fully paying the earthly satisfaction due for their sins. This doctrine holds that even after sin has been pardoned by God through Christ, some kind of human payment is due for that sin.

Luther: The Holy Trade Is Wholly Wrong!

Indulgence preachers—and there were many besides Tetzel—were severely criticized in many camps, even though their sermons included the standard Catholic Church teachings. They were seen by many as nothing more than religious hucksters whose only goal was to "shear the sheep"—of their money, that is!

The critics of the indulgence sales as well as those who were in positions of authority who put some action behind their opposition (Duke George of Saxony prohibited them in his territory, and Cardinal Ximenes forbade them in Spain) held that the sales of indulgences exploited the uneducated and ignorant—those who could least afford to be separated from their money—and that they misrepresented the true teachings of the church and of the Scriptures.

Who Needs Confession When You Have an Indulgence?

Martin Luther found out what was going on when Wittenbergers, who had traveled to Jüterbog and Zerbst to see Tetzel, came to him in confession and reported that they had received pardons for sin from Tetzel. Luther was deeply concerned about the spiritual condition of the penitents, and when he told them they needed to change their ways—to repent of their sins—some of them went so far as to show him the indulgences they had purchased from Tetzel. They honestly believed that the indulgences not only provided pardons for their past sins, but also entitled them to forgiveness for sins they hadn't even committed. In short, the indulgences had come to be seen as a "license to sin."

In his preaching prior to the beginning of the Reformation, Luther never warned his hearers against indulgences—only against the abuse of indulgences. By this time, Luther was at the very least well on his way to developing a new understanding of the forgiveness of sins. He was coming to the conclusion—if he hadn't already—that forgiveness of sins had more to do with an inner attitude toward God and his holiness and less to do with following the traditions and practices of the church.

Now, Luther recognized that there were people within the church who were openly abusing their positions by making wild and unscriptural promises concerning indulgences. He believed that the trade of indulgences was completely unwarranted, by church tradition or by the scripture. The people were being sold a bill of goods, and the church was making a bundle exploiting the ignorance of the common people.

Luther knew it was time to do something about what he saw.

Luther's Message to the Church: "Let's Talk!"

Martin Luther lived in a place and time when it was acceptable to challenge the local church leadership to debate on spiritual matters. In Wittenberg, it was the custom to hold religious debates on a weekly basis, and the door of Castle Church there was considered the official bulletin board of the university. If someone wanted to debate a certain issue, all he had to do was post theses for discussion and debate on the door of the church.

Luther's views on the sale of indulgences went public after October 31, 1517, a day that would change forever the face of the Christian faith in Europe and beyond. After thinking through what he wanted to say, Luther wrote the theses—the most important of which spoke of what Luther considered a problem with the way some preachers handled indulgences—then posted them on the church door. He then sent a copy of the theses to Archbishop Albert and included a letter explaining his actions.

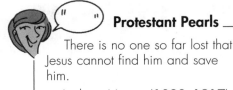

Protestant Pearls

There is no one so far lost that Jesus cannot find him and save him.

—Andrew Murray (1828–1917), Preacher in Scotland and South Africa

When Luther nailed the 95 Theses to the church door, his intent was not to be rebellious or radical, or to bring embarrassment to the church, or to cause any kind of split in the church. At the time, Luther had respect for the church and even for the priesthood and papacy.

"In the desire and with the purpose of elucidating the truth," the preface of the 95 Theses read,

> A disputation will be held on the underwritten propositions at Wittenberg, under the presidency of the Reverend Father Martin Luther, Monk of the Order of St. Augustine, Master of Arts and of Sacred Theology, and ordinary Reader of the same in that place. He therefore asks those who cannot be present and discuss the subject with us orally, to do so by letter in their absence. In the name of our Lord Jesus Christ. Amen.

In the 95 Theses, Luther stated that he agreed with many of the beliefs and practices of the Catholic Church, including the sacraments and offices of the church. He even went so far as to condemn those who would deny the right of the pope to grant indulgences. He defended the pope in his writings and stated that the pope's authority could be damaged by the way the indulgence preachers had exaggerated their claims of what indulgences could do.

Luther wrote the 95 Theses in Latin and not in German, which many historians say underscores the fact that Luther was not looking to start any kind of widespread revolution, but just debate within the church. But someone, without Luther's permission, published the 95 Theses in German and distributed them widely.

That, it turns out, was the beginning of the end of the peaceful life of a monk for Martin Luther.

Public Support and Papal Anger

Martin Luther had posted his now-famous 95 Theses on the Castle Church door in hopes of bringing the issue of the sale of indulgences to some kind of peaceful, constructive debate.

Looking at the history of indulgences, Luther should have known better than to think his words wouldn't raise the ire of the church. John of Wesel (1420–1489), for example, had been tried by the Inquisition in 1479 for heresy and condemned to death for preaching against indulgences. John, who was a German theologian and also a member of the Brethren of the Common Life, was one of many reformers who got themselves in trouble with the church for speaking out against indulgences. He died in prison.

After Luther posted the 95 Theses, Archbishop Albert immediately reported him to Rome. At first, Pope Leo X shrugged off Luther's words and actions as those of a man who had been drinking too much and would later "sober up" and come to his senses. Luther later suggested that his obscurity turned out to be a blessing to him because the pope didn't take him seriously enough.

As thousands of copies of Luther's 95 Theses made their way around Germany, the people got solidly behind him. There had been a growing sense of resentment among Germans that they were being exploited by Rome, that they were being taxed to the point of poverty just to further adorn the Roman papal court.

It wasn't long after the posting of the theses that Luther was branded a heretic. John Eck, a professor of theology and chancellor at the Bavarian university at Ingolstadt and a former friend who would become one of Luther's fiercest opponents, severely criticized Luther. Cardinal Prierias, who was an advisor to Leo X, accused Luther of heresy. Luther felt compelled to answer the charges against him, and he did so in 1518 in his *Resolutions Concerning the Virtue of Indulgences*, in which he explained the 95 Theses. In *Resolutions*, Luther implied that as humans, even popes could err.

In May of 1518, Luther wrote to the pope and *very* respectfully—he referred to the pope as "Holy Father" and "your Holiness"—explained that he hadn't intended to start any kind of conflict when he posted his 95 Theses: "They were made public at the University of Wittenberg, and intended only for this university … They are theses; they are neither teachings nor doctrines; as is customary, they are cast in obscure and ambiguous language." Luther went so far as to say that if he'd had any idea what kind of problems the theses

> **Protestant Pearls**
>
> Life is a hard fight, a struggle, a wrestling with the Principle of Evil, hand to hand, foot to foot. Every inch of the way must be disputed. The night is given us to take breath, to pray, to drink deep at the fountain of power. The day, to use the strength which has been given to us, to go forth to work with it till the evening.
>
> —Florence Nightingale (1820–1910), English nurse

were going to create, he would have taken more time to carefully state them. He also submitted himself to the pope for whatever discipline the pontiff found fitting.

Later, Pope Leo X summoned Luther to Rome to answer for the things he had written. Luther knew that if he appeared in Rome, he likely wouldn't make it back to Germany, that he would either be tried as a heretic and executed or imprisoned. The university and elector Frederick the Wise intervened and negotiated a hearing closer to home. Cardinal Cajetan (Thomas de Vio) gave Luther his hearing in Augsburg, Germany.

A Hero's Welcome in Augsburg

On October 7, 1518, Luther arrived on foot in Augsburg, where he was received by many prominent citizens as a hero. He didn't know about the political moves made on his behalf prior to his trip to Augsburg, so he expected to be tried for heresy and burned. On October 12, Luther appeared at the first of three hearings before Cajetan.

It would be an understatement to say that the meetings with the cardinal didn't go well— at least as far as Luther's reconciliation with the church's positions was concerned. Luther refused to budge from some of his stated positions without being shown in the Bible why he was wrong. Cajetan lost his temper with Luther and called him a "wretched worm," and Luther replied that the cardinal was as fit to judge in spiritual matters as "an ass is to play a harp."

Luther and Cajetan were at an impasse. No additional talks or debate was going to bring them to any kind of agreement. So, on the night of October 20, Luther slipped out of Augsburg and headed back to Wittenberg. On his way home, Luther saw a copy of a papal brief, dated August 23, which declared him a heretic and told Cajetan how to deal with him.

> **Protestant Pearls**
>
> It is time that Christians were judged more by their likeness to Christ than their notions of Christ.
>
> —Lucretia Mott (1793–1880), Preacher and campaigner against slavery

But things were going to be getting warmer for Luther in the coming year.

When the Gap Widened to a Gulf

One event, the famed Disputation at Leipzig in June and July of 1519, marked a time of widening division between Luther and those who agreed with his teaching and the Catholic Church. The debate was to be held between representatives of Luther's university at Wittenberg and the University of Ingolstadt. The two debaters were Andreas von Carlstadt, Luther's colleague at Wittenberg, and John Eck of Ingolstadt.

People You Should Know

Andreas Von Carlstadt (1480–1541) was a German Protestant reformer. As early as 1516, Carlstadt presented theses denying free will and asserting the doctrine of salvation by grace alone. In 1518, he supported Luther against the attacks of John Eck by maintaining the supremacy of Scripture and in 1519 he appeared with Luther against Eck in the public disputation at Leipzig. In time, he became known as one of the more radical Wittenberg reformers.

Andreas Von Carlstadt and Eck were set to debate one another on the subjects of free will and divine grace, but Luther soon entered the arguments. From July 4 to July 14, Luther and Eck debated several subjects—for example, purgatory, indulgences, and penance. The most explosive of the subjects was the supremacy of the office of pope. Luther had set himself up to enter the debate by publishing theses against Eck, the last of which defiantly expressed doubt over whether there was historical justification for the power of the pope.

Luther had raised eyebrows by taking the position that the idea of the supremacy of the pope was less than four centuries old and that if the denial of papal supremacy was a heresy, then all the leaders of the early church were heretics. He stated that if Christ was the head of the church, then there was no need for a pope. Further, he took the position that since Christ had done the work of reconciliation between God and humans, there was no need for any further mediation between humans and God.

In the debate, Eck did what he could to associate Luther's beliefs and teachings with those of John Huss, the Bohemian reformer who paid for his work with his life. Huss's followers, the Hussites, had been severely persecuted since his death in 1415 following the Council at Constance. Eck knew that if he could attach Luther's beliefs with those of Huss, he could then label Luther as not only heretical, but anti-German. In the end, Luther admitted that not all of Huss's ideas and positions were wrong.

Eck had won the debate, but Luther had won in that it brought him and his beliefs to even broader attention. He had become something of a hero to the German people. Luther was also strengthened in his beliefs concerning the ultimate authority of the Bible, the church as a body of believers, and the papacy as a completely human institution.

Following the debate with Eck, Luther called not just for reforms or adjustments in the Catholic Church but for a complete housecleaning—from the top down. He made his call using paper and pen.

I'll Put That in Writing!

Luther did some of his most important Reformation writing in 1520, the year following his famous and momentous confrontation with John Eck. In the second half of that year, he published what are considered *the* key essays on the Reformation: He wrote *Address to the Christian Nobility* in August, *The Babylonian Captivity* in October, and *On the Freedom of the Christian Man* in November.

These three writings constituted the essentials of Lutheranism. In them, Luther spelled out the harm the Roman Church had done to Germany, proposed that the church reduce the number of sacraments from seven to two (baptism and the Lord's Supper), stated that the Bible was the ultimate authority, and asserted that humans had direct access to God through Christ and needed no human mediators.

The first of these pamphlets, *Address to the Christian Nobility*, was widely circulated and read. It was an appeal to German princes to unite, oppose the rule of Rome, and reform the church in Germany. It presented the complaints of Luther—as well as many other Germans—against Rome. Luther addressed this pamphlet to the German nobility because he believed that the clergy had vested interests in keeping the system the way it was. He argued that in special cases, secular officers who were Christians had the God-ordained responsibility to step in and take positions of leadership in the church.

Going Deeper

The Babylonian Captivity of the Church was one of Luther's most important pamphlets. It summarized Luther's theology and stated his position on justification by faith alone. In it, he condemned the papacy and the church for depriving Christians of their freedom to approach God individually.

In *The Babylonian Captivity*, Luther argued that only baptism and the Lord's Supper were legitimate sacraments, that the other five were human-initiated and false. He stated that the church had placed too many of its own ideas or doctrines on the sacrament of the Lord's Supper, including that of transubstantiation. He also stressed the priesthood of individual believers and rejected the idea of a priesthood separate from the rest of the church.

In *On the Freedom of the Christian Man*, which is considered among the very best of Luther's writings, he stressed justification by faith:

> It is clear then that to a Christian man his faith suffices for everything, and that he has no need for works for justification. But if he has no need of works, neither has he need of the law; and if he has no need of the law, he is certainly free from the law.

Luther's writings in 1520 had a dual effect. They had been widely read and loved by the citizens of Germany and beyond, and that rallied public support for him. On the other hand, they also put him in even more hot water with the church.

In addition to the writings we've already covered, in June of 1520 Luther had written *On the Papacy at Rome*, in which he called the pope "the real *Anti-Christ* of whom all the Scripture speaks."

You Can Look It Up

The **Anti-Christ,** or Antichrist, is referred to in the Bible (specifically in the book of Revelation) as "the Beast." He is to be the embodiment of all evil who makes his appearance in the end times, just prior to the apocalypse. In his June of 1520 writing *On the Papacy at Rome,* Luther demonstrated his contempt for the office of pope when he referred to him as "the real Anti-Christ of whom all the Scripture speaks."

Luther was able to communicate his message directly and forcefully through his writings, and that helped him garner the public support he needed for his movement. But he also had the support of the man who would prove to be his most important ally.

Martin Luther's Right-Hand Man

Luther first became acquainted with Phillip Melanchthon in 1518 at the university at Wittenberg, where both men were professors. Melanchthon's first address at the university, titled *Discourse on Reforming the Studies of Youth*, caught Luther's attention. Luther introduced Melanchthon to his own theology, and Melanchthon taught Luther Greek. Luther also quickly persuaded the younger Melanchthon to join him in his Reformation movement and also motivated him to turn to the study of theology.

At Wittenberg, he studied and taught theology and other subjects, including rhetoric. Melanchthon was among the more popular lecturers at Wittenberg, and his lectures were attended by hundreds of students. His lectures were so popular that students copied and published them.

Luther and Melanchthon were different in many ways. Luther was an ordained Roman Catholic Priest and a Doctor of Theology, while Melanchthon was a layman who never earned a doctor's degree and was never ordained. They were also greatly different in their personalities. Luther was hardly one to pull a punch when he had something to say, while Melanchthon seemed to dislike conflict and controversy.

Melanchthon and Luther formed a deep friendship during their time together. Luther had deep love and respect for his younger colleague and was impressed with his knowledge and ability. Luther once said, "In my teaching profession I do not respect anything more than Philip's advice," and Melanchthon once said of Luther, "I would rather die than be separated from this man."

Beginning in 1519, Melanchthon worked the rest of his life learning and defending the belief system behind the Reformation. In June of that year, he accompanied Luther and Carlstadt to the Disputation at Leipzig, where Luther debated the theologian John Eck. Melanchthon did not officially take part in the debate, but he is said to have helped Luther via written notes that gave biblical passages contradictory to the Church's claim of papal preeminence.

Luther worked hard at defining his "new" system of beliefs, but he never took the time to systemize his theology. In 1521, Melanchthon published the first summary of reformation theology, which is called the *Loci Communes*, or *Theological Common-Places*. Melanchthon finished the book in April and sent the proof-sheets to Luther, who was staying at Wartburg Castle at the time (more on that in Chapter 9). Luther was so enthusiastic about the book that he even wanted to include it in the Bible.

Melanchthon's work is a biblical explanation of the doctrines of sin, grace, repentance, and salvation. His main objective in writing the *Loci Communes* was to show that humans couldn't be saved by their good works or merits, but only through the grace of God as revealed in the gospel of Christ.

The pope had been receiving all kinds of reports concerning Luther and his movement, and with the things he had been writing in 1520, it was only a matter of time before the pope used his authority against him.

The Burning of the Bull

Pope Leo X responded to Luther's writings with the famous *Exsurge Domine*, a bull (a "bull" is a proclamation by the pope) of excommunication, meaning that unless Luther disavowed himself of his views and writings (that is, unless he recanted), he would be cut off from the Catholic Church. The bull condemned Luther for heresy and demanded that he retract his views within sixty days. It also warned all Christians to reject Luther's heresies and to burn all his writings.

The bull, which had been signed by the pope in June, reached Wittenberg in October, but it was a few months later that Luther provided a defining moment for himself and for the Protestant Reformation.

On December 10, at the end of the sixty-day "grace period" the pope had given him to recant, a defiant Martin Luther took Leo's bull, as well as numerous books supporting the authority of the papacy, to the eastern gate of Wittenberg and burned them publicly as enthusiastic students and faculty from the university gathered around and sang the *Te Deum*, or song of praise to God.

This wasn't the first time a papal bull had been publicly burned. Before, bull burnings were done by powerful monarchs who had less to fear from the pope than did Luther or others in his position. It was the first time a mere monk had done it. The German response to the bull had been overwhelmingly in Luther's favor, and the response to his burning of the bull was even greater.

Luther Opens Another Can of Wörms

In January of 1521, Luther was finally excommunicated, and two months later he was summoned to appear before newly crowned Holy Roman Emperor Charles V at the imperial *Diet* of Wörms. Historians consider this one of the most important scenes in Western history, for it was here that Luther stood and flatly refused to recant his earlier statements about the Christian faith, the Catholic Church, and the pope.

Luther was promised safe passage to and from Wörms, a city in southwestern Germany, but his friends were still worried over what might happen to him. They remembered how just over a century before, Bohemian reformer John Huss was promised safe passage, only to be imprisoned, tried, and burned as a heretic. Luther knew of the dangers of traveling to Wörms, but that wasn't going to stop him. As it was later said, Luther would have gone to Wörms if there were "as many devils in it as there were tiles on the roofs of the houses."

> **You Can Look It Up**
>
> A **diet** is a legislative assembly where any number of issues is addressed.

The road to Wörms was safe for Luther, and it was anything but lonely. As he proceeded along in the horse-drawn carriage, crowds greeted him as a hero at every turn and every stop of his journey. After two weeks' travel, Luther and his party arrived in Wörms, where they were greeted by a huge crowd of people.

> **Going Deeper**
>
> The Diet of Wörms (January 27–May 25, 1521) was the first diet of Holy Roman Emperor Charles V, who wanted to consolidate his power and set the guidelines for peace and government in the empire. The Diet of Wörms is best remembered for the "Luther issue." Luther was brought to the diet at the urging of Frederick the Wise of Saxony, who wanted to have the professor/priest heard by the officials. Luther, in defiance of both the emperor and the pope, refused to recant his writings and teachings.

Luther appeared before the Diet of Wörms twice. He was accused of breaking church laws and teaching heresies. Luther was never given a chance to explain himself. He was told that the doctrines and practices of the church were not open for discussion. He was simply told to recant.

What? Me, Recant?

On the second day of the diet, Luther refused to recant. He said he would not recant unless someone could refute his ideas directly, using the scriptures as the basis of the argument. Speaking respectfully, Luther told the assembly, "your Imperial Majesty and Your Lordships … unless I am convinced of error by testimony of scripture or by clear reason … I cannot and will not recant anything, for it is neither safe nor honest to act against one's conscience. On this I take my stand. I can do no other. God help me. Amen."

For a week, various theologians argued with Luther trying to sway him. But he would not back down. When it became obvious that there was no room for compromise or agreement, Luther asked for permission to leave for Wittenberg. The emperor, seeing that any further discussion of Luther was a waste of time, allowed Luther to leave the city. He headed back for Wittenberg on April 25.

At this point, Christianity was divided and the battle lines for the Reformation were set. The Reformation Luther had started when he nailed the 95 Theses on the church door was picking up even more steam.

Luther Going Underground

Luther was on his way home from Wörms when he mysteriously disappeared. All of Germany was abuzz over where he had gone, and rumors of his death spread like wildfire.

But Luther was fine. Before Luther had left Wörms, Frederick the Wise, the Elector of Saxony, had organized a "kidnapping" in order to protect Luther. On May 4, Luther and his party were traveling through the Thuringian Forest when they were intercepted by some "friendlies" who took Luther and whisked him off to the Wartburg Castle, which overlooked the city of Eisenach.

Meanwhile, back at Wörms, Luther was declared a heretic and an outlaw in the Edict of Wörms, which Emperor Charles V signed on May 25. This edict stated that since

People You Should Know

Charles V (1500–1558) was Holy Roman Emperor from 1519–1558. Charles fought to keep the Roman Catholic empire together in the face of emergent Protestantism and outside pressure. At 19, Charles bribed the electors to take the position of Holy Roman Emperor.

Luther refused to recant of his writings and preaching, the emperor was bound by law to enforce the papal bulls against him. Luther was placed under an imperial ban, meaning that he was without physical protection and that all subjects of the empire were forbidden to help him out or communicate with him. Luther was a man without a church, a man without a home, a man without an empire.

> **Going Deeper**
>
> The Edict of Wörms was signed by Emperor Charles V on May 25, 1521. It was an edict against Martin Luther declaring him a heretic and an outlaw and accused him of disobedience to the established political authority. Luther, then, was placed under an imperial ban, meaning that all subjects in the empire were forbidden to help him in any way or even to communicate with him. In addition, all of Luther's books were to be gathered up and burned.

Life in Wartburg Castle

Luther stayed in the safety of Wartburg Castle for almost a year. While there, he allowed his hair to grow, threw away his monk's habit, and masqueraded as "Knight George." During this time, and at the motivation given by Melanchthon, Luther concentrated on translating the New Testament into German so it could be read by the general public. Like so many of Luther's works, this translation sold in large numbers. In the two months after its release, it sold 5,000 copies and continued to sell strongly for many years to come.

While he stayed at Wartburg Castle, Luther expected that Melanchthon would keep the movement he had started going forward. What Luther didn't seem to take into account is that Melanchthon, while a great teacher and theologian, didn't have the kind of personality it took to lead that kind of movement. Melanchthon was by nature a timid man, and that gave Andreas von Carlstadt the opportunity to become the prime influence on the movement at Wittenberg.

Carlstadt began making some changes in the worship services in Wittenberg. They were largely popular among the people, but they did cause some unrest. Luther feared that Carlstadt was placing too much emphasis on external reforms—for example, he simplified the services and rid the churches of traditionally Catholic images—and threatening to overshadow Luther's emphasis on justification by faith.

Knowing that there were problems in Wittenberg, Luther left Wartburg Castle after ten months and returned to Wittenberg, where he continued his writing and resumed his preaching. In doing this, Luther defied the imperial edict against him.

No Matter What the Pope May Say, Reformation's Here to Stay!

Luther's excommunication by the Roman Catholic Church, as well as his being branded an outlaw and a heretic, did nothing to stop his teachings but rather fanned the flames of Reformation. Under Luther's leadership, this "new" religious movement was launched, and it was a movement that would change the course of Western history for good.

Like the reformers who had gone before him, Martin Luther courageously stood up to the religious power structure of his time and in the face of serious threats to his life. He did this because he had the same goal as earlier reformers: to see the church return to the model described in the New Testament and demonstrated in the book of Acts.

History records that the Protestant Movement spread like wildfire—first throughout Europe, then eventually to the New World and beyond. And all because a man, at the right time in history, had the courage to stand up and be counted.

The Least You Need to Know

- Indulgences meant paying money as penance for sins and being relieved of earthly punishment, as well as the possibility of setting others free from some of their temporal punishment.
- Luther's objection to indulgences later expanded to other doctrines such as papal supremacy, the seven sacraments, the authority of the Bible, and the corruption of the clergy.
- At the Diet of Wörms, Luther made his final decision not to reverse his own teachings in the face of opposition, stating that unless someone could refute him from the Bible, he would continue to stand on his beliefs.

Chapter 9

The Ups and Downs of Lutheranism

In This Chapter

- Martin Luther's triumphant return to Wittenberg
- The effect of the Peasants' Revolt on the Lutheran Movement
- Religious wars of the sixteenth century and their effect on the Lutheran Movement
- Lutheranism's struggle for legitimacy in the Holy Roman Empire

The Reformation was well on its way to becoming a world-changing historical event by the time Luther made his triumphant return to Wittenberg on March 6, 1522. When Luther took to the pulpit on Sunday, March 8 for the first of seven days of preaching, he knew that what had started as a simple challenge to debate had the potential to become a violent revolution.

Luther knew that he needed to settle down the people of his church. He needed to do that because Andreas von Carlstadt, who had more or less taken over while Luther was staying at Wartburg Castle, had stirred up the people with more radical preaching. For example, he attempted to institute more radical changes in church worship and removed all images from the churches. In his own preaching, Luther's message was one of tolerance, patience, and love.

He warned the Wittenbergers that it was wrong, even dangerous, for anyone to force religious reform down the throats of those who resisted:

> Dear friends, a man must not insist in his rights, but must see what is useful and helpful to his brother. I would not have gone as far as you have done if I had been there. What you did was good, but you have gone too fast, for there are brothers and sisters on the other side who belong to us, and must still be won. ... Faith never yields, but love is guided according to how our neighbors can grasp or follow it. There are some who can run, others who must walk, but still others who can hardly creep. Therefore we must not look on our own, but on our brother's powers, so that he that is weak in faith ... may not be destroyed. ... Let us therefore throw ourselves at one another's feet, join hands and help one another ... I will do my part, for I love you even as I love my own soul. ... We must first win the hearts of the people. And that is done when I teach only the Word of God, preach only the Word of God, and if you win the heart, you win the whole man. ...

> I have opposed indulgences and all the papists, but never by force. I simply taught, preached, wrote God's Word ... otherwise I did nothing ... The Word did it all. Had I desired to foment trouble, I could have brought great bloodshed upon Germany.

Luther Stands Tall in Wittenberg

Following his return to Wittenberg, Luther seemed to be in charge. He reversed much of the "reform" Carlstadt had brought to the church at Wittenberg, and he tailored his sermons to fit the needs of the congregation. Not long after his return, he showed his German translation of the New Testament to Melanchthon, then had it published in the summer of 1522. He then began working, with the help of a translation committee made up of his colleagues, on the translation of the Old Testament. In time, he embarked on a long preaching tour throughout Saxony, which was entirely pro-Reformation.

And of course, there was the writing. Luther continued to turn out volume after volume of materials related to his faith and beliefs. In 1523, Luther published a guide for ministers responsible for worship in their congregations. It was titled *Formula Missae et Communionis (The Reformed Communion Service)*. In this work, Luther stated that it was never the goal of the Lutheran movement to abolish the formality of the Catholic form of worship, only to remove those things that were not scriptural. That same year his *On the Order of Divine Worship* stressed that individual believers should read their Bibles daily and follow that up with prayer and thanksgiving to God.

In 1526, Luther wrote *Mass in German*, in which he described the ideal mass for the ordinary parish as one that could be of use to the common people and the young:

But, above all, the Order is for the simple and for the young folk who must daily be exercised in the Scripture and God's Word, to the end that they may become conversant with Scripture and expert in its use, ready and skillful in giving an answer for their faith, and able in time to teach others and aid in the advancement of the kingdom of Christ. For the sake of such, we must read, sing, preach, write, and compose; and if it could in any wise help or promote their interests, I would have all the bells pealing, and all the organs playing, and everything making a noise that could.

Lutheranism on a Roll!

At this time, Luther and the Reformation movement seemed to be flying high. Lutheran ministers all over Germany were preaching from the Bible and using Luther's books and pamphlets. Religious revolt was stirring to the east and to the north of Germany, as well as in Switzerland and some areas of France. It seemed as if Luther was at least on his way to uniting Germany, rather than dividing the country along religious lines. But it didn't happen. Before long, the Lutheran Movement would lose some needed support.

The years 1524–1525 marked a tragic event that badly hurt Luther's cause in a large part of Germany.

What a Revolting Development!

Europe had been for more than a century a cauldron of discontent on many fronts. One of those fronts was that of the peasantry in Germany.

The peasants were the common farmers and laborers. There were peasants all over Europe in the sixteenth century, and the discontent wasn't limited to those in Germany. Peasants throughout Europe had endured the misery of exploitation by the nobility and the resulting economic injustice. They worked hard, but didn't get to fully enjoy the economic fruits of that work. They had to pay their feudal lords (the actual owners of the land on which they farmed) money for the use of the land, and many of them were forced to labor for the lords in addition to keeping their own farming businesses running.

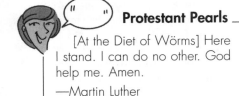

Protestant Pearls

[At the Diet of Wörms] Here I stand. I can do no other. God help me. Amen.

—Martin Luther

In addition, the Roman Catholic Church demanded its tithes and other payments. As if that weren't enough, prices were rising steeply during the first quarter of the sixteenth century, and the peasants received little or none of the benefits of the additional revenues.

Most peasants didn't need much in the way of farming equipment, but often they could barely afford to buy the tools they did need. When all the work was done and everyone was paid, the average peasant had little left over with which to care for himself and his family. Most peasants weren't starving, but they had little hope of moving upward economically.

Martin Luther foresaw the coming troubles, and he saw them as God's judgment on unjust princes and rulers. In January 1522, from Wartburg Castle he wrote:

> The people are everywhere restless and their eyes are open. They ... will no longer submit to oppression by force. It is the Lord who is directing all this and who is concealing this threat and imminent peril from the princes. It is he who will bring it all to pass through their blindness and their violence; it looks to me as though Germany will be drenched in blood.

In some circles, Luther has been criticized for inciting the peasants to revolt. Others say that he knew of the peasant's lot in life and realized that a violent uprising was inevitable. Either way, Luther's prediction that "Germany would be drenched in blood" would come to pass within just a few years after he wrote it.

In June of 1524, the peasants marched on Waldshut. From there, the revolt spread quickly.

Twelve Things ... This Is All We Ask!

The peasants' demands were put on paper in the form of the "Twelve Articles," which began to circulate in February of 1525. These twelve articles demanded, among other things, the right of a community to choose its own pastor, the elimination of some forms of tithing, the right to hunt and fish and gather wood on what would now be called "public lands," relief from excessive feudal dues and forced labor, and the fair payment for lands seized from the peasants. The twelfth article stated the peasants' willingness to withdraw any of the previous articles, if they were shown to be contrary to the teachings of the Bible.

The peasant revolt was in some ways encouraged by the Reformation. The peasants, who had endured their miserable lot in life for centuries, were encouraged to revolt by the reformist positions of liberation from the control of the church and equality of men before God, as well as its stand against the Roman Catholic Church's financial abuses. Luther didn't encourage the revolt—in fact, he stood strongly against it—but the revolutionaries saw his teachings as a basis for their demands and for their actions.

The Peasants' Revolt had as one of its supporters Thomas Münzer, as well as other
"Anabaptists." The Anabaptists were a sect
that seemed at first to have a lot in common
with Luther but whose practices and ideas
were a little more radical. (More on the
Anabaptists in Chapter 15, "The Radical
Side of the Reformation.")

> **Protestant Pearls**
>
> Here must the spirit rise to
> grace, or else neither the body
> nor it shall there rise to glory.
> —Lancelot Andrewes (1555–
> 1626), Anglican Bishop and
> Bible translator

The Peasants' Revolt began relatively peacefully in June of 1524, and early attempts by
the princes to negotiate with the rebels proved unsuccessful. By the beginning of 1525,
the revolt had spread to about a third of Germany. Early that year, the protests turned
violent. Before the nobles realized what was happening, more than 40 German monasteries
and castles were destroyed.

The Big—and Costly—Misunderstanding by the Peasants

Luther recognized that the grievances of the peasants were valid, and he himself was concerned with how they had been treated. In April of 1525 he wrote *Admonition to Peace in
Response to the Twelve Articles*, in which he criticized the nobility, whom he said had caused
the revolt in the first place. He spoke affectionately of the peasants, using terms such as
"dear brethren" and "friends."

At the same time, Luther said that the peasants had made the mistake of confusing the
gospel of Christ with the cause of earthly human rights. He suggested that Christians
had no right to take matters of justice into their own hands, but should expect to suffer
injustice, as Christ had told them they would.

As the uprising began to pick up steam, Luther seemed guarded in his response to it. He
even traveled, at risk to himself, to the central German city of Thuringia in an attempt to
reason with the peasants and persuade them to negotiate with Frederick the Wise, who was
willing to hear them. But as the movement expanded and became more violent, Luther was
horrified. He saw that the actions of the peasants presented a danger not only to his own
cause, but to the social order of Germany. He spoke out, urging violent responses to the
uprising, if need be.

Historians have stated that it was a mistake on the part of the peasants to believe that
Luther's religious rebellion against Rome would translate into a political rebellion against
the princely authority of Germany. But Luther, a man who believed strongly in submission
to authority, was no rebel in this area. He stood on the side of the princes against the rebels—
Carlstadt and Münzer, in particular—who took up the political cause of the German com-
moner against their rulers.

Luther: "Stop the Madness, by Any Means Necessary!"

Luther responded harshly against the Peasants' Revolt. In his tract *Against the Murdering, Thieving Hordes of Peasants*, Luther called on the princes of Germany to "knock down, strangle, and stab … and think nothing so venomous, pernicious, or Satanic as an insurgent. Such wonderful times are these that a prince can merit heaven better with bloodshed than another with prayer." Luther held that it was the princes' duty, as "God's sword on earth," to put down such a revolt, using reason first but using violent force if reason didn't work.

It's hard to say whether Luther's writings encouraged the princes' responses to the peasants, or merely foretold them. Throughout much of Germany, the princes put down the Peasants' Revolt with stunning cruelty and brutality. More than 6,000 peasants were slaughtered in the one-day battle of Frankenhausen, and more than 100,000 had died in battle or were executed before the "war" was over. What's more, the peasants who managed to survive didn't see much if any improvements in how they were treated. The peasants ceased to matter in the political world of Germany. The princes had laid a firm hold on power, and they weren't going to let go.

Where Did the Peasants' Uprising Leave Us?

Luther was later roundly criticized for his advocacy of such a severe response to the peasant uprising. And after the princes had defeated the peasants with finality, he wrote the pamphlet *The Terrible Story and Judgment of God concerning Thomas Münzer*, in which he appealed to the princes to deal mercifully with the peasants (sadly, some of them did not). He also wrote *Circular Letter concerning the Severe Booklet against the Peasants*, in which he condemned those who continued to mistreat the peasants, even after the uprising had been fully defeated.

Protestant Pearls

In a true church of Christ gathered together by God, not only into the belief of the principles of Truth, but also in the power, life and Spirit of Christ, the Spirit of God is the orderer, ruler and governor.

—Robert Barclay (1648–1690), Scottish Quaker apologist

At any rate, the Peasants' Revolt and Luther's response to it cost the Lutheran movement the appeal that it once held among the common people. The peasants had revolted believing that Luther, who was obviously a man of great influence, would support them in what they were doing. Luther, on the other hand, believed that the peasants had through their actions betrayed the true message of the gospel. It was for that reason that he backed the authority structure of his time to restore the peace that he saw as a necessity if he was to spread his message.

This turn of events brought about great mistrust between Luther, who felt that the peasants' actions undermined his message, and the peasants, who felt that Luther had betrayed their trust by not coming to their defense during their uprising. In many areas of Germany, particularly in the southern regions and other areas where the revolt had been most violent, the peasantry and townspeople began turning away from the Lutheran Movement to more radical religious movements that sprang from the Reformation.

The tragic event that came to be known as the Peasants' Revolt was the first of the major Reformation-era wars, but it was hardly the last. For the following three decades, the arrival of Lutheranism continued to cause violent conflict in Europe.

Just Where Do These Lutherans Fit In?

In the mid-1500s, the Holy Roman Empire, which covered much of central Europe, consisted of more than 300 territories, some of which were larger principalities and some of which were individual cities. As the Lutheran movement spread, many of the German territories began to convert from Catholicism to Lutheranism. The Catholic Church, from the pope and the emperor down, saw Lutheranism as heresy. By 1521, Charles V, Holy Roman Emperor and secular leader of the church, had pledged to purge the Lutheran movement from the empire, and he was ready to use force if necessary.

There was no war right away; the political and military situation of the time made it impossible for Charles V to move against the Lutherans. After all, he needed all the help—politically, militarily, and economically—he could get, and the Lutherans, although they opposed his role with the church, were a great resource. Yet a series of events over the next few decades made an eventual armed conflict between the two sides almost inevitable.

When They Became "Protestants"

At the 1526 Diet of Speyer—which Holy Roman Emperor Charles V was unable to attend—the Lutherans, who were well represented by several Lutheran princes from northern Germany, received major concessions. At this diet, it was decided that the empire would allow each state to choose for itself between Roman Catholicism and Lutheranism. This was hardly a final solution to the problem of the two religious factions, and it was decided to put off dealing with that problem.

But the decision of the 1526 Diet of Speyer was reversed when in 1529 Charles demanded that the diet assemble again, revoke its 1526 edict, and move against Lutheranism. In effect, this decision prohibited Luther's teaching. It was an attempt to stop the Reformation once and for all. Most of the German estates complied with the emperor, but some of them—the elector of Saxony, the governor of Brandenburg, and others—entered a protest against the decision of the 1529 Diet of Speyer. Followers of the movement came to be known as "Protestants," and the name stuck. From then on, advocates of the movement started by Martin Luther were called "Protestants," and the movement itself called "The Protestant Movement."

> **Going Deeper** _____
>
> The 1526 and 1529 Diets of Speyer presented greatly different outcomes for the Lutherans. At the first diet, it was decided that the empire would allow each state to choose for itself between Roman Catholicism and Lutheranism. That decision was reversed at the 1529 diet and, in effect, prohibited Martin Luther's teaching. It was as a result of the protests following the second diet that the movement came to be known as the Protestant Movement.

In a span of less than three years, the Protestant Movement had been given free reign, only to have that free reign rescinded. In short, nothing had been decided, and the Protestant/Catholic conflict continued.

When Peace Turned to War

A year after the second Diet of Speyer, all sides of the issue again met in an attempt to settle the dispute between the Protestants and Catholics. This was the 1530 Diet of Augsburg. Luther was not able to attend the Diet of Augsburg due to the Edict of Wörms, which had declared him an outlaw and a heretic. He stayed at nearby Coburg Castle, receiving regular updates on the diet.

By this time, Charles V had enjoyed some military successes, and he wanted to use the opportunity to unite the empire. Charles had just returned from Rome, where the pope had crowned him emperor, and he wanted to take care of the Lutheran "heresy." The Catholic majority at the Diet of Augsburg wanted to settle the matter using a general church council. The pope wanted to use force to settle things. Charles was seeking a peaceful, diplomatic solution to the split, so he asked the Lutherans to come to the diet ready to present and defend their beliefs.

It was at the Diet of Augsburg that Philip Melanchthon presented his famous "Augsburg Confession of Faith," the statement of Protestant beliefs, which is to this day embraced by the Lutheran Church. Luther had read and approved the Augsburg Confession, which was read before the emperor and the diet on the afternoon of June 25. Melanchthon had prepared the Confession using earlier writings by Luther and other Wittenberg theologians.

Going Deeper

The Augsburg Confession is the most widely accepted Lutheran statement of faith. It was prepared by Philip Melanchthon and approved by Martin Luther as a summary document to be read for the German nobility at the 1530 Diet at Augsburg. The Confession was rejected at the Diet of Augsburg and later amended. The Confession—together with several other creeds and catechisms—constitutes the written system of beliefs for tens of millions of Lutherans.

The Confession consisted of two parts. The first part was twenty-one short articles outlining the Protestant beliefs in the positive—what they believed in. The second part was a rejection of some Roman Catholic beliefs and practices, such as denial of the cup to the laypeople at the Lord's Supper, celibacy for priests, and the Catholic Church's use of confession, fasts, penances, and monastic vows.

Melanchthon's "Confession" was moderate in tone, but it spelled out many of the differences between Lutheranism and Catholicism. It avoided the most contentious areas of disagreement between the two sides. While the tone was in many ways conciliatory, many of the Catholics could not compromise with the Lutherans, and they presented Charles V with the "Confutation at Augsburg." Charles rejected the Augsburg Confession and accepted the Confutation and renewed the Edict of Wörms, which banned Luther's ideas. Nothing was settled at this diet; the conflict continued.

The Rise of the Schmalkaldic (That's Right, Schmalkaldic) League

When they saw what had happened in Augsburg, the Protestant princes of Germany—as well as Luther himself—knew that Emperor Charles V intended to go to war against them to enforce the pope's desire to end the Protestant "threat" to religious unity in the empire. The princes realized it was time to organize against what seemed almost certain attacks on the Lutheran estates.

Two of the top Lutheran princes—Landgrave Philip of Hesse and Elector John of Saxony—set up a meeting in Schmalkalden in Thuringia in December of 1530. In that meeting, eight princes and eleven cities came together and early in 1531 formed the Schmalkaldic League, a defensive alliance against aggression by the empire. They adopted the Confession of Augsburg as their statement of faith and agreed that if one of the territories or cities were attacked because of its religious affiliation, the others would come to its defense.

People You Should Know

Philip of Hesse (1504–1567), a German nobleman, was one of the founding leaders of the Schmalkaldic League, an alliance of princes and cities formed to defend themselves against aggression by the Holy Roman Empire. The League began to lose its power in 1540, when Philip was found to be a bigamist, a crime punishable by death according to imperial law. Philip was instrumental in putting down the Peasants' Revolt. In 1527, he founded the first Protestant university (Marburg).

The Protestants fully expected an attack to come around the middle of April 1531. But the attack never came. Charles V wanted more than anything to end the "Protestant problem" by the use of force, but that was going to have to wait: The Turks were preparing to attack the Austrian lands, and Charles needed all the support—from Protestants as well as Catholics—he could get. In the summer of 1532, Charles "made nice" with the Protestants with a declaration of peace that again postponed the final settlement of the conflict. This agreement allowed the Protestants to adhere to the terms of the Augsburg Confession and stated that no attacks would be made against the Protestant estates, at least until a meeting of a church council to finally work out the conflict. The "Peace of Nuremberg," as it was called, was never published or signed by anyone, but the Protestants trusted the emperor to keep his end of the bargain and supported him in his war with the Turks.

People You Should Know

John Frederick I (1503–1554) was elector (1532–1547) and duke (1547–1554) of Saxony. Like his father and predecessor John the Steadfast, John Frederick was a devout Lutheran. A leader of the Schmalkaldic League, he vacillated in loyalty to Holy Roman Emperor Charles V, but he was thrown into opposition when Charles undertook the Schmalkaldic War to crush the independence of the imperial states in Germany and to restore Christian unity.

A final settlement of the religious conflict was going to have to wait until later.

The Loss of a Great Leader

On February 18, 1546, Martin Luther, the unquestioned leader and founder of the Protestant Reformation, died in Eisleben, his place of birth. He had traveled to Eisleben to help settle a dispute between two nobles concerning the division of some lands. He was buried February 22 in the Castle Church in Wittenberg, the same Castle Church on whose door he posted his 95 Theses.

Luther left a legacy he could never have imagined on that fateful day when he first challenged the leaders of the church at Wittenberg to a debate. What Luther had hoped to be a simple academic discussion had spiraled into an all-out animosity, with Luther and his followers on one side and the centuries-old Catholic Church on the other.

No one could look at Luther's history and say that he was perfect in everything he did. Far from it! His oftentimes-fiery and occasionally hot-headed temperament caused him to do and say things that, in hindsight, he might have been better off not doing or saying (his wife, Catherine von Bora, once told Martin that he was oftentimes "too rude"). His criticisms of those who disagreed with him were sometimes strong, even to the point of being crude and nasty. Luther's words and actions tell us that he cared deeply for his fellow man, but they also tell us that he wasn't perfect in how he demonstrated his "brotherly love."

As he aged—and as he suffered with several illnesses, including some recurring ones (arthritis, heart problems, digestive problems)—Luther became more and more impatient and irritable with those who disagreed with him. For example, in his earlier years, Luther strongly advocated brotherly love and mutual toleration between Christians and Jews. But some of his later writings have been branded as "anti-Semitic," although Luther's criticisms of the Jews weren't racial or ethnic in tone, but religious. Luther just couldn't understand how the Jews didn't recognize Christ as the Messiah the Old Testament promised would come. Still, the criticism was harsh (the contents of his 1543 pamphlet *The Jews and Their Lies* matched its title for harshness). Luther had believed that when the church reformed itself, Jews would be more willing to reconsider the Christian faith. To the very end of his life, Luther had hoped that some of the Jews would be convinced to convert to Christianity.

Luther wasn't perfect, but his accomplishments as a preacher, teacher, theologian, and man of God left a profound mark on the Christian world, a mark that can be easily seen to this day.

Religious War—It Was Only a Matter of Time

During the 1530s the Schmalkaldic League—under the fiery leadership of a Philip of Hesse—grew in numbers, in territory, and in strength. And in response to the formation and growth of this league, a Catholic League was formed in 1538 under the leadership of Charles V. Both sides now actively prepared for armed conflict. The Treaty of Frankfurt, which was drawn up in April of 1539, resulted in another temporary peace between the two sides. During this temporary peace, Charles V tried again to settle the religious conflict, but again failed. It became more evident as time went on that a conflict was unavoidable.

Through the middle of the 1540s, the Schmalkaldic League supported and defended cities that had converted to Lutheranism. The league was also on occasion aggressive in its approach. In 1542, the league attacked the Duchy of Brunswick-Wofenbüttel, the last Catholic land in northern Germany. At that point, Charles V was occupied in the conflict with France, and he couldn't respond to the actions of the league.

Going Deeper

The Treaty of Frankfurt, drawn up in April of 1539, called for a truce between the Holy Roman Emperor, Charles V, and the Schmalkaldic League. It was one of many truces and treaties between the two sides, all of which failed to prevent the later Lutheran/Catholic wars of the 1540s.

By 1545, all of the northern part of the Holy Roman Empire had gone Lutheran, and Lutheranism was spreading to the south. Finally, in 1546, the emperor, his hands free from other military endeavors, prepared for action. Charles gathered an army of men from across the empire, and Pope Paul III sent a force led by his grandson as support.

The Schmalkaldic War was fought in the years 1546–1547. The Schmalkaldic League had superior numbers in the conflict, but lacked the organization it needed to be successful against the imperial forces. The issue was decided on April 24, 1547, at the Battle of Mühlberg, a decisive victory for Emperor Charles V over the league. John of Saxony and Philip of Hesse were both taken prisoner, and the emperor stripped 28 Lutheran cities of their independence.

So What's Next for the Lutherans?

The death of Martin Luther and the imperial victory over and the destruction of the Schmalkaldic League looked like crushing blows to Lutheranism. But the movement was far from finished. Lutheranism as a belief system had become too dug in and established in Germany, and it was only a matter of time before the empire would have to deal again with the Protestants.

Many of the Lutheran territories that had been conquered flatly refused to "reconvert" to Catholicism. In many ways, the situation remained the same as it was in the 1530s. Civil war raged on and off for several years. The emperor attempted to make peace again with the 1548 Interim of Augsburg, which was published at the conclusion of an imperial diet. This interim made two important concessions to the Protestants: the marriage of clergy and communion of both kinds (the bread and the cup).

The Interim of Augsburg didn't make anyone happy. The Catholics thought it went too far in the Protestants' favor, and the Protestants objected because it maintained Catholic rule. In the end, this interim failed to keep the peace, and the wars continued.

Peaceful Coexistence at Last

After decades of rancor, mistrust, and outright war, both sides of the Lutheran/Catholic conflict came to the table at the 1555 Diet of Augsburg to try to hammer out a peaceful resolution of their differences.

Neither the emperor nor the pope—Paul IV at this time—were present. And most of the German princes and electors chose not to appear. The majority of the representatives at the diet were Catholic princes or their representatives, though Protestants at that time made up a larger portion of the general population of Germany.

People You Should Know

Born Gian Pietro Carafa in 1476, Pope Paul IV served as head of the Catholic Church from 1555–1559. Paul IV was the successor of Marcellus II. He was also considered a reformer, as he labored to purify the clergy and abolish corruption and worldliness from the papal curia, thus promoting reform. This reform movement came to be known as the Counter-Reformation (see Chapter 16, "The Catholic Church's Own Reformation," for more on the Counter-Reformation). He was succeeded by Pius IV.

It took months of negotiations (from February to late September) and compromising for the Catholics and Lutherans to hammer out the terms of the Peace. Many disagreements between the two sides remained unsettled; both sides more or less agreed to tolerate their differences of opinion or religious conviction. On September 25, 1555, the Peace of Augsburg was completed.

What Do You Mean, "Peace of Augsburg"?

In many ways, the Peace of Augsburg reaffirmed the outcome of the 1526 Diet of Speyer. It was basically an edict of toleration of Lutheranism. It stated that the emperor would surrender his right to interfere in the religious affairs of the various states within the empire. Each prince was free to choose between Lutheranism or Roman Catholicism for his territory (this was called *cuius regio, eius religio*, which didn't actually appear in the Peace) and dissenters were allowed to emigrate to the cities where their religion was practiced. The free cities were required to allow both Catholics and Lutherans to practice their religions.

You Can Look It Up

Cuius regio, eius religio, which means that each individual prince should determine his territory's own form of religion, was the outcome of the Peace of Augsburg. *Cuius regio, eius religio* didn't actually appear in the Peace, and it was a little misleading, because the only two choices were Lutheranism and Catholicism. Other reform religions weren't included in the peace.

The Peace of Augsburg formally recognized Lutheranism. But it wasn't a total victory for the Reformation movement, as the other reformed faiths—for example, Calvinism and Zwinglianism, both of which we will discuss in Chapter 10, "The Reformation Expands"—were not recognized in the Peace.

Following the 1555 Diet of Augsburg, Emperor Charles V, knowing he had failed at bringing his dream of religious unity in Europe to fruition, abdicated the throne in 1556. His brother Ferdinand, to whom Charles had given authority to handle the terms of the Peace of Augsburg, took over as emperor. Charles withdrew to live near a Spanish monastery. He died in September of 1558.

In a sense, the Peace of Augsburg was a compromise between those who believed in the absolute rule of Rome over all religious matters and those who wanted local congregations to choose between Roman Catholicism and Lutheranism. According to this agreement, the ruler of a principality or city determined the religious makeup of the area he ruled. Some of the principalities (those in southern Germany) remained loyal to Rome and some (mainly those in the north) embraced Lutheranism. This kind of church/state relationship became the rule and stayed that way into the twentieth century.

The Peace of Augsburg gave Germany and that area of Europe a religious peace it had not known for decades. And for the first time, Lutheranism had taken a place of officially recognized legitimacy in Europe.

The Least You Need to Know

- Martin Luther and his movement grew in influence following his return to Wittenberg. It was then that he did some of his most important writing.
- The Peasants' Revolt and Martin Luther's response to it hurt the growth of Lutheranism in a large part of Germany and in other parts of Europe.
- The Peace of Augsburg marked an end—a temporary end, at least—of hostilities between Roman Catholics and Protestants in the empire.

The Reformation Expands

In This Chapter

- ◆ The rise of Lutheranism in Scandinavia
- ◆ Ulrich Zwingli and the Reformation in Switzerland
- ◆ Conflicts between Martin Luther and Ulrich Zwingli
- ◆ The pre-reformer life and times of John Calvin

Early on in the Reformation, Luther's words and writings greatly influenced many countries in Europe and the New World. While most non-German countries didn't embrace Lutheranism—meaning Luther's *specific* teachings— itself, they still underwent their own historic religious reformations. Christian leaders such as Ulrich Zwingli (Switzerland), John Knox (Scotland), and William Tyndale (England) were pivotal reformation leaders in their respective home- lands.

In the Scandinavian countries, however—Denmark, Finland, Sweden, Norway, and Iceland—it was a different story. It was in these countries that Luther- anism became the dominant religion, if not the official state religion. Their embrace of Lutheranism came from the very top—from the heads of their governments. Often, but not always, the movement was helped out by its pop- ularity among the people.

Lutheranism Goes Scandinavian

The ideas of Luther were introduced in Scandinavia largely by young men who had studied under him at Wittenberg or who had become familiar with his writings, which had spread far and wide throughout the first half of the sixteenth century.

In Scandinavia, as in other parts of Europe, the Reformation got a foothold due to the social, political, economic, and religious climates of the time.

Sweden Welcomes Lutheranism

The Reformation in Sweden got its start largely through the work of two disciples of Luther—brothers Olaf and Lars Petri (in the original language, their names were Olavus and Laurentius Petersson), who were sons of a blacksmith from Orebro. Both of the brothers studied under Martin Luther and Philip Melanchthon. Their personalities reflected those of the Wittenberg reformers. Olaf was much like Martin Luther in that he excited and moved people with his zeal and eloquence. Lars was like Melanchthon, in that he was thoughtful and calm in his approach. He became dean of the cathedral school at Strengnäs, where he was influenced by Archdeacon Lars Anderson, a theologian and reformer who aided the Petri brothers in bringing the ideas of Martin Luther to the Swedish people.

The Petri brothers, like Luther and the other reformers who had gone before, faced opposition from the Catholic Church and from the pope. The church did all it could to stir up the people against Olaf and get them to oppose his teachings. Several times, Olaf was confronted by angry mobs and barely escaped with his life.

While these two reformers were opposed by Rome, they received approval and protection from King Gustavus Vasa (1523–1560), who had led Sweden in winning independence from Denmark in 1523. In Sweden, the people had suffered through years of poverty and oppression under Roman Catholic rule. Having no access to the Bible for themselves, they were dependent upon the church for all things spiritual. To make matters worse, rival factions within the nation made life harder on everyone. The king wanted to reform both the state and the church, and he was grateful for the help of the Petris.

Protestant Pearls

Here must the spirit rise to grace, or else neither the body nor it shall there rise to glory.

Lancelot Andrewes (1555–1626), Anglican Bishop and Bible translator

In the face of the opposition from Rome, Olaf Petri defended the reformed faith with great passion and courage. He held that all teachings—from the Church Fathers, from Rome, or from the local church—should be in alignment with the Bible. He maintained that the Bible was the ultimate authority over all things having to do with the Christian faith.

Gustavus Vasa favored Protestantism over Catholicism and did everything he could to help it spread throughout his country. It wasn't long before the whole country became Lutheran. In 1527, the Reformation was established by Swedish law. Once it was no longer under what was at the time oppression from Rome, Sweden became one of the bastions of Lutheranism.

Finland, which was a possession of Sweden at the time, followed in its adoption of Lutheranism. The first Lutheran preacher in Finland was Peter Särkilahti, who had studied in Germany before he began preaching in 1524. Another important reformer in Finland was Michael Agricola (1508–1557), who also studied in Wittenberg. Agricola published a New Testament in Finnish in 1548. He followed that in 1551 with translations of the Psalms and some of the Old Testament prophets.

Denmark, Norway, and Iceland—Northern Reformation Dominoes

Lutheranism also spread to Denmark, Norway, and Iceland (which was a possession of Norway but later became a Danish province). King Frederick I, although he had promised to prevent any heresies from coming to Denmark, pushed for church reform, even going so far as to appoint "reforming" preachers and priests. The result was a major abandonment of the Catholic Church in favor of Lutheranism. Young Danish preachers—in particular Hans Tausen, who studied under Luther at Wittenberg—preached reforming doctrines with great effectiveness.

Tausen, who has been called "the Reformer of Denmark," was from a peasant family. Early in his life, he demonstrated the intelligence and passion it would take to do great things for the church. Tausen was given the opportunity to receive an education at any university he wanted, as long as it wasn't Wittenberg, where his spiritual superiors knew Luther was teaching his "heresies." He enrolled at the university in Cologne, which was a center of support for Roman Catholicism. But while there, he got his hands on some of Luther's writings, and he wanted to know more. He wanted to attend the university at Wittenberg and be taught by the Reformer. He knew that a decision to attend Wittenberg meant the probability of losing the support he had from home.

> **People You Should Know**
>
> Hans Tausen (1494–1561) has been called "the Reformer of Denmark." Tausen studied at Wittenberg before returning to his monastery in Denmark. He later broke with the Roman Catholic Church and began teaching Lutheranism. He had the support of King Frederick I, who had appointed Tausen one of his court chaplains.

Tausen returned to his monastery in Denmark, where no one had any idea that he had adopted for himself Lutheran beliefs. He kept his new religious leanings to himself, opting instead to simply open his Bible and explain its true meaning. In other words, he preached the same things Luther had been preaching, teaching, and writing about. When his superiors, who believed Tausen would be a staunch supporter and defender of the old church in Rome, found out what he had been doing, they moved Tausen from his monastery to another and placed him under strict supervision.

By 1524, Tausen had openly broken with the Catholic Church and began preaching Lutheran beliefs. In 1527, at the Diet of Odense, the Danish Catholic bishops attempted to stop the strongly Lutheran-leaning King Frederick I, who had appointed Tausen and other Lutherans as his court chaplains, from supporting the Lutheran cause. They failed, and after that the Reformation spread rapidly throughout Denmark.

After a period of civil war in Denmark, in 1536 King Christian III became king of Denmark and Norway (Norway gave up its status as a kingdom and became a province following the Danish civil war). Christian began taking steps to make Lutheranism the recognized state religion. In addition, the kingdom of Denmark took steps to put down Roman Catholic and Anabaptist dissidence, and confiscated the lands and properties of the old church. As Lutheranism spread directly into Norway, the bishops who fled the country or who died off were replaced with Reformation ministers.

People You Should Know

Christian III (1503–1559), was the king of Denmark and Norway from 1534 to 1559 and a key figure in the Protestant Reformation of Scandinavia. Christian III established Lutheranism as the state religion in all his dominions. In doing so, he defeated strong Roman Catholic opposition, then confiscated the properties of the old church. He was succeeded by his son Frederick II.

Icelander Oddur Gottskalkson, who had studied in Germany and returned to Iceland as a Lutheran and who published an Icelandic translation of the New Testament in 1540, introduced the Reformation to his home country. At first, the Icelandic populace was reluctant to embrace Lutheranism; it was imposed by force, over the opposition of Bishop John Aresson, between 1539–1551. Many Icelanders resented the new state church, but that began to change when Gudbrandur Thorlakson, an Icelandic bishop from 1571–1627 who was also a Lutheran, began persuading them to accept it. Thorlakson also translated the Bible into the Icelandic language.

Switzerland—Different Country, Different Reformation

Reformation broke out in Switzerland at roughly the same time as in Germany. While the theology surrounding the Swiss Reformation was a lot like that in Germany, Switzerland's movement was mostly independent of Germany's. Both reformation movements enjoyed widespread public support.

At the time, Switzerland was a loose network of thirteen small "cantons," or states. The northern and eastern regions of Switzerland were populated by people who spoke German and held to German culture. The western part spoke French, and the southern part Italian.

The German-speaking part of the country was led by reformer Ulrich Zwingli, who initiated the Swiss Reformation while serving as a priest in Zürich. The Reformation spread from Zürich to other cantons of German Switzerland. But that development didn't translate into religious or political unity. Some of the cantons remained strongly Roman Catholic, and as happened in Germany, parts of Switzerland and other areas were thrown into religious war.

The Life and Times of Ulrich

Ulrich (or Huldreych) Zwingli was born New Year's Day of 1484—seven weeks after the birth of Martin Luther—in Wildhaus, Switzerland. Zwingli was the third of eight sons from a fairly prominent middle-class family in Wildhaus. His father, Ulrich, was for a time mayor of the town of Wildhaus and the brother of Bartholomew Zwingli, the pastor of Wildhaus. In 1487, Bartholomew took the position of pastor and dean of Wesen, where the younger Ulrich Zwingli received at least part of his primary education.

Ulrich Zwingli began his university-level studies at the University of Vienna, where he was influenced greatly by the humanism that was a large part of the educational scene of the time. He completed his studies at the university at Basel, where he sat under the teaching of reformer Thomas Wyttenbach (1472–1526), receiving his Master of Liberal Arts in 1506. That same year Zwingli, who, unlike Luther, hadn't earned a doctorate in divinity, was ordained and began his priesthood in the Swiss town of Glarus. It was in Glarus that Zwingli spent much of his spare time studying the writings of humanists such as Desiderius Erasmus of Rotterdam.

> **Protestant Pearls**
>
> In a true church of Christ gathered together by God, not only into the belief of the principles of Truth, but also in the power, life and Spirit of Christ, the Spirit of God is the orderer, ruler and governor.
>
> —Robert Barclay (1648–1690), Scottish Quaker apologist

Glarus was a well-known recruiting center for Swiss mercenary soldiers for many of Europe's armies, and twice during fighting on foreign soil Zwingli served as chaplain for the soldiers. Having seen some of the horrors of the wars the mercenaries fought, Zwingli wrote against the mercenary system. Before long, he was forced to leave Glarus. In 1516, he went to Einsiedeln, located southeast of Zürich, where he began to have doubts about some of the practices of the Roman Catholic Church. Those doubts would eventually lead him to the point of renouncing the Church.

Martin Luther's story included a personal religious crisis in which he questioned his own standing before God. It was through solving that personal crisis that Luther realized the need for church reform. But Zwingli's story was different from Luther's. Zwingli became a reformer through his studies, which brought him to a point of questioning the teachings of the Roman Catholic Church.

What Zwingli Thought of the Bible and the Church

While in Einsiedeln, Zwingli had a chance to spend some time with Erasmus, and he also read and memorized Erasmus's Latin translation of the New Testament. After reading Erasmus's work, Zwingli began to preach that many of the church's teachings and practices strayed from the simple message of the Bible. He criticized as "unscriptural" practices such as the adoration of saints and relics and the abuse of indulgences.

Ulrich Zwingli's direct and honest affirmation of the authority of the Bible won him great support and popularity in Switzerland. He also remained in the good graces of the pope, and on his thirty-fifth birthday—January 1, 1519—he was rewarded with an appointment as priest at the Grossmünster (in German, the "Great Cathedral") in Zürich, a position he had badly wanted.

The stage was now set for reformation in Switzerland. Zürich was to become to the Reformation in Switzerland what Wittenberg was to the Reformation in Germany.

How and When Zwingli Became a Reformer

It has been said that the Reformation in Switzerland started the day Ulrich Zwingli took the position of parish priest in the Great Cathedral. Soon after Zwingli's arrival at Zürich, large audiences began to come to the Great Cathedral to hear his preaching. In a lot of ways, Zwingli's preaching indicated that he had remained a good Catholic, but there were inklings of reformation theology in his preaching early on. He broke with Catholic tradition by preaching the New Testament Scriptures from the original Greek and Hebrew Scriptures. Prior to this, priests had used Vulgate, the Latin translation of the Bible, and the writings of the Fathers of the Church in their sermons.

> **Protestant Pearls**
>
> Wherever we see the Word of God purely preached and heard, there a church of God exists, even if it swarms with many faults.
>
> —John Calvin

In 1519, one of Ulrich's admirers provided him the use of a printing press, allowing him to spread his ideas outside of Zürich. That same year, Zwingli got hold of some of the writings of Martin Luther, many of which had been printed in Basel and distributed throughout the Swiss cantons. Zwingli became an ardent follower of Luther, and during the latter half of 1519—following his near death from the plague, which claimed the lives of nearly a third of the people in Zürich—he embraced for himself many of the German reformer's doctrines.

In his preaching, Zwingli attacked the abuses of the Catholic Church, as well as social and political ones. He preached against fasting, confession, the celibacy of the clergy, Mass, monasticism, and the use of pictures and music in church services. Zwingli faced opposition for his reforms, but he had support on the Zürich city council. In 1520, Zwingli persuaded the council to ban religious teachings that weren't founded on the Bible.

Going Deeper

Celibacy of the clergy was one of the points of contention between Ulrich Zwingli and the Roman Catholic Church. The Catholics believed that their clergy should renounce marriage. There is nothing in the Bible to support making celibacy of the clergy mandatory. But in Matthew 19:12, Jesus commends those who remain unmarried for the sake of the kingdom of God. And the apostle Paul does the same in 1 Corinthians 7:7,8 and 32–35.

One of those teachings was the church's prohibition against eating meat during *Lent*. In 1522 several prominent people in Zürich deliberately broke the church's rule against eating meat during Lent and were arrested. Zwingli jumped to the defense of these "criminals," and they were released with what we might call "a slap on the wrist." In that same year, Zwingli published *Architeles*, which clearly stated his position on believers' freedom from the control of the Roman Catholic hierarchy.

Not long after that, Zwingli sent a letter to the Bishop of Constance asking for permission for the clergy to marry. The request was denied, but Zwingli defied the bishop by secretly marrying a widow by the name of Anna Reinhart Meyer. That act of defiance, although it was not made public knowledge until 1524, was accompanied by Zwingli's

You Can Look It Up

Lent is a forty-day period—excluding Sundays—of preparation for the death and resurrection of Jesus Christ on Easter Sunday. The season begins with Ash Wednesday, when pastors mark Christians' foreheads with ashes as a reminder that they will return to the dust from which they were created. Lent ends on Holy Saturday, which is the day before Easter Sunday.

open preaching against celibacy. This preaching stirred up the public to the point where the city council of Zürich called a public meeting to discuss religious subjects.

It was there that Zwingli presented the Swiss equivalent of Martin Luther's 95 Theses.

Sixty-Seven This Time, Not Ninety-Five

Around 600 people appeared at the Zürich Disputation, where Zwingli would have a chance to explain and clarify his beliefs. On January 29, 1523, Zwingli appeared before the Zürich council. The Disputation was attended by hundreds of educated men, including representatives from Rome and representatives of the Bishop of Constance. There, Zwingli presented his specially prepared Sixty-seven Theses (sometimes they are called the Sixty-seven Conclusions or Sixty-seven Articles), which laid out his patently Protestant positions. Among those positions were:

◆ That the Bible was and is the rule for faith

◆ That Jesus Christ is the one and only mediator between man and God

◆ That those who put their faith in Christ are members of His body, and therefore members of the church

◆ That it is by the power from God that any Christian can perform any good act

◆ That Jesus Christ is the only eternal priest

◆ That the mass is not a sacrifice but simply a commemoration

◆ That monkery, and all the practices that pertain to it, should be rejected

◆ That Scripture permits all men to marry

◆ That Christians owed obedience to the government, except where the government contradicted the Bible

◆ That God alone can pardon sin

◆ That every kind of food could be consumed on any day of the week

◆ That there is no purgatory after death

After deliberation on the theses and other information presented at the Disputation, the council supported Zwingli and gave him the right to preach from the Bible and to initiate his reforms. The council also withdrew the Zürich canton from the jurisdiction of the Bishop of Constance and affirmed the ban on preachings and teachings not founded on the Scriptures. In taking these steps, the Zürich council officially adopted Zwingli's Reformation.

To the Victor ...

Zwingli's victory at the Zürich Disputation led to sweeping reforms in the churches. Monasteries were converted into hospitals, organs and religious images were removed from the churches, mass and confession were eliminated, priests were allowed to marry, and communion was made into a commemorative feast. In 1524, Zwingli publicly celebrated his marriage, which he had illegally contracted two years previously. In 1525, the Catholic Mass was replaced by a reformed service at Zwingli's church in Zürich.

The Inroads of Zwinglianism

The Reformation started by Ulrich Zwingli gained popular support in the larger and wealthier cantons of Switzerland. Zwingli worked hard to spread his reforms beyond Zürich, and his efforts paid off. One of the first of the cantons to follow the lead of Zürich and Zwingli was the largest, Bern, which adopted Zwingli's reforms in 1528. The leading reformers of Bern were teacher/pastor Berchtold Haller, a friend of Philip Melanchthon, and layman Niklaus Manuel, a writer who helped spread Protestant beliefs through religious plays.

The wealthy city of Basel, which was greatly influenced by Erasmus and other Christian humanists, was next to follow Zürich. The Reformation leader in Basel was Johannes Oecolampadius (1482–1531), a one-time humanist and follower of Erasmus who converted to Protestantism. Oecolampadius, a friend and supporter of Zwingli's, was a brilliant scholar who became pastor of St. Martin's Church in Basel and later introduced the Reformation to Basel.

> ### People You Should Know
>
> Johannes Oecolampadius was a sixteenth-century Protestant reformer. He brought reformation to the canton of Basel in Switzerland. In his youth, he was a humanist and a follower of Erasmus, who he worked with on the great humanist's translation of the New Testament. After becoming interested in the works of Martin Luther, Oecolampadius converted to Protestantism and became a friend and supporter of the leader of the Reformation in the German-speaking portion of Switzerland, Ulrich Zwingli.

In the canton of St. Gall, the man most responsible for bringing Zwingli's Reformation was physician Joachim von Watt (1485–1551). He was assisted by teacher/preacher Johannes Kessler (1502–1574).

In Glarus—the same Glarus where Zwingli began his career as a priest—reformation broke out and most of the congregations of the canton turned to Zwinglianism. In

Grisons, Zwinglianism made great gains largely because it was populated by refugees of the Italian Inquisition who settled there around mid-sixteenth century. One of those refugees was Pietro Paolo Vergerio, a lawyer who had actively persecuted Protestants before converting in 1548. After fleeing to Glarus, he began preaching Reformation beliefs.

The spread of Zwingli's beliefs wasn't limited to Switzerland. It made some headway in Martin Luther's homeland of Germany.

A "New" Last Supper

During Holy Week in April of 1525, the churches in Zürich celebrated communion the way Zwingli had wanted, using the examples of the ancient church as their model. Zwingli took his place at the head of the table, which was covered in a white linen cloth. After they prayed and read the appropriate Bible passages, Zwingli and his associates ate and drank the bread and the wine, which were contained in cups and wooden plates on the table. They then went pew to pew and served the rest of the congregation.

In describing this new rite, Zwingli wrote:

> As soon as the sermon is over, unleavened bread and wine shall be placed upon a table on the floor of the nave, and then the ordinance and actions of Christ, in accordance with His institution of this memorial, shall be recited openly and intelligibly, in German, as hereafter follows. Then the bread shall be carried round by the appointed ministers on large wooden trenches from one seat to the next, and each shall break off a bit or a mouthful with his hand and eat it. Then they shall go round with wine likewise; and no one shall move from his place. When that is done, in open and clear words praise and thanksgiving shall be offered to God in an audible and distinct voice; and then the whole multitude of the congregation shall say "Amen" at the end.

To Zwingli, this was merely a literal and accurate reconstruction of the Last Supper, using the New Testament text that describes Christ's meeting with his twelve apostles prior to his arrest, conviction, and crucifixion.

It was a radical departure from the sacramental practices of the Roman Catholic Church, but it was also a point of great argument with Martin Luther.

Zwingli versus Luther—The Battle of the Reformers

Zwingli came into conflict with the Lutherans over doctrinal differences concerning the nature of the Eucharist, or *the Lord's Supper*. Originally, both Luther and Zwingli had opposed the Catholic doctrine of transubstantiation, which held that the elements in the Lord's Supper—the bread and the wine—actually became the body and blood of Christ. Both had also opposed the idea of the Mass being a sacrificial gathering.

You Can Look It Up

The Lord's Supper is the Protestant rite of commemorating Christ's Last Supper with the twelve apostles. At the Protestant Reformation, the leaders in general rejected the traditional Roman Catholic belief in the sacrament as a sacrifice and as an invisible miracle of the literal physical changing of the bread and wine into the body and blood of Christ. The Protestants in general held to the belief that the Lord's Supper mystically unites believers with Christ and with one another.

The two were in agreement over many aspects of the Lord's Supper. Both saw it as instituted by Jesus Christ himself and therefore important to the spiritual life of the church as a whole and to believers as individuals. But that is where the agreement concerning communion ended. Zwingli saw it more as a commemorative practice that celebrated the believers' union with Christ. In his mind, Christ's "This is my body" at the Last Supper could be taken as "This *represents* my body." Zwingli had, therefore, rejected the idea of Christ's physical presence at the Lord's Supper. Luther, on the other hand, believed in *consubstantiation*, interpreting Christ's words to mean that his physical body was present in the form of the bread and the cup. While they didn't literally become the body and blood of Christ—the bread remained bread and the wine remained wine—they were a vehicle for God's grace and a means for union with Christ.

Neither Luther nor Zwingli would swerve from their respective positions. Protestant theologians and religious leaders began taking sides in the issue, and in 1527 Luther and Zwingli began to openly attack one another's positions. Zwingli published *Friendly Exposition*, which criticized Luther's views on the Lord's Supper as he explained in his 1526 tract *Sermon on the Sacrament of the Body and Blood of Christ against the Radicals*. These writings were followed over the next few years by further attacks and counter-attacks, including Luther's *Confession Concerning the Lord's Supper*, which he wrote in order to set straight those he considered "heretics."

It is recorded that Zwingli was in the name of unity willing to "agree to disagree" on issues such as the Lord's Supper. Luther, on the other hand, would have nothing to do with those he considered to be misinterpreting or misusing the message of the Bible.

You Can Look It Up

Consubstantiation is the belief on the part of the Lutheran branch of the Reformation that there is a change by which the body and blood of Christ join with the bread and wine in the Lord's Supper. Swiss reformer Ulrich Zwingli rejected this belief and held that the bread and wine were only symbolic and a commemoration of Christ's death. This difference led to a bitter dispute between Zwingli and Martin Luther.

Time for Some Unity, Guys!

As the arguments between Luther and Zwingli raged on, there was potential trouble brewing for all the Protestants. By 1529, Holy Roman Emperor Charles V had defeated the French in a war that had kept him from focusing on ending the empire's religious division between the Protestants and Catholics. With that war out of the way, the Protestant princes in Germany knew that Charles could concentrate on ending the Protestant "heresy" that threatened to tear the empire apart.

Philip of Hesse, alarmed at the new "threat" and hoping to present a united Protestant front against the Catholic princes, called the two sides together to meet at his castle in Marburg to try to work out their differences. Zwingli (who had visions of a united Protestantism for both religious and political reasons), was all for the meeting, but Luther was at best lukewarm toward the idea because he didn't believe in going to war to decide issues of religion and faith. Eventually, however, Luther agreed to attend the meeting, which came to be known as the Marburg Colloquy.

Who's Down for a Colloquy?

Luther came with Philip Melanchthon (himself hesitant because he didn't want to offend Catholics by attending, as he had hoped for a peaceful solution to the Lutheran/Catholic conflict) and other "Lutherans." Zwingli attended with Johannes Oecolampadius of Basel. They and other figures in the dispute met on October 1–3, 1529, in Marburg, Germany, for the Colloquy.

At the request of Philip of Hesse, Martin Luther drew up 15 articles for debate at the Marburg Colloquy. They included:

- The Trinity (the belief in one God who had revealed himself in the person of the Father, the Son, and the Holy Spirit)
- The incarnation (Christ's coming to earth as a human)
- The simultaneous divinity and humanity of Christ
- Original sin (the doctrine that all people are born into the sin of Adam and Eve)
- Justification by faith
- The work of the Holy Spirit
- Baptism
- The role of good works in the life of the Christian
- Confession
- Civil government
- Christian liberty
- The Lord's Supper

This was the first-ever council among Protestants as well as the first-ever attempt to unite them. The desire for unity can be seen in Zwingli's prayer as he entered the conference:

> Fill us, O Lord and Father of us all, we beseech Thee, with thy gentle Spirit, and dispel on both sides all the clouds of misunderstanding and passion. Make an end to the strife of blind fury. Arise, O Christ, Thou Sun of righteousness, and shine upon us. Alas! while we contend, we only too often forget to strive after holiness which Thou requirest from us all. Guard us against abusing our powers, and enable us to employ them with all earnestness for the promotion of holiness.

Luther and Zwingli came to the Marburg Colloquy with their own notions about one another. To Luther, Zwingli was at best a radical, and more than likely not a Christian at all. (Prior to the Colloquy, Luther declared that the Swiss were "of another spirit.") To Zwingli, Luther was a man who may have meant well but who hung on too tightly to some of the outdated beliefs of the old church.

Agreement and Unity—To a Point

Luther and Zwingli came to agreement on fourteen of the points but could not come to full agreement concerning the fifteenth, the Lord's Supper. They agreed on some points concerning communion. For example, they both held that the bread and the cup was for all believers. Where they couldn't agree was on the physical presence of Christ at the Lord's Supper.

Both reformers remained adamant in holding to their positions, but they did come to an agreement to disagree without taking further shots at one another. They agreed to cease their feud and, in the spirit of brotherly love, continue to study the issue.

In the end, the Marburg Colloquy didn't bring lasting peace between the two sides. It became clear that the points of contention between the different arms of Protestantism were profound ones and that they weren't going to be solved with a simple meeting of those of different belief systems. The movement called Protestantism remained divided between the Lutherans of Martin Luther and the Reformed Protestantism of Ulrich Zwingli.

Trouble for Zwinglianism

Although Zwingli's reformation movement had made great strides in German-speaking Switzerland, he faced some potential crises in the form of agitation by the Anabaptists. The Anabaptists wanted more radical reforms than Zwingli offered. Zwingli also faced the armed resistance of what had come to be known as the "Forest Cantons," an alliance of Swiss cantons that had remained loyal to the Roman Catholic Church, even as Zwingli's brand of Protestantism made great gains.

Going Deeper _____

The Forest Cantons were a group of five Swiss cantons (cantons can be defined as states)—Uri, Schwyz, Unterwalden, Lucerne, and Zug—that remained staunchly Catholic. In 1524, these cantons formed an alliance whose purpose it was to check the growth of heresy (especially Protestantism). This alliance came into conflict with Zwingli and some of the Protestant cantons.

The Anabaptists

Anabaptism in Switzerland was something of an offshoot of Zwinglianism. Anabaptists, many of whom were scholars of the Bible, objected to infant baptism, a practice they considered unbiblical. Instead, they held that the scriptures supported the baptism of adults who had been spiritually converted.

Around 1524, some of the Anabaptists refused to have their children baptized, and in January of 1525 they debated the issue of infant baptism with Zwingli and some of his followers. The Anabaptists—who were led by Conrad Grebel, Felix Manz, and Wilhelm Reublin— argued their point, but Zwingli would not budge. The Anabaptists were ordered to baptize their children or face banishment from Zürich.

As they fled Zürich, many of the Anabaptists preached their beliefs in the surrounding areas. Many of them, with the blessings of the city council and of Zwingli himself, faced imprisonment and even death.

It wasn't long before the Anabaptist "threat" was permanently ended in Switzerland.

Zwinglianism Takes the Hit at the War of the Cantons

The end of the spread of Zwinglianism in Switzerland came with the 1531 religious civil war between Zwinglians and Catholics. Six Swiss cantons had been converted to Protestantism, but five—Uri, Schwyz, Unterwalden, Lucerne, and Zug—remained staunchly and militantly Catholic. These five came to be known as the "Forest Cantons," and there was serious friction between them and the Zwinglian cantons.

Eventually, what had been hostility between the cantons became an all-out civil war. Starting in June of 1529, both sides marshalled their forces near Kappel, but the battle was delayed by a treaty called the "First Peace of Kappel." The treaty was drawn up on June 26 and it allowed the Forest Cantons to remain Catholic.

Over the next two years, tensions between the two sides continued. The tensions grew to anger, and the anger played itself out in violence by both sides. The final straw was a trade embargo imposed on the Forest Cantons by Zürich that deprived them of much-needed grain, wine, salt, and metal. Out of sheer desperation, the Forest Cantons responded to the embargo by attacking Zürich in 1531. The Forest Cantons attacked with some 8,000 troops and were met with the 2,000 men from Zürich. The battle ended quickly, with Zürich losing many important religious and civic leaders.

Zwingli Meets His Demise

Zwingli had accompanied the Protestant armies to battle as a chaplain, but he ended up as one of the casualties in the battle. On October 10 or 11, 1531, Zwingli, acting as chaplain for the Protestant forces but bearing arms himself, was wounded at the Battle of Kappel. Troops from the Forest Cantons found Zwingli wounded and immediately killed him, and quartered and burned his body.

After Zwingli's death, a peace treaty was signed by Zürich and the Forest Cantons on November 20. The treaty stated that the Forest Cantons were allowed to remain Catholic and that Zürich was allowed to remain Protestant. This spelled the end of the growth of German Swiss Protestantism.

Protestant Pearls

How, then, shall others presume to enact dogmas at their pleasure, and impose them as things necessary to salvation?
—Olaf Petri, Swedish reformer

Zwingli's place as leader of the Reformation in Zürich was taken by his son-in-law, Heinrich Bullinger, but after 1536, John Calvin, a young preacher working in French-speaking Geneva, took the reins of leadership. At first, Calvin stuck to Zwingli's doctrines, but in time he developed his own theology, which rejected most of Zwingli's more radical teachings.

Calvin would become much better known than his predecessor—Zwingli would later be called "the Third Man of the Reformation," behind Luther and Calvin. He is even referred to as "the forgotten Reformer." But it was the relatively obscure Ulrich Zwingli who paved the way for the works of John Calvin, which were to profoundly influence Protestantism not only in his time, but into the twentieth century and beyond.

The Molding and Making of the Reformer Calvin

John Calvin was born on July 10, 1509 in Noyon, France, around sixty miles from Paris. John's father was Gérard Calvin, a notary for the city of Noyon, and his mother was Jeanne le Franc, the daughter of a fairly wealthy innkeeper.

Early in his life, John Calvin seemed destined for the priesthood. In 1523, when John was 14—and during an outbreak of plague at Noyon—his father sent him to Paris for further education in theology. There, he first enrolled at Collège de la Marche, where he studied under Mathurin Cordier, who would later convert to Protestantism and who would be a part of Calvin's life years later. After his time at Collège de la Marche, Calvin was transferred to Collège de Montaigu, which counted as one of its former students the great humanist Desiderius Erasmus. At both institutions, John Calvin was an outstanding student.

A Different Kind of Law

John Calvin seemed destined for a brilliant career serving the Catholic Church, but in 1528, Gérard Calvin had a change of heart when it came to what he wanted his son to do; he encouraged young John to take up the study of law instead. Gérard Calvin may have wanted his son to have a more lucrative career, but it is also likely that he was motivated by his own problems within the ecclesiastical circles of Noyon. Gérard had been involved in a dispute over accounts with the cathedral in Noyon, and he knew that because of that his son's career as a priest might not pan out.

Being the dutiful son he was, John enrolled at the universities at Orléans and Bourges, where he studied law under a highly regarded jurist by the name of Pierre Taisan de l'Étoile. Again, he was an outstanding student. At Bourges in 1529, John studied the humanities. A year later, one of his friends, Melchior Wolmar, joined him in Bourges and taught him Greek and studied the New Testament with him.

Gérard Calvin died in 1531, and again John changed the course of his educational life. He moved back to Paris, where he studied the ancient classics and continued his studies in Greek and also took up the study of Hebrew.

John Calvin—Another Protestant "Convert"

Calvin received what can be called a "Renaissance education," meaning that he learned the value of the works of humanity. Calvin learned philosophy, law, and classical literature and arts. This educational background was the basis for Calvin's belief that individual people—the "common" people, and not just princes and bishops—should have a part in making political and religious policy.

As Calvin studied the Scriptures—in light of the whole of his education—he came to the point of believing that there was something wrong with the way the Roman Catholic Church was doing things. It was during this time of personal enlightenment that Calvin "converted" to Protestantism.

Calvin, who was from a Catholic background, had a personal experience of "sudden conversion" somewhere between the years 1532 and 1534. John never publicly discussed the details of his conversion, but it seemed obvious he was referring to this experience in a letter he wrote to Cardinal Sadoleto, who had written against reforms in Geneva Switzerland. Calvin wrote:

> The more closely I considered myself, the more my conscience pricked with sharp goadings, so much so that no other relief or comfort remained to me except to deceive myself by forgetting. … Then however there arose quite another form of teaching, not to turn away from the profession of Christianity but to reduce it to its own source, and to restore it, as it were, cleansed from all dirt to its own purity.

Calvin apparently wanted a Christianity that more resembled the faith he read about in the Bible. Through this private study, he came to a point of rejecting the absolutions, the penances, the intercessions, and many of the other practices of the Roman Catholic Church. It wasn't long after Calvin's embrace of Protestantism that he was forced to leave Paris, which was the site of an anti-Protestant drive that could have been dangerous to him and his Protestant friends.

For about three years, Calvin was a man without a country. He wandered around France, Germany, and Switzerland before settling for a time in Basel. Still a very young man of 26, Calvin made his break with the Roman Catholic Church public when he published the first edition of *Institutes of the Christian Religion* (1536), which is considered to this day to be the definitive statement of Protestantism.

As profound as the effect *Institutes* would have on Protestantism in the coming centuries, it was only the start for Calvin.

The Least You Need to Know

- ◆ Lutheranism spread outside of Germany to the Scandinavian countries, though it did not make great strides elsewhere.
- ◆ Reformation did come to many European Countries, under the leadership of their own reformers.
- ◆ Although he had conflicts with German reformer Martin Luther, Ulrich Zwingli can be seen as the father of the Reformation in Switzerland.
- ◆ After Ulrich Zwingli's death, John Calvin rose to the place of leadership of the Reformation in French-speaking Switzerland.

Chapter 11

The Reformation Changes Hands

In This Chapter

- ◆ John Calvin's *Institutes of the Christian Religion*
- ◆ A first attempt at sweeping reformation in Geneva
- ◆ Calvin's return to Geneva and his success there
- ◆ John Calvin's legacy in Christianity

Frenchman John Calvin was one of what are called the "second-generation reformers"—he continued the work begun by Martin Luther, Ulrich Zwingli, and others. Calvin was eight years old in 1517, the year Martin Luther nailed his 95 Theses to the Castle Church door. When Calvin began his work as a reformer in the city of Geneva, Switzerland, Luther was 52 years old and near the end of his days as a reformer.

The Beginnings of Calvinism

John Calvin is the source of the Protestant system of beliefs that has come be known as Calvinism. Central to Calvinism is the belief in the absolute sovereignty of God, which is a theological way of saying that God and God alone controls everything that happens or will happen. Calvin also held to the

Lutheran belief in justification by faith alone as well as the doctrine of *predestination*, which holds that after the fall of man (another term for the original sin of Adam and Eve) human beings are incapable of *free will* when it comes to salvation and that God "elects" certain people for salvation and others for eternal damnation. Calvin also shared with Luther the belief in the Bible as the absolute standard for the life of faith.

Calvin had studied the writings of Martin Luther, and he deeply respected them and the German Reformer. Calvin even called himself a disciple of Luther, and referred to him as "that … apostle of Christ, through whose labors the purity of the gospel has been restored to this age." However, there were some differences between Lutheranism and Calvinism. For example, Calvin differed from Luther in his ideas about the relationship between church and state and in his interpretation of the Lord's Supper.

Calvin's theology was spelled out in his *Institutes of the Christian Religion*, which he intended as an aid to the interpretation and study of the Bible.

Institute-ional Christianity

Institutes has been one of the most widely read statements of belief of the past four-plus centuries. Calvin published his first edition of *Institutes* in 1536, then revised the work at least five times throughout his lifetime, publishing several editions in Latin and French. Calvin translated this final edition of the *Institutes* into French in 1560. From there, *Institutes* was published in several languages. Early translations of *Institutes* were done in Dutch (1560), English (1561), German (1572), Spanish (1597), Czech (1617), Hungarian (1624), and Arabic (before 1667).

Institutes was a clear explanation of the reformer's beliefs, and it launched Calvin into a position of leadership in the Protestant movement. The first edition of *Institutions*, which was published in Basel, contained six chapters. It covered, among other things, the Ten Commandments, faith, prayer, the Lord's Prayer, the sacraments of baptism and the Lord's Supper, and the "false" sacraments of the Roman Catholic Church.

Calvin's work on *Institutes* over the years greatly expanded this statement of his beliefs. The final edition of *Institutes*, published in 1559, included four articles—one on God the Father, one on God the Son, one on God the Holy Spirit, and one on the church.

Calvin states that imperfect humans can comprehend God only imperfectly and that they are not capable of living truly religious lives on their own. God, Calvin says, is a personal being who is absolutely holy, perfect, and good.

In contrast to the God who is perfect in everything he does is mankind, who is sinful and depraved in every way and to the core of his being. Calvin held that it is only through God's grace, poured out on corrupt mankind through the works of Jesus Christ, that the Creator gave humankind a true revelation of himself. Furthermore, there is no good deed anyone can do to justify himself before God, and it is only those who recognize the truth about their own sinfulness and imperfection who can turn to God, repent, and find salvation in him.

If that weren't enough, Calvin states that on its own, humankind is completely incapable of turning to God for salvation, apart from God's own calling. In other words, humans can do nothing to save themselves. Even the desire to do something about their sinful condition amounts to nothing without God's "calling." According to Calvin, sin isn't just what humans do, it's at the core of their very nature. Even infants, Calvin believed, were born into condemnation.

Going Deeper

The Doctrine of Original Sin refers to the universal condition of sinfulness of each and every human born since the fall of man, which occurred in the Garden of Eden when Adam committed the first sin of disobedience to God. The term "original sin" doesn't appear in the Bible but is implied in several passages (Romans 5:12–19, 1 Corinthians 15:22, for example).

Protestant Pearls

They [the Catholics] suspect everything we say. If I simply said it was daytime at high noon, they would begin to doubt it.

—John Calvin

Calvin defines what is called "saving faith," or faith that justifies sinful man before God. That faith, Calvin asserts, isn't a mere intellectual agreement with the truth of the gospel message as laid out in the New Testament, but an attitude of trust in the work of Jesus Christ on the cross. Calvin reaffirms his position that each human being deserves eternal damnation but that through Christ, who is seated at the right hand of God and making intercession, the "elect" can have new life and eternal life.

Calvin writes about the role God's Holy Spirit plays in salvation. It is the Holy Spirit, he says, who gave to humans the Word of God, the Bible, and it is he who enables us to comprehend that Word. Furthermore, the Holy Spirit enables each believer to grow in Christ and to live a life worthy of one who calls himself "Christian." It is also the Spirit of God who gives the believer assurance of his salvation.

Calvin defines the church and explains its role in the *Institutes*. He wrote that the church exists to edify, or build up, the elect and for the good of the world around it. The true church of Jesus Christ can be recognized by the fact that it receives and preaches the Word of God and through the proper use and administration of the sacraments, which he held were external signs of what had been done to the believer internally. Calvin also held that church leaders should be those who live their lives as true disciples of Christ.

Calvin's World-Changing Detour

After he had published the first edition of the *Institutes*, Calvin intended to travel to Strasbourg, where he hoped to engage in a quiet life of study. In July of 1536, Calvin was on his way from Italy to Strasbourg, but because of a war raging between the Emperor Charles V and the King Francis I of France, he had to take a detour through Geneva to get there. In his mind, it was to be a one-night stay, after which he would continue on his journey the following morning.

People You Should Know

Guillaume Farel is a sixteenth-century reformer whose work in Geneva laid the groundwork for what John Calvin would do there later. It was Farel who convinced a reluctant Calvin, passing through on his way to Strasbourg, to stay in Geneva.

Those plans changed when Calvin met a fiery reformer by the name of Guillaume (or William) Farel. By the time Calvin, a young man of 27, arrived in Geneva, Farel had labored long and hard to bring reform to the city. In fact, Farel had already been run out of Geneva once, thanks to his uncompromising reformist preaching.

A Forerunner to Calvin

Farel's first stay in Geneva didn't last long. When he arrived in Geneva in 1532, it was completely a Roman Catholic city. The people practiced the rituals of Rome, and they also took part in the depravity and worldliness that was so readily available in Geneva at that time. Farel saw the need for reform, and reform is what he began preaching.

There were some Christians in the city who had been influenced by the teachings of Luther, Zwingli, and other reformers, and Farel at first limited his preaching to the homes of these people. But soon, what was said in private made its way into the public square. In short order, Farel had to take his preaching to the general public in Geneva.

It wasn't long before Farel was called before an Episcopal council, which saw him as a threat to the authority of Rome. Although Farel's preaching had won him popularity with at least some of the Genevans, it had exactly the opposite effect with the council, which insulted and mocked him.

One of the clerics on the council shouted out, "Come, you filthy devil. Who gave you authority to preach?" No doubt Farel knew that his very life was in danger, but he wouldn't back down. "I have been baptized in the name of the Father, the Son, and the Holy Ghost, and am not a devil!" he shot back.

> I go about preaching Christ, who died for our sins and rose for our justification. Whoever believes in him will be saved; unbelievers will be lost. I am sent by God as a messenger of Christ, and am bound to preach him to all who will hear me. I am ready to dispute with you, and to give an account of my faith and ministry. … So I say, it is you and yours, who trouble the world by your traditions, your human inventions, and your dissolute lives.

After hearing this, one enraged councilor shouted out, "He has blasphemed. We need no further evidence. He deserves to die!" Farel barely escaped Geneva with his life. He was chased with clubs, and even shot at. Though Farel was forced to flee Geneva, his work in the city was far from finished. He sent other reformers to continue what he had started, then returned to Geneva in 1533. He picked up where he left off, preaching and teaching in a place where doing so put him in great danger.

In time, Farel and the reformers who worked by his side made great headway in Geneva. People began turning from Roman Catholicism to Protestantism. At this point in history, Geneva was governed by two city councils: the Little Council of twenty-five members and the Council of Two Hundred. On April 27, 1535, the Council of Two Hundred passed the formal declaration that converted the city of Geneva to Protestantism. The mass was abolished and images and relics were removed from the churches. Daily sermons were preached and the sacraments were administered according to the Scriptures. The council also passed laws against activities such as gambling, drunkenness, and dancing, but these laws had little effect on the behavior of Genevans.

Though Protestantism made huge gains in Geneva, Farel and the other reformers believed there was still much work to be done. Geneva was still, in their minds at least, a place of at best moral indifference. There were still social, moral, and religious problems that needed solving. And in Farel's mind, John Calvin was just the man to help him solve them.

A Little Help Here!?

John Calvin had no desire to become embroiled in any kind of political or religious movements. He just wanted to study and write. But when Farel found out that Calvin was in Geneva, he called for him and begged him to stay there and help him with his work.

When Farel met Calvin, he could easily see that the young Frenchman was just the kind of teacher and preacher needed for the job at hand. Farel asked him to stay and preach in Geneva, but Calvin had no desire to stay. Calvin already had his plans made, and besides, he didn't feel rightly equipped for the kind of work Farel was suggesting. His answer to the Genevan reformer was "Thanks, but no thanks!"

Some Spiritual Arm-Twisting

Farel wasn't taking "No" for an answer. He tried everything he knew to persuade Calvin to stay in Geneva, but to no avail. Finally, when pleas for help didn't result in the answer he wanted, Farel turned to threats.

Calvin later recalled his encounter with Farel in the introduction to his *Commentary on the Book of Psalms*:

> … finding that he gained nothing by entreaties, he proceeded to utter an imprecation that God would curse my retirement, and that tranquility of the studies which I sought, if I should withdraw and refuse to give assistance, when the necessity was so urgent. By this imprecation I was so stricken with terror, that I desisted from the journey which I had undertaken. … I was terrified by Farel's words and made conscious of being a coward.

There's no other way to put it but to say that Farel had pronounced a curse from God on Calvin if he didn't stay in Geneva. Farel's words made Calvin shake with fear, as he wrote later: "God had stretched His hand upon me from on high to arrest me."

In Calvin's heart and mind, it was settled. He had no choice but to stay in Geneva.

Making the Law of God the Law of the Land

John Calvin's work in Geneva was not going to be easy. It was going to be done in the presence of those who wanted to return Geneva to the rule of the old church, as well as against a backdrop of long-established practices of immorality in the city. Calvin held to a theology that included good, Bible-based moral behavior, and he was bringing that code to a place that knew little of any kind of moral teaching, even under the city's clergy, which was known for its laxness in teaching or enforcing moral conduct.

Protestant Pearls

God wants to come down to us … and we do not need to clamber up to him, he wants to be with us to the end of the world.

—Martin Luther

By today's standards, the behavior of the people of Geneva doesn't look at all unusual. They danced, they gambled, they cursed and swore, they fought, they took part in all sorts of sexual immorality. And they did all those things to excess. But Calvin and Farel believed that reform meant changes not just in what the people believed, but in their moral practices.

Calvin started his work in Geneva preaching from the letters of the apostle Paul at St. Peter's Cathedral. He took his work several steps further by instructing the citizens of Geneva on the "new" reformed faith. He and Farel compiled Articles Concerning the Government of the Church. These articles were written by Calvin and laid out the fundamentals of the Christian faith as well as the system of discipline for citizens who failed to keep those fundamentals.

On January 16, 1537, the Little Council and the Council of Two Hundred adopted Calvin's twenty-one articles. Regulations were laid down for proper conduct. These regulations outlawed activities such as gambling, dancing, and the singing of songs considered obscene or blasphemous. The hours of taverns were shortened, and people were required to be in their homes by 9 P.M. The articles also provided for a panel of ministers whose job it was to help provide moral discipline in Geneva and to deal with those who violated the city's code of conduct. The punishments for unrepentant sinners ranged from simple excommunication to banishment from the city.

Calvin's articles were hardly observed, and Calvin and Farel were compelled to try to enforce them. From the pulpit, Calvin was uncompromising when it came to the "Christian" standards adopted by the city in the form of the twenty-one articles. Naturally, many Genevans resented the rules and regulations, and most opposed them. In hindsight, it appears that it was only a matter of time before the citizens revolted against the *theocracy* of Calvin.

> **You Can Look It Up**
>
> A **theocracy** is a system of civil government that is centered on a deity or a system of religious beliefs. In a theocracy, generally, the lawmakers are clergy, ministers, or priests.

A Revolt We Could See Coming

The revolt against Calvin's sweeping reforms came from an opposition party, which came to be known as the Libertines. The Libertines demanded the abolition of the new code of conduct in the city, and the councils responded by issuing an edict commanding that they leave the city. But the council didn't enforce that order, and the Libertines grew in strength and confidence. In the annual election on February of 1538, the Libertines took the majority in the council.

This situation put Calvin and Farel in conflict with the city councils, which informed the reformers that they were to stop trying to enforce their rules of conduct and stick to preaching the gospel. The general population also grew more hostile toward the two "foreigners." But Calvin wouldn't budge. He believed it was his job as spiritual leader to enforce the disciplines laid out in the twenty-one articles and that the council should stay out of it. Both Calvin and Farel strongly denounced their opponents from the pulpit.

What had been a problem turned into a crisis when the Council of Two Hundred voted to accept what are called the "ceremonies of Bern," which included the observances of several religious holidays, as well as the use of unleavened bread in the Lord's Supper. To Calvin and Farel, the use of unleavened bread in communion was a nonissue, but the same couldn't be said for the Libertines.

As Easter approached, many of the Libertines were creating an uproar in the streets over how communion should be served. The Libertines wanted the churches to use unleavened bread in communion. They ran through the streets, yelling, discharging their firearms, and creating general chaos. The closer Easter came, the worse the confusion grew.

The situation came to a head on Easter Sunday of 1538, April 21, when Calvin took the pulpit at St. Peter's and Farel at St. Gervais and both refused to serve communion at all. Both looked out over their congregations and could see the Libertines, and they knew the risks of taking the stand they took. But they did what they had to do. They explained the nature of the Lord's Supper, that to serve communion to those who had been engaging in blasphemy and immorality—meaning the Libertines—would be to desecrate the sacrament. Therefore, there would be no communion that morning. In an almost unthinkable scene, swords were drawn in the church services, and angry men rushed the pulpits. But both preachers stood their ground, defying the order of the council to use unleavened bread in communion.

Protestant Pearls

To be the people of God without regeneration, is as impossible as to be the children of men without generation.

—Richard Baxter (1615–1691), Nonconformist pastor and writer

On the following Monday, the Council of Two Hundred met and banished Calvin and Farel from the city. They were ordered to leave within three days. Before he left, Calvin was threatened in the streets, and crowds gathered around his home, shouting threats and mocking him by singing vulgar songs. "Had I been the servant of man, I should have received but poor wages," Calvin replied, "but happy for me it is that I am the servant of him who never fails to give his servants that which he has promised them."

In early June, Calvin and Farel fled to Basel, where they went their separate ways. Calvin traveled on to Strasbourg, his intended destination from the beginning, where he worked as a minister. Farel fled to Neuchâtel, where he had preached before.

Let's Try This Again Later ...

Calvin's brand of reform, which was for a fact both authoritarian and theocratic, failed because the people of Geneva were not ready for the kind of discipline he supported. The city councils of Geneva, which had basically declared Calvinism the city's official religion, didn't realize the problems that adopting Calvin's kind of rule would create within the general population. In the end, it was that authoritarianism that would doom Calvin's first attempt at reformation in Geneva.

Calvin would have to wait another day to institute lasting reforms in Geneva. That day would come, but only after Calvin spent a couple of years in Strasbourg.

Time Away from Geneva

Strasbourg was an unusual city at the time in that it was known for its religious tolerance. The city itself had been introduced to the Reformation late in the first quarter of the sixteenth century. Although Protestantism had a strong hold on the population, Catholic-style worship was still tolerated. The clergy of the city also welcomed religious fugitives from all over Europe.

While in Strasbourg, John Calvin was greatly influenced by Martin Bucer and Wolfgang Capito, who were both prominent reformers in the city. These two men saw that Calvin was a passionate, gifted young man, and they invited him to pastor a church attended by 400 French exiles living in Strasbourg. Calvin served in that capacity from 1538 to 1541.

During his time in Strasbourg, Calvin didn't just preach. He also taught and wrote. He lectured on the gospel of John and on Paul's first letter to the Corinthians. He also produced several important writings, including his commentary on the book of Romans, and he helped prepare a Protestant liturgy that Bucer had developed. The year 1539 saw the first of several revisions of *Institutes*. That same year, Calvin completed a project on the Psalms.

> **People You Should Know**
>
> Martin Bucer (1491–1551) was the third most influential German reformer, behind Martin Luther and Philip Melanchthon. Bucer attempted to mediate in the dispute between the Lutherans and Zwinglians. He gave shelter and a position in ministry to John Calvin in Strasbourg after he was banished from Geneva. His teachings greatly influenced the young Frenchman.

> **People You Should Know**
>
> Wolfgang Capito (1478–1541) was a well-known German Protestant reformer. He was a humanist who helped open communication between Desiderius Erasmus and Martin Luther. He also worked with Martin Bucer in his attempt to unify the Evangelical churches of Germany, France, and Switzerland. Like Bucer, he influenced John Calvin during his stay in Strasbourg.

Calvin was in Strasbourg at the same time Holy Roman Emperor Charles V was attempting to forge some kind of unity between Catholics and Protestants, who had been in often-violent conflict in the empire. In 1539, the emperor sponsored a conference to attempt to achieve that goal, which Calvin and Bucer attended. Calvin also attended the diets of Hagenau (1540), Wörms (1540–1541), and Regensburg (1541).

Calvin's nonstop schedule proved to be a drain on his health, which had never been strong anyway. At the advice of Bucer and others, Calvin decided to get married. He was looking for a woman who was, in his words, "modest, decent, plain, thrifty, patient, and able to take care of my health." After one failed engagement, in August of 1540 Calvin married Idelette de Bures, a widow from Liége. Theirs was a happy marriage, but it had more than its share of tragedy. Their one child, Jacques, born in July of 1542, lived only a few days. Idelette died after only nine years of marriage.

Meanwhile, Back in Geneva

While Calvin lived and worked in the peace of Strasbourg, Geneva was falling apart. The city lacked religious leadership, and the moral climate was quickly deteriorating. Political strife threatened the stability of the city.

Catholics sensed a chance to reclaim Geneva. In 1541, a Catholic cardinal by the name of Jacopo Sadoleto wrote the council of Geneva and asked if the city would like to return to the Roman Catholic Church. The city was torn; the population hated the Roman church but had also responded negatively to many of Calvin's reforms. By this time, Calvin's enemies on the two city councils had fallen from power, and councilors more friendly to him had taken their place. The councils asked Calvin to reply to Sadoleto, and he responded by writing *Reply to Sadoleto*, which defended the beliefs and principals of Protestantism. Not long after that, the Geneva councils asked Calvin to return to the city.

People You Should Know
Jacopo Sadoleto (1477–1547) was a Catholic cardinal, humanist, reformer, and distinguished lawyer. He was favored by Pope Leo X, who made him his secretary. In 1517, Sadoleto was appointed Bishop of Carpentras near Avignon. Sadoleto lived a blameless life and was vigilant in doing all his duties as a priest and bishop. In 1541, he wrote the city council of Geneva to inquire if the then-Protestant city would like to return to the Roman Catholic fold.

Calvin still had a place in his heart for Geneva, and he believed God had initially called him to serve there. But he remembered the treatment he had received there a few years earlier. Geneva, which he had referred to as "that place of torment," wasn't at the top of his list of places to go. But his friends in the city begged him to return and try to help put things right, and Farel appealed to Calvin as well. Reluctantly, he agreed. "I submit my mind bound and fettered to obedience to God," he said of his impending return to the city that had once terrified him.

On September 13, 1541, John Calvin, at the age of 31, returned to Geneva to a noisy, excited welcome. And what he had failed to achieve in his first stay, he would more than accomplish in his second and final stay in the city, which would be his home for the rest of his life.

The Bonding of Church and State

Calvin's goal upon returning to Geneva was simple: He wanted to pick up where he had left off three years before. He immediately asked for a city council–appointed committee to help him produce a church constitution. Calvin drafted the constitution in three weeks. *Ecclesiastical Ordinances* would be the foundational document for his reformation in Geneva. On November 20, 1541, the Geneva city councils and general assembly approved *Ordinances* with some changes.

Upon his return to Geneva, Calvin vowed to the city councils that he would be "forever the servant of Geneva." He was all that and more. Calvin wasted no time in taking up a schedule that was at least as busy as the one he had kept in Strasbourg. He preached seven days a week every other week, and he taught theology three days a week. He held meetings, wrote books and commentaries, and argued theology with those who opposed Calvinism.

Though Calvin never held any elected or public office in Geneva, the effects of his presence would be felt for decades. His reforms covered not just the religious lives of Genevans, but their political, social, and economic lives as well.

Calvin used his position to make many improvements in the life of the average Genevan. He supported a bigger and better infrastructure, including the building and operation of quality hospitals and an effective sewage system. He also supported the introduction of new industries into Geneva. He was also a strong advocate of a universal education system for children and for adults.

Calvin also established a system of personal attention to the citizens. Once a year, every family in the city was to be visited by a minister. He made sure that the sick and poor were tended to, and that people laid up in hospitals were visited. With everything else he had to do, Calvin himself wanted to visit the hospital during an outbreak of the plague, but the city councils stopped him from exposing himself to the disease through these visits.

Protestant Pearls

Wherever we find the Word of God surely preached and heard, and the sacraments administered according to the institution of Christ, there, it is not to be doubted, is a church of God.

—John Calvin, in the *Institutes*

In Geneva, John Calvin was a dynamo of energy. He studied without ceasing, preached faithfully, and answered the flood of correspondence coming from reforming churches and governments all over Europe interested in what was happening in Geneva.

Calvin's schedule was an overwhelmingly busy one, particularly for a man of frail health. He later wrote to a friend, "I have not time to look out of my house at the blessed sun, and if things continue thus, I shall forget what sort of appearance it has."

When Religion Becomes the Law of the Land

John Calvin's ultimate goal was to create what has been called a "city of God" in Europe, in which the church and the government ruled side by side as those called by God to rule. And Geneva was to be just the beginning. Calvin envisioned the spread of his doctrine and of this kind of church/government rule.

Like Luther, Calvin believed that worldly government was established by God and that the church and state had their own roles in the lives of the people. Unlike Luther, Calvin believed that government—no matter what form it may take—could and should have a role in protecting the church and in regulating the lives of the people in accordance with "moral law" as found in the Bible.

Calvin taught that according to the Bible, it was the Christian's duty to obey the civil authorities, even if they were corrupt. His reasoning was that one day God would judge the people and those who ruled over them, and corrupt rulers would be punished for their actions. He taught that there was one exception to this rule, and was that situation in which rulers laid down laws that were in contradiction to God's law.

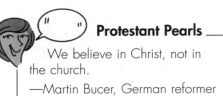

Protestant Pearls

We believe in Christ, not in the church.

—Martin Bucer, German reformer

That Calvinistic belief was at the heart of what was called "the consistory," a panel of 12 elders and ministers whose job it was to oversee disciplinary matters. In the consistory system used in Geneva, citizens charged with the rejection of Calvinist doctrine or with engaging in "un-Christian" conduct were called before the panel to be warned, reprimanded, or, in some cases, punished. The more serious cases were turned over to the city councils.

The Genevan consistory tackled its job with great gusto, going so far as to invade the privacy of families by questioning the children of parents suspected of wrongdoing. Some of the crimes and misdemeanors the consistory prosecuted included absence from church services, some kinds of dancing, playing cards, family squabbles, and other infractions.

Sadly, the city government was known to have gone too far in its attempts to keep the people on the "straight and narrow." During this time there were tortures, excommunications, banishments, and even executions in Geneva for the more serious crimes. Between 1542 and 1546 alone, 58 Genevans were executed for crimes such as heresy, adultery, blasphemy, and witchcraft. (It should be noted, however, that those were all crimes punishable by death throughout most of Europe.)

A Blot on Calvin's Record

As he had in his first stay in Geneva, Calvin faced opposition from those who felt that his rules were too confining. Occasionally, his responses looked, at least by today's more permissive standards, excessive. For example, there was a member of Geneva's Little Council who had tried to discredit Calvin because the Genevan laws hurt his business (he sold playing cards). Calvin responded by forcing him to march through the streets in disgrace.

But probably the darkest blot on Calvin's record in Geneva involved a Spaniard by the name of Michael Servetus (1511–1553), a theologian and physician who held religious views that had him in trouble with Catholics and Protestants alike. Servetus was under a death sentence by the Inquisition for opposing the doctrine called the *Trinity*. In 1531, Servetus renounced the idea of a triune God in his *On the Error of the Trinity*.

You Can Look It Up

The **Trinity** is the Christian doctrine that states that though there is but one God, he has revealed himself in the form of three distinct personalities: namely the Father, the Son, and the Holy Spirit.

Around 1545, Servetus escaped from prison and contacted Calvin to ask for permission to visit Geneva. Some historians assert that Servetus was only in Geneva to stir up trouble against Calvin and his reforms in the city. While attending a church service there, he was arrested and put on trial for heresy and blasphemy. The city's official policy was to expel those found guilty of such crimes, but Servetus was sentenced to death by burning.

Calvin didn't want Servetus burned and is reported to have spent many hours with him, begging him to recant so that his life could be spared. Calvin also lobbied for a more humane form of execution. But in the end, Calvin did nothing to stop the execution. Michael Servetus was burned at the stake on October 27, 1553.

Apologists for Calvin have pointed out that the reformer lived in a time when executions for heresy—mostly executions of Protestants by Catholics—were rampant in Europe. According to that interpretation of the facts, the execution was more a part of the European culture of the time than a policy of Calvin's Geneva.

Calvinism Hits the Road ... And It Never Stops

Although Calvin faced stiff opposition for the reforms he wanted to make, and although some of his reforms and even some of his doctrine may seem extreme, the city of Geneva became, to many, a model of Protestantism in action. Calvin worked long and hard, and he demonstrated extreme patience, and eventually, Geneva became a city where persecuted Christians from all over Europe could find refuge as well as an inspiring ministry.

The fact that Geneva became a refuge for Protestants of every European country added to the success of Calvinism. That is because those who sought refuge in Geneva during tough times would return home and spread the message when the fire died down. In a relatively short period of time, Calvinism spread to France, to the Church of Scotland, and to the Reformed Churches of Germany, Hungary, and Holland.

From there, the expansion continued into the seventeenth century and took on different forms and expressed itself in movements such as Dutch Arminianism, the Huguenot movement of France, and the Puritan movement in England, which would eventually settle in New England.

The Long and Living Legacy of Calvin

John Calvin lived an amazing life and accomplished incredible things for the Christian faith. He squeezed a mind-boggling amount of work into what would turn out to be a short life. In the physical sense, he was never a healthy man—he suffered from chronic asthma, digestive problems, severe headaches, and other problems—and late in life, the workload began to take a toll on him. On February 6, 1564, Calvin preached his final sermon, and on May 27 of that year, at the age of 54, he passed away. He was buried in an unmarked grave in Geneva.

To the very end, Calvin maintained the humility that was such a part of his character. As his death approached, Calvin addressed the elders in Geneva and said,

> I have had much infirmity that you have had to bear, and the sum total of all that I have done has been worth nothing. Evil men will catch at this word, but I still say that all I have done has been worth nothing, and that I am a pitiable creature. Yet I can say that I desired your good and that my faults have always displeased me, and the root of the fear of God was in my heart.

John Calvin's incredible humility notwithstanding, he left behind a legacy that would benefit the church into and beyond the twentieth and twenty-first centuries. His writings, particularly those of the *Institutes*, became the basis for most of the non-Lutheran Protestant movement. He also wrote commentaries on most of the books of the Bible as well as hundreds of letters to fellow reformers. In addition, his sermons and manuscripts were recorded on paper and have lived on and influenced Christianity centuries after his death. There is no way to know who, if anyone, would have taken the lead and accomplished what Calvin did. But in the hindsight of many church historians, it appears that the Reformation could have died out had it not been for the work of John Calvin.

Historians also point out that Calvinism has had a profound effect on the economies of the Western world. Calvin taught that thrift, industry, and hard work were virtues and that a successful business was a sign of God's grace. In Calvin's day, these views helped to create an atmosphere that was friendly toward commerce. Therefore, it is widely believed that Calvinism played a role in the establishment of the capitalist system.

Calvin also left a legacy of the encouragement and inspiration of other great reformers who were to follow. One of the men he most greatly influenced was John Knox, who took the doctrines of Calvinism to Scotland. We'll learn about him in Chapter 12, "The Spread of the Reformed Faith."

The Least You Need to Know

◆ Originally, John Calvin had no intention to travel to Geneva, Switzerland, but through a series of events, he felt that God had called him to lead the reformation in that city.

◆ Calvin attempted and failed, then succeeded in creating a Christian theocracy in Geneva.

◆ In his *Institutes of the Christian Religion*, John Calvin laid out a system of beliefs that would be the cornerstone of a long-lasting religious reformation.

◆ John Calvin left a legacy that included his system of beliefs (doctrines) as well as a growing and expanding Calvinistic Christendom.

The Spread of the Reformed Faith

In This Chapter

- ◆ The spread of reformed theology into France, Germany, the Netherlands, and Scotland
- ◆ The early life and development of Scottish reformer John Knox
- ◆ The Reformation in Scotland
- ◆ The development of Presbyterianism

There was something about the way John Calvin founded the Reformed faith—also known as Calvinism—that lent it to expansion far and wide. It is true that Calvin worked hard to take his doctrines throughout the known Christian world of the mid- and late-sixteenth century.

But there were other factors that helped in the spread of Calvinism, namely the fact that Calvin's Geneva was a haven for Christian dissidents from throughout Europe. When those dissidents, who were fleeing persecution, arrived in Geneva, they were exposed to Calvin's teachings and way of life. When they returned to their homelands or to their places of ministry, they took Calvinist doctrines with them.

Calvinism Goes International

While the doctrines of Lutheranism took hold mostly in Germany and in the Scandinavian countries, Calvinism, at least in different forms, spread throughout Germany, England, France, the Netherlands, and, eventually Scotland. In addition, Calvinism made inroads into Eastern European countries such as Poland and Hungary. From England and Holland, it spread to the New World and became the major religious influence in the United States.

Calvin was especially concerned about taking his doctrine to France (that made sense, since he was a Frenchman!), and his *Institutes*, in addition to the Bible printed in French and other reformed publications, helped get the French Protestant Reformation moving.

As the sixteenth century progressed, the Roman Catholic Church in France (as in so many other areas of Europe) descended further and further into a mire of corruption and slackness. As the Reformation picked up steam, it seemed that the Catholic leadership was more concerned with putting down the Protestant "threat" than it was in providing positive spiritual leadership.

In spite of the persecution, the Protestant Movement in France spread like wildfire. It has been estimated that near the middle of the sixteenth century, there were more than 400,000 Protestants in France. These people, who met in more than 2,100 individual congregations, came to be known as "Huguenots."

> **Protestant Pearls**
>
> Christ's deeds and examples are commandments of what we should do.
>
> —John Wycliffe (1330–1384)

Largely because of the influences of Erasmus and the Brethren of the Common Life, both Lutheran and Calvinistic teachings were enthusiastically accepted in the Low Countries (Belgium, Luxembourg, and the Netherlands).

Calvinism came to the Low Countries largely by Protestants fleeing the sometimes-violent persecution in France and England. It was also spread directly and intentionally by preachers who brought its message from Geneva. The people of the Low Countries seemed drawn to Calvinism's emphasis on the Bible and on its form of church government.

John Calvin greatly admired Martin Luther and the Lutheran Movement in Germany. While Calvin didn't intentionally try to interfere directly with the Protestant Reformation in Germany, his doctrines took hold in some parts of Germany, mostly through preaching and teaching of Christian refugees from France, England, and the Low Countries. The movement in Germany was also helped along by Martin Bucer and other Strasbourg preachers.

Eventually, Calvinism made its way into the last of the European countries to take part in the Protestant Reformation: Scotland.

Better Late Than Never! Scotland Gets into the Reformation Act

Anti-Catholic "heresy" made its first appearance in Scotland early in the fifteenth century, when the Lollards, the followers of John Wycliffe (see Chapter 4, "Rebels, Rabble-Rousers, and Revolutionaries: The Reformers"), fled the persecution in England and crossed the border into Scotland. As in the rest of Europe, some of the reformers who found their way into Scotland paid for their beliefs with their lives. For example, Lollard James Resby was martyred in 1407, and in 1433, a Bohemian by the name of Paul Crawan, a "Hussite" or follower of John Huss (see Chapter 4), was arrested while studying at St. Andrews University and burned as a heretic.

One of the more important forerunners to the Reformation in Scotland was a martyr by the name of Patrick Hamilton. He was born in 1503 and traveled extensively before land-ing in Scotland, where he preached reformist-type messages. Not surprisingly, the Roman church saw Hamilton as a threat. He was summoned to St. Andrews, Scotland, where he was tried as a heretic and burned on February 29, 1528, at the age of 25. His death was a horrible and slow one.

People You Should Know

Patrick Hamilton (1503–1528) was not just a forerunner of the Protestant Reformation in Scotland, he was also one of its lightning rods. Hamilton had been labeled a Lutheran and fled Scotland for fear of persecution. When he returned, he preached Protestant beliefs and was arrested on charges of heresy and sentenced to death. Hamilton was hailed as a hero by the reformers, and he deeply influenced John Knox.

Church historians point to the death of Patrick Hamilton as a key moment in the refor-mation of Scotland. But it was still almost two decades later that the movement got started in full there.

Time for Changes!

In the early sixteenth century, while much of Europe was in the throes of Reformation, Scotland stayed behind. Sixteenth-century Scotland was known for being somewhat back-ward and behind the times. Long periods of weak or absent leadership left Scotland well behind the curve as the rest of Europe was being prepared for Reformation.

The Catholic Church in Scotland at this time took corruption to depths not seen in the rest of Europe. Aside from the excesses and abuses of power straight from Rome, the local Scottish priests habitually engaged in drunkenness, depravity, and immorality. Those things were facts of life in the clergy throughout Europe, but they found a comfortable home in Scotland. According to some historians, clerical immorality made its way down through the ranks of the church, all the way to the laypeople.

But while reform was slow in coming to Scotland, it did come eventually. The Scottish church was influenced by Lollards and other reform-minded movements, and as the sixteenth century wore on, the writings of Martin Luther and others made their way onto the scene in Scotland—this despite legislative attempts to stop the "heresies" from making their way into the hearts and minds of the people. Within a decade of Luther's posting of the 95 Theses, Protestant tracts and books were being smuggled into the country.

As in other parts of Europe, one of the key factors in the starting of the Scottish Reformation was the citizens' reading of the Bible. Scottish bishops, seeing that the authority of Rome was challenged when people read the Bible for themselves, prohibited the reading of it in the people's own language. Still, the people of Scotland acquired and read Bibles in their own language.

With all the ingredients for revolutionary religious changes in place, all Scotland needed was a leader to provide the spark to get the fire going.

The Leader of the Scottish Reformation

The foremost leader of the Scottish Reformation, as well as the founder of Presbyterianism in that country, was John Knox.

 Going Deeper

> Presbyterianism is a form of church government found in the Presbyterian and Reformed denominations. Presbyterianism includes church government by elders, who can be clergymen or laypeople. These elders govern a congregation, appointing its leader and themselves being linked to the broader Presbyterian Church through historical covenants.

Not a lot is known about the early years of John Knox. He was born in Haddington, Scotland, but the year is disputed. Traditionally, he is thought to have been born around 1505, but in recent years historians put the year of his birth as late as 1515. His father's name was William Knox, and he was probably a farmer. John Knox received his primary education in the Haddington grammar school, but there is no record—from his own writings or from any other accounts—of his having graduated from any university. It is thought that he was sent at the age of sixteen to the University of Glasgow.

Knox left the University of Glasgow without receiving a Master's degree, then did some teaching at the University of St. Andrews, before becoming a Roman Catholic priest around the year 1530, and then served the church in different capacities for more than a decade.

A Man John Knox Could Look Up To

Around 1543, John Knox became interested in the preaching and teaching of one of the forerunners of the Scottish Reformation, George Wishart (1513–1546). Wishart had studied under Martin Luther but held more closely to the teachings of Ulrich Zwingli regarding the Lord's Supper. Wishart was forced to flee to England to avoid the persecution in Scotland. When he returned to Scotland (in 1543 or 1544), he began traveling around preaching Protestant beliefs.

Wishart was definitely a man who put his faith into action and not just into words. He fasted every fourth day, ate only twice a day, and lived humbly, even though he was from a fairly well-to-do family. He looked out for the needs of his fellow man as best he could, even risking his own life by visiting and caring for those who had come down with the plague, which had swept through Scotland around that time.

Wishart was a role model, mentor, and confidant for John Knox, who described him as "a man so full of grace there was none that had come before to whom we could compare him." Knox marveled at Wishart's spiritual insight and at what he saw as his gift of prophecy. Knox felt deep respect and affection for Wishart, and it is recorded that Knox took the role as kind of a bodyguard for the preacher.

Words to Live—or Die—By

Like the reformers who had gone before him, George Wishart preached against the corruption and errors of the Roman Catholic Church. Also like the reformers who had gone before him, Wishart fell into deep disfavor in Rome. Those loyal to the pope and to the Catholic Church were so angry with him that an attempt was made on his life. In 1545, persecution of Protestants in Scotland was growing, and those loyal to Wishart and his teachings warned him to lay low for a time. Wishart acknowledged that he would one day be martyred, but he refused to stop preaching.

Knowing of the threats against Wishart's life, Knox would sit in the congregation Wishart was preaching to, with his sword drawn in case Wishart needed protection. However, George Wishart's days were numbered. John Knox was with his friend when Wishart was arrested in a small village not far from Haddington. Wishart knew what was ahead for him, and he wouldn't allow Knox to follow him any further. "Nay, return to your home and God bless you. One is sufficient for a sacrifice," Wishart told him.

Wishart was taken to St. Andrews and tossed into the dungeon at the castle of Cardinal David Beaton. Later, he was tried and convicted of heresy. On March 1, 1546, Wishart was taken outside the castle and burned to death.

People You Should Know
David Beaton (1494–1546), was a Scottish cardinal of the Roman Catholic Church. He was made a cardinal in 1538 and succeeded his uncle, James Beaton, as Archbishop of St. Andrews. Beaton was a relentless and merciless persecutor of Scottish reformers, and his execution of George Wishart, a friend and confidant of John Knox, led to his own murder as an act of vengeance almost three months later.

Wishart was now out of the picture, but that wasn't the end of the Protestant movement in Scotland. Many of his supporters were present at his execution, and they were set on not just avenging Wishart's death, but on ending the tyrannical rule of a man who had threatened others who held Wishart's views with violence.

Knox later wrote of this incident in his *History of the Reformation in Scotland*: "Men of great birth, estimation and honour, at open tables avowed, that the blood of the said Master George should be revenged, or else they should cast life for life." Knox's words rang true. Almost three months after Wishart's death, Scottish Protestants responded violently to Cardinal Beaton's actions. On May 29, 1546, 16 men broke into the Cardinal's castle and stabbed him to death, then hung his body on the castle wall where the citizens of St. Andrews could see it.

This violent scene marked the beginning of the work of the reformer John Knox, who was asked by the friends of George Wishart to pick up where the martyred reformer had left off.

To the Galleys with You!

After what had happened to his friend, Knox knew there was a good chance his life was in danger, so he decided to leave Scotland, at least until the fire died down. But some associates of Wishart's persuaded him to stay at the castle of St. Andrews, where he would be safe.

But it turned out there weren't many safe places for Protestants in St. Andrews. In 1547, Scottish Catholics joined forces with France and took St. Andrews. Knox, as well as the others who shared refuge at the castle, were taken prisoner and given life sentences as galley slaves aboard French ships.

Month after endless month, Knox endured the suffering and humiliation of his sentence. He and his associates sat chained on rowing benches, often next to violent criminals. They survived on small meals of stale biscuits and an oil-and-bean soup. At night, they were allowed to sleep, under their rowing benches, still chained to one another.

Finally, in February 1549, after nineteen months of captivity, Knox was freed. Historians credit King Edward VI, under whose rule England was Protestant, with intervening on Knox's behalf. The English had been negotiating with France for the release of English and Scottish Protestant prisoners in exchange for French prisoners.

Once freed from the French, Knox traveled to England, where he joined the ministry of the Church of England. He preached for two years in Berwick, England, where his sermons exposed the errors and corruption of the Roman church. After his stay in Berwick, in 1550 Knox was transferred to the town of Newcastle, where he stayed until 1553. It was during this time that Knox met Marjorie Bowes, who would later become his wife. In 1551, Knox was also appointed as one of the six chaplains of Edward VI.

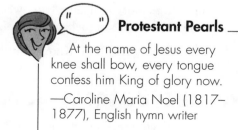

Protestant Pearls

At the name of Jesus every knee shall bow, every tongue confess him King of glory now.
—Caroline Maria Noel (1817–1877), English hymn writer

The Beginning of the End for Knox in England

On Christmas Day of 1522, Knox preached a dangerous sermon in Newcastle, England. He had received word that King Edward VI was terminally ill, and he knew that after he died, the Catholic Mary Tudor (later Mary I of England, or "Bloody Mary" as she would later be called) might soon come to the throne, meaning a return of Catholicism in England. Knox, in a move that put his life at risk, warned the congregation of a return to Catholic rule.

The Protestant King Edward VI died in July 1553, and soon after, Mary Tudor took the throne as Queen of England. As Knox had warned, Mary I attempted to turn England back to Catholicism. That began a time of violence and terror in England.

Knox had openly opposed Mary's appointment to the throne, and he knew his life would likely be worthless if he stayed in England. He fled to Geneva, where he stayed for a time observing the accomplishments of John Calvin. Knox was impressed with what he saw, and he accepted an invitation to preach at an English church in Frankfort, Germany. Knox was at the Frankfort church for only about six months before resigning over quarrels concerning some of the church's ceremonies he disagreed with. He resigned on March 26, 1555. In August of that year, Knox returned to Scotland.

Just Here for a Visit!

Almost immediately after his arrival in Scotland, Knox began preaching Protestant doctrines in different parts of the country. He found in Scotland a country ready for real and lasting reforms. He also found opposition.

Knox knew that Scotland was nearly ready for reformation, but the time wasn't right. He left Scotland the following July and returned to Geneva, where he resumed his ministry. While in Geneva, Knox preached and took care of other pastoral tasks. During that time, he carried on what would turn out to be some vitally important correspondence with people in England and Scotland. Three years after his 1555–1556 visit to Scotland, the Protestant leaders there invited him to return and lead the way to reform. Using language similar to that of Guillaume Farel when he persuaded John Calvin to stay in Geneva, they warned Knox not to rebel against God by refusing to come.

In January of 1559, John Knox returned to Scotland to stay.

Scotland: On the Verge of Something Big

Knox arrived in Edinburgh on May 2, 1559, and he was greeted by a Scotland nearly in a state of civil war. While Knox was away, reformers had become more numerous and more aggressive in their demand for change. Mary of Lorraine, appointed to rule Scotland by her daughter, Mary Queen of Scots, who was in France at the time, was a Frenchwoman and a Catholic, and she wanted to stop the Protestants, using force if necessary. At first, Mary of Lorraine attempted to reconcile with the Protestants, but when that didn't work, she turned to the stake. One of the victims was an eighty-year-old Protestant by the name of Walter Mill, whose last words were, "If I be burned, there shall a hundred rise from my ashes better than I."

Mill's words were almost prophetic. Civil war seemed certain, but cooler heads prevailed, and war was avoided. However, it was only a matter of time until Protestant revolt swept the country.

> **People You Should Know**
>
> Mary Queen of Scots (1542–1587), or Mary Stuart, was the daughter of James V, king of Scotland. She became queen before she was a week old. Raised in France, she returned to Scotland in 1561, after the Protestant revolt and Scotland's embrace of Protestantism. She later attempted to reintroduce Catholicism to Scotland.

Knox and One Little Boy: The Straws That Stirred the Drink

Upon his return to Scotland in 1559, John Knox became the leader the country's reformers had hoped he would be. His strong and forceful speaking style moved people to action. He preached against what he saw as the corruption of the Roman Catholic Church. He spoke out against the Mass in particular, referring to it as "idolatry."

The result of Knox's teaching was open revolt against the Roman church, and one morning a young boy started something that neither Knox nor the Catholic Church in Scotland could stop. During the Mass in the city of Perth, a young boy yelled out in protest, and the officiating priest, responding to this rudeness, slapped him. The boy responded by throwing a rock and breaking one of the images in the church. That started what Knox later referred to as the "rascal multitude ... purging" the churches of their "idolatrous" images. In Perth and in other cities of Scotland, church images and statues, as well as monasteries, were destroyed, and some of the churches were looted. While Knox did not condone this action, he didn't speak out against it. To him, what was happening was nothing more than a much-needed overthrow of an idolatrous religion.

From that point forward, events unfolded at breakneck speed, and it wasn't long before Scotland was a plainly Protestant land.

And in This Corner ...

As in other parts of Europe, the Reformation had political as well as religious overtones. It was a case of the reformers and Scottish nationalists opposing the Catholics and the French, who had been sent to Scotland to help stamp out Protestantism. The Scottish reformers, who on June 29, 1559, had control of Edinburgh, wanted to be free not just from Rome, but from France, and they had no problem looking to England for assistance.

Knox appealed to Queen Elizabeth I of England, who had very recently taken the throne, for support against the French. The two didn't much care for one another, as Knox had riled up the Queen with an earlier writing concerning female leadership titled *The First Blast of the Trumpet Against the Monstrous Regiment of Women*. But there was a mutually beneficial arrangement to be made, so England and Scotland became allies against the French. Knox, the reformers, and the nationalists received the help they needed with the signing of the February 26, 1560, Treaty of Berwick, which held that Scotland and England would provide mutual aid against France.

In 1560, Mary of Lorraine died, and on July 6, 1560, the Treaty of Edinburgh was signed. This treaty provided for the withdrawal of most of the French troops from Scotland. It also excluded Frenchmen from holding public office. And it sealed Scotland's destiny as a Protestant nation. On August 17, Scotland's parliament ratified the *Scots' Confession of Faith*, thus officially abolishing Roman Catholicism and its forms of worship in that nation. The *Scots' Confession of Faith* was drawn up primarily by Knox, with minimal assistance from five other men named "John"—John Winram, John Spottiswoode, John Willock, John Douglas, and John Row—who came to be known as "the Congregation."

> **Protestant Pearls**
>
> Holiness is a state of soul in which all the powers of the body and mind are consciously given up to God.
>
> —Phoebe Palmer (1807–1874), North American Methodist

The *Scots' Confession of Faith* was drawn up in just four days, and it was made up of twenty-five chapters. The first 15 chapters dealt with doctrine from the Bible, which it held to be the absolute authority over believers and the church. The remainder of the *Confession* dealt with topics such as the composition and character of the church and the definition of proper use of the two "true" sacraments, baptism and the Lord's Supper.

The *Scots' Confession of Faith* sought to abolish Roman doctrine that wasn't in keeping with the teachings of the Bible. It wanted to restore worship and discipline to the model demonstrated in the book of Acts. It also provided for revenues to support the ministry, the promotion of education, and the relief of the poor.

The *Scots' Confession of Faith* wasn't a complete system of theology, but it reflected the democratic nature of Presbyterianism when it requested its readers to bring to the attention of the writers any errors—based on the Scriptures—in the *Confession*. This was clearly a break with the more-authoritarian Roman Catholic tradition of the infallibility of the clergy.

The *Confession* held a place of great importance in Scotland, before it was replaced in 1647 by the more comprehensive *Westminster Confession of Faith*.

Knox Puts It All in Writing

In 1561, Knox and his associates also completed *The First Book of Discipline*, which provided for the organization and operation of the "Kirk" in Scotland. (The Church of Scotland was called the *Auld Kirk*, which meant "Old Church.") This book, though it was never approved by the parliament, was an attempt to spell out the nature of a true Christian community, or church. It attempted to provide uniformity in doctrine, sacraments, and in the operation of the church.

According to *The First Book of Discipline*, baptism was to be performed publicly and communion was to be celebrated four times a year. It also recognized five church offices—minister, lay-leader, superintendent, elder, and deacon—and provided for the election by the local congregation of ministers, who were then to be examined and approved by the public.

Going Deeper

The Church of Scotland was born in 1560 through the efforts of Scottish reformer John Knox. On December 20, 1560, the first general assembly of the Church of Scotland was convened in Edinburgh. The church is also called the Auld Kirk, meaning Old Church. Its doctrine is Calvinist. Politically, it is Presbyterian.

Knox's *Book of the Common Order* was his book of church liturgy, and it was approved by the General Assembly in 1564. It was intended as a guide for the practice of the sacraments and for ceremonies such as marriages and funerals. It also gave instructions for the holding of church elections for positions such as superintendents, ministers, elders, and deacons. In addition, subjects such as church discipline were covered.

The writings of Knox and his associates have lasted through the centuries, and they have come to be seen as the teachings and doctrines of Presbyterianism.

The Legacy of Knox: Presbyterianism in Scotland

Presbyterianism is a type of church government practiced to this day. Originally, Presbyterianism was an attempt to return to the ancient church practice of appointing elders, as described in the New Testament. This system of church government is characterized by the authority given elders in the church. In fact, the word Presbyterian in its original Greek literally means "elder."

In many ways, this system of church government is in direct opposition to the Roman Catholic hierarchical system, which rules locally through an individual bishop. In Presbyterianism, both clergy and laity may be elders, which supports the Lutheran and Calvinist position that individual believers in Christ are called to be his priests.

Presbyterianism is a system that provides a "balance of power" between clergy and laity and between congregations and a church's larger governing bodies. There are some variations in the structure of Presbyterian Church government. Each congregation is governed by a ruling body composed of the pastor and the elders, who are elected by the congregation. Individual congregations belong to a *presbytery*, which governs the activities of congregations in a given geographic area. The members of a presbytery include all the pastors and elected representative elders from each of the congregations.

In Presbyterianism, the presbytery has the power to ordain ministers. This is different from Episcopal forms of church government, in which a bishop ordains the ministers, and from the congregational church government, in which the congregation has the power to ordain. Each presbytery belongs to a *synod*, which is a larger geographic unit of the church. A general assembly, or general synod, unites the entire church.

You Can Look It Up

A **presbytery** is a larger church body made up of multiple congregations in a geographic area and governs their activities. The members of a presbytery include all the pastors and elected representative elders from each of the congregations.

You Can Look It Up

Synod (from the Greek *synodos*, "assembly") is a term for an ecclesiastical (religious or church-related) council. In Presbyterianism, presbyteries belong to larger general assemblies called synods. For example, the Reformed Church in America is incorporated as The General Synod of the Reformed Church in America, a Protestant organization.

If you wanted to describe Presbyterianism in one word, the word *democratic* would be a good one. From the beginning, John Knox's Reformation was embraced by the people of Scotland (as opposed to many other places, where reformation was imposed, or at least introduced, by the authority of government). Knox's system of church government assured that no one man—no pope, cardinal, or bishop—would dominate or rule. Under Knox, for the first time ever in Scotland, the layman had actual power within the church.

The question for Knox and for the Reformed Church in Scotland was, "Would it last?"

A Return of Roman Catholicism to Scotland?

In August of 1561, the devoutly Catholic Mary Queen of Scots returned to Scotland. The Queen had one goal in mind upon her return: to restore Roman Catholicism as the religion of Scotland. And she was prepared—and, historians tell us, able—to use her charms and powers of persuasion to get what she wanted.

At this time, Knox was preaching at Saint Giles Cathedral in Edinburgh and he publicly condemned Mary's policies and personal conduct. As Queen, Mary was sworn to uphold the laws of Scotland, which outlawed Mass. But she was permitted to attend her own private Mass in the palace chapel. Even this small concession troubled Knox deeply, as he saw it as the first step back to Catholicism.

After hearing of one of Knox's sermons, Mary summoned him to the palace for a series of five personal interviews. Knox later acknowledged that Mary had a sharp mind and stated her positions clearly and persuasively. In fact, Mary had managed to win over the nobles in Scotland. But Knox would have none of her charm, and from the first meeting he was inflexible, harsh, and confrontational. He refused to bend on any essential of his faith. And all this as he talked with the Queen!

When Mary realized that her attempts to persuade Knox had failed, she turned to bribery and even threats. In time, however, her actions alienated both Protestants and Catholics and brought on the anger of her subjects. She was arrested and imprisoned. She escaped prison and in 1568 was forced to flee to England, where she was later beheaded for scheming to have Queen Elizabeth killed so she could take the throne of England and Scotland.

> **Protestant Pearls**
>
> To be in a state of true grace is to be miserable no more; it is to be happy forever. A soul in this state is a soul near and dear to God. It is a soul housed in God.
>
> —Thomas Brooks (1608–1670), Congregational minister

Over the next few decades, the Scottish Presbyterians faced their share of struggles as they fought to keep their religion in place. Finally, in 1590, after periods of civil war and attempts by outsiders to introduce new beliefs and doctrines, Presbyterianism was formally recognized as Scotland's official religion.

The End of a Full and Productive Life

John Knox made an incredible difference not just in his own time, but in generations to come. It has been said that the Scottish Reformation was "Knox's Reformation," and that it would never have happened had this man of amazing vision and conviction not burst on the scene.

In 1572, Knox returned to Edinburgh, and on August 31, 1572, he preached his final sermon before falling ill. On November 24, after tending to some personal financial business, Knox died. It was recorded that on his deathbed, Knox asked his wife to read aloud the seventeenth chapter of the Gospel of John, which he referred to as "where I cast my first anchor."

Knox's body was buried near St. Giles Cathedral. His epitaph reads, "Here lieth a man who in his life never feared the face of man."

It is a fitting epitaph for a man who was willing to stand up for what he believed in, no matter what the cost.

The Least You Need to Know

- The "Reformed" faith of John Calvin expanded far and wide into Europe—including Lutheran Germany and Scotland—during the sixteenth century.
- Scotland was late to the Reformation party, but when the time was right for change, John Knox led the movement.
- Knox's impassioned preaching was in part the motivation the Scottish people needed to rise up against Catholicism.
- John Knox worked to institute the Reformation in Scotland, then later worked to keep Protestantism as Scotland's religion.

Part 3 — Results of the Reformation

As the Reformation spread, it took on different looks in different parts of the world. It also brought different kinds of responses from the power structures—religious and political—of the time. It also helped bring about what is called the "Counter-Reformation" or the "Catholic Reformation," which was Catholicism's attempt at reform from within.

Sadly, the Reformation also was a time of terrible warfare, persecution, and martyrdom on both sides of the issue. But it was a time where freedoms were won and advances were made in politics, education, science, arts, music, literature, and other important areas of life in the Western world.

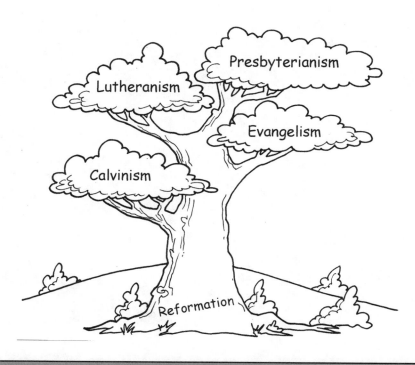

England's Own Brand of Reformation

In This Chapter

◆ John Wycliffe's groundwork for the English Reformation

◆ The life, times, and work of reformer and Bible translator William Tyndale

◆ The role of King Henry VIII in the English Reformation

◆ Thomas Cranmer and the Anglican Church

The reformation movements of the sixteenth century were religious movements, but in a lot of ways they were more. It wasn't a case of some rabble-rouser deciding they wanted a new kind of religion. These reformations were the culmination of centuries of social, political, economic, and, of course, religious upheaval.

England was no exception. The seeds of reformation were sown long before the "official" arrival of the Protestant Reformation in England. Those seeds were sown by the "Morning Star of the Reformation," John Wycliffe, and by his followers, the Lollards. In the mid- to late-fourteenth century, Wycliffe, preaching like the reformer he was, spoke out against the rampant papal abuses and materialism within the church. He attacked Catholic doctrines such as transubstantiation and papal supremacy. He also denounced monasticism and spoke in favor of marriage for the clergy.

Most important, Wycliffe held that the Bible was the ultimate source of authority for the Christian and that all believers should have a Bible in their own language. To that end, Wycliffe worked to translate the Bible into English (the project wasn't completed until after his death). The Lollards, despite persecution and at great risk to their own lives, traveled throughout England distributing copies of Wycliffe's translation.

Going Deeper

The Wycliffe Bible was the first translation of the Scripture into English, and it was done by John Wycliffe in the fourteenth century. It was distributed by the Lollards, Wycliffe's followers and disciples, and at great personal danger to them. Unfortunately, the Wycliffe Bible had numerous errors, mostly because it was translated from Jerome's *Vulgate*, the Latin translation of the Bible that originally contained the errors.

Lollards: Thorns in the Pope's Side

While the Lollards were supported by the common people throughout England, their activities flew in the face of the Catholic Church. The church didn't approve of the Bible falling into the hands of the common man; its position was that the Bible in the hands of the uneducated was dangerous because it was bound to be misunderstood. Wycliffe disagreed and was condemned for his actions. (He died a natural death in 1384, but long after his burial his bones were dug up and burned.)

In 1408, the English bishops, who desperately wanted to guard and preserve their power, met at the Convocation at Oxford, where it was formally declared illegal for anyone to possess or read an English version of the Bible or to translate it into English without a license from a bishop.

> The Holy Scripture is not to be translated into the vulgar tongue, nor a translation to be expounded, until it shall have been duly examined, under pain of excommunication and the stigma of heresy … We therefore enact and ordain that no one henceforth on his own authority translate any text of Holy Scripture into the English or other language, by way of a book, pamphlet, or tract, and that no book, pamphlet, or tract of this kind be read … Whoever shall do the contrary is to be punished in like manner as a supporter of heresy and error.

When Intolerant Words Turn to Persecution

Over the next several years, the Lollard movement faced great persecution, and a 1414 Lollard uprising was met and crushed. The repression continued after that, and eventually, the movement was forced underground. From that time on, activities by the Lollards were scattered, and they often resulted in martyrdom.

On the surface, it appears that the Lollard movement was a failure. But this movement was vital in preparing the way for reform, which would start more than a century after the death of John Wycliffe. It has been said that it is "impossible to unring a bell already rung." That may be what the English bishops attempted to do at the convocation at Oxford. Yes, they made the reading and translation of the Bible illegal, but by that time the Book had already become available to many of the commoners in England. And as the English read it, discontent arose as they became aware of the differences between the teachings of the Bible and the practices of the Roman Church. That discontent continued through the fifteenth century and into the sixteenth, when another would pick up where John Wycliffe left off.

Wycliffe Hands Off to Tyndale ...

William Tyndale had something in common with John Wycliffe: He wanted more than anything to see the Bible in the hands of all people in England. Deeply and passionately, Tyndale held the conviction that everyone who desired one should possess a Bible they could read for themselves.

Tyndale was born between 1490 and 1495 in Gloucestershire, England, a center for the growing wool and cloth trade. In modern terminology, Tyndale's family would probably be called "upper middle class." Starting in about 1510 he studied at Oxford University, where he received his Bachelor of Arts degree in 1512, and his Master's degree in 1515. From there, he moved on to Cambridge University, which at the time was a hotbed of Lutheranism. It has been guessed that this was where Tyndale first began to subscribe to Protestant beliefs.

Protestant Pearls

The strong hands of God twisted the crown of thorns into a crown of glory: and in such hands we are safe.

—Charles Williams (1899–1945), English poet and novelist

During his time in the university system in England, Tyndale became proficient in Greek and learned to read the Bible in its original languages. However, he wasn't completely pleased with how the universities taught theology. He seemed to resent the fact that he had to study "theology" and couldn't study the Bible. Later he said, "In the universities they have ordained that no man shall look on the Scripture until he be [filled with] heathen learning eight or nine years, and armed with false principles with which he is clean shut out of the understanding of the Scripture."

Already, Tyndale was beginning to demonstrate a heart for taking the Bible to the "common people" of England.

The Making of a Bible Translator

Around 1521, Tyndale left the world of education and joined the household of Sir John Walsh at Little Sodbury Manor, north of Bath. By this time he had been ordained, but little is known about his activities or role in the household. One thing is certain: Tyndale had a chance to meet the local clergy, and he was appalled and shocked at their lack of knowledge of Scripture. It was at this time that Tyndale started becoming a bit of a troublemaker.

Tyndale wasn't shy about sharing his convictions about the Scriptures. A story is told about how Tyndale engaged in a heated exchange with an English clergyman who stated, "The Bible is not necessary. It is all foolishness to talk about translating it into English for the people to read. All they need is the word of the pope. We had better be without God's laws than the pope's laws!"

Enraged at what he had just heard, Tyndale is said to have stood up and pounded the table in front of him and shouted, "I defy the pope and all his laws! And, if God spares me, I will one day make the boy that drives the plow in England to know more of the Scriptures than the pope does!"

Tyndale's answer to the assertion that people didn't need the Bible as long as the pope was around harkened back to a well-known quotation from the Dutch humanist, Desiderius Erasmus, who stated in the preface of his Greek New Testament,

> I wish that the Scripture might be translated into all languages, so that not only the Scots and the Irish, but also the Turk and the Saracen might read and understand them. I long that the farm laborer might sing them as he follows his plow, the weaver hum them to the tune of his shuttle, the traveler beguile the weariness of his journey with their stories.

Erasmus is considered one of the greatest humanists of all time. Humanism, which included a revival of learning and reading, helped prepare the way for the works of Wycliffe and Tyndale in that it encouraged an interest in reading and learning, and by the 1490s that included reading and learning what was in the Bible. Erasmus was a committed Catholic, but he saw the importance of allowing people to read the Bible in their own language.

Tyndale certainly agreed with Erasmus that all people needed the Bible, and he demonstrated his convictions when he said,

> Scripture is a light, and showeth us the true way, both what to do and what to hope for, and a defense from all error, and a comfort in adversity that we despair not, and feareth us in prosperity that we sin not ... Suck out the pith of Scripture and arm thyself against all assaults.

Protestant Pearls

When you have read the Bible you will know that it is the word of God, because you will have found it the key to your own heart, your own happiness, your own duty.

—Thomas Woodrow Wilson (1856–1924), President of the United States

Time for a Change of Scenery ... and Purpose

Before long, Tyndale was reprimanded for the things he had said to the clergy, and after that he realized it was best for him to move on. In the summer of 1523, he left the household of Sir John Walsh and traveled to London.

Tyndale knew that it was against the law in England to translate the Bible into English. He intended to comply with the law, and he hoped to get approval for his project from the newly appointed Bishop of London, Cuthbert Tunstall, who happened to be a friend of Erasmus and a scholar who had humanist leanings himself.

People You Should Know

Bishop Cuthbert Tunstall was the Bishop of London and later Bishop of Durham. He was born in Yorkshire in 1474 and died at Lambeth Palace in 1559. He was a friend of Erasmus and a scholar in his own right. William Tyndale visited Tunstall hoping to get permission from the Roman church for his work in translating the Bible into English. The meeting came to nothing, and Tyndale went on to do the work without permission from the pope.

But Tyndale's visit with Tunstall turned out to be a disaster and a dead end. He had only been in Cuthbert's presence a short time when he realized that he wouldn't be receiving the blessings or permission for his Bible translation. Tyndale left the meeting discouraged. He later said, "Not only was there no room in my lord of London's palace to translate the New Testament, but also that there was no place to do it in all England."

But Tyndale was far from finished.

An Underground Operation

At this time, William Tyndale was staying in London with a merchant named Humphrey Monmouth, who was sympathetic with Protestantism. Monmouth supported Tyndale financially and allowed him to work on his Bible translation out of his home.

In short order, word got out about Tyndale's work, and the English Catholic bishops and priests became enraged. The authorities turned against him, and even Monmouth was powerless to help him, other than to arrange his departure in 1524 from London to Hamburg, Germany. With the financial support of Monmouth and other English merchants, Tyndale continued his work in an environment that was safer than that of London. Even then, he wasn't completely secure, because the English clergy had hired spies to hinder his work.

A New Way of Translating Some Really Old Manuscripts

Tyndale translated the New Testament directly from the original Greek. This was a different approach than the one used by Wycliffe, who started from the Latin translation, Jerome's *Vulgate*. The problem with that method was that the *Vulgate* proved to have had a number of errors in the translation. Therefore, Wycliffe's version had some errors.

The spelling and style in Tyndale's first Bible show that it was intended for the commoners in England, as demonstrated in this passage from an edition printed in 1526, Romans 12:1–2:

> I beseeche you therefore brethren by the mercifulness of God, that ye make youre bodyes a quicke sacrifise, holy and acceptable unto God which is youre reasonable servyge off God. And fassion note youre selves lyke unto this worlde. But be ye chaunged (in youre shape) by the renuynge of youre wittes that ye may fele what thynge is good, that acceptable and perfaicte will of God is.

Finally, in 1525, Tyndale's English translation of the New Testament was ready to go to a press he'd found in Cologne. Tyndale had intended to keep his work secret for the time being, knowing that the English Catholic bishops would have him arrested if they knew where he was and how close his project was to being completed.

Then it happened. One night, one of Tyndale's printers had a few too many glasses of wine and said too much about the project. Johannes Dobneck (also known as Cochlaeus), a devout Catholic and a violent opponent of reform theology, got word of what was going on and planned a raid on the printing press. Tyndale found out about the planned raid, which included threats against his life. He fled, taking with him the copies that had already been printed. The printing press Tyndale was using was destroyed in the raid, but Tyndale took his work and moved on to Wörms, where the first version of his New Testament was published the following year.

You Can't Keep a Good Book Down!

With the printing finished, it was time for Tyndale to see the fruit of his work: English Bibles in England! He and his assistants had them smuggled into the country in large numbers. When the Catholic bishops found out what was happening they did everything they could to stop the flow of Bibles into England.

Ironically, the Catholic Archbishop of Canterbury actually helped finance the printing of more and more copies. He purchased all the copies from a German merchant, thinking that this would stop the spread of the English Bibles. What the archbishop didn't know was that this particular merchant happened to be a friend of Tyndale's.

The German merchant knew that Tyndale needed more funding to print additional Bibles, so he approached the archbishop and offered to buy up as many Bibles as he could get his hands on and turn them over for burning. "My dear sir," the archbishop said, "do your best to get them for me, all of them, for they are very bad books. I will gladly pay you whatever they cost, for I intend to burn them all and end this matter." The merchant purchased a large printing of the testaments at an inflated price, then sold them to the archbishop at an even more inflated price. This arrangement provided Tyndale with all the money he needed to print and send a torrent of Bibles into England. Later, a man arrested for trafficking in the books informed the authorities that it was the Archbishop of Canterbury who had funded additional printings!

Many of the Bibles were incinerated, but as time went on many more of them made it into the homes, offices, and meeting places of English people. There was nothing the bishops could do to completely stop them. As one of the bishops put it, "It passeth my power, or that of any man, to hinder it now!"

William Tyndale, a Winner Who Paid the Price

The victory that Tyndale had achieved for his country came at a personal cost. As his New Testament made its way around England and other parts of the world, Tyndale accepted that he couldn't return to his homeland. He loved England, and he missed his home and his family. But he knew that returning would be a self-imposed death sentence, so he became something of a refugee in Germany. He couldn't walk the streets in daylight for fear that a representative (make that spy) of the English Catholic bishop, or of the pope himself, would see him and have him arrested.

Tyndale later settled in Antwerp, where his translation of the Pentateuch (the first five books of the Old Testament—Genesis, Exodus, Leviticus, Numbers, and Deuteronomy) was printed in 1530. By this time, there had been several editions of the English New Testament printed. Tyndale also planned to translate the remainder of the Old Testament.

In 1535, a fellow Englishman named Henry Phillips befriended Tyndale, but it turned out that the pope had sent him to trap Tyndale. One night Phillips lured Tyndale out on the streets of Antwerp, where a band of men ambushed him and took him to a dark prison in the castle of Vilvorde, near Brussels. There was no trial, but Tyndale knew his days were numbered. On October 6, 1536, after a year and a half in captivity, Tyndale was hanged and his body burned at the stake. It was reported that his last words were, "Lord, open the King of England's eyes."

Tyndale Makes His Mark

Though he never completely accomplished his goal of translating the entire Bible into English, William Tyndale came to be known as "The Father of the English Bible." Tyndale was careful and meticulous in his work. His translations served as the basis for the complete English translation of the entire Bible, which was completed in 1535 by Miles Coverdale. Tyndale's work was so accurate that about 90 percent of his words from his last revision of the New Testament made their way into the King James Version, which was published in 1611.

> ### People You Should Know
>
> Miles Coverdale (1488–1569) was the Bishop of Exeter. He was born in Coverdale, Yorkshire, England, educated at Cambridge, and died in London. He was a Catholic who later became one of the earliest supporters of the Protestant Reformation in England. In 1535, he produced the first complete printed Bible in English. After spending a great deal of time in Germany, he returned to England following the death of King Henry VIII, "when the gospel had a free passage and did very much good in preaching of the same."

Tyndale was a reformer in every sense of the word, and by far his greatest contribution to the cause of the English Reformation was the translation, production, and distribution of an English New Testament. It was through his work that English-speaking people became reacquainted with the Bible. After Tyndale's death, other reformers took up Tyndale's cause of distributing the Scriptures to all people, and by 1539 a few of those reformers persuaded King Henry VIII to order that every parish church make a copy of an English translation of the Bible available to all its parishioners.

One of those persuasive reformers was Archbishop of Canterbury, Thomas Cranmer, who would take his place as one of the leaders of the Reformation in England.

A Backdoor Route to Reformation

Thomas Cranmer was born in the village of Aslacton in Nottinghamshire, England, on July 2, 1489. He was the son of a village squire and at a young age he became an accomplished archer and horseman. He attended the local schools before attending Jesus College in Cambridge. In 1526, Cranmer received a Doctor of Divinity degree and was ordained. He was such a good student that he was elected a fellow of the college, where he lectured.

Cranmer played a key role in an incident in English history that, while not a direct cause of the Reformation, brought about changes that provided the final spark needed. This incident was King Henry VIII's divorce of Queen Catherine of Aragón.

Henry VIII had a number of reasons for wanting out of the marriage with Catherine. First, he was concerned about who would ascend to the throne following his death. Catherine had given birth for Henry seven times, and only one of the children—the future (and notorious) Queen Mary Tudor—survived to adulthood. Henry wanted a male heir to the throne, but when it became apparent that Catherine was no longer able to bear children, Henry looked elsewhere.

Then there was the issue of "the other woman." Henry VIII had had numerous affairs during his marriage to Catherine, but around 1527, he fell hopelessly in love with a beautiful young woman named Anne Boleyn.

> **Going Deeper**
>
> Cranmer's Bible, so titled because Thomas Cranmer wrote the preface, was used in the English parishes after it replaced a translation by Miles Coverdale. Cranmer's Bible, also called the Great Bible, was based on the translation by William Tyndale and was used until the publication of the King James version.

A Repentant Henry VIII?

Some historians assert that Henry was genuinely grieved that he had ever married Catherine. It was Catherine's second marriage, and her first had been to Henry's brother, Prince Arthur of Wales. Arthur and Catherine were married in 1501, but just five months later, Arthur died. The law of the church wouldn't allow a man to marry the widow of his deceased brother, but in 1504, Pope Julius II allowed Henry to marry Catherine. Henry knew that it was against the law of the church to marry as he had.

Protestant Pearls

A true Christian is a man who never for a moment forgets what God has done for him in Christ, and whose whole comportment and whole activity have their root in the sentiment of gratitude.

—John Baillie, Scottish theologian

There had been a time when King Henry VIII was passionately loyal to the pope. When Martin Luther started the Protestant Reformation in Germany, Henry criticized him and his movement and took to the defense of the Roman church. It was then that Pope Leo X gave him the title "Defender of the Faith," which would become a title hereditary to the King of England.

Being the loyal Catholic he was, Henry appealed to Rome to grant an annulment of the marriage, but the decree was stalled in Rome because Pope Clement VII was afraid of the reaction it would bring from Holy Roman Emperor Charles V, who happened to be Queen Catherine's nephew. The year was 1527, and the imperial troops had just overtaken Rome. Charles V wasn't going to allow his aunt to be dishonored publicly, and the pope, afraid of what could happen in Rome if he allowed the divorce to proceed, gave in to Charles.

Henry VIII knew he wasn't going to get any help from Rome in dissolving his marriage, but when Anne became pregnant in 1532, it was time for the matter to be solved. It was at this time that Cranmer, who happened to be a friend of Anne Boleyn, gained the favor of Henry by suggesting that the king didn't need to wait for Rome to annul the marriage. In March of 1533, Henry appointed Cranmer to the position of Archbishop of Canterbury. In May, the king secretly married Anne Boleyn.

Cranmer, who was loyal to the king, used that position to quickly nullify the marriage between Henry and Catherine. He also declared the marriage between Henry and Anne Boleyn valid. The pope responded to that by a threat of excommunication. Against the orders of the pope, Henry remained married to Boleyn and had her crowned Queen of England.

The following year, the English Parliament passed what is called the "Act of Supremacy," which stated that the King of England, and not the pope, was the true head of the Church of England.

It was then that the English Reformation was "officially" underway.

Oh Henry! Where Is Your Protestantism?

The English Reformation, while its roots went far back beyond the appearance of Henry VIII, didn't go on without some opposition. This is largely because most of the people, although they wanted reforms in the Roman church system, and despite the legislation of king and Parliament, remained Catholic.

This situation led to more than a decade of religious violence and confiscation of property for those who maintained any loyalty to Rome. From 1534, the year of the Act of Supremacy, to well into the 1540s, more than 300 people were executed for treason, mostly for re-belling against Henry's new religious order. Among those killed was Sir Thomas More, a member of Henry's court, as well as many bishops and prominent nobles.

After the English break with Rome, Henry VIII needed money to fight a series of wars, and he began confiscating what was an enormous amount of wealth of the Catholic Church (the Church's holdings were said to be around three times that of the English kingdom's). He began closing monasteries around England and confiscating their property, which he then sold to the nobles and upper classes of England.

For a man who had basically declared himself the ultimate head of church and state, King Henry VIII really didn't do a lot to bring any kind of Protestant theology into England, and it has been suggested that near the end of his reign he did more to hurt the Protestant cause than to help it. Although he did bring changes to the religious climate in England, his beliefs continued to reflect Catholicism until his death. In 1539, he got Parliament to pass the *Six Articles*, whose purpose it was to restore to the English Church the fundamentals of the Catholic faith.

> ### Going Deeper
>
> King Henry VIII's Six Articles, which have been referred to as "the bloody whip with six strings," were an attempt on Henry's part to re-reform the Church of England and bring back many of the practices, beliefs, and traditions of the Roman Catholic Church. For example, it reaffirmed transubstantiation and forbade priests from marrying. In the Lord's Supper, the cup was to be withheld from laypeople, and binding monastic vows were brought back.

In the end, Henry's reformation was little more than the transfer of religious power from Rome to the throne of England. Henry died on January 28, 1547, and was succeeded by Edward VI, a nine-year-old boy.

Cranmer Has His Heyday with Edward

Edward VI was the only son of Henry VIII and Jane Seymour, the third of his six wives. He came to the throne less than a month after the death of his father. When he ascended to the throne, his maternal uncle, Edward Seymour, the First Earl of Hertford, was named Lord *Protector*, meaning he would rule until Edward was able to take over for himself.

You Can Look It Up

A **Protector**, in English history, is someone appointed ruler of the kingdom during a time when the true monarch is unable or unready to serve in that capacity. The Protector of King Edward VI, who was only nine years old when he took the throne following the death of his father, Henry VIII, was Edward Seymour, Edward's uncle and the First Earl of Hertford.

The reign of Edward VI was a great time for the English Reformation and for Thomas Cranmer; Edward Seymour and Edward VI were both supporters of the Reformation. They repealed Henry VIII's Six Articles and in 1549 they, with the help of an Act of Uniformity from the Parliament, imposed the first *Book of Common Prayer* (or the First Prayer Book of King Edward VI, or *Book of Common Prayer and Administration of the Sacraments and Other Rites and Ceremonies of the Church*). Cranmer and Nicholas Ridley compiled and produced the book.

The first *Book of Common Prayer* was strongly opposed by the Roman Catholics in England but came into general use as the official prayer book of the Church of England and of the Anglican churches of other countries, including some in the United States. Cranmer and Ridley had set out to produce a book that contained the Protestant equivalent of the books of Roman Catholic liturgy. The book, when it was used with the Bible and an authorized hymnal, provided instruction for Anglican worship, as well as morning and evening prayers and the sacrament of communion.

Going Deeper

The Anglican Church, or Church of England, was England's arm of Protestantism. It was formed largely out of the efforts of Thomas Cranmer (1489–1556).

The second *Book of Common Prayer* was a radically revised version of the first book. It is sometimes called the *Second Prayer Book of Edward VI*, and it first appeared in 1552, when its use was imposed by the English Parliament. In the second book, the structure of the communion service was changed and many of the ceremonies of the first book were eliminated. The references to transubstantiation were also removed.

Cranmer also produced the *Forty-two Articles of the Reformed Faith* in 1553. The articles seemed to be influenced by the *Lutheran Augsburg Confessions of Faith* and by Calvinist doctrines, and their purpose was to achieve doctrinal uniformity in the Anglican Church. The purpose of the Forty-two Articles was to fix the doctrinal errors in the previous Church of England writings. They sought to reject the errors and heresies on the part of the medieval papacy and to avoid the excesses of the radical reformers. The Forty-two Articles were reduced to thirty-nine articles in 1571, under the reign of Queen Elizabeth. In that form, they are still the definitive and authoritative word on Anglican doctrine.

Coming Around to Reformation Thinking

It seemed that in the decades leading to the reign of Edward VI, Cranmer's beliefs were moving closer and closer to those of the other reformers. In 1525, the better part of a decade before Henry VIII and the English parliament gave official sanction to a Reformation that had been brewing in England, Cranmer began speaking openly against the abuse of papal power in his country. He also had embraced the doctrine of justification by grace through faith, a belief central to the Reformation.

By 1535, Cranmer was speaking out against prayers for the dead, prayers to saints, and celibacy of the clergy. Prior to 1537, Cranmer held to the Catholic doctrine of transubstantiation, but he began taking the Lutheran view of the Lord's Supper in 1538. In the 1540s, he adopted a view of communion more in line with Ulrich Zwingli. (See Chapter 11, "The Reformation Changes Hands.")

Cranmer's works did much to advance the Protestant Reformation in England, and to establish the Anglican Church, or the Church of England. His compilations and writings were translated into the language of the common people in England from many books of medieval worship and prayers.

Cranmer's stands won him great support among the people of England, but they also won him more than his share of adversaries. And when the reign of Edward VI ended, Cranmer would be faced with a most dangerous enemy.

> **Protestant Pearls**
>
> The Scripture is that wherewith God draweth us unto him. The Scriptures sprang out of God, and flow unto Christ, and were given to lead us to Christ. Thou must therefore go along by the Scripture as by a line, until thou come at Christ, which is the way's end and resting place.
>
> —William Tyndale

Cranmer's Last Stand

Early in 1553, King Edward VI became gravely ill, and on July 6 of that year, he died at the age of 15. At the death of Henry VIII, Cranmer had promised to see to the succession to the throne of Mary Tudor, Henry's daughter by Catherine of Aragón. But he switched course and honored the request of Edward VI on his deathbed that Cranmer support the transfer of the crown to Lady Jane Grey, the great-granddaughter of Henry VII. Lady Jane was queen for nine days, but on October 1 of 1553, Mary Tudor was crowned Queen of England at a ceremony at Westminster Abbey. Queen Mary was a devout Catholic, who wanted two things: the restoration of England to the papacy and revenge against Cranmer.

> **Protestant Pearls**
>
> God's glory is at work in all things. Everything that exists, exists because it is held, sustained, enlivened by God's wisdom and God's power. The Word of God who is God, God expressing himself towards his creation, wills at all times to work the mystery of his embodiment.
>
> —Arthur MacDonald, Allchin Anglican pastor and writer

Having taken the throne of England, "Bloody Mary" had her chance to bring England back to the Catholic fold. Many of the Reformers in England saw the danger Mary represented, and they left the country in droves. Those who stayed behind lived in an England going through a horrible time of persecution against Protestants. More than 50 Protestants were burned at the stake in 1555.

Thomas Cranmer saw the danger too, and he sent his family from the country, but he stayed behind. That decision would prove to be the beginning of the end for Cranmer, who faced the Holy Inquisition and a sentence of death by burning at the stake. For over a year, he was in solitary confinement and was daily counseled by two Spanish monks. He was offered a phony deal: recant, and he would live. He did recant of his Protestant beliefs and stated that he believed in the teachings and practices of the Roman Catholic Church. Though he had signed several recantations, he was sentenced to death. Before his execution at the stake on March 21, 1556, Cranmer "recanted of his recantations," and died as a martyr (see Chapter 17, "Martyrdom: The Darker Side of the Reformation").

Go Ahead! Try to Stop This Reformation!

The death of Cranmer, as well as two of his fellow Protestant leaders, was a turning point for the Protestant movement in England. Mary Tudor believed that the persecution—particularly the killings of the leaders—would stop the movement in its tracks. But it had the opposite effect. Her actions earned her disrepute and disgust among the masses in England. In the end, Mary herself did as much or more than anyone to bring Protestantism to England.

Mary Tudor's final years were lived in pain, failure, and sorrow. She died on November 17, 1558 and was buried in a nun's habit. Queen Mary left behind a legacy of violence and disgrace. Thomas Cranmer, on the other hand, left behind an England ready for the kind of reformation he wanted.

The Least You Need to Know

- John Wycliffe and the Lollards laid the foundation for what would become the Protestant Reformation in England.
- William Tyndale led in the Reformation in England by helping make the Bible available in the English language.
- King Henry VIII, although he wasn't a Protestant reformer in the same way as people such as Luther, Zwingli, and Calvin, played a key role in bringing reform to England.
- Thomas Cranmer died a violent death but it was his death that fanned the flames of reform in the country of England.

Chapter 14

The Struggles for Reformation in England

In This Chapter

◆ The ups and downs of the Anglican Church

◆ The attempts to return England to Catholicism

◆ The Puritan Movement under Elizabeth, James I, and Charles

◆ The English Civil War and Oliver Cromwell

The end of the reign of "Bloody Mary" Tudor was a welcome relief to the English population in general. She was followed to the throne in 1558 by her half-sister Elizabeth I, the daughter of Henry VIII and his second wife, Anne Boleyn. The reign of Elizabeth I has been called the "Golden Age" or the "Elizabethan Age."

Almost immediately, Queen Elizabeth was going to have to settle some questions of religion in England.

Pick a Religion and Go with It!

When Mary Tudor came to the throne, she immediately took England back to Catholicism. When Elizabeth arrived on the scene, the English people weren't altogether sure where she would take the country in regard to religion. Even to this day it isn't certain where Elizabeth stood when it came to her Christianity. Scottish reformer John Knox once said that Elizabeth was "neither good Protestant nor yet resolute Papist."

It was Knox who had appealed to the newly crowned Queen Elizabeth I for support against the French (see Chapter 12, "The Spread of the Reformed Faith"). Although the Queen didn't like Knox (the feelings were mutual, as Knox had written against women in roles of government leadership), she sent both money and ships to help out the Scottish nationalists and reformers, who were being threatened with a forced return of Catholicism. The assistance from Elizabeth helped the Scots repel the French forces who threatened their sovereignty and their attempts at religious reform. This assured that Scotland would remain a Protestant nation, and in short order, the Scottish Parliament ratified the *Scots' Confession of Faith*, which abolished Roman Catholicism in Scotland.

Although the personal religious leanings of Elizabeth I are still very much open to debate— did she favor the formalism and ritualism of the Catholic faith, or did she favor the "back-to-the-basics" doctrines of the Protestants?—it wasn't long before England had its direction as far as religion was concerned.

Getting It All "Settled"

Elizabeth's first Parliament, in 1559, revoked the Catholicism of the previous monarchy, and by an Act of Uniformity commanded the English ministers to use the second *Book of Common Prayer*, which had been compiled by Thomas Cranmer under the rule of Elizabeth's father. Also, a new confession of faith was adopted, as Cranmer's Forty-two Articles were reduced to thirty-nine and adopted by the English Parliament.

Most important, however, the 1563 Elizabethan Settlement reestablished the Church of England, the church set up under Elizabeth's father but later persecuted and abolished by Mary Tudor. In the settlement, Elizabeth also showed herself to be a master politician, as she took the title of "supreme governor" of the church, rather than the previous title of "supreme head of the church." This was in an attempt to avoid offending both Catholics, who saw the pope as the head of the church, and Protestants, who recognized Christ as the head of the church.

Going Deeper

The Elizabethan Settlement of 1563, which was imposed under the reign of Queen Elizabeth I, reestablished the Anglican Church in England following the Catholic reign of Mary Tudor. The terms of the Elizabethan Settlement were popular in England, but they aroused opposition from devout Catholics and from radical Protestants.

The Elizabethan Settlement was met with overwhelming public approval, but there were some who weren't happy with it, namely the more loyal Catholics and the more radical Protestants. Seventeen of Mary Tudor's Catholic bishops remained when the Elizabethan Settlement went into effect, and all but two of them refused to take oaths that they would hold to its conditions.

The Catholic Church was always on the lookout for ways to make inroads back into England, but some of its attempts strengthened Protestantism's hold on the kingdom. Early in her reign Queen Elizabeth did all she could to keep from offending Rome. Because of the weakened state of the country and of the queen's throne, Elizabeth couldn't afford to make enemies with the Catholics.

You've Made a Big Mistake, Buddy!

It turned out that Elizabeth's quest for peace was a one-sided affair. The Roman Catholic Church made a series of mistakes that cost it any chance of being reestablished in England. The first of these provocations came in 1570, when Pope Pius V published a bull of excommunicating Elizabeth and removing her from the throne, a move that stunned and angered much of Europe. The last of the provocations came from Pope Gregory XIII, who essentially gave his blessing to anyone who wanted to assassinate the queen. Attempts were made on her life in 1581 and 1584. In addition, Catholics attempted to make progress through the use of schools to train young Catholics as missionaries to England.

The harder the church pushed, the more it alienated the country. The English, by and large, loved their country and the queen, and they resented attempts from "outside" to influence or change their chosen course. To further seal Catholicism's doom in England, laws were passed in the country against Catholic practices. Fines were levied against those who took part in Mass, and arrest and imprisonment was threatened. And England's response to the Catholic missionaries was a resounding "Get lost!"

For the remainder of Elizabeth's reign as Queen of England, Catholicism had absolutely no chance of reestablishing itself. However, that did not mean there would be no religious conflict in England. For several decades to come, the English would have to settle the question of whether they would embrace Anglicanism or another belief that came to be called "Puritanism"—or whether both forms of Protestantism could somehow coexist in the same country.

Going Deeper

The Anglican Church, or the Church of England, was established under the reign of King Henry VIII. Catholic Queen Mary Tudor returned England to Catholicism, but Queen Elizabeth returned England to Anglican rule. Anglicanism is more formal than most forms of Protestantism, and it has many similarities to Catholicism.

What Does Puritanism Really Mean?

It's not often that a compromise completely pleases either side in a bitter dispute, and the Elizabethan Settlement, while popular with a big majority in England, didn't do much to settle things between the Catholics and the radical Protestants. In fact, if anything it created a new religious conflict.

At this time in the history of England, there was a movement of radical Protestants who opposed Elizabeth's form of reformation. They were called "Puritans." In our culture, we associate the word *Puritan* with those who try to live what some people might consider overly strict with their morals. While the early Puritans certainly stressed living the "clean" life, the name "Puritan" actually referred to the group's ultimate goal of a completely "non-Roman" church. They wanted the church to follow more literally the example of the church as it was set up during the times of the apostles and the church fathers.

There was no real organization to the Puritan movement. There was no Puritan party or Puritan Church. In fact, there were different sects of Puritanism, each with its own ideas and convictions. The word Puritan came into usage in around 1564, one year after the Elizabethan Settlement. Many of the Puritans were religious exiles—Protestants—who fled England during the reign of Mary Tudor. At first, they were like most of the Catholic reformers of the Middle Ages, in that they attempted to make changes in the church from within the church.

The Puritans were unhappy with the Elizabethan Settlement because they saw it as a reconciliation of the irreconcilable, namely the ceremony and traditionalism of Catholicism and the Bible-based doctrine of Protestantism. The Puritans wanted more radical reforms than provided for in the Elizabethan Settlement. They wanted the total abolition of any religious rites or ceremonies that in any way resembled those of Roman Catholicism. Many of the Puritans raised the issue of whether the office of bishop had any basis in the Bible and they wanted the English Church to adhere to a more "Presbyterian" form of government.

Protestant Pearls

The Bible and the Bible only is the religion of Protestants.

—William Chillingworth (1602–1644), English theologian

The Beginning of the Conflict

In hindsight, the details of the first conflict between the Anglicans and Puritans—called the "Vestiarian Controversy"—may not seem like a big deal. It took place in 1563 and had to do with certain articles of clothing the queen had prescribed for the clergy to wear during religious services.

The Puritans objected to the rules regarding church vestments, and they also protested other things in the church services, including the use of the sign of the cross at baptisms, the requirement that parishioners kneel at communion, the use of organs in churches, and the observance of too many "holy days."

The old saying goes that if something looks like a duck and quacks like a duck, it must be a duck. Well, to the Puritans, the practices prescribed by Elizabeth for the church looked very Roman Catholic, and they objected.

In 1572, a more serious development took place. That year, a Puritan conference in London published a document titled "First Admonition," in which the Puritans—who were under the leadership of Thomas Cartwright, a fellow of Trinity College in Cambridge—stated their view that bishops should be replaced by ministers who were democratically elected by the individual congregations. Cartwright, in the "Second Admonition," presented a Puritan idea for church government that included the popular election of ministers as well as other ideas that looked very "Presbyterian."

Puritans like Cartwright had no intention of seceding from the Church of England but hoped to reform it from within. But some of the Puritans came to be known as "Separatists," and they completely withdrew from the Church of England over the issue of rituals and of the government's control of their religion. The first of these Separatists was an English clergyman from Cambridge by the name of Robert Browne, whose followers came to be known as "Brownists." Browne held that the Church of England had been so corrupted by "Romanizing" influences that anyone who considered himself or herself a true Christian should "separate" from it and form independent churches. During the seventeenth century, the Separatists joined with other dissident Puritan groups and began calling themselves Independents.

Around 1580, Brown founded what is called a "Congregational" church in Norwich. *Congregationalism* is a form of church government in which each local congregation governs itself and elects its own ministers. This form of church government differed greatly from the hierarchical systems of Catholicism, Episcopacy, and Presbyterianism. Episcopacy—which is the system of church government of the Church of England—is a system in which an order of bishops exercises authority over the church congregations. Presbyterianism is the system in which local congregations are governed by the actions of presbyteries (see Chapter 12).

You Can Look It Up

Congregationalism is a form of church government in which individual congregations govern themselves without outside authority by bishops or presbyteries. This form of church government has its roots in English Puritanism.

You Can Look It Up

An Episcopal form of church government is one that asserts the authority of bishops over church congregations. This is the form of church government practiced in the Anglican Church, and it is part of what led England to the Puritan Revolution in the seventeenth century.

In later years, Robert Browne was pressured to recant and was restored to office in the Church of England. But his ideas about church government lived on and were established among denominations such as the Baptists, the Unitarians, and the Disciples of Christ (now known as the "Christian Church").

(Mis)Handling the Anglican/Puritan Conflict

Separatism was in direct conflict with the idea of a national church, specifically the Church of England, and that conflict is what brought action from the Queen and other authorities in England, including the Archbishop of Canterbury, John Whitgift. Whitgift was the third of Queen Elizabeth's archbishops. The first two were Matthew Parker and Edmund Grindal, and they were more moderate in how they dealt with the Puritans.

When Whitgift became Archbishop of Canterbury in 1583, one of his main goals was to subdue the growing Separatist movement in England. On November 17, he preached his first sermon as archbishop, and in that sermon he made it clear that he was going to do whatever he needed to in order to bring the Puritans back into the fold.

In Whitgift's "Six Articles" of 1583, he demanded submission to the supremacy of the queen when it came to all issues of religion and government and to the *Book of Common Prayer* and the *Thirty-nine Articles*. He put some teeth behind his demands by imposing severe penalties for those who defied the Six Articles. In short order, more than two hundred Puritan ministers were suspended.

In 1586, Whitgift tried to further suppress Puritan ideas by prohibiting any publication of manuscripts without the approval of himself or the Bishop of London. This measure backfired, as defiant and determined Puritans published the "Martin Marprelate Tracts," which were anonymously written documents that branded the Church of England bishops as "petty antichrists, proud prelates, intolerable withstanders of reformation, enemies of the gospel and covetous wretched priests."

Obviously, the Puritans weren't going to submit to the rule of the Queen over their religion without a fight, and Whitgift responded to their rebelliousness with even more severe measures. Many hundreds of Puritans were arrested and imprisoned, and many more fled England for Holland, where they founded their own churches.

Despite the opposition and despite the emigrations to other lands, the Separatist movement continued strong in England into the first half of the seventeenth century.

Although the Puritans did have some support in the English Parliament, the long-term prospects for peace between the Anglicans and the Puritans weren't good. The persecution they had suffered at the hands of Elizabeth and Whitgift had strengthened their resolve, and it had also caused resentment to rise within the movement, resentment that would one day explode into all-out rebellion.

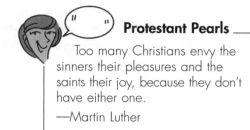

Protestant Pearls

Too many Christians envy the sinners their pleasures and the saints their joy, because they don't have either one.

—Martin Luther

That resentment would continue through the reign of England's next monarch, James I, who accomplished some great things as king of England but failed to bring about a lasting peace between the Anglicans and the Puritans.

King James Takes the Throne

King James I (born James Charles Stuart) was the son of Mary Queen of Scots and Lord Darnley, who was murdered before James was a year old. He was born on June 19, 1566, at Edinburgh Castle in Scotland. James served as king of Scotland (as James VI) for thirty-six years. He had been crowned when was just over a year old. John Knox preached the sermon at his coronation. He had aspired to be king of both Scotland and England, and he accomplished that in 1603 when Queen Elizabeth died and he took the throne of England.

King James believed in what he called Divine Right of Kings and in the king's duty to reign according to the Word of God, while paying attention to the good of the public. He believed that as king, he was responsible to God alone, for it was God who placed him on the throne in the first place.

King James's view of the Bible was patently Protestant, as demonstrated in this excerpt from some correspondence with his eldest son, Prince Henry:

> Diligently read his word, & earnestly ... pray for the right understanding thereof. Search the Scriptures saith Christ for they will bear testimony of me. The whole Scriptures saith Paul are profitable to teach, to improve, to correct, and to instruct in righteousness, that the man of God may be perfect unto all good works.

As a Scotsman and a Protestant holding the throne of England, King James had more than his share of enemies, and that included the Roman Catholic Church. The relationship between King James I and the Catholics was simple: He didn't like them, and they didn't like him. On a number of occasions, the "Papists," as James called them, made attempts on his life. One of the best-known assassination attempts was in 1605, when a Roman Catholic by the name of Guy Fawkes attempted to blow up Parliament with the king present. Fawkes's conspiracy was uncovered, and he and his associates in the plan were executed.

King James was a Protestant, which automatically made him an enemy of Rome. One prominent Catholic said of King James: "He is a Protestant…the King tries to extend his Protestant religion to the whole island. The King is a bitter enemy of our religion."

The Crowning Achievement of King James

King James was the first English monarch to unite England, Scotland, and Ireland into what he called "Great Britain." But he is also remembered for one of the most important, influential pieces of literary/religious work of history, the Authorized Version, or King James Bible.

In January of 1604, James called the Hampton Court Conference, where Christian leaders were allowed to air what they believed was amiss or wrong in the church. At the conference, John Reynolds, a Puritan, told the court that a new translation of the Bible was needed because the ones done during the reigns of Henry the VIII and Edward the VI were corrupt.

King James agreed with Reynolds that the church needed a new English translation of the Bible, and in July of the same year, he appointed a translation committee made up of 54 of the best linguists and scholars in the world. These were incredibly qualified men who had a grasp of the Hebrew, Aramaic, and Greek languages of the Bible. All of them had written, translated, and edited works in Greek. On top of that, and most important to King James, they were all devout Christians.

The committee was organized into six subcommittees, which met in the cities of Westminster, Cambridge, and Oxford. Of course, their work met with opposition from Rome, as pointed out in the preface of the original King James Bible. The translators wrote of the Catholics who opposed their project: "So much are they afraid of the light of the Scripture, that they will not trust the people with it … Sure we are that not he that hath the good gold, that is afraid to bring it to the touchstone, but he that hath the counterfeit."

> **Protestant Pearls**
>
> Trust God and keep your powder dry.
> —Oliver Cromwell (1599–1638)

The work went on despite the Catholic opposition, and the result quickly became one of the most cherished and influential pieces of literature in history. It is the best-selling book of all time, and it remains so to this day. Christians have praised the King James Bible for its accuracy and those in the secular world have praised it for its quality as a literary work.

James and the Puritan Problem

Queen Elizabeth I gave the Puritans little or nothing during her reign, and King James I didn't give them much more, if anything.

Some more moderate Puritans, those who were loyal to the Anglican Church but wanted to reform it from within, appealed to James to relax some of the terms of the Elizabethan Settlement that had to do with "objectionable" ceremonies and rites. Their appeal was respectful and in moderate language, but James, who believed that "one doctrine and one discipline, one religion in substance in ceremony" was necessary for unity and peace in England, wasn't going to compromise with them. "I will make them conform themselves," he threatened, "or I will harry them out of the land, or do worse."

James had the opportunity to bring religious peace, if not unity, to England, but his inflexibility only aggravated the tensions. James I was never a very healthy man, and on March 27, 1625, he died at the age of 59. King James accomplished many great things in his life, all but thirteen months of which was spent as a monarch, most notably a now-world-famous translation of the Bible. But he is also remembered for allowing—through his inaction and inflexibility—religious tensions to continue in England.

Welcome to Leave

England and Scotland had something in common with one another, but something that was not shared by the rest of Europe. From the time of Queen Elizabeth on, England and Scotland were the only European nations that allowed religious dissidents—they would brand them "heretics"—to leave and practice their religion elsewhere. In other nations, those who had differences with the official religion of that state were persecuted, arrested, and oftentimes martyred. Although those things took place in England, there was some freedom to leave for those who didn't like the Anglican Church.

In the early 1600s, a group of about a hundred people from the church in Leyden, Holland, which was set up by John Robinson in 1607–1608, boarded the Mayflower and set sail for Virginia. Although they missed their destination, they wound up making a home in Plymouth Rock, Massachusetts, where they set up a church.

During the next few decades, a steady stream of people made their way out of England. During the rule of Charles I, more than 20,000 men and women made their way across the Atlantic Ocean to settlements in New England.

The ones who left faced many dangers and hardships, but they were a hearty, brave people. And in hindsight, it may have been better if some of them had left England, considering the events that took place during the reign of Charles I.

What Not to Do When Faced with a Revolution

In 1625, Charles I succeeded his father, James I, as king of England, Scotland, and Ireland. He was James's second son, but became the heir to the throne when his older brother, Henry, died. Like his father, Charles believed in the divine right of kings. That belief would prove to be his undoing.

Charles inherited from his father a country full of religious conflict and discontent. And not only did Charles do nothing to improve the situation, but he did everything he could to make it worse. With the help of William Laud, who became the Archbishop of Canterbury in 1633 and who was a loyalist to the throne and to the Anglican Church, Charles attempted to crush the Puritan movement.

Under Charles's rule, even the most trivial religious deviation was punished severely, and it appeared that the measure employed by Charles and Laud was having the desired effect of putting an end to the Puritan problem. It looked as if there would be religious unity in England.

All was not as it appeared, though. Charles likely believed he was in control of the situation, but he had no idea of the strength and resiliency of the Puritan movement. In 1642, all that peace and unity came to a halt in the English Revolution, a.k.a the Puritan Revolution, and known in history as the English Civil War.

The Man Who Could Have Been King

Oliver Cromwell was born in Huntingdon, England, on April 25, 1599. As a boy, he was educated at the grammar school in Huntingdon. He spent a year at Sidney Sussex College at the University of Cambridge, but he returned home to care for his mother after the death of his father.

In 1620, Cromwell married Elizabeth Bourchier, the daughter of a well-to-do London merchant. The Cromwells weren't what you might consider a prosperous family early on. In fact, as his family grew, his income declined. In 1636, he inherited from an uncle both lands and a minor office in the eastern cathedral town of Ely, England. Cromwell worked as an estate manager and a tax collector, and in time he became one of the richest men in Ely.

Sometime between his marriage and when he found financial success in Ely, Cromwell underwent what can be described as a life-changing religious conversion. He came to a point of believing in the doctrine of predestination (although he probably didn't call it that), and he believed that he was one of God's "elect." After his conversion, Cromwell began spending more and more time with friends and associates who shared his religious convictions and political outlook.

In time, Cromwell and his friends became more and more agitated about the way Charles I was running things. First of all, they didn't believe he was doing enough to suppress Catholicism in England.

The final move toward war came when Charles attempted to impose Anglicanism on Scotland, which had been Presbyterian. In 1635, the *Book of Canons* was published. This book, which declared the king the absolute head of the "Kirk" in Scotland, was put into effect without the approval of the General Assembly or the Parliament. The last straw for the Scots came when Charles authorized a book that required the churches in Scotland to follow more Anglican practices.

These moves by Charles were opposed in Scotland, even to the point of violence. But the king wouldn't bend. In April of 1640, he called Parliament for the purpose of raising money for the military actions that would be needed to end the rebellion in Scotland. The Parliament refused to fund Charles's war, instead insisting on peace with Scotland and presenting to him a list of complaints against his rule. Charles went around the Parliament and raised funds for the war on his own.

When the money for his war ran out, Charles called another Parliament later in 1640. The Parliament was called the "Long Parliament," because it lasted for twenty years. When the Parliament met, Oliver Cromwell and a group of his friends, who had been selected to serve, entered the House of Commons. Cromwell served as a member of the Parliament with a group of dissident members called the "fiery spirits." For most of the next two years, the relationship between the king and the Parliament grew worse and worse.

Finally, the crisis came to a head as Charles appeared at the House of Commons and attempted to arrest some of those who had most strongly opposed him. The response to this action was so strong that the king was forced to flee from London with his family.

From there, things went from bad to worse for England. The Parliament raised its own army, and the stage was set for the English Civil War. Those loyal to the king, called the Cavaliers, would oppose those in the army of the Parliament, the Roundheads.

The Look of a Revolutionary Leader

At first, it looked as though there was nothing about Oliver Cromwell to indicate that he would be the key leader of the Parliamentary forces during the English Civil War. But he was a devout Calvinist with seemingly inborn military ability. On top of all that, he is remembered by historians as a natural leader, as one with the kind of personality that demanded the attention and respect of those around him. Those personality traits proved to be essential for the one who would have to hold together competing groups involved in the war against King Charles and his loyalists.

Cromwell established himself as leader of the Puritans in the October 23, 1642, Battle of Edgehill. It was Cromwell's first military action, and it was not decisive for either side of the conflict.

Going Deeper

The Battle of Edgehill was the first major armed battle of the English Civil War. It was fought on October 23, 1642 in Edgehill, Warwickshire. In the battle, Parliamentary troops, fighting under the Earl of Essex, took on the royal troops under the Earl of Forth. The battle settled nothing, and it would take several more to settle this civil war.

In 1643, Parliament got some needed help when it received the support of the Scottish army in what was called the "Solemn League and Covenant." This support came in return for a promise that the Westminster Assembly (1643–1647) would force the Anglican Church to conform to the Presbyterian Church of Scotland. This development would bring a reaction from Independents and other radicals, who opposed the idea of any nationalized church, be it Presbyterian, Catholic, or any other system.

Meanwhile, Cromwell was promoted to the position of colonel of a cavalry regiment. It turned out that Cromwell, who had no experience in battle prior to the civil war, was a master military tactician as well as a fierce warrior. He very quickly rose in the ranks, and in 1644, he was promoted to lieutenant. That year, he made key contributions to the Parliament's victory in the July 2 Battle of Marsten Moor.

After that, he was named general of the cavalry—which earned him the name "Ironsides"—and again played a key role in another military victory at the pivotal 1645 Battle of Naseby. Although the royal forces dragged the war out for several more months, the Battle of Naseby was effectively the end of the civil war. The fighting continued another year, but the king's military forces were in ruin, and it was just a matter of time before the results were finalized. Finally, Cromwell, serving as second in command to Thomas Fairfax, helped the Parliamentary forces to a final victory when they took Oxford in 1645. Charles I escaped and fled to Scotland, but in January of 1647, the Scots returned him to England.

People You Should Know

Thomas Fairfax (1612–1671) was the commander in chief of the Parliamentary army during the English civil wars between the royalists and the parliamentarians. He was a highly skilled military tactician who helped lead the parliamentary forces to victories in northern and southwestern England. After Oliver Cromwell's death, he helped General George Monck restore Parliamentary rule in England.

The Civil War Is Over, So What's Next?

Following the first phase of the English Civil War, there was conflict between the victorious army and the Parliament. The Parliament wanted to disband the army, which had served its purpose, come to terms with the king, and deal with the radical religious elements, which Cromwell had encouraged. But the army, which was alienated by the Presbyterian rule of the Parliament, would have none of that, and soldiers took King Charles and marched him to London.

In the confusion of these events, Charles escaped and fled to the Isle of Wight and made an agreement with the Scots, who pledged to help bring him back to the throne if he would make Presbyterianism the official religion of both England and Scotland. The result of all this was the second civil war, which started in the spring of 1648. There were uprisings in different parts of England, but the parliamentary forces quickly suppressed them. A Scottish army had invaded England, but on August 17–19, Cromwell defeated the invading Scots at the battle at Preston.

The army was now firmly in control of the nation, and the next step was what came to be called "Pride's Purge" after Thomas Pride, which took place in December of 1648. This purge removed the Presbyterian members from Parliament, which left behind what was called the "Rump Parliament." Cromwell stayed in the northern part of England until the purge was finished, and when he arrived back in London in 1649, it was time to deal with King Charles. Cromwell took part in a commission to try the king for treason. Charles was found guilty of treason and on January 30, 1649 he was beheaded. For Cromwell, the execution of the king was a divine judgment against a tyrant.

With the execution of Charles out of the way, the Rump Parliament formed the Commonwealth of England, which was to be ruled by a Council of State that included members of the Rump Parliament.

For the next two years, Cromwell dealt with military matters. There were powerful enemies to be dealt with, particularly in Catholic Ireland and in Scotland, where Charles II, son of Charles I, was proclaimed king. Cromwell organized his forces and went to Ireland, where he conducted a brutal campaign aimed at ending Catholic power there. Cromwell defeated the Scots in two battles, one at Dunbar in 1650 and one at Worcester in 1651. Both Ireland and Scotland became parts of the Commonwealth.

Protestant Pearls

Grace can pardon our ungodliness and justify us with Christ's righteousness; it can put the spirit of Jesus Christ within us; it can help us when we are down, it can heal us when we are wounded; it can multiply pardons, as we through frailty multiply transgressions.

—John Bunyan (1628–1688)

All that remained for Cromwell and his army was to establish a permanent government for the Commonwealth. He didn't want military rule in England, but he was also growing impatient with the Rump Parliament. Rump did its best, but its membership was divided over which specific programs it should implement and how it should implement them. In April 1653, Cromwell had the Rump Parliament forcibly removed from the House of Commons and replaced it with a nominated Parliament often called the "Barebones Parliament," and its members were chosen from among those loyal to the army and to London's Puritan congregations.

The Barebones Parliament proved no more effective in implementing the reforms Cromwell and the army wanted, so it lasted just a few months. In December 1653, Cromwell accepted the "Instrument of Government," a written constitution developed by General John Lambert that created a protectorate consisting of himself as Lord Protector (or the chief executive) and a one-house Parliament. Lambert wanted a king to head the new government in England, but Cromwell wouldn't rule without constitutional law. Under the provisions of the Instrument of Government—England's only written constitution—Cromwell governed as Lord Protector from 1653 to 1658.

During that time, Cromwell tried to establish many of the reforms that Puritans had demanded prior to and during the two decades of revolution. These measures included more religious toleration in England, as well as the stricter morals the Puritans had always favored. During his reign, all but the most extreme religious movements enjoyed tolerance. In addition, the stricter moral codes were enforced.

None of the Puritan policies under Cromwell enjoyed widespread support, and it was only a matter of time before discontent arose among the people. The Protectorate, which was a minority government in England, was on unstable footing from the very beginning. Cromwell's government took measures to try to quiet royalist uprisings, which began almost from the start. But they were unsuccessful.

People You Should Know

General George Monck (1608–1670) was an English soldier and politician who in the spring of 1660, while he served as commander of the Scottish army, marched into London and recalled the Long Parliament, which then restored the monarchy to England. The monarchy had been temporarily deposed following the English Civil War.

On his deathbed in the fall of 1658, Oliver Cromwell nominated his eldest son, Richard, to succeed him as Lord Protector. He died on September 3 of that year. Richard Cromwell's reign as Lord Protector didn't last long. Richard wasn't a strong leader, and before long England was in a state of near anarchy. In the spring of 1660, General George Monck, the commander of the Scottish army, marched into London and recalled the Long Parliament, which restored Charles II to the throne. The monarchy, though it would forever be altered by the revolution, had returned, and the Anglican Church was also restored.

The Legacy of the Puritan Revolution

In many ways, the revolution led by Oliver Cromwell was a failure. The Commonwealth of England lasted just over a decade, and its presence in that nation was not accepted by the majority of the English people.

But not all was lost for the Puritans. The English Revolution set the stage for a more tolerant religious climate in England. Religious liberty would be granted in 1689 in the Act of Toleration, which kept the Anglican Church as England's official religion but also guaranteed freedom for all Protestant dissenters.

This development would have lasting implications for the religious climates in England and later in what would become the United States. From the Puritan Revolution sprang the numerous sects and denominations that made their way to America.

The Least You Need to Know

- When Queen Elizabeth I ascended to the throne, she reestablished the Anglican Church as England's official church.
- The Anglican Church as it was reestablished by Elizabeth met with opposition from two camps: Catholics and radical Protestants, including the Puritans.
- The English Revolution, also known as the Puritan Revolution, was led by Oliver Cromwell, and it temporarily ended the monarchy in England.
- The Puritan Revolution, while it ultimately failed in its goal of bringing a new church and government to England, had lasting positive effects when it came to religious toleration.

Chapter 15

The Radical Side of the Reformation

In This Chapter

- ◆ The beginnings of Anabaptist movements
- ◆ The Anabaptists face persecution
- ◆ The spread of different forms of Anabaptism
- ◆ The lasting influence of the radical reformations

In a world where Catholic and Protestant ideas clashed with sometimes-deadly outcomes, there was another important sect of Christianity that arose and made its mark in Europe and later in the New World. It was a movement of people who held to a more radical view of the Christian faith, one that neither the Catholics nor the Protestants came close to holding. These radicals are the people who came to be known as the Anabaptists.

Like the Protestant movement, the Anabaptist movement includes several sects (today, we would use the word *denominations*) and sub-movements. There was no individual "Anabaptist movement" as such, but a loose grouping of movements whose beliefs and practices were outside the "mainstream" of the Protestant movement.

Who Were the Anabaptists?

The term "Anabaptist" covers a variety of groups, many of which still exist today. "Anabaptist" was not a complimentary term during the days of the Protestant Reformation, and the different Anabaptist movements never accepted the label. Today, it might be considered a religion-based epithet. "Anabaptist" is a term that came from the movements' enemies, and it meant "rebaptizer," because these sects believed in the practice of adult baptism even for those who had been baptized as infants. The Catholics and most of the mainstream reformers believed in infant baptism.

The movement can be traced back to the early 1520s, when several religious leaders began to question some of the practices of the Roman Catholic Church and to preach against some of the practices in Switzerland, Germany, and Austria. Among those men was Conrad Grebel, who is considered the earliest leader of the Anabaptist movement. He was joined by Hans Denck and Balthasar Hubmaier, who with other early dissidents came to be known as "the Swiss Brethren." They believed that there was no basis in the Bible for infant baptism or for the Mass. They also preached against the church hierarchy and against the role of civil authorities in religious matters.

Their preaching and activities got them in trouble with the city council at Zürich. Many of their followers and fellow preachers were persecuted or even martyred for their beliefs. Many of them left the city, taking their radical message with them into Germany and Moravia, where Anabaptist movements flourished, despite the persecution.

Anabaptist movements arose in many different areas of Europe, but they were especially common in Germany, the Netherlands, and Switzerland. Anabaptist beliefs and practices appealed most to the poor and uneducated peasants and to the artisans of Europe.

> **Protestant Pearls**
>
> Faith is nothing at all tangible. It is simply believing God; and, like sight, it is nothing apart from its object.
>
> —Hannah Whitall Smith (1832–1911), devotional writer and founding member of the Women's Christian Movement

What the Anabaptists Believed

It isn't really practical to define what the Anabaptists as a group believed, mostly because there were so many different groups within the movement, each with their own particular set of beliefs. The beliefs of Anabaptists were as varied as the personalities in the movement, but there are some basics of belief we can mention for the early Anabaptists.

The common denominator when it came to Anabaptist beliefs seems to be the opposition to infant baptism. The Anabaptists were in agreement with Lutherans and Calvinists when it came to the importance of personal faith in God as opposed to the ritualism of the Roman church. But there were some differences between the two positions.

Some of the Anabaptist groups established Christian communities that in modern days might be called "Christian communes." They took the idea of separation from the world to such an extreme that they opposed any kind of participation in civil affairs.

According to the earliest Anabaptists, the church services were to be very simple and were not to contain anything not in keeping with the primitive church or in the Book of Acts. Baptism was to be saved for those who were personally penitent, who had confessed faith in Christ, and who had been instructed of its significance. That meant that only adults could be baptized. Baptism was seen as a confession of faith and a commitment to live the "new life" of one who had been truly converted.

The Anabaptists had a view of the Lord's Supper that was radically different from that of the Protestants or Catholics. They saw it as a remembrance (as Christ had said, "Do this in remembrance of me") and they practiced it as a meal of Christian fellowship, which was to be served in private homes and not in the church. This was a very literal reenactment of Christ's "Last Supper" with the disciples in the upper room prior to his arrest and execution.

In Anabaptism, pastors were to be selected and supported by the congregations. The pastors' duties included the reading of the scriptures, and teaching and preaching from them. The pastors were to lead the church services and care for the spiritual welfare of the congregation. They were also responsible for administering discipline and, when it was called for, banning those unfaithful to the message of Christ as recorded in the Bible.

Anabaptists saw themselves as missionaries whose job it was to take their message to the Catholic world, to the Protestant world, and to the nonreligious world. To the average Catholic or Protestant, the Anabaptist message was a hard one to hear and a harder one to practice. It was a radical message of discipleship, one that many people rejected outright, but others gladly accepted. The Anabaptists had a system for evangelizing Europe, and they sent missionaries out by twos and threes.

Show Me Your Faith!

When Luther started the Protestant Reformation with his 95 Theses, he brought the doctrine of justification by faith to the forefront of religious discussion. Luther believed that no amount of good works would justify sinful man before a holy God. That justification, he taught, came through the works of Jesus Christ, whose death and resurrection demonstrated God's grace. That grace could only be accessed through faith in Jesus Christ.

Anabaptists, while they believed in the idea of justification by faith, would add a condition to the formula. The typical Anabaptist would agree with the doctrine of justification by faith, but he would say that one's faith should be demonstrated by one's actions. In other words, real saving faith in Christ will demonstrate itself in tangible ways in the life of the true believer.

Because they were different in how they approached their faith, and because their approach to religion was well outside what was legally recognized in Europe, the Anabaptists were subject at times to severe persecution. And, according to their own beliefs, there was nothing they could do about that persecution, other than to see it as a fulfillment of Jesus' promise that opposition would come to those who lived for him.

But they differed from the two main branches of the Reformation in that they advocated pacifism (nonviolence, even in the face of the most severe persecution) and the establishment of state churches.

Tough Times for the Anabaptists

There wasn't a whole lot Catholics and Protestants could agree on in the sixteenth century, but one thing they had in common at that time in Europe was the conviction that something had to be done about these radicals. Both sides of the Reformation conflict believed that Anabaptists were not just heretics, but a danger to the stability of Europe as a whole.

Because they were seen as a threat, Anabaptists in Europe suffered under intense persecution from all sides: from the nobility, from the governments, from the Catholic Church, and from the leaders of the orthodox Reformation movements. They were persecuted because they saw both Catholicism and Protestantism as corruptions of the church as God had intended it to be, and their words and actions reflected that belief.

The persecution and opposition started before 1525 in the days of Conrad Grebel, a friend of Swiss reformer Ulrich Zwingli in Zürich, who had expressed questions about infant baptism. But in time, Grebel and the others known as the Brethren, became more and more unhappy with Zwingli, because they thought he was abandoning biblical principles. Soon, Zwingli and others in Zürich began denouncing the Brethren from the pulpit. The issue between the two camps was infant baptism.

Anabaptists Facing off with Zwingli and Zürich

In January 1525, Zwingli and his colleagues faced off with Grebel and his friends in a public disputation in Zürich. The Brethren gave a spirited and eloquent defense of their views, but the Zürich city council sided with Zwingli and outlawed meetings of the Brethren and ordered all parents in the city to have their infants baptized within eight days if they hadn't already done so. Those who defied the order were to be expelled from the city.

The defiant response to the city council's order came on January 21, when Grebel, who was a layman, baptized an ordained priest named Georg Blaurock in the home of Felix Manz. It was the first recorded adult baptism, and it marked a new dimension to the

Anabaptist movement. From that day on, the movement spread quickly. The Brethren preached in the surrounding areas, and won many "converts." But in October of 1525, Grebel, Manz, and Blaurock were arrested and put on trial for their radicalism. All three were sentenced to prison.

In the winter of 1525, as the three Anabaptist ring leaders sat in a Zürich prison, their movement continued to expand. The following spring, the original 3—plus 14 others, including 6 women—were tried again and sentenced to life in prison. At that time, the Zürich city council issued a decree against "rebaptizing" and set as the penalty death by drowning. (The council seemed to be asking those who would "rebaptize" just how much they like going into the water.) Two weeks later, Grebel, Manz, and Blaurock escaped from prison and set about preaching their faith.

Meanwhile, Zwingli's approach to the Anabaptists grew more and more severe. In November, the Zürich council passed a decree sentencing people to death for just listening to Anabaptist preaching. One month later, Manz and Blaurock were captured and tried (Grebel had died in August). Blaurock was not a citizen of Zürich, so he was whipped and banished from the city. Manz, a native of the city, was sentenced to death and executed by drowning, a fate he met on January 5, 1527—with Zwingli's approval.

The First Martyr, but Hardly the Last

Manz was the first Anabaptist martyr, but far from the last. All over Europe Anabaptists were treated with mind-boggling cruelty. Men and women alike were put to their deaths by drowning, burning, hanging, burial, and other equally horrible methods. Menno Simons (who we will discuss shortly), a later Anabaptist leader, wrote of this time:

> Some they have executed by hanging, some they have tortured with inhuman tyranny, and afterwards choked with cords at the stake. Some they roasted and burned alive. Some they have killed with the sword and given them to the fowls of the air to devour. Some they have cast to the fishes. … They are hated, abused, slandered and lied about by all men.

Clearly, there was no treatment that was too harsh for the radical Anabaptists. This is considered by many historians to be the darkest hour of the Reformation. But the persecution didn't stop the Anabaptists. They continued their preaching and teaching, and their movement continued to expand all over Europe. Eventually, the persecution of the Anabaptists would die down, and they would make huge contributions to history and to the religious world of Europe and later what would be known as the New World.

The Creation of a Münster

In 1534, a group of Anabaptists came to power in the northwest German city of Münster, where they engaged in shocking excesses. They believed that Christ would soon return to the world to reign for a thousand years before executing the final judgment.

This strange scene got started in 1525, when a Lutheran-turned-Anabaptist by the name of Bernard Rothmann began preaching the most radical of Anabaptist ideas. He preached that infant baptism was unlawful and that the wealth and possessions of all in the city should be shared for the common good. In a short time, the news of Rothmann's preaching made its way around the region, and the city was overrun with radical Anabaptists seeking a haven from the persecution as well as a home where their beliefs would be practiced to the extreme.

Bishop Count Francis of Waldeck and those loyal to him were driven from the city and other "ungodly" people were expelled. All books but the Bible were burned. The Anabaptists were now in complete control of the city, and in short order a man named John of Leyden became something of a tyrant. He decreed that all adults in the city must either be baptized or leave and that all food and clothes were to be shared among the citizens. He even introduced polygamy (he himself had four wives, one of which he beheaded during a fit of rage).

Protestant Pearls

My very soul was flooded with celestial light ... for the first time I realized that I had been trying to hold the world in one hand and the Lord in the other.

—Fannie Crosby (1820–1915), North American hymn writer

This strange theocracy ended on June 25, 1535, when an army made up of Lutherans and Catholics—and led by Philip of Hesse and the deposed Bishop of Münster—stormed the city. The Anabaptist leaders of the city were arrested, tortured, and executed.

Word of the goings-on in Münster made their way around Europe, and the Anabaptist movement fell into even more disrepute among the people. It was "guilt-by-association" for other Anabaptists, and it wasn't fair. But the situation would be addressed by the work of Anabaptist leader Menno Simons.

Menno Simons Saves Anabaptism

Historians have credited the survival of the Anabaptist movement—though it has undergone major changes since its beginnings in the 1520s—to the work of Menno Simons (about 1496–1561), a former Catholic priest who broke with the Roman church and joined with the Anabaptists.

Menno Simons was born in Friesland, the Netherlands. After being ordained as a Catholic priest in 1524, he began having doubts concerning the doctrine of transubstantiation. He wondered whether the elements of the Eucharist *literally* became the body and blood of Christ. His doubts motivated him to search for the truth in the New Testament. Later, he began to have other questions, specifically on the subject of "rebaptism." He searched the Bible, and began to question the practice of infant baptism. He eventually came to the conclusion that infant baptism wasn't in the Bible.

During his search, Menno Simons began to examine his own life—first against what he saw in the Bible, then later against what he saw in the lives and deaths of some 300 Anabaptists who were slaughtered in April 1535. It was then that Simons realized that something was missing in his life, and that he hadn't taken his Christian faith as seriously as he should.

Though he had problems with some of the practices and beliefs of the Catholic Church, Simons remained in the priesthood until 1536, when he publicly renounced his allegiance to the pope and to the church and began spending his time with some Anabaptists he knew. Not long after that, Menno Simons was "rebaptized."

When he learned of what had happened in Münster, he was moved to action. Simons wanted to do what he could to heal and strengthen the Anabaptist movement. He immediately repudiated the excesses of the Anabaptists in Münster, criticizing John of Leyden, the ringleader of those excesses, as an antichrist.

The Time for a Good Man to Act

From 1536 to 1543, Simons worked in the Netherlands and from 1543 until his death in 1561, he worked in northern Germany. He worked to bring moderation to the Anabaptist movement. He renounced the movement's more fanatical elements, as well as the apocalyptic ideas held by some Anabaptists. He worked to establish community churches of men and women who had been regenerated by faith in Christ—such as those in the first century church. He stressed personal conversion and discipleship, and that the act of adult baptism was an outward sign and seal of those things.

In spite of the persecutions of Anabaptists, Menno Simons held strong to the movement's principle of nonresistance:

> The regenerated do not go to war, nor engage in strife. They are the children of peace who have beaten their swords into plowshares and their spears into pruning hooks … Since we are to be conformed to the image of Christ, how can we then fight our enemies with the sword? Spears and swords of iron we leave to those who, alas, consider human blood and swine's blood of well-nigh equal value.

The Mennonite Legacy

In 1536, Menno Simons gathered the scattered northern European Anabaptists into congregations. It was these people who took on the name *Mennonites*. By the latter part of the sixteenth century, the Mennonites, who were more moderate than the earlier Anabaptists, were tolerated in the Netherlands under the protection of William the Silent, Prince of Orange.

You Can Look It Up

Mennonites are those who hold to the teachings of Menno Simons, who was a reformer of the Anabaptist movement in the sixteenth century. Simons was a former Catholic priest who later ascribed to the general ideas of the Anabaptists.

From Holland, the Mennonites spread into other lands, including Poland, Russia, the Ukraine, southern Germany, eastern France, and, eventually, to North America. Today, there are close to a half-million baptized members of this church in Switzerland, France, Germany, North America, South America, and Russia. It has been estimated that half of those make their homes in the United States.

Today, there are several "sub-sects" of the Mennonite church. Some are more conservative and more withdrawn from modern society than others. However, all Mennonites hold to the model of the religious community as demonstrated in the New Testament book of Acts. Most of the prominent Mennonite beliefs can be found in a confession of faith that was first circulated in Dordrecht, the Netherlands, in 1632.

According to the Mennonite statement of faith, the Bible as it is interpreted by the individual conscience is the sole authority on doctrinal matters, and the ministry has no power or authority as mediator between God and the individual human. Adult baptism is administered as a confession of faith, and infant baptism is rejected.

Mennonites hold to the principle of separation of church and state. They were among the first to condemn slavery. Mennonites traditionally obey all civil laws, but many of them refuse to take up arms or to support violence in any form. They also refuse to take judicial oaths or to hold public office.

The Mennonites also have a great legacy of influence on other "denominations" that have made their way into North America. They greatly influenced the Baptists. They also are credited with indirectly influencing the Amish, founded by Jacob Amman; the Hutterites, which were founded by Jacob Hutter; and the Quakers (Friends), who were founded by George Fox.

The Amish—A New Kind of Anabaptist

The Amish people are direct descendants of the Anabaptists. More specifically, the Amish religion branched off of the Swiss Mennonites. This group received its name from its founder, Jacob Amman, who was born on January 19, 1656, in Switzerland but later moved to Alsace. There he was an elder and a spokesman for the Anabaptists.

The *Amish* religion was founded as a result of the reforms Amman wanted to make in the religion during the second half of the last decade of the seventeenth century. His proposed reforms caused a disagreement between Amman and other Mennonite leaders. Amman had proposed that the Mennonite congregations meet twice a year for communion. Before that, Swiss Mennonites had observed communion once a year. When the other church leaders rejected his idea, Amman moved on to other topics for discussion. After several disagreements on several issues, the Swiss Mennonites rejected Amman's reforms outright. He responded by excommunicating the Swiss ministers. Later, he tried to make up with the Mennonites, but the damage was done. A new division of the Mennonites had to be formed, and it was called the Amish.

The Amish hold the Bible sacred and interpret it literally and directly. In addition to the Bible, the Amish observe unwritten rules concerning morals and their way of life. These unwritten rules are known as "The Ordnung" and the Amish follow them closely.

You Can Look It Up

The **Amish** religion got its name from its founder Jacob Amman, a Swiss-born Anabaptist. The religion sprang out of some disagreements between Amman and other Swiss Anabaptist preachers.

Protestant Pearls

It also pleased God by the revelation of his holiness and grace ... to bring home to me my sin ... I was turned from a Christian to a believer, from a lover of love to an object of grace.

—Peter Taylor Forsyth (1848–1921), Congregationalist pastor

Where the Amish differ from other Anabaptist movements is their acceptance and observance of the Dordrecht Confession of 1632, which endorses the Amish practice of avoidance and foot washing. Anabaptists practice avoidance, meaning that those who fall into sinful lifestyles should be shunned until they make needed changes in their lives. Jacob Amman's interpretation of this practice was stricter than that of the Anabaptists. For example, his followers were to shun all members who leave the Amish church and those who marry an outsider. He also preached that one should not buy from, sell to, or even eat at the same table as the excommunicated individual. Such strict traditions have been passed down from generation to generation and have kept the Amish lifestyle stable.

The Amish met with persecution in eighteenth-century Switzerland. Many of them immigrated to North America, where most of them settled in Lancaster County in Pennsylvania (still one of the best-known Amish communities even today). There are also Amish populations in rural areas of the Midwest. As of 1995, there were an estimated 30,000 Amish in North America and 134,000 worldwide.

Today, the Amish still live quiet lives of separation from the outside world. They practice the separation of church and state, but more than that they separate themselves from modern society—an amazing achievement, especially in the United States, where mainstream culture is very different.

Hearing It for the Hutterites

Another lasting sect of the Anabaptist movement is the Hutterites, who got their name from their founder, Jacob Hutter, a hat maker who joined an Anabaptist group in Austerlitz, Moravia, in 1529. Though he was serving the church in Austerlitz, he stayed in an area of Austria called Tyrol. On two occasions, the Moravian Church called him in to settle conflicts, and in 1533 he moved to Moravia, where he became an elder of the church.

The Hutterite religion was another radical form of Anabaptism, and it is based on the communal way of living as suggested in Acts 2:44–45. As with other forms of the Anabaptist faith, life as a Hutterite was not easy. Hutterites were subjected to severe persecution during the early years of the movement. In 1535, around 2,000 Austrian Hutterites were executed. In November of that year, the movement's founder was arrested, and tried for heresy and treason. On February 25, 1536, he was put to death. His wife was executed two years later.

After Hutter's death, his followers sought refuge in Moravia, where they received protection from persecution and were exempted from military service or taxation. This ended when war broke out between the Hapsburg Empire and Turkey in 1593. When the Turks occupied Moravia, many of the Hutterites were killed or taken into slavery. In 1622, the Hutterites fled Moravia to avoid persecution by Protestant and Catholic forces, who were at war in central Europe. The persecution continued into the eighteenth century, and many Hutterites fled to Russia.

In 1874, a group of Hutterites emigrated to the United States, where they settled in South Dakota. Life in the United States was good for the Hutterites until World War I. It was then that the Hutterites, as pacifists, refused to support the war or serve in the armed forces. This brought them ridicule and harassment. The Hutterite communities migrated to Canada, where they settled in Alberta and Manitoba.

After the war ended, some of the Hutterites gradually returned to the United States, where to this day they live quiet, communal lives and have little to do with the outside world.

Another movement that was influenced by the Anabaptists—one that is better known than the Amish or the Hutterites—was the Friends, or Quakers as they are better known.

The Beginnings of Quakerism

George Fox was born in Fenny Drayton, Leicestershire, in 1624, and is considered the founder of the Religious Society of Friends, also known as the *Quakers*. He was the son of a weaver and worked as an apprentice to a Nottingham shoemaker.

From the time he was a youth, Fox thought deeply about religion. In the mid-seventeenth century, he began walking around England talking with priests and other authorities on religion, trying to find out about true religion. Instead, what he found was a lot of men with some amazing knowledge of the Christian faith, but who had little if any personal connection with God. Fox later reported hearing the voice of God speaking to him: "And when all my hopes in them and all men were gone … I heard a voice which said, 'There is one, even Christ Jesus, that can speak to thy condition,' and when I heard it, my heart did leap for joy."

You Can Look It Up

Quakers, another term for the Society of Friends, was originally coined as a derisive term. It originated in a courtroom in Derby, England, where George Fox told a judge who had sentenced him for blasphemy that he should "tremble in fear of God." "You folks are the tremblers, you are the Quakers," replied the judge. The name stuck.

This personal "enlightenment" took place in 1647, when Fox was a young man of 23. From that time on, he began a traveling ministry in which he encouraged seekers to hear and obey the voice of Christ within them. He also encouraged them to be honest, compassionate, and to support the ministry of their local churches.

The more people were converted by his preaching, the more opposition and persecution he faced. He was beaten, imprisoned, and bodily thrown from the churches where he preached. He even spent a year in prison for his efforts.

In 1652, Fox climbed up the desolate Pendle Hill in northern England, where he had a vision of "a great people to be gathered." Fox took this vision as God's instruction for him to preach and proclaim Christ's power over sin so that there could be an ingathering of people. He did just that, and by 1660, just eight years after his "hilltop" vision, he had more than 50,000 followers. Fox's followers included a group of devoted young men and women who came to be called "the valiant sixty," and who joined him in preaching in every setting where people could hear them.

Early on, Fox's followers called themselves "Children of the Light," "Publishers of Truth," and "the Camp of the Lord." In time, their title became simply "Friends," after Christ's promise in John 15:14 that those who were obedient to him were his "friends." Eventually, they came to be known as the "Society of Friends." "Quakers" came from an exchange between a judge and Fox having to do with "quaking before God."

People You Should Know

Edward Burrough (1634–1663) lived much of his short life working for the Quaker cause. He began associating himself with the Quakers at the age of nineteen. This caused him to be rejected by his family. He was one of the leaders in the establishment of Quakerism, particularly in London. He was seen by some as George Fox's right-hand man. He was imprisoned in the early 1660s and died at Newgate prison in 1663.

The Quakers Move On

The Friends refused to accept many of the social customs and religious rules of their time, and they were often persecuted because of it. For example, after 1656 the Friends, because they rejected the organized church, refused to attend the Anglican services or to pay the church tithes. This resulted in Fox's arrest. They also got in trouble with the authorities because they met publicly for worship, which violated the provisions of the Conventicle Act of 1664, which made it a crime to meet for worship, other than that with the Church of England.

Fox survived his stay in prison, but many of his followers weren't so fortunate. During the reign in England of King Charles II—from 1660 to 1685—more than 13,000 Quakers were arrested and imprisoned in England. Of those, more than 300 died in prison or from wounds they received when their meetings were assaulted.

After his release from prison in 1666, Fox and the Quakers developed an organization for the Friends movement. They elected elders and overseers for the organization. In 1669, Fox married a widow by the name of Margeret Fell.

In the 1660s, the Society of Friends began to immigrate to the American colonies. They settled particularly in New Jersey, where they purchased land in 1674, and in the Pennsylvania colony, which was granted to William Penn in 1681. By 1684, approximately 7,000 Friends had settled in Pennsylvania. In the colonies, the Quakers ran into continuous persecution, particularly in Massachusetts. The Quakers were also active in opposing slavery in the colonies.

Before his death in 1691, George Fox had occasion to visit Barbados, Jamaica, America, Holland, and Germany. Fox was accompanied on his travels by William Penn, one of the best known of the early Quakers. In 1661, Fox founded the American Quaker Colony of Pennsylvania and he continued preaching until his death. At the time of Fox's death, there were more than 100,000 Friends worldwide, mostly in England, Scotland, and the American colonies.

In addition to what he accomplished while he was alive, George Fox left behind the legacy of the Quaker system of beliefs.

What Do Quakers Believe In?

The foundational belief of the Quakers is that God gives the individual divine revelation. Each and every person may receive the word of God internally, and each should endeavor to receive that word and heed it. The first Friends termed this revelation the "inward light," the "inner light," or "Christ within." Scottish Quaker Robert Barclay (1648–1690) wrote the first complete doctrinal statement concerning this "inner light," which was titled *An Apology for the True Christian Divinity, as the Same Is Held Forth and Preached by the People Called in Scorn Quakers* (1678). This writing was considered the most important theological work for Quakers.

The Quakers rejected the formal creeds and regarded each worshiper of God as a vessel of divine revelation. For that reason, there wasn't the same need for paid clergy or priests to bring the Word to people. Quakerism also holds to the idea of human goodness, on the basis of the fact that there is something of God in each and every person. But it also recognizes the presence of evil in every human.

The Quakers place great emphasis on living by Christian principles. They greatly value truth and honesty in all their dealings with others. The Friends attempt to emulate Christ by avoiding excessive luxury and by dressing and speaking with simplicity.

Many of the doctrines of the Society of Friends were taken from the influence of earlier religious groups in England—particularly the Anabaptists and Independents—who believed in the leadership of laypeople, the independence of individual congregations, and the complete separation of church and state.

Quakers take two passages of scripture quite literally, the first of which is Christ's words "Do not swear at all" (Matthew 5:34). In obedience to those words, Quakers as a group refuse to take oaths or make promises. Instead, they allow their yes to be yes, and their no to be no. The second passage of this kind is Christ's words "Do not resist one who is evil" (Matthew 5:39). In light of that, Quakers have always preached against war and other forms of violence, even when human logic says that it is justified.

The Society of Friends is not one of the bigger Christian denominations. As of the late twentieth century, their worldwide membership was approximately 200,000 people in about 30 countries. The United States is by far the home of the largest number of

Robert Barclay (1648–1690) was a prolific Quaker writer/ theologian who wrote the first complete Quaker doctrinal statement, which was titled *An Apology for the True Christian Divinity, as the Same Is Held Forth and Preached by the People Called in Scorn Quakers* (1678).

Friends—around 117,000 in about 1,100 congregations nationwide. The Friends also have congregations in Africa, the United Kingdom, Central America, Australia, Canada, and New Zealand.

In a world where the more "visible" denominations— those founded on the doctrines of Martin Luther, Ulrich Zwingli, John Calvin, and John Knox—dominate the non-Catholic religious scene, there are still the remnants of what was once the more radical Protestant movements, and they still hold an important place in the history of the Reformation.

The Least You Need to Know

- While many of the Protestant movements led by Luther, Calvin, Zwingli, and Knox gained some form of official acceptance or support, the more radical Anabaptist movements were rejected and persecuted by both Protestants and Catholics.
- Despite the persecution from all sides, the radical Anabaptist movement survived and grew in Europe.
- Catholic-turned-Anabaptist Menno Simons was the key figure in keeping the Anabaptist movement alive despite intense persecution.
- The remnants of the radical Protestant movements are still part of the religious scene in the United States today.

Chapter 16

The Catholic Church's Own Reformation

In This Chapter

- ◆ Catholic calls from within for Reformation
- ◆ The mystics and the humanists: different approach, same goals
- ◆ The reforms from the Council of Trent
- ◆ The part of the Roman Inquisition and the Jesuits in the Catholic Reformation

There are a couple of ways to look at the sixteenth-century event known as the Catholic Reformation. You could say that it was the natural and necessary response to the Protestant Reformation that got its official start in Wittenberg, Germany, in 1517.

There is no question that the Catholic reformers were concerned about the Protestant movements and that some of the things they did were answers to those movements. But you could say that the Protestant Reformation only brought about what was bound to happen in the Catholic Church anyway.

It is true that the Roman Catholic reformers were as troubled by the corruption in the church as were the Protestant reformers. And it was those reformers in the sixteenth century who led the Catholic Reformation, also known as the Counter-Reformation.

Calls for Reformation—From Within

For centuries, there had been calls from within the church for reforms, and not just from those who wanted to break away from Rome. These calls came from Catholics, devout men and women who loved the church but who were saddened and angered by the corruption and the materialism that had become such a huge part of it. They knew something had to change.

There had been previous attempts at reform. From the early part of the twelfth century onward, there were calls from all sorts of people within the church for reform (see Chapter 4, "Rebels, Rabble-Rousers, and Revolutionaries: The Reformers"). Men and women from all over Christendom made their desires for change known. Between 1215 and 1545, there were nine Catholic Church councils whose primary goal it was to bring reform. But those councils accomplished little in the way of significant reform. The abuses and corruption continued mostly unchecked.

> **Protestant Pearls**
>
> Some books are copper, some are silver, and some few are gold; but the Bible alone is like a book of bank notes.
>
> —John Newton (1725–1807), Evangelical hymn and letter writer

The calls for reform became harder and harder for the church to ignore following Martin Luther's historic posting of the 95 Theses in Wittenberg. In fact, those calls just became louder and louder as the sixteenth century progressed. The events that followed that historic day made reform within the Catholic Church a necessity.

Many of the reformers were people who wanted a different kind of religion, one they could feel and experience for themselves. They were the "mystics."

A Mystical Kind of Reform

An important part of the Catholic Reformation was the new emphasis on inner spirituality and a more personal relationship with God. This kind of religion is known as "mysticism," and during the time of the Protestant Reformation, it resulted in many new writings and movements that stressed personal devotion to God.

The medieval Catholics had a problem with mysticism because it suggested that many of the practices of Catholicism weren't necessary for true devotion to God. The mystics downplayed the importance of the sacraments and mediation between God and humans through priests and stressed practical, heartfelt, individual faith in God.

Remember, it was the mystics who centuries before the Protestant Reformation had attempted to make reforms within the Catholic Church. One of the most important of the mystical movements came to be known as the Brethren of the Common Life. One of the best known of the Brethren was Thomas à Kempis, who wrote the classic *The Imitation of Christ*, which emphasized an inward kind of Christianity.

The pre-sixteenth century mystics didn't accomplish much, if anything, in the way of true church reform, but they helped lead the way to later reformation movements, including the Protestant Reformation and the Catholic Reformation that followed.

Spain's Contribution to the Catholic Reformation

Spain wasn't exactly a center of Protestantism, but it contributed much to the Reformation of the Catholic Church. One of its most important contributions to that end was a movement of mystics who worked toward reformation of the old church.

Among the most important of those mystics was Teresa of Avila (1515–1582), a Spanish nun whose given name was Teresa de Cepeda y Ahumada. Teresa, one of ten children in her family, was inspired to become a nun when she read some of the letters of Jerome, and in 1536, at the age of 20, she entered the Carmelite convent in Avila. In her early years at the convent, she became seriously ill, to the point of being partially paralyzed.

Teresa's illness was said to have caused her great doubt and anguish, to the point that she considered ending her career in the con-

> **Protestant Pearls**
>
> God is a tranquil being, and abides in a tranquil eternity. So must thy spirit become a tranquil and clear little pool, wherein the serene light of God can be mirrored.
>
> —Gerhard Tersteegen (1697–1769), German Protestant devotional writer

vent. She left the convent in order to recuperate, and when she returned her prayer life deepened and intensified, and she started having visions of heaven and hell and of the Holy Spirit. She also began to experience a deeply felt sense of God's presence in her life. It was at this time in her life that she had a "reconversion" and began living a life of radical devotion to Christ.

Teresa was troubled by what she learned were the lax spiritual conditions of the Spanish monasteries, and around 1560, she resolved to do something about it. With the support of wealthy friends and family, in 1562 she founded a reformed convent called St. Joseph's of Avila.

People You Should Know

Jacopo Sadoleto (1477–1547) was a member of a group of Roman Catholic reformers called "The Oratory of Divine Love." He served as secretary to popes Leo X and Clement VII. He was not only a reformer, but also a reconciler. He corresponded with Lutheran Philip Melanchthon as well as John Calvin in an attempt to reconcile them with the Catholic Church.

Teresa then received permission from Rome to continue with her reform program, and she traveled all over Spain founding new convents and reforming the ones already in existence. By the time her work was finished, she had established 17 houses called Carmelites of the Strict Observance. The houses were small and poor, but they were strictly disciplined.

Teresa was aided in her work by a devoted follower called John of the Cross (1542–1591), another Spanish Mystic. John joined the Carmelites in Medina in 1563, then studied at the University of Salamanca before being ordained. After he was ordained, Teresa asked him to join her in her reform activities.

It was through the work of Teresa and John that a movement of practical Christianity—meaning Christianity that could be experienced and practiced from within the believer—started among Spanish Catholics. This kind of reform was one of the factors in keeping the Protestant Reformation from taking hold in Spain. After all, people who already had a faith that stressed personal devotion to God had no reason to explore a way of faith that offered essentially the same thing.

Protestant Pearls

Though our Savior's passion is over, his compassion is not.
—William Penn (1644–1718), English Quaker and founder of Pennsylvania

While the mystics of the sixteenth century played a huge role in the Catholic Reformation, they were only part of the story. Another group, one we discussed earlier, was vital to the cause of reform.

The Humanists and What They Did for Reformation

In the fifteenth and sixteenth centuries, there arose in the Catholic Church a group of people known as Christian humanists. Many of these humanists were familiar with the Bible, and they knew that the Catholic Church needed to be reformed from within if it was going to look anything like the church they read about in the book of Acts.

While both the humanists and the mystics favored reform in the church, they differed in how they wanted to do it. The humanists favored what was called a "scholastic" approach, which was based on intellect and learning, while the mystics attempted to reform the church from within the hearts of the people.

Among the influential humanists of this time were John Colet (about 1467–1519), Sir Thomas More (1478–1535), and Desiderius Erasmus of Rotterdam, the Dutchman who is considered one of the greatest humanists ever. Each of these men believed in reformation for the Catholic Church. It has been said that Erasmus, while he opposed the Lutheran Reformation, had helped make the Protestant Reformation almost inevitable with his re-formist writings. To look at some of the writings of Erasmus, it's amazing to think that he was a devout Catholic. He was open about his disapproval of the abuses and excesses of the papacy, and he was with Luther in disapproving of the abuse of indulgences. Among his writings was *The Praise of Folly*, a scathing satire of the papacy that he wrote while staying with More in London. But Erasmus, as well as many of his fellow Christian humanists, accepted the authority of the Catholic Church, and he didn't want to, as the old saying goes, "throw the baby out with the bath water."

Around 1517, there arose in Rome a small group of reformers who called themselves the Oratory of the Divine Love. The group consisted of about 50 men, some of them clergy and some of them laymen, and many, if not most, of them were Christian humanists. They met often for prayer, meditation, and discussion about how the Catholic Church might be reformed. These men were not radicals—in fact one of them, Gian Pietro Carafa, later served the church as Pope Paul IV and others served as cardinals under Pope Paul III. They were committed Catholics who saw the problems in the church and favored reform along the lines of those favored by Erasmus.

As an advocate for reform in the Catholic Church, the most important of these men may have been Gasparo Contarini, who was a layman when the Oratory of Divine Love was formed but who was later named a cardinal under Pope Paul III. Contarini was a Christian humanist, and his ideas about reform reflected those of Erasmus and the others who went before him.

Contarini, it turns out, would play a large role in the reformation of the Catholic Church and of the papacy. In 1536, Paul III, who is considered one of the leading reformer popes, named him to lead an important papal reform commission.

We Can't Go On This Way!

Contarini and the commission pulled no punches when they drew up their formal report on the papacy for Pope Paul III. The report, which was submitted early in 1537, stated that one of the many causes of disorder in the Catholic Church was the secularization, the materialism, and the abuses from the office of pope. The report gave specific examples of all kinds of abuses and immorality on the part of the papacy. It wasn't a pretty picture, but Paul III wanted to take steps to make some reforms.

Paul III faced great opposition on the part of several powerful cardinals, but he took action against some of the problems the reform commission had brought to his attention. Paul made changes in the government of the papacy and he put an end to old papal practices such as simony, or the taking of money in exchange for church appointments.

Unfortunately, Paul didn't make all the changes recommended by the commission. But he took an action that had the potential to lead to even greater reforms when he called the famous Council of Trent.

Paying Off an Old Debt

One of the conditions of Paul's election to the papacy in 1534 was a promise to convoke a council in which reforms could be made and doctrine could be better defined. In 1537 and again in 1538, Paul III attempted to call Catholic Church councils, but they didn't happen.

For more than a century there had been calls for councils for the purpose of reform in the Roman Catholic Church. The Fifth Lateran Council was held under the papacy of Leo X, but it didn't settle any of the issues the German monk Martin Luther had raised. Around 1520, Luther himself had called for a council to reform the church. Lutherans as well as Catholics agreed with Luther, but Pope Clement VII—himself a reformer pope—resisted for fear that such a council would undermine his authority.

But Pope Paul III was finally able to bring together the Council of Trent, the nineteenth ecumenical council of the Roman Catholic Church and perhaps the most important council in the history of the church.

A Long and Often Interrupted Council

The Council of Trent was a series of conferences held by the Roman Catholic Church. Trent was a city in what is now northern Italy. The council met during three separate periods between 1545 and 1563—in 1545–1547, in 1551–1552, and in 1562–1563. The interruptions in the council were due to events in Europe such as wars and serious religious arguments.

The church's purpose in calling this historic council was to clarify its beliefs and to deal with the teachings of the Protestant movements. There was also the hope that there could be some reconciliation between Protestants and Catholics, but there was little chance of that, as the Lutherans refused to attend.

There was disagreement among the key figures in the council over what was to be accomplished. Holy Roman Emperor Charles V wanted a more sweeping reformation of the Catholic Church, and Pope Paul III wanted a definitive statement of the Catholic faith.

Paul III, after intense negotiations with Charles V and with King Francis of France over the location of the meeting, called the council in 1542, but it didn't open until December 13, 1545. The sessions of the Council of Trent were often marred by intense and heated disagreements. One of those arguments was how or whether Protestants and Catholics could be reconciled. The reconciliation camp was led by Christian humanists Reginald Pole and Girolamo Seripando, both of whom were cardinals. On the other side of that debate were those who favored the defeat of all "heresies" against the church, including Gian Pietro Carafa and Ambrogio Catarino.

The Beginning of Something Big

During its first session—which was attended by only four archbishops, twenty bishops, and four heads of monastic orders—the Council of Trent began with a debate over what should be debated and when. Should the council concentrate on doctrinal matters, or should it work on the abuses and excesses of the Catholic Church? After deciding that both issues should be addressed together, the council proceeded to address the pivotal doctrinal issues raised by the Protestants.

At the first session, the council affirmed the Catholic position that Scripture and tradition (meaning the writings of the apostles, the pronouncements of the pope and of the councils, and the ages-old customs of the Catholics) were equally valid when it came to issues of the faith. This amounted to a rejection of the Protestant principle of "Scripture alone." It was also decided that Jerome's *Vulgate* was the authentic text of the Bible. It also decreed that the Catholic Church alone had the authority to interpret Scripture, which was in effect a rejection of the Protestant view of the "priesthood of the believer."

Going Deeper

Tradition, in the context of the Council of Trent, refers to the writings of the apostles, the historical pronouncements of the pope and of the church councils, and the customs of the church that had developed over the centuries. The Council of Trent decided that tradition and the Bible were equally valid when it came to deciding issues of faith and church government. This decision flew in the face of the Protestant position of "Scripture only."

The council rejected the Protestant beliefs on salvation and sin—namely that humans were completely sinful after the fall of man in the Garden of Eden. The Council of Trent decided that Catholics would take the position that humans were cursed with the consequences of the original sin, but not the sin itself.

The first session of the Council of Trent ended in March of 1547. It ended due to political conflicts between Paul III and Charles V. In November of 1549, Paul III, who wanted to make further reforms through the council, died and was replaced by Cardinal Giovanni del Monti, who took the papal chair as Julius III.

In May of 1551, the Council of Trent reconvened.

The Protestants Have Something to Say, but Is Anyone Listening?

The second session of the Council of Trent is known as the session boycotted by the French, who were in political conflicts with Pope Julius III. It was also the session that Protestants, due to the workings of the emperor, were allowed to attend. Charles V had pulled some strings to get the pope to allow Protestants to attend. The pope gave into his demands, but he would not allow them to have a vote in the proceedings.

Although the Protestants were allowed to raise some of their concerns at the second session, nothing really came of their presence. No Lutheran showed up, but Protestant delegations from Brandenberg, Württemburg, and Strasbourg arrived at Trent late in 1551. They left in March of the following year, disillusioned and sure that there was nothing further they could do in Trent to bring about some kind of reconciliation between themselves and the Catholics.

At the second session, the council turned its attention to the sacraments. The council decided that all seven sacraments were essential to salvation and that they were to be administered only by the clergy. Still, many issues were left to be resolved.

The Council of Trent adjourned in April of 1552, and did not reconvene for nearly a decade.

The Council of Trent Ends—Finally

In November of 1560, Pope Pius IV issued a papal bull ordering the third and final gathering for the Council of Trent on Easter of 1561. The debate of the third session began on January 18, 1562. For the Catholics, the third session would be the most productive of the three.

Most of the Catholic beliefs and practices from the Middle Ages were reaffirmed, and several issues that had been debated but decided in the first two sessions were finally resolved. The council reaffirmed the controversial and highly un-Protestant doctrine of transubstantiation as well as the Catholic doctrine of justification by faith and works. If that weren't enough, the final session affirmed the seven sacraments, the celibacy of the clergy, and the existence of purgatory. It also approved of the practice of prayers to the saints and clarified practices surrounding Mass and other Catholic practices.

The council did strike something of a middle ground when it came to the granting of indulgences, the abuse of which brought Luther into the Reformation picture. The council affirmed the use of indulgences, but abolished the position of indulgence sellers and took steps to correct the abuses surrounding the sale of indulgences. The council also passed decrees to establish seminaries to train priests.

On January 16, 1564, Pius IV issued the bull *Benedictus Deus*, which confirmed all the decrees of the Council of Trent and stated that the pope alone had the right to interpret those decrees. The bull was later signed by all the prelates present at the council and by proxies for those who were absent. The bull then became part of Catholic doctrine. In September of the same year, Pius summarized the doctrines from Trent in *The Creed of Pope Pius IV*.

The Protestants were hardly surprised at the outcome of the Council of Trent. Martin Luther himself had looked at the council with skeptical eyes and held that it was going to be impossible to reform something that was irreformable. In the minds of the Protestants, nothing had changed.

The Council of Trent didn't achieve its goal of establishing unity within Christendom, but it succeeded in putting together a definitive statement on Catholic doctrine. It also raised the office of pope from where it had fallen prior to the start of the Reformation and dealt with the Catholic Church's most glaring abuses and doctrinal problems.

While the Catholic Church remained patently Catholic, it did manage to make significant reforms at the Council of Trent. For that reason, the Council of Trent was a key part of the Catholic Reformation.

But there was another part, and it was something that in some ways took the church back to the Dark Ages.

Reformation by Inquisition

Another tool used by the Catholics in the Counter-Reformation was the Inquisition. The Inquisition used in the sixteenth century—in Italy and Spain, especially—was basically the same as the Inquisition used in medieval times. The Netherlands was hit hard by the Inquisition, but Protestantism still remained strong there. But in other parts of Europe—Italy, Spain, Portugal, and Belgium, for example—the Inquisition was effective in quelling some of the effects of the Reformation.

In the early 1540s, Pope Paul III became alarmed at the spread of Protestantism throughout Europe, particularly into his homeland of Italy. In 1542, Paul took the advice of Catholic reformers such as Cardinal Carafa and established the Congregation of the Inquisition, also known as the Roman Inquisition, or the Holy Office. Carafa was one of six cardinals in the Congregation, which had power over the whole church. Carafa and his associates in the Congregation were known as "Inquisitors General."

The Roman Inquisition was similar to the medieval inquisitions, but there were great differences in function and in form. The Roman Inquisition was concerned with maintaining the Catholic orthodoxy.

Carafa had long been critical of efforts on the part of some Catholics to bring Protestantism and Catholicism to some sort of reconciliation. He saw the Protestants as the heretics, and to him, heretics were the worst of the worst criminals. Carafa believed Protestants deserved to be dealt with harshly, and in some areas of Europe, they were. The Roman Inquisitors often used terror, torture, and threats of death to extract confessions and recantations from the heretic Protestants. In the cases where they saw the death penalty as appropriate, the heretic was handed over to the secular authorities for execution. That is because it was against church law for men of the church to kill.

In the first decade or so of the Roman Inquisition, its work was limited mostly to Italy. But in 1555, Cardinal Carafa became Pope Paul IV and he desired a more energetic pursuit of heresy and heretics. In Paul's mind, rank had no privilege when it came to the pursuit of heretics. Even bishops and cardinals were subject to inquisition.

Later popes also saw the Roman Inquisition as a tool for maintaining the purity of the Roman Church. In Italy, Pope Pius V (1566–1572) granted the Inquisition a free hand in dealing with the heretics. In Rome, as well as other cities where Protestantism had gained a foothold, many heretics were tried, condemned, and burned at the stake. In many other countries, heresy was dealt with via excommunication.

Reading and Writing—But Only What the Church Says You Can

Another tactic of the Roman Inquisition was the effort on the part of Pope Paul IV to prohibit the possession and reading of certain books he saw as heretical or encouraging of heresy. In 1559, Paul IV approved and published the first Index of Forbidden Books. It was an extensive list that listed prohibited books, passages, authors, and printers. It wasn't the first time the Catholic Church had used such a list in an attempt to protect its own turf. In the early sixteenth century, several lists of this kind were circulated, along with "encouragements" for Christians not to read them.

At the last session of the Council of Trent, a list of prohibited books and other writings, titled the Tridentine Index, was produced. It was then handed over to Pope Pius IV for enforcement. Incredibly, this list censored almost three-quarters of the books in print in Europe during that time. About the only books that escaped this "blacklist" were the *Vulgate* Bible and Catholic devotionals.

A Revival of Monasteries and Monasticism

In a time when the idea of monasticism (meaning the life of one who serves God through life in a monastery) was under attack from the Protestants, it seems strange that a big part of the Counter-Reformation was the rise of that lifestyle. But indeed the rise of Protestantism was mirrored by a revival of monasticism in Europe. It was a new kind of monasticism in that it stressed reform within the Roman Catholic Church.

These reforming monastic orders of the Catholic Reformation were known for their concern for the social and religious needs of the people. Among those orders were the *Theatines* (founded in 1524), the Sommaschi (1528), *Barnabites* (1530), and the *Capuchins* (1529). Also, reformed convents such as the Ursulines (founded in 1535 by Angela Merici) began to appear.

Among the most important and influential of these new orders was the Society of Jesus (the Jesuits).

You Can Look It Up

The **Theatines** were an order of Catholic reformers founded in 1524 by Gaetano de Thiene (1480–1547). Gaetano was a member of the Oratory of Divine Love. The Theatines lived lives of extreme asceticism and poverty. In 1527, the order set itself up in Venice, and a branch was started in Naples in 1533. Pope Paul IV was influenced by the Theatines.

The **Barnabites**, also known as Clerks Regular of St. Paul, was another order of Catholic reformers. This order was founded in 1530 by Italian noblemen Anton Maria Zaccaria, Barthelemy Ferrari, and Jacopo Morigia. This order had houses in Italy, Germany, Bohemia, and France. This order had a female counterpart, which was founded in 1535 and called the Congregation of the Holy Angels, or Angelice.

The **Capuchins** were an order of reformers who stressed the care of the physical and spiritual needs of the common people. The founder of the Capuchins was Matteo da Bascio (1495–1552), who believed in the vows of poverty such as those taken by Francis of Assisi. He and his followers dressed as Francis dressed, and they donned hoods like the one he wore. They became known as the "little hooded men."

A Different Kind of Reformer

The Society of Jesus was founded by Ignatius of Loyola, who could be seen as the Catholic Reformation's equivalent to Martin Luther. Loyola has been referred to as one of the most important—if not the most important—figures of the Catholic Reformation.

Loyola was born Inigo de Oñez y Loyola around 1491. He was born at his family's ancestral castle in Guipúzcoa. When he was old enough, he entered the military service, where he served until 1521 when he was seriously wounded in battle. During his recovery from his wounds, he read about the lives of the saints of the church, and he was motivated to devote his life to spiritual service. He hung up his sword and spent a year in prayer and meditation at a cave near the Manresa monastery. While there, Loyola fasted, knelt in prayer for seven hours a day, and flagellated himself to the point of endangering his health.

Loyola later described this time as an incredible "mystical" experience during which he had blinding visions of heaven and hell and Christ and Satan. He saw Jesus as "a big round form shining as gold." He later wrote of this time in his life in a book he titled *The Spiritual Exercises*, in which he also emphasized obedience to Christ and to the church at Rome.

Going Deeper _____

The Spiritual Exercises by Ignatius Loyola, first published in its entirety in 1548, was the story of Loyola's spiritual journey as well as a manual for the Society of Jesus, the Jesuits. It consisted of about 160 pages of rules and directions for a deeper spiritual life. It includes an appendix titled Rules for Thinking with the church, which states the position that the Catholic Church is the body of Christ on earth and that believers need to conform themselves to its teaching and instruction.

After that, Loyola made a pilgrimage to Jerusalem, and when he returned, he began his formal education in Barcelona, Alcalá, Salamanca, and Paris. By the time he started his studies, he was thirty-eight years old, broke, and without much of an educational background. He graduated from the University of Paris in 1528.

A Magnificent Seven

Following his graduation, Loyola stayed in Paris for a time, and on August 15, 1534 he and six recruits—Francis Xavier, Peter Faber, Diego Laynez, Alfonso Salmerón, Simon Rodriguez, and Nicholas de Bobadilla—took vows of poverty and celibacy and devoted themselves to service to God. It was this small group that developed in the next few years into the Society of Jesus.

At first, the seven men had vowed to take a missionary journey to Jerusalem to attempt to convert the Muslims there, but war between Venice and the Turks made that impossible. Instead, they stayed in Venice, where they preached, did works of charity, and recruited men for their group. They also vowed to keep themselves completely and unquestioningly at the disposal of the pope.

Over the next few years, this new group of "Jesuits" grew in numbers, and in 1538, some of the members journeyed to Rome, where they sought the approval of Pope Paul III. The group was founded on the principle of absolute obedience to the Pope, and they awaited his confirmation of the order, which came in 1540 with the papal bull *Regimini militantis ecclesiae*. The following year, the Jesuits elected Loyola as the first general of the order.

The Growth and Work of the Jesuits

Although Loyola took an approach of "quality over quantity" when it came to welcoming men into the Jesuits, the order of the Jesuits grew very rapidly. Loyola and the Jesuits welcomed only those whose spirituality reflected his and those who were willing to engage in unquestioned obedience to the pope. Any applicant who had even a hint of bad character or lack of orthodoxy was rejected.

Still, by 1566, just a little over a quarter century after the Jesuit order was founded, there were more than 1,000 Jesuits living and working mainly in Spain, Italy, and Portugal. By this time some were also working in France, Germany, the Low Countries, India, Brazil, and Africa. By the late 1620s, there were more than 13,000 Jesuits.

Loyola had high standards for entrance into the Jesuits because he also had a high purpose for the group. This purpose was reflected in the order's motto *Ad majorem Dei gloriam*, which is Latin for "to the greater glory of God." The mission of the Jesuits was to educate the young, to lead the people back from Protestantism to Catholicism, and to take the Catholic message to new areas of the world.

They were successful in all three endeavors.

Catholic Reformation Through Education

The philosophy of the Jesuits regarding education was a simple but effective one. They believed that if they could get hold of a young mind, they could mold it into a mind that understood and embraced the Catholic faith. One of their sayings regarding the education of the young was, "Give me a child until he is seven, and he will remain a Catholic for the rest of his life."

Protestant Pearls

Rock of Ages, cleft for me, let me hide myself in thee.

—Augustus Montague Toplady (1740–1778), Calvinist clergyman and hymn writer

The Jesuits provided high-quality education, and that helped them to turn the opinion of society in general in favor of the Catholic faith. Through their educational efforts, many people, including the educational elite, had been educated into accepting the Catholic faith. For more than a century and a half, the Jesuits were leaders in European education.

By 1556, the year of the death of Loyola, the order had founded famous educational institutions such as the Roman College and the German College, both of which were subsidized by the pope. By 1640, they had founded more than 500 colleges in Europe. By the mid-1700s, the number of Jesuit-founded universities had risen to more than 650. In addition, the Jesuits had established more than 200 seminaries and houses of study.

Jesuit education during the latter half of the sixteenth century was designed to steady Roman Catholicism against the expansion of Protestantism. For that and other reasons, the Jesuits were key figures in the Counter-Reformation.

What the Jesuits Were Known For: Missions

The Jesuits also stressed missionary work, and they were very successful at spreading Catholicism throughout Europe and beyond. In doing that, they also expanded the size of the Jesuit order itself. Jesuit priests hit the mission field by boarding Spanish and Portuguese ships that sailed in search of both material wealth and places to colonize. These missionary priests traveled to Africa, to Asia, and to the Americas looking for new converts.

The most famous of the Jesuit missionaries was Francis Xavier, one of the original seven Jesuits, who took the Jesuit message to India, Japan, and Indonesia. In 1542, Xavier landed at Goa, the Portuguese settlement in India, and began preaching reforms to the settlers, attacking their corruption, greed, and brutality. From there, he continued his travels before returning to Goa in 1548. After that, he went to Japan, where he worked for two years.

Xavier died in December of 1552 on an island near Canton. During his time as a missionary, he reportedly converted hundreds of thousands of Asians to the Christian faith.

The Jesuits most successful missionary endeavors of the sixteenth century took place in South America, specifically Brazil, where they had the support of a Portuguese king who was a Catholic. In Brazil, they opposed the enslavement of the natives, and they worked at civilizing them and teaching them Christianity.

Though the Jesuits would later suffer through opposition of their own, they were a vital part of what came to be known as the Catholic Reformation.

Where Did This Reformation Leave Us?

At the time when the Catholic Reformation—or Counter-Reformation, if you prefer—began, there was great concern in many quarters of Catholicism that the old church, with all its history and tradition, could be in trouble.

Something had to be done to counter what the Protestants were doing. And when that something was done, Catholicism had re-established itself as a religious force to be dealt with.

The legacy of the Catholic Reformation of the sixteenth century is plain to see in Europe and in other parts of the world. To this day, Italy, France, Ireland, Spain, Portugal, the southern part of Germany, and other areas are mostly Roman Catholic. At the same time, the legacy of the Protestant Reformation can be seen in Europe, as England, Scotland, Switzerland, and the north and east of Germany, Scandinavia, and parts of Eastern Europe have largely remained Protestant.

The Least You Need to Know

- One of the many effects of the Protestant Reformation was the Catholic Reformation, which became a necessity in the sixteenth century.
- The Catholic Reformation was moved forward by the teachings and ideas of both humanists, those who stressed reform on an intellectual basis, and the mystics, who stressed inner spiritual growth.
- One of the most important developments in the Catholic Reformation was the rise of reformed monastic orders and convents, the most important of which was the Jesuits.
- The Catholic Reformation helped assure the survival of the Roman church, particularly in places such as Italy, France, Ireland, Spain, Portugal, and the southern part of Germany.

Chapter 17

Martyrdom: The Darker Side of the Reformation

In This Chapter

- ◆ The Reformation's legacy of persecution and martyrdom
- ◆ Persecutions and martyrdoms in England
- ◆ Opposition to Protestantism in other areas of Europe
- ◆ St. Bartholomew's Day Massacre and its aftermath

There is an aspect of the history of the Christian religion that both Protestants and Catholics would erase if they could. The Protestant Reformation—and the Catholic Reformation that accompanied it—wasn't always pretty. In fact, there were times when it was really, really ugly.

The history the Reformation and the events and developments leading up to it include a long legacy of religious wars, inquisitions, and persecutions. Both Catholics and Protestants had their hand in the violence, and each side had more than its share of martyrs. Many historians say that the various persecutions resulted in literally tens of millions of deaths. Neither side was innocent; Catholics killed Protestants, Protestants killed Catholics, and in some cases, each side killed members of their own faith! If the Catholics were responsible for the deaths of more people—and they were—it is only because they had been around longer. In other words, if the roles had been reversed, it is likely that the Protestants would be the ones with the most blood on their hands.

And all that over a religion headed by a man who was called the Prince of Peace!

How Could This Have Happened?

In hindsight, it's difficult to imagine how so many people would have to die for their religious faith. It's one thing to realize that the first- and second-century Romans, who felt politically, religiously, and socially threatened by this new religious sect, resorted to horrible persecutions. But it is something else to realize that in the wars and persecutions between Catholics and Protestants, people killed one another over differences in their approach to what was basically the same religion.

In our more "enlightened" times, it's probably not possible to fully understand everything that was behind the Christian-on-Christian persecution. But it is helpful to keep in mind that the time and place of the Reformation was radically different from our own. It was a time and place when church and state were in many ways one, a time when whoever controlled the religious climate of a nation controlled everything else.

It was also a time of religious exploration and rediscovery, a time when men and women began questioning where they stood with God and what it took to make themselves acceptable to him. It was a time when there were sharp disagreements over things that had to do with people's eternal souls.

Most of all, it was a time—like now—when fallible, imperfect human beings tried to settle those religious disagreements and disputes, sometimes using force.

Protestant Pearls

The Bible is full of logic, and we must never think of faith as something purely mystical. We do not just sit down in an armchair and expect marvelous things to happen to us. That is not Christian faith. Christian faith is essentially thinking.

—Martyn Lloyd-Jones (1899–1981)

People You Should Know

John Hooper (1495–1555) was an Augustinian monk who converted to Protestantism and then had to flee England after his conversion. He settled in Zurich for a time. He returned to England and became bishop of Gloucester and Worcester. He was one of the martyrs who died under the reign of Queen Mary Tudor, dying at the stake in 1555.

Persecution and Martyrdom of the Pre-Reformation Reformers

In order to have a complete understanding of the place the Protestant Reformation has in the history of Western civilization, it is important to understand the role persecution and martyrdom plays in the different movements that make up the Reformation. Let's start by looking at martyrdom prior to 1517, the year Martin Luther posted his now-famous 95 Theses.

John Wycliffe's Lollards

The beliefs and teachings of John Wycliffe were a lot like those of Luther, Calvin, Zwingli, Knox, and other reformers. He condemned what he saw as the false teachings of the church and also criticized the church's materialism and greed. He condemned the church teachings concerning purgatory, and he also criticized the abuses and false teachings of the church. He criticized the sale of indulgences and denied the doctrine of transubstantiation. He taught that the pope was infallible only when his decrees were based on the Bible and that Christ, not the pope, was the true head of the church.

Of course, in that day and age—nearly a century and a half before the start of Martin Luther's Reformation—taking those kinds of stands could get a body in trouble. That's exactly what happened. In a 1377 edict, Pope Gregory XI condemned 18 of Wycliffe's statements. That same year, the English bishops attempted to put Wycliffe on trial for heresy.

Wycliffe somehow managed to avoid martyrdom—no small feat at the time—and he died a natural death in 1384. But at the Council of Constance in 1415, the church listed 45 "errors" or "heresies" on Wycliffe's part and decreed that his bones be dug up and burned. That act was carried out in 1428, more than four decades after his death.

Immediately following Wycliffe's death the Lollards were a growing, thriving group. But their numbers started decreasing under the reigns of kings Henry IV and Henry V. The Lollards remained a factor until the early years of the reign of Henry VI, when intense and systematized persecutions, including a mass hanging and many burnings at the stake, caused the movement to become more of an underground one.

Wycliffe didn't die a martyr's death. He died in 1384 of a stroke. But this next reformer wasn't able to escape the executioner.

Going Deeper

Lollards Tower was a prison in London where many "Lollards," followers of John Wycliffe, were tortured and murdered for "heresy." The tower still stands as a memorial to the suffering of the Lollards in the early fifteenth century.

Going Deeper

The Council of Constance (1414–1418) was a Catholic Church council called to end the Great Schism, in which three men claimed to be pope at once. From the Protestant perspective, this was one of the saddest of the councils, as it was here that John Huss and later Jerome of Prague were tried and condemned to death for heresy. Also, John Wycliffe, who had been dead three decades, was condemned for heresy. It was decreed that his bones be dug up and burned.

People You Should Know

Thomas Arundel (1353–1414), the Archbishop of Canterbury in the late 1390s and early 1400s, produced in 1408 the *Constitutions of Thomas Arundel,* which made it illegal to read any of John Wycliffe's writings or translations within the province of Canterbury. The constitution also decreed that all copies of Wycliffe's work would be destroyed and that no one was to translate any part of the Scripture into English or any other language. Arundel's constitution provided for death by burning at the stake.

John Huss

The Bohemian reformer John Huss (1374–1415) gained fame as a martyr for his cause. Huss, like John Wycliffe, condemned abuses in the Roman Catholic Church and wanted to see reforms. He believed that all Christians are members of the Church and that Christ, not the pope, is the head of that church. He also believed in the ultimate authority of the Scriptures. In 1410, the pope ordered Huss to stop preaching. Huss refused to stop, and he was condemned at the Council of Constance.

John Huss was barely given a chance to speak at the council. Finally, he dropped to his knees and lifted his hands toward heaven and prayed, "O God I commend my cause to thee." The whole scene had been a setup. Emperor Sigismund had guaranteed Huss safety if he came to Constance to appear before the council. But when the proceedings turned threatening, Sigismund disappeared. Huss stood at the council a condemned man, barely allowed to plead his case to the authorities.

On July 6, 1415, Huss was condemned to death for heresy and turned over to the secular authorities to be executed. They placed a paper crown on his head inscribed with the words, "THIS IS A HERETIC," and led him away to die. As Huss and the procession made their way to the place of execution, Huss saw a bonfire burning in the street. The priests were fueling the fire with his and John Wycliffe's books. Huss, knowing that they could burn the books but couldn't stop the truth contained in them, smiled and continued in the process, reciting the thirtieth Psalm.

"Do not believe that I have taught anything but the truth," he told the crowd as he approached the stake. Huss was tied to the stake, and the executioner stood with his torch. One last chance to recant.

"Renounce your error!" the Duke of Bavaria shouted.

"I have taught no error," Huss calmly replied. "The truths I have taught will be sealed with my blood."

"Burn him!" the Duke commanded, and the executioner obeyed. As the flames made their way upward, Huss used his last breath to sing praises to his God.

John Huss was gone—even his ashes had been cast into the river and carried away—but his followers, the Hussites, and their movement remained. The Bohemian people were angered at his death, and in the following years, that resentment led to the Hussite wars, which cost Bohemia thousands of lives.

Jerome of Prague

Like Huss, Jerome of Prague (1370–1416) was influenced by the writings of John Wycliffe, and also like Huss, those views kept him in trouble with the authorities. In 1407, he met Huss in Prague, where the two joined forces. When Huss was examined at the Council of Constance, he was accompanied by Jerome, who hoped he could help in his friend's defense. As it turned out, there was nothing he could do, and he fled Constance. Later, Jerome was arrested and brought back to Constance and thrown in prison. His legs were placed in stocks that were attached to a long chain. He sat in prison in this miserable condition for several days.

After Huss's execution, a terrified Jerome recanted of his defense of Huss and Wycliffe, but the authorities didn't believe he was sincere, so they kept him in prison. In 1416, nearly a year after Huss's death, he had a chance to recant again, but took that opportunity to publicly withdraw his recantation.

After several days, the council condemned him to die at the stake. Two days after his condemnation, the authorities placed on his head a paper crown with red devils painted on it. When he saw the crown, he said, "Our Lord Jesus Christ, when he suffered death for me, a most miserable sinner, did wear a crown of thorns upon his head; and I for his sake will wear this adorning of derision and blasphemy."

> **Protestant Pearls**
>
> Make it the first morning business of your life to understand some part of the Bible clearly, and make it your daily business to obey it in all that you do understand.
>
> —John Ruskin (1819–1900)

On May 30, 1416, Jerome was led to the stake. Like his friend John Huss, he sang hymns of praise as he was tied up and put to a horrible death.

The Martyrs and the Inquisition

The Lollards, Huss, and Jerome are just a few of the pre-Reformation reformers to die as martyrs for beliefs that were a lot like Luther's and Calvin's. There were many others. For example, the Italian reformer Girolamo Savonarola was hanged and burned in Florence in 1498. The Waldensians, the followers of twelfth-century French reformer Peter Waldo, were persecuted long after his death.

You Can Look It Up

The Inquisition was the Roman Catholic Church's forceful response to the teachings of the pre-Luther reformers in Europe. The inquisitors were appointed by the Catholic Church to travel all over Europe to search for those who opposed the church and what it stood for. They used torture and death threats in order to get confessions, recantations, and the names of other "heretics."

There were many, many thousands of others, some of whom died or suffered torture in the Inquisition. This was the Roman Catholic Church's response to the spread of the "heretical" doctrines of the early reformers among the people. During this time in history, the church appointed inquisitors to go all over Europe to search for those who opposed the church and what it stood for. They used torture and death threats in order to get confessions and recantations, as well as names of other "heretics." Often, the victims were executed at the stake.

The Inquisition was used extensively in Spain and Italy prior to the Reformation, and it continued even after Protestantism had gained legal recognition in Europe. Many thousands of Europeans lost their lives in the Inquisition, and still more lost their property and families.

The pre-Reformation persecutions and the Inquisition made life tough for the reform-minded Christians in medieval Europe. But in a way, just as the early reformers prepared the way for the likes of Luther, Calvin, Zwingli, and Knox, the pre-Reformation martyrs prepared the way for those who would risk or lose their lives for their Protestant faith after 1517.

One of the most famous—and most influential—of the Reformation martyrs is William Tyndale, "The Father of the English Bible."

Tyndale: All This over a Bible Translation!

William Tyndale, who is best remembered for his translation of the Bible into English, also met an early death as a martyr for his beliefs. About the time he began printing his translation of the New Testament, he narrowly escaped arrest and probable death for defying a law against translating the Bible into English.

With the help of some men—many who showed themselves to be very clever smugglers—who sympathized with Tyndale's goal of putting an English translation of the Bible into the hands of everyone who wanted one, Tyndale was able to get his Bible distributed in England. This despite the efforts on the part of the authorities to stop the flow of Bibles into England.

Tyndale continued his work, and was hounded all over Europe. After spending time in Germany, where he worked on publishing his English New Testament, Tyndale settled in Antwerp, where he finished his translation of the Pentateuch (the first five books of the Old Testament) and printed it in 1530. About this time, he had planned to translate the remainder of the Old Testament into English.

Protestant Pearls

Men never do evil so completely and cheerfully as when they do it from religious conviction.

—Blaise Pascal (1623–1662), French scientist and man of letters

But William Tyndale would never get the chance to finish his project.

William Tyndale's martyrdom was a story of betrayal on the part of a fellow Englishman named Henry Philips, who in 1535 befriended the great Bible translator only to arrange his arrest by the authorities. All of this was at the instruction of the pope. Philips was to have dinner with Tyndale one night, and when they entered the place where they were to dine, Philips invited Tyndale to go ahead of him. When they entered the door, Philips gave the sign, and two officers arrested Tyndale and took him to a dark prison in the castle of Vilvorde, near Brussels.

While in prison, Tyndale is said to have talked to the castle guards about his faith, and they later said that if Tyndale wasn't a good Christian man, then they didn't know anyone who was. Tyndale is said to have converted his keeper, as well as the keeper's daughter and other members of his family.

During that time, Tyndale wrote to a friend a defense of his English Bible translation, which many Catholic authorities said was full of heresies and errors: "I call God to record against the day we shall appear before our Lord Jesus, that I never altered one syllable of God's Word against my conscience, nor would do this day, if all that is in earth, whether it be honor, pleasure, or riches, might be given me."

Tyndale was offered legal counsel, which he declined, for he intended to defend himself against the charges. Day after day he waited, with no trial scheduled. Tyndale knew of his fate, and it finally came on October 6, 1536. He was taken to the town of Vilvorde, where he was hanged and his body burned. He last words weren't words of condemnation for his accusers. He simply cried out in a loud voice, "Lord, open the King of England's eyes."

Tyndale never finished translating the entire Bible into English, but his work paved the way for the acceptance of an English translation of the Bible. Others picked up where he left off, and in time the Bible became readily available in English.

Throughout the first half of the sixteenth century, there would be times of persecutions and times of peace for English Protestants. But it was during the reign of Queen Mary I that English Protestantism endured a horror show.

Queen Mary I and Her Martyrs

The reign of Queen Mary I in England was marked by horrible and relentless persecutions of Protestants. Mary Tudor, also known as "Bloody Mary," came to power following the reign of Henry VIII, who had taken steps to make England a Protestant nation under the Anglican Church, and Henry's son Edward VI. Mary's first goal was to reconvert England to Catholicism, and she pursued that goal with a vengeance.

There was great resistance on the part of the Protestants to Mary's attempts to restore England to Catholicism, and she responded to those people with violence. From 1555 to 1558, almost 300 Protestants—men and women, clergy and laity—were put to death for their faith.

The Fate of Thomas Cranmer and Friends

The persecutions under Mary Tudor began with the deaths of five Anglican bishops, all of whom were replaced by Catholics. The most famous of these "heretics" to meet with death at the hands of Mary Tudor were Thomas Cranmer and his associates Nicholas Ridley and Hugh Latimer.

On October 16, 1555, Ridley and Latimer were taken to be executed. When they came to the site of the execution, Ridley embraced Latimer and said, "Be of good heart, brother, for God will either assuage the fury of the flame, or else strengthen us to abide it." Then, they knelt by the stakes, prayed together and had a short private conversation.

The two men were tied to the stake, and the fire was lit. As the flames made their way up, Latimer offered Ridley one final word of encouragement. "Be of good cheer, Ridley; and play the man," he said. "We shall this day, by God's grace, light up such a candle in England, as I trust, will never be put out."

As Ridley saw that the fire was about to take him, he cried out loudly, "Lord, Lord, receive my spirit." On the other side of the stake, Latimer cried out equally loudly, "O Father of heaven, receive my soul!"

Thomas Cranmer's Double Reversal

Thomas Cranmer knew the danger he faced if he stayed in England following the ascension to the throne of Queen Mary I on October 1, 1553. He was aware of an exodus from England on the part of Protestants. Cranmer knew that Mary wanted to return England from the Anglicanism of the previous English monarchs to Catholicism, and that she would likely resort to violence to accomplish that goal. He also knew that Mary had some personal scores to settle with him, because he had opposed her taking the throne.

Thomas Cranmer sent his family out of England, but stayed behind himself. In short order, he was arrested and tried for treason, then heresy. He was sentenced to death but told he would be allowed to live if he would recant of his Protestantism. He signed six recantations, each stronger than the one before.

One of Cranmer's recantations read,

> I, Thomas Cranmer … do renounce, abhor, and detest all manner of heresies and errors of Luther and Zwingli, and all other teachings which are contrary to sound and true doctrine. And I believe most constantly in my heart, and with my mouth I confess one holy and Catholic Church visible, without which there is no salvation; and therefore I acknowledge the Bishop of Rome to be supreme head on earth, whom I acknowledge to be the highest bishop and pope, and Christ's vicar, unto whom all Christian people ought to be subject. … To conclude, as I submit myself to the Catholic Church of Christ, and to the supreme head thereof, so I submit myself unto the most excellent majesties of Philip and Mary, king and queen of this realm of England, etc., and to all other their laws and ordinances, being ready always as a faithful subject ever to obey them. And God is my witness, that I have not done this for favor or fear of any person, but willingly and of mine own conscience, as to the instruction of others.

Cranmer had said the things Mary and the Catholic Church wanted to hear, but that wasn't going to save his life. In March of 1556, his final recantation was placed before Queen Mary. It turned out that the deal offered him was a sham, and that Mary, who sought revenge for his support of Lady Jane Gray, intended to have him put to a violent death no matter what he said. Wanting not just to end Cranmer's life but to humiliate him, Mary ordered both his death and the publication of the recantations.

A Time of Reversal

Cranmer, now a man not only sentenced to die but tormented by his own conscience for denying what he believed deeply was the truth, knew he had nothing to lose. In one final effort to humiliate Cranmer, he was taken to St. Mary's Church where he was to preach his last sermon and publicly renounce his faith. But he did nothing of the sort. He begged the congregation to forgive him for recanting, then he proceeded to retract every word of the recantations:

> … now I come to the great thing which so much troubleth my conscience, more than any thing that ever I did or said in my whole life, and that is the setting abroad of a writing contrary to the truth, which now here I renounce and refuse, as things written with my hand contrary to the truth which I thought in my heart, and written for fear of death, and to save my life, if it might be; and that is, all such bills or papers which I have written or signed with my hand since my degradation, wherein I have written many things untrue. And forasmuch as my hand hath offended, writing contrary to my heart, therefore my hand shall first be punished; for when I come to the fire it shall first be burned.

Cranmer finished his recantation-of-a-recantation with these words: "And as for the Pope, I refuse him as Christ's enemy, and antichrist, with all his false doctrine." The congregation was stunned at Cranmer's reversal, and with the order issued to "Lead the heretic away," Cranmer was dragged from the church to the same place where Latimer and Ridley had been executed.

Cranmer was stripped to his undergarments, then he knelt at the stake to pray. When he got up to prepare himself for the fire, two friars tried to talk him into recanting again, but he refused. He said his good-byes, then was chained to the stake. The fire was lit, and as the flames made their way up, Cranmer thrust his right hand—the one he had used to write his recantation—down into the fire and held it there until it was burned to a crisp. He looked toward heaven, repeating the words "this unworthy right hand." As the flames engulfed him, Cranmer's dying words were "Lord Jesus, receive my spirit."

Mary's persecutions of the Protestants helped doom her reign. The English people equated Roman Catholicism with the harm they saw being done to many of the country's religious leaders, and for that reason they were drawn to Protestantism. Mary Tudor left the throne a failure who was hated by her own people. She died in November 17, 1558, a bitter, defeated woman.

Mary was gone forever, but the Protestantism that Cranmer, Latimer, and Ridley died for lived on.

Next, let's take a look at a different kind of religious persecution, a kind where Protestants persecute Protestants.

Anabaptists: Paying the Price for a Different Kind of Reformation

The orthodox Protestants' early dealings with a group called the Anabaptists have been called one of the saddest moments in the history of the Protestant movement. Certainly, it can be seen as a blot on the record of the great Swiss reformer Ulrich Zwingli.

From the very beginning, the Anabaptists suffered persecution from all sides: from the Catholics because they opposed the organized rule from Rome, from the Protestants because they opposed the church governments proposed in Protestantism, and from the secular authorities because they were seen as threats to the stability of the government and society.

The persecutions of the Anabaptists started early in their movement. In January of 1525, some of the leaders of the early Anabaptist movement faced off with Swiss reformer Ulrich Zwingli in a public disputation in Zürich, Switzerland. The two sides debated the issue of infant baptism, which Zwingli favored and the Anabaptists opposed. The results of the disputation were that the city council ordered all parents to have their infants baptized within eight days or face expulsion from the city.

The Anabaptists responded peacefully but defiantly, and the movement quickly spread in Zürich and beyond. That winter, the ringleaders of the Anabaptists were arrested and thrown into a Zürich prison. Others followed. The response of Zwingli and the Zürich city council to the Anabaptists grew harsher and harsher. The council passed a decree making just listening to Anabaptist preaching punishable by death.

With the approval of Zwingli, Felix Manz, one of the first of the Anabaptist leaders, was sentenced to death, then executed by drowning on January 5, 1526. Manz's death was just the beginning. From that time on, Anabaptists all over Europe—in Switzerland, southern Germany, Thuringia, the Austrian lands, and the Low Countries—were hunted down and put to death with numbing cruelty. Men and women alike met their deaths by drowning, burnings, hangings, and other methods. Some were even buried alive. By 1530, no fewer than 2,000 Anabaptists had been martyred by Catholic and Protestant persecutors, and the persecutions continued till about 1560.

All of this persecution was done against a people who for the most part were pacifistic in their beliefs, meaning that they would not fight back, no matter how cruelly they were treated. Part of the reason for the persecution was a fear on the part of Catholics and Protestants of a religious movement that was spreading all over Europe. Zwingli himself predicted that the Protestant struggle with the Catholics was "but child's play" compared with what was ahead if the Anabaptist movement wasn't stopped. As it turns out, the core beliefs of the Anabaptists rendered this fear groundless.

This Anabaptist cause was hurt by what had happened, but the movement was far from defeated. The Anabaptists continued their preaching and teaching, and their movement expanded all over Europe.

While the persecution on the Anabaptists cost the movement many thousands of lives, it didn't stop the movement. In fact, the Anabaptists seemed fearless in the face of horrible torture and death, and even seemed to see it as part of their calling as those who lived "true Christian lives." For a fact, the more tortures and killings that took place, the greater following the movement earned. One official who had overseen the execution of hundreds of Anabaptists was heard to say, "What shall I do? The more I kill, the greater becomes their number!"

In time, the Anabaptists would be tolerated, even accepted, in Europe and beyond. The Anabaptist movement produced, or at least influenced, some new sects of Christianity—the Hutterites, the Mennonites, the Amish, the Quakers—many of which played a huge part in bringing the Christian religion to the New World and to the United States and Canada specifically.

Martyrdom in the "Low Countries"

Protestantism made a successful entry in the Low Countries, and the Pope was not happy about it. Emperor Charles V also strongly opposed the rise of Lutheranism in that part of the world, as did Charles's successor as king of Spain, King Phillip II. It was the Spanish Duke of Alva who conducted a campaign of terror against the Protestant movement that claimed the lives of up to 100,000 people.

Clergy and laypeople alike were martyred for their Protestant faith, and many of them met with horrible deaths.

Foxe's Book of Martyrs gives accounts of victims including:

◆ A Protestant widow who refused to "convert" was put to death for her faith. At the insistence of a friend, she was strangled rather than burned at the stake.

◆ A Protestant clergyman was tied up in a sack and thrown into a river to drown.

◆ A Protestant minister who was ordered to attend the beheading of 16 other Protestants and, being a chaplain himself, was beheaded after the 16 had met their fate.

◆ A well-known and well-liked Protestant in the city of Antwerp was put to death by drowning in a large tub in prison when the authorities decided that executing him publicly would cause public unrest. The execution was botched when the man struggled to keep his head above water and the executioner had to stab him to death.

It seems that almost every nation touched by the Protestant Reformation had its legacy of horror and persecution. England had Mary Tudor, Switzerland had the persecution of the Anabaptists, and the Low Countries had their persecutions started by the Duke of Alva.

France had its legacy of terror against Protestants, too. It was a horrible day in 1572 that led to the deaths of thousands of unarmed Calvinists.

The Tragedy on St. Bartholomew's Day

Perhaps the most horrifying day of martyrdom of Protestants was the St. Bartholomew's Day Massacre. This horrible event started in Paris on the morning of August 24, 1572, and the violence spread from Paris to the outlying provinces.

The victims were the Protestants, specifically *Huguenots*, who were French followers of John Calvin. As it had in most parts of Europe, the Protestant Reformation had made its way to France, where it quickly spread and became the faith of a third of the French population by the middle of the sixteenth century. Around that time, however, Catholic/Protestant conflict also appeared on the scene.

You Can Look It Up

Huguenots were French Protestants of Calvinist persuasion. Protestantism appeared in France in the early 1520s, but it met with great persecution and had little support. The Huguenots first appeared on the scene in the late 1550s, when a group of Calvinists formed a congregation in Paris. The Huguenots enjoyed times of protection and endured times of persecution in Paris, but they increased in number. They were violently opposed in 1572 in the St. Bartholomew's Day Massacre, when up to 100,000 of them were slaughtered within a few days.

Times of Conflict, Times of Peace

The French Roman Catholics and Huguenots fought bitterly throughout the mid-1500s. The conflict grew worse because the Huguenot movement had attracted so many followers that the Catholics worried that they might take over the French government, which was Catholic at the time.

The Huguenots, on the other hand, were becoming a political force in France. In 1559, the first French national Calvinist synod was held, and that same year a Presbyterian Church opened. A large number of the French nobility turned from Catholicism to Calvinism, and that only made the situation more dangerous. In 1562, civil war broke out. During this period, the Huguenots were no longer satisfied with toleration for their Protestantism, but wanted to wipe out the "papists and idolaters" of Catholicism. But in 1570, the Peace of Saint Germain gave the Huguenots amnesty and freedom of religion and other rights. This treaty also allowed the Huguenots to have four fortified cities and restored Catholicism in areas where the Huguenots had suppressed it.

It appeared that there would be peace in France, at least for a while. Still, the French Catholics feared the potential power of a rapidly growing Huguenot movement, and plans were made to do something about that threat.

In an attempt to strengthen the grip of royal power, Catherine de Médicis, the mother of King Charles IX and his regent (he was just a child when he ascended to the throne), and Duke Henry of Guise arranged for the assassination of Gaspard de Coligny, one of the leaders of the Huguenots. Coligny was one of Charles's ministers, and Catherine and Henry of Guise both resented Coligny's influence on Henry. The first attempt on his life failed, and when word of the assassination attempt went public, there was great tension in the city of Paris.

But that tension was nothing compared with what was about to take place.

A Bad Time and Place to Be a Huguenot

Huguenots had flocked to Paris from around France to celebrate the marriage of another of their leaders, Henry of Navarre (later King Henry IV of France), to King Charles's sister, Margaret of Valois. The wedding took place on August 18, 1572 outside the Cathedral of Notre Dame.

Less than a week later, Paris was the sight of a bloodbath.

There is some controversy over whether the events on St. Bartholomew's Day of 1572 were planned as a citywide—then nationwide—massacre. The events of that day may have been orchestrated by the enemies of Coligny and the Huguenots, but they may have been a case of one act of assassination that got out of hand.

A mob of men, led by Henry of Guise, set out to find and kill Coligny. The Huguenot leader heard the commotion outside, and as the noise intensified—he could hear the gunfire—he arose and began to pray. But he still felt a sense of assurance for his own safety. After all, he was one of the king's advisers, one in good standing, and it was only a matter of time before the commotion was stopped and order was restored.

Coligny soon realized that he was the target of the mob, and that they intended to kill him. He sent his associates and assistants away, and prepared himself for what was to come. The mob murdered the guard at the door and burst through the door of his chamber, swords drawn.

"Are you Coligny?" one of the mob demanded.

"Yes, I am he," Coligny fearlessly replied. "But you, young man, respect these white hairs. What is it you would do? You cannot shorten by many days this life of mine." With that, one of the murderers killed Coligny with his sword, then disfigured his body to a point that it was barely recognizable.

Coligny's body was taken from his quarters and thrown out in the street, where it was further mutilated, hanged, burned, and thrown into the river. Paris was filled with rumors of what was happening and why, and the militia and the general population of France got in on the murderous rampage.

The St. Bartholomew's Day Massacre was underway. Men, women, and children—unarmed and taken completely by surprise—were slaughtered and their bodies left in the streets. The killings spread from Paris to other areas of France—the provinces of Rouen, Lyons, Bourges, Orleans, and Bourdeaux—all were the sites of killings of Huguenots. The killings went on for three days, and the city councilors and the king were powerless to stop them.

A Time of Unspeakable Horror

It still isn't known for sure just how many people died in this massacre. Estimates range from 2,000 to 3,000 in Paris and between 70,000 and 100,000 and more nationwide. Many Huguenots who survived the massacre were imprisoned or taken as slaves. Still others were able to escape to countries such as Germany, Switzerland, England, Ireland, and, later, America.

Protestant Pearls

Believe God's word and power more than you believe your own feelings and experiences.

—Samuel Rutherford (1600–1661), Scottish minister and theologian

One eyewitness to the horror gave this account:

> Suddenly—and without warning—the devilish work commenced. Beginning at Paris, the French soldiers and the Roman Catholic clergy fell upon the *unarmed* people, and blood flowed like a river throughout the entire country. Men, women, and children fell in heaps before the mobs and the bloodthirsty troops. … In one week, almost 100,000 Protestants perished. The rivers of France were so filled with corpses that for many months no fish were eaten. In the valley of the Loire, wolves came down from the hills to feed upon the decaying bodies of Frenchmen. The list of massacres was as endless as the list of the dead!

The news of the massacre spread throughout Europe and was greeted with a lukewarm response among everyone but the Protestants, who were horrified at what had happened. This event was the beginning of a new hatred between Protestants and Catholics in that part of Europe, and a series of new religious wars resulted.

The St. Bartholomew's Day Massacre devastated the Huguenot leadership in France, but it didn't stop the movement. In time, new leadership arose in France and in the areas outside France where Huguenot refugees settled.

In the days following the massacre, there were rumors of celebrations in Rome and throughout the Catholic world over the deaths of the "heretics" in France. There is debate among historians as to exactly how the Catholic Church responded to the tragedy in Paris, just as there is debate as to the actual causes of the massacre.

However, historians are united in agreeing that the St. Bartholomew's Day Massacre was one of the darkest moments in the history of Christendom and of the Reformation.

It Has to Stop Somewhere!

In time, the Catholics and Protestants would find a way to live together in relative peace. There would still be incidences of violence from time to time, but the days when thousands died in a single incident were over.

When the religious wars and the Christian-on-Christian persecutions ended, when there was finally peace between Protestants and Catholics, the faith had not only survived but continued to thrive and grow and expand. Even today, many Christians don't like to think about that part of their religious heritage. But it is that part of the heritage that stands as a testament to the strength and perseverance of the Christian faith, even in the hands of fallen humanity.

The Least You Need to Know

◆ Martyrdom and persecution have been a part of the Christian religion from the very beginning.

◆ The persecutions of reformers started long before the arrival of Martin Luther. Reformers like John Huss and Jerome of Prague met with martyrdom.

◆ The persecutions of the radical Protestant movement called the Anabaptists were inflicted largely by fellow Protestants.

◆ The St. Bartholomew's Day Massacre was one of the darkest moments in the history of the Protestant Reformation.

Chapter 18

Wars, Rumors of Wars, Then a Lasting Religious Peace

In This Chapter

- ◆ The business left unfinished by the Peace of Augsburg
- ◆ Continued tension between Catholics and Protestants in Europe
- ◆ The Thirty Years' War—a war of religion, then politics—and its aftermath
- ◆ The final religious settlement: the Peace of Westphalia

You can't have gotten this far in the book without realizing that Europe was a place of tremendous religious and political conflict following the beginning of the Protestant Reformation in 1517. For the rest of the sixteenth century and into the seventeenth, Protestantism—in its many forms, including Lutheranism and Calvinism—struggled to establish and sustain itself. On the other hand, Catholicism tried to hang on to its power and influence in the face of the spreading Protestant threat.

Sadly, the results of this struggle were violent. Literally millions of Europeans died in the various religious wars that accompanied the Protestant Reformation and Catholic Reformation. The Peasants' Revolt (1524–1525), the Kappel Wars (1529–1531), and the Schmalkaldic War (1546–1547) were some of the major military conflicts in the first four decades of Protestantism.

In order to understand the importance of these events—as well as the final peace treaty that would come in the seventeenth century—in the bigger picture of the Protestant Reformation, we need to review some of the conflicts, armed and otherwise.

The End of Protestantism As We Know It?

The Schmalkaldic War was a decisive victory for the Catholic forces of the Holy Roman Empire. The Schmalkaldic League, which was formed as a defensive alliance against rising Catholic aggression in the empire, had superior numbers in the conflict, but were disorganized and badly led and fell with finality on April 24, 1547 at the Battle of Mühlberg.

Protestant Pearls

Some ministers would make good martyrs. They are so dry, they would burn well.

—Charles Haddon Spurgeon (1834–1892), Baptist preacher

On paper, the defeat of the Schmalkaldic League looked like the end of the Lutheran movement in the empire. But by that time, Lutheranism had established itself for good in Germany. Many of the Lutheran territories of Germany that had been conquered flatly refused to reconvert to Catholicism. In short, nothing had been permanently decided in the Schmalkaldic War. For several years, civil war continued to rage on and off between the Lutherans and the Catholics in the empire.

Can't We All Just Get Along?

Holy Roman Emperor Charles V, who wanted more than anything to unite the empire under one religion—Catholicism—attempted to make a final peace between the two sides with the 1548 Interim of Augsburg. This interim, though it made some concessions to both sides in the conflict, didn't settle anything. Catholics didn't like it because they thought it gave the Protestants too much, and Protestants didn't like it because it maintained Catholic rule in the empire.

The Augsburg Interim couldn't keep the peace between the Protestants and Catholics for long. Civil wars continued for the better part of another decade. Finally, in 1555, both sides came to the table at the Diet of Augsburg, where the Peace of Augsburg, another temporary settlement between the warring factions, was reached.

It Isn't Perfect, but at Least It's Peace!

The Peace of Augsburg was more or less an edict of toleration of Lutheranism. It held that the emperor would no longer interfere in the religious affairs of the various states and principalities of the empire. It held that each prince was free to choose between Lutheranism or Roman Catholicism for his territory. Some of the principalities (those in southern Germany) remained loyal to Rome and some (mainly those in the north) continued as Lutheran states.

The Peace of Augsburg gave Germany a much-needed reprieve from years and years of religious war. But it is fair to say that it was at best an uneasy peace. The bitterness, tension, anger, and distrust continued between the Lutheran north and the Catholic south. The Catholics believed that the Lutherans had designs on their territories, and the Lutherans believed it was only a matter of time before they and their movement faced annihilation.

And there was something to what both sides believed during this time, too. There was genuine animosity and distrust, as both sides would have loved more than anything to see the other eliminated—or at least their system of beliefs.

Protestant Pearls

I used to ask God to help me. Then I asked if I might help him. I ended up by asking him to do his work through me.

—James Hudson Taylor (1832–1905), Medical missionary and founder of the China Inland Mission

A Hamstrung Peace from the Beginning

In hindsight, it's not hard to see why the Peace of Augsburg didn't settle anything with finality. To start with, it was received in a lukewarm fashion. It wasn't backed by or even attended by many of the key players in the conflict. Emperor Charles V wasn't there, and neither was Pope Paul IV. And most of the German princes and electors, though they obviously had a huge stake in what was going on in Augsburg, turned up their noses at the 1555 diet.

At best, the Peace of Augsburg was a stopgap measure. It still left many conflicts between Catholics and Lutherans unresolved, and it benefited only the Catholics and the Lutherans. No other reformation movement was recognized. The Zwinglians, Calvinists, and others of the "reformed" persuasion were left to fend for themselves.

In the long run, that lack of inclusion would prove to be at least part of the undoing of the Peace of Augsburg.

A Chance for Unity Within Protestantism

Some church historians believe that the developments of the mid-1550s might have resulted in a more permanent religious peace in Europe had there been unity within Protestantism. Sadly, however, there were great divisions between Lutherans and Calvinists, and that led to a more vulnerable Protestantism throughout Europe.

Remember, Emperor Charles V wanted a religiously united Europe, and he wanted it united under Catholicism. If not for a series of wars—for which he needed the help of the Protestant territories in the empire—and political developments, Charles would likely have used force against the Protestants in accomplishing that goal of unity.

But in 1529, the Holy Roman Empire was finally at peace with its neighbors, and Charles V had an opportunity to move against the Protestants. Some of them saw that they were living in a threatening situation, and they called for unity in the Protestant world. One of those people, Philip of Hesse, arranged a meeting between the two key players in that situation—German reformer Martin Luther and Swiss reformer Ulrich Zwingli. That meeting was the Marburg Colloquy of October 1529.

An enthusiastic and encouraged Zwingli and his associates met a reluctant Martin Luther and his associate and right-hand man Philip Melanchthon at the Marburg Colloquy, where many Protestants hoped for the establishment of some kind of unity. They came close, too. Of the 15 articles for debate at the Colloquy, Zwingli and Luther agreed on 14. The sticking point had to do with their differences over the Lord's Supper.

Both reformers held firm to their positions, and when the Marburg Colloquy was over, nothing was settled, and Protestants remained divided between the Lutherans of Martin Luther and the Reformed Protestantism of Ulrich Zwingli. In the end, the Marburg Colloquy was a blown opportunity for Protestants to come together in a united front against the Catholic threat. And with the Calvinists and Zwinglians—not to mention the persecuted Anabaptists—in a state of disunion, the situation remained a dangerous one for the Protestants clear into the early part of the seventeenth century.

The division within Protestantism made for an uncomfortable situation, and it was made worse by changes in Catholicism.

Catholic/Protestant Conflict in France

While the different Protestant movements moved forward independently of one another, the Catholic Reformation—also known as the Counter-Reformation—strengthened and united the Catholics, setting the stage not only for the conflicts in Germany between 1547–1555, but also for conflict in France between the French Calvinists (Huguenots) and the Roman Catholics.

The French Roman Catholics and Huguenots fought bitterly throughout the mid-1500s. The Catholics were threatened by the growth of this aggressive Protestant movement, which wanted to wipe out the "papists and idolaters" of Catholicism. The Huguenots grew in power and influence, and violent conflict ensued.

In 1562, civil war broke out, but it was quieted for a time by the 1570 Peace of Saint Germain, which gave the Huguenots amnesty and freedom of religion and other rights. That peace was broken in 1572 when Catholics attempted to murder Huguenot leaders, then engaged in the infamous St. Bartholomew's Day Massacre (see Chapter 17, "Martyrdom: The Darker Side of the Reformation"). In time, all this violence brought the nation of France to a point of complete exhaustion, and the result was the 1598 Edict of Nantes, which granted the Huguenots various religious freedoms, the right to legal protection and to hold public office, and other political rights. In addition, the Huguenots received political control of parts of France.

> **Protestant Pearls**
>
> For the attainment of divine knowledge, we are directed to combine a dependence on God's Spirit with our own researches. Let us, then, not presume to separate what God has thus united.
>
> —Charles Simeon (1759–1836), Evangelical clergyman

The Edict of Nantes didn't satisfy the extreme fringes of the Huguenot and Catholic camps, but it succeeded in keeping the peace in France into the 1680s, when King Louis XIV revoked it. Many of the Huguenots then left France for Geneva, Germany, England, and even America—places where by that time, they could practice their brand of Protestantism in relative safety and security.

While France enjoyed relative religious peace during most of the 1600s, Germany suffered through a great deal of that time as the prime battleground of one of the worst conflicts in European history.

The Thirty Years' War: The Mother of All Religious Conflicts

The last of the religious wars—and it should be kept in mind that all these wars had very political overtones—was the Thirty Years' War, which had been broken down into four historic periods: the Bohemian period (1618–1623), the Danish period (1623–1629), the Swedish period (1630–1635), and the French period (1635–1648). Different historians label the four periods of the Thirty Years' War differently, and there are some differences in the actual dates as well.

In a nutshell, the Thirty Years' War can be seen as a three-decade-long conflict with German Protestant princes and allied foreign powers—France, Sweden, Denmark, England, and the United Provinces—facing off against the Holy Roman Empire and the German Catholic princes. When the war began in 1618, it was a decidedly religious conflict. But during its final thirteen-year period, religion was only a minor point.

When and Where the Whole Thing Started

Catholic/Protestant tensions were already high at the beginning of the seventeenth century. Under the reign of Holy Roman Emperor Rudolph II, violence against Protestants had become widespread in Germany. Churches there were destroyed and restrictions were placed on Protestant worship. In general, it was an attempt on the part of the emperor and his people to reestablish Roman Catholic power in places where Protestants had ruled before. In 1608, the Evangelical Union, a defensive alliance of Protestants, was formed, and it was followed by the formation in 1609 of a similar organization for Roman Catholics.

The tension ran thick in Germany at that time. It was only a matter of time before another round of religious violence broke out. In 1617, Holy Roman Emperor Matthias, a devout Catholic, knew his reign was coming to an end, and he wanted to make sure that a Catholic succeeded him to the throne, so he had the zealously Catholic Ferdinand II placed on the throne in a largely Protestant Bohemia. From there, Ferdinand would take the throne as Holy Roman Emperor. Of course, the Bohemians found the appointment of Ferdinand as their king offensive, and they protested.

> **Going Deeper**
>
> The Battle of Pilsen was fought on November 1, 1618. In response on the part of the Bohemian Protestants called for help from Ferdinand of Austria. An army of 20,000 soldiers crossed the Bohemian border and marched on the city of Pilsen, which was a Catholic stronghold about 50 miles southwest of Prague. The army was under the command of Count Ernst von Mansfeld. It took 15 hours of fighting before Mansfeld's men captured the city.

By 1618, anti-Protestant violence had become rampant in Bohemia, and some Bohemian Protestants appealed to Ferdinand to intervene on their behalf. Ferdinand did nothing to help the Protestants, and tensions only grew worse.

Finally, on May 23, members of the Evangelical Union, led by a radical Protestant noble by the name of Heinrich von Thurn, took matters into their own hands. The Prague Protestants stormed the royal palace, and after an exchange of bitter words, they threw two of Ferdinand's ministers and their secretary out a window. The ministers, who fell 50 feet to the palace moat, survived the fall and escaped, but they were badly injured. This incident came to be known as the *Defenestration of Prague*, and it preceded a major uprising by the Protestants in Bohemia, again led by Heinrich von Thurn. The Protestant uprising quickly spread, and soon what had been an uprising escalated into the start of the Thirty Years' War.

You Can Look It Up

The **Defenestration of Prague** is seen as the spark that started the fire of the Thirty Years' War. In this incident, Protestants, led by Heinrich von Thurn, a Protestant nobleman, stormed the royal castle in Prague in Bohemia, then threw two of Holy Roman Emperor Matthias's ministers out a window and into the castle moat. Both ministers survived the fall. This incident was in response to Matthias's lack of action over anti-Protestant violence.

The first part of the Thirty Years' War went very badly for the Protestants. In November of 1620, the Catholics, led by Johannes von Tilly, quickly routed the Protestant Bohemians, who were led by the newly crowned Bohemian King Frederick V and Thurn, at the Battle of White Mountain (or Battle of White Hill). By the spring of the following year, the Protestant uprising had been completely suppressed throughout Bohemia. That was followed by a period of ruthless persecution in which many of the Protestant leaders were tried and executed.

People You Should Know

Johannes von Tilly (1559–1632) was a commander for the Catholic League during the Thirty Years' War. Tilly was a devout Catholic who did all he could to restore the influence of Catholicism in central Europe. Tilly won important victories over the Bohemians and the Danes early in the war. In 1631, Tilly was defeated at the Battle of Breitenfeld by Swedish King Gustavus Adolphus. He then went to work raising a new army to oppose the advancing Protestants.

The Second Leg of the Thirty Years' War: The Danish Period

In the Danish period of the Thirty Years' War, the German Protestant states, many of them the victims of violence, sought out and received assistance against the Catholics. In the spring of 1625, Christian IV, the King of Norway and Denmark, put together a large army and invaded the German territory of Saxony. Meanwhile, the Duke of Fiedland, Albrecht von Wallenstein, put together an army of his own to fight on behalf of Ferdinand II, who had taken the seat of Holy Roman Emperor after the death of Matthias in March of 1619. Unfortunately for the Protestant cause, Christian's army was poorly trained and poorly led, and by spring of 1629 the Danish army had been defeated. Christian was forced to accept the Peace of Lübeck in May 22 of that year. Under this treaty, Christian was to renounce all rights to German bishoprics (dioceses) and pledge to stay out of German politics.

Christian was also forced to accept the conditions of the Edict of Restitution, which enforced the Peace of Augsburg with a strictly Catholic spin. That included the exclusion of Calvinists from the provisions of the edict. Had it been literally and fully enforced, it would have effectively ended Protestantism in Germany.

Protestantism did survive this part of the Thirty Years' War, and things took a decidedly positive turn during the next stage of the war.

People You Should Know

Armand Jean du Plessis Richelieu (1585–1642) was a French cardinal turned prime minister whose work helped pave the way to his country's ascendancy in Europe in the seventeenth century. Richelieu was an able politician who played the participants in the Thirty Years' War to France's advantage. He provided funds to help pay for the invasion of Germany by Swedish King Gustavus Adolphus. Later, he made France an active ally of the German Protestants by committing French troops to fight in the Thirty Years' War.

Moving On: The Swedish Period

The third period of the Thirty Years' War began in 1630, when Sweden entered the war under King Gustavus Adolphus, who came to be known as the "Lion of the North." Sweden's king wanted to stand up for Protestantism, but he also wanted to protect Sweden's supremacy in the Baltic Sea—it is said he wanted to make the Baltic a "Swedish Lake"—and in expanding the Swedish empire.

People You Should Know

King Gustavus Adolphus (1594–1632), who was king of Sweden from 1611 to 1632, was a key player in Protestantism's fight for survival during the Thirty Years' War. He led Sweden to victorious war efforts against Denmark, Poland, and Russia before leading an army into Germany in 1630 to help save Protestants from Roman Catholic domination. He came to be known as "the Lion of the North."

In June of 1630, Gustavus Adolphus landed a well-disciplined army of 13,000 in Pomerania, but at first some of Germany's Protestant princes refused to join him. For more than a year, Gustavus was unopposed in Germany. He later earned the support of the Protestant princes in the September 1631 *Battle of Breitenfeld*. Leading an army of his own men and the Saxon troops, Gustavus took a decisive victory at Breitenfeld over the imperial forces, who were fighting under Johannes von Tilly, the commander of the Catholic League. This win gave Adolphus and the Saxons northern Germany and earned him the support of nearly all the Protestant princes in Germany.

The victory at Breitenfeld was the first of several military triumphs for Gustavus, and it also marked the beginning of a great surge of success for the Protestant forces. The Protestants also won at the 1632 Battle of Lützen. Unfortunately for them, Gustavus was fatally wounded in that battle. Still, the Protestants carried on. The war dragged on for three more years, and on September 6, 1634, the imperial army inflicted a demoralizing attack on the Protestants in Nordlingen, Germany.

The Protestants had defeated the Catholics at battles in Breitenfeld and Lützen, but the Catholics had been victorious in a key battle in Nordlingen. It became obvious that the Catholic forces couldn't overtake the Protestants in northern Germany, nor could the Protestants make any headway against the Catholics in the south.

By this time, the people of Germany were weary of war. On May 30, 1635, the *Peace of Prague* was signed, ending the Swedish phase of the Thirty Years' War. This treaty helped bring peace between Catholics and Protestants. It was accepted by almost all of the German princes—Protestant and Catholic alike. For a short time, it seemed that there would be peace and stability in central Europe under Ferdinand II.

You Can Look It Up

The **Battle of Breitenfeld** in September of 1631 was a key battle of the Swedish period of the Thirty Years' War. In this battle, King Gustavus Adolphus led an army of his own men as well as the army of Saxony against the Catholic League, who were led by Johannes von Tilly. This victory, which was decisive, earned Adolphus the support of almost all the Protestant princes in Germany.

You Can Look It Up

The **Peace of Prague** (May 30, 1635) was signed at the end of the Swedish period of the Thirty Years' War. It dealt with what would be done with church-held lands in the empire and also solved some of the political disputes. It was welcomed by the Germans, who had grown weary of war by that time.

But there would be one more phase to the Thirty Years' War, one that had little to do with the religious struggles in Germany and more to do with political ones.

An Ending That Just Won't End: The French Period of the Thirty Years' War

Up to 1635, the Thirty Years' War had a distinctly religious flavor to it. But that changed in the fourth and final period of the war, when France got into the fray. At that point, the Thirty Years' War became a struggle for political, economic, and military supremacy in Europe.

Prior to the Peace of Prague, France didn't play a big part in the Thirty Years' War, offering mostly diplomatic and political input and next to no military help to any of the combatants. In May of 1635, France declared war on Spain, and with that, the fourth and final phase of the Thirty Years' War had begun. Before long it was a war pitting France, the Netherlands, and Sweden against Spain, Austria, and other German states. This phase of the war used most of Europe as its battlefield, especially Germany. Fighting between Spain and France and its allies took place in the Low Countries, as well as in Italy. Of course, fierce fighting was also taking place in war-ravaged Germany.

The French period of the war—which has been referred to as "the International Phase"—was the longest of the four periods of a war that devastated much of Europe, particularly Germany. By the time it was finished, Germany was in a social and economic shambles.

A Devastated Continent, a Shattered Germany

The Thirty Years' War was an unspeakably horrible time for Europe, particularly Germany. Hundreds of thousands of people—even those not directly involved in the fighting—died, and many others lost their homes or were permanently separated from their families. Children whose parents were killed in the fighting were left to fend for themselves. Severe food shortages left people starving, and there are some accounts of starving people resorting to cannibalism to survive. At some points, even the soldiers doing the fighting had no food.

Germany suffered the longest-lasting repercussions from the war. Some historians have estimated that the total population in Germany fell from roughly 16 million in 1600 to around 11 million in 1650. Deaths from the war and from its aftermath took a lot of lives, but many Germans left for safer places. Almost all of Germany had it bad during the Thirty Years' War, but the smaller villages suffered the most. Due to the losses in population—as well as in farmland and infrastructure—the German economy took a century to recover from the effects of the war. All aspects of the economy in Germany—agriculture, commerce, and industry—were devastated.

It's a Whole New World with the Peace of Westphalia

The Thirty Years' War had been dragging on sporadically for more than two decades before the negotiations for a settlement in Europe were started. The main cast of characters in the negotiations were Germany and its allies Sweden and France, and their opponents in the conflict, Spain and the Holy Roman Empire. In 1643, the negotiations were moved to the German province of Westphalia. Finally, after eight long years of give and take, on October 24, 1648 the Peace of Westphalia was signed in Münster.

The Peace of Westphalia wasn't technically one treaty, but a series of treaties whose purpose it was to spell out the political, as well as religious, terms of peace following the Thirty Years' War. The "Peace" changed the course of European history, and not just because it saved lives when the fighting stopped.

Politically, the Peace of Westphalia in effect marked the end of the Holy Roman Empire as it had been known and began the system of individual governments in Germany and the rest of the empire. Emperor Ferdinand III, the son of Ferdinand II, signed the Peace of Westphalia. After that, the more than 300 principalities and cities that once made up the Holy Roman Empire were more or less autonomous political bodies, free to make their own decisions. It also established Switzerland and the Netherlands as independent nation states. It also ensured that France would emerge as the chief power of Europe.

People You Should Know

Ferdinand III (1608–1657) was the emperor of the Holy Roman Empire from 1637 until his death. Ferdinand tried to promote his authority over the German states of the empire and to strengthen the Roman Catholic Church in them. Ferdinand III succeeded his father, Ferdinand II, as emperor and continued his father's policies in the Thirty Years' War. Following several military defeats, he signed the Peace of Westphalia, which weakened the authority of the Holy Roman Emperor.

The Peace of Westphalia provided for what we today might call a "separation of church and state." That separation was limited, as the churches were still run and controlled by the individual states. But the Peace of Westphalia put an end to the strong political influence of the pope, which the pontiff had enjoyed for many centuries. It also put limits on the authority of the emperor over the affairs of the churches.

Pope Innocent X refused to recognize the Peace of Westphalia, but the Catholics and Protestants largely ignored his objections. This was a whole new world of freedom, both religiously and politically.

In the religious arena, the Peace of Westphalia settled once and for all the major religious conflicts in Germany. The provisions basically affirmed the Peace of Augsburg with one addition: Now, Calvinism and other forms of Protestantism were included in the agreement. Instead of the princes being just Lutheran or Catholic, they could be Lutheran, Catholic, or Calvinist.

In effect, the long era of religious warfare in what was the Holy Roman Empire was now over. Europe was now a continent divided by religion, and that division was officially sanctioned. The Protestants continued dominance in England, Scotland, Holland, Scandinavia, and parts of Germany and Switzerland. The Roman Catholic Church retained its dominance everywhere else.

There would still be struggles, but they would not be on nearly as large a scale. The Peace of Westphalia also ended a long-time dream of Roman and Holy Roman emperors alike: that of an empire united under one religious rule.

Instead, it would be a Europe—and later, other parts of the "Christian" world—where it was legal and relatively safe to practice different forms of the Christian faith.

The Legacy of the Thirty Years' War and the Peace of Westphalia

The Thirty Years' War, which many historians say was the worst time of war in the history of Europe, ended forever the notion of a completely religiously united Europe as well as the idea of complete domination by the Protestants or the Catholics.

> ### Protestant Pearls
>
> By holiness I mean not fasting, or bodily austerity, or any other external means of improvement, but the inward temper, to which all these are subservient, a renewal of the soul in the image of God, a complex habit of lowliness, meekness, purity, faith, hope, and the love of God and man.
>
> —John Wesley (1709–1791)

The Peace of Westphalia created a basis for a lasting peace between Catholics and Protestants of all persuasions. That didn't mean that the sides in what had once been a bitter conflict didn't still have their differences. They did and still do. Occasionally, those differences have caused outbreaks of violence in different parts of the world. But in general, those religious differences are talked out in a peaceful fashion. Sometimes the differences are settled, but many other times the sides in the disagreements "agree to disagree."

There are several different ways to see the Peace of Westphalia and its resulting lack of armed—with a few exceptions—conflict over the past three-plus centuries of Christendom. It could be said that both sides simply got tired of the violence and somehow have found a way to get along. On the other hand, it could also be said that they have "remembered history" and have chosen not to relive it. It could be that each side has realized that the other isn't going away, that it is here to stay—therefore, why fight it?

Many, if not most, historians say that the Thirty Years' War and the Peace of Westphalia that ended it marked the actual end of the Protestant Reformation. That may be true, but that doesn't mean that it was the end of reformation for churches (notice, that's reformation with a little "r"). The Catholics, the Lutherans, the Calvinists, the Anabaptists, and all other offshoots of the original Protestant Reformation continue to this very day and beyond to reform and change themselves. Interestingly, some of those changes are the churches' efforts to "keep up with the times," while others are efforts to keep the church what it was originally intended to be all those thousands of years ago.

Catholics and Protestants alike have witnessed and taken part in all kinds of reformations, revivals and renewals since the end of the Protestant Reformation and the resulting Catholic Reformation. But the beauty of it now is that even if they disagree with one another in how things should be done, they can do it the way their teacher, Jesus Christ, as well as the early church fathers would want them to do it: peacefully.

The Least You Need to Know

- Tensions between Catholics and Protestants started almost from the moment Luther posted the 95 Theses.
- Despite the provisions of the 1555 Peace of Augsburg, Catholic/Protestant tensions continued in Europe well into the seventeenth century.
- The last major "religious war" was the Thirty Years' War, which included four different phases.
- The Peace of Westphalia allowed for peaceful coexistence between Catholics and Lutherans, and it also recognized other forms of Protestantism.

Chapter 19

The Renewals and Revivals of Europe

In This Chapter

- ◆ The church's need for renewal in the 1700s
- ◆ The Methodist Revival and its main characters, John and Charles Wesley and George Whitefield
- ◆ The roots of the Methodist movement
- ◆ The reformist legacy of the Methodist Revival

It's been pointed out that Christianity is an amazingly resilient religion. Over the centuries it has survived threats from without and from within, and it continues to grow and to sustain itself. That resilience has demonstrated itself throughout history through the ability of the faith to reform or renew itself when necessary.

The Protestant Reformation, which started in 1517 and ended sometime in the mid-1600s, was the most sweeping of the reformations the church had gone through. But, as you read in earlier chapters, it was hardly the first. And it wasn't going to be the last, either. Since the end of the Protestant Reformation, the church—both Catholic and Protestant—has continually renewed and reformed itself.

The Evangelical Revival

One of the most important and dramatic of those renewals—and most important as far as Christianity in the United States was concerned—was what has come to be known as the Evangelical Revival (also known as the Methodist Revival), which started in the late 1730s and affected England and what would later be the United States. The Methodist Revival was led by brothers John and Charles Wesley and their friend and colleague George Whitefield (pronounced WIT-field).

These three men are credited with starting a movement called *Methodism* and with laying the groundwork for the creation of the Methodist Church.

You Can Look It Up

Methodism is a Christian religious movement started by Charles and John Wesley and George Whitefield, three eighteenth-century evangelists in England. The movement started in reaction to the spiritual apathy of England in the early eighteenth century. Methodism stresses personal conversion and holy living, which were lacking in the church when the movement started. It also stresses a more "methodical" approach to the Christian faith.

John Wesley was the foremost leader of the Methodist movement. Charles Wesley made his contribution to the revival as a traveling preacher and as one of the most prolific and gifted hymn writers in the history of Christianity. Whitefield fanned the fire of the revival though his preaching, which is said to have been the most powerful since the apostle Paul and to have touched the hearts and lives of hundreds of thousands—more likely millions—in England and in America.

You could also call this revival the "Wesley Revival." Though it took place more than 200 years after Martin Luther's 95 Theses provided the spark that started the flame of Reformation in Germany and abroad, it owed much of its success to the works of the reformers—Luther, Zwingli, Calvin, and the rest. It was these sixteenth-century men who gave the Methodists' approach to God a platform in England.

That this revival movement had its roots in the works of the reformers of the sixteenth century can be seen in these quotes from George Whitefield:

◆ "Works? Works? A man get to heaven by works? I would as soon think of climbing to the moon on a rope of sand!"

◆ "It is an undoubted truth that every doctrine that comes from God, leads to God; and that which doth not tend to promote holiness is not of God."

- ◆ "Let a man go to the grammar school of faith and repentance before he goes to the university of election and predestination."

- ◆ "I embrace the Calvinistic scheme, not because of Calvin, but Jesus Christ has taught it to me."

- ◆ "Good works have their proper place. They justify our faith, though not our persons; they follow it, and evidence our justification in the sight of men."

The Look of Pre-Revival England

Before we go into the particulars and details of the work of the Wesley brothers and Whitefield, let's take a brief look at post-Reformation England. It wasn't a pretty picture!

By now you know that during the centuries heading into the actual era of the Protestant Reformation, the Roman Catholic Church had become awash in immorality, materialism, and corruption. Move ahead 200 years in England, and that is what the general population looked like once again.

By the beginning of the eighteenth century, many thought that England was becoming something of a European Sodom and Gomorrah. Immorality of every imaginable kind was rampant, as well as open drunkenness and violence. The treatment of many people, particularly children, in England had fallen behind the times—medieval times, that is! Forced child labor was common in England, as were barbaric practices such as infanticide and slavery.

To make matters worse, religion in England at this time had become less than an after-thought. The Anglican Church was in operation and there were people in attendance, but the spiritual life of the parishioners was cold and stale. Many of the English were so apathetic toward religion that they stayed away from church altogether.

John Wesley himself summed up the Christian perspective of the moral and spiritual morass of early-nineteenth-century England when he said, "What is the present characteristic of the English nation? It is ungodliness. Ungodliness is our universal, our constant, our peculiar character."

Clearly England and its culture were in trouble, and there was nothing that even the leaders of the country could do about it. This was going to call for a nationwide spiritual revival.

It was into this culture that the revivalists/reformers of the Methodist Revival came, ready and armed to make a difference through their preaching, teaching, and writing. And before they were through, the spiritual landscape of England and of America would undergo radical change.

The Wonderful Work of the Wesleys

John and Charles Wesley's family life was radically different from that of George White-field. They were the sons of Samuel and Susanna Wesley. Samuel held a high position in the family's Anglican church in the village of Epworth, where the Wesleys lived. John was born in 1703 and Charles in 1707. John and Charles were 2 of the 18 children born to Samuel and Susanna.

> **Protestant Pearls**
>
> I felt my heart strangely warmed. I feel I did trust in Christ, Christ alone, for salvation; an assurance was given me that he had taken away my sins, even mine, and saved me from the bore [burden] of sin and death.
> —John Wesley (1703–1791), Founder of the Methodists

John and Charles Wesley would one day be among the most influential and important evangelists in the history of Christianity, but it was only after near death for both of them that they were able to fulfill that calling. In 1709, when Charles was two years old and John six, John nearly lost his life in a fire at the rectory where they lived. John's life was saved by two brave villagers who saw him peeking out through an upstairs window. This incident may have happened when he was a small child, but it left an impression on John Wesley, who in later life often referred to himself as "a brand plucked from the burning fire," in reference to the Old Testament verse Zechariah 3:2.

Charles Wesley was also rescued from the fire, but as a toddler he was among the first evacuated from the rectory. Charles had a fight for his life, but his had to do with his poor health as a baby. He had been born prematurely and struggled to stay alive during his first few years.

John and Charles attended different preparatory schools in London, but both of them attended Oxford University. John studied at Christ Church and was ordained an Anglican priest in 1728. Charles began his studies at Christ Church just as John was leaving. While John was away from Oxford, Charles founded the "Holy Club," a group of young men with a common goal of the strengthening of their faith. When John returned to Oxford, he assumed the leadership of the group.

The members of the Holy Club pledged themselves to the spiritual disciplines of daily private prayer and Bible reading, and they also met every evening to do the same as a group. They also devoted themselves to social service, such as caring for the sick, the poor, and people in prison. These devoted young men received several labels from their fellow students—"Enthusiasts," "Bible Moths," and "Sacramentarians" were among them. But one name stuck: Methodists. "Methodist" was originally a derisive term that referred to the group's methodical approach to their sense of Christian duty and ritual.

This group would be the beginning of great things in England and abroad, but before that would happen, the Wesley brothers had to figure out where they stood with the God they wanted to serve.

The Missionary Trip, Then Conversion of the Wesleys

In 1735, John and Charles set out on a missionary journey to the North American colony of Georgia, where they had hoped to convert some of the natives. But neither of them had much success, and they left disappointed. That trip, however, turned out to be a life-changer for both men. It was on the trip to Georgia that John and Charles had a chance to talk to some Moravian Christians, who challenged them concerning their personal salvation.

People You Should Know

James Oglethorpe (1696–1785) was the founder of the American colony of Georgia. He was born in London and attended Eton and Oxford. He joined the British Army at the age of 14 and was elected to Parliament in 1722, at the age of 26. In 1732, Oglethorpe and a group of associates received a charter from George II for the colony of Georgia, which was to be established on territory between the Savannah and Altamaha rivers.

It was a timely conversation, as both John and Charles lacked the assurance that they had true "saving faith" in Christ. In fact, upon their departure from Georgia, a disillusioned and disappointed John Wesley said, "I went to America to convert the Indians. But, oh, who shall convert me?" The answer to that question came when the Wesleys returned to England, where another Moravian Christian, Peter Boehler (1712–1775), played a part in leading both John and Charles to not just an understanding of their faith, but a personal experience of it. It was through these experiences that the Wesleys, who grew up in a very religious home, would become "converted" to what they would later think of as the Christian faith.

On Sunday, May 21, 1738—*Whit Sunday*—Charles, who was recovering from an illness, read Martin Luther's commentary on Paul's epistle to the Galatians. That day, for the first

People You Should Know

Peter Boehler (1712–1775) played a huge role in the Methodist Revival, as he helped bring John Wesley to a point of assurance about his own relationship with God. The discussion between Boehler and Wesley took place when Wesley returned to England after a three-year stay in Georgia, where he attempted to win natives to Christ. However, he himself lacked "assurance" of his own salvation.

time, Charles came to a point of personal faith in Christ. In other words, he had been converted. He later wrote of that experience, "I now found myself at peace with God, and rejoiced in hope of loving Christ. I saw that by faith I stood; by the continual support of faith."

You Can Look It Up

Whit Sunday is another term for the Christian feast of Pentecost, which takes place fifty days after Easter. It has been celebrated since the third century, and was originally a commemoration of the descent of the Holy Spirit on the believers in Jerusalem in the first century, as recorded in the book of Acts.

Three days later, John had the same kind of experience at a meeting on Aldersgate Street in London—a meeting he wasn't especially pleased to be attending—where someone read the words from Luther's preface to his commentary on Romans. He later wrote in his *Journal* these now-classic words: "I felt my heart strangely warmed. I felt I did trust in Christ, Christ alone, for salvation; an assurance was given me that he had taken away my sins, even mine, and saved me from the bore [burden] of sin and death."

This conversion experience was the beginning of an incredible career of traveling evangelism. It was also the beginning of amazing spiritual changes in the people of England.

John and Charles Wesley: Never the Same Again

Following their conversion, the Wesleys embarked on an amazing life of preaching and evangelism. Both John and Charles Wesley believed that the gospel of Christ should be preached to all people in England, and that they were to do everything in their power to see that it happened—all over England.

They preached in English churches when they were welcomed, which, because of their unorthodox methods and message, was not always the case. They had, in fact, gotten themselves in a little hot water with the Anglican Church. When their requests for pulpit time was denied, they took their message anywhere there were people to hear them—in streets, in public squares, in centers of commerce.

Protestant Pearls

I have found in the Bible words for my inmost thoughts, songs for my joy, utterance for my hidden griefs and pleadings for my shame and feebleness.

—Samuel Taylor Coleridge (1772–1834), English poet and literary critic

John Wesley spent most of his time in poor neighborhoods, preaching to the industrial and agricultural workers who scratched out a meager living. His message was one of God's love for sinful mankind. He assured those who attended his meetings that they could be "saved from sin and made holy" if they responded to God's love. He also preached about personal morality, and he warned people against the evils of gambling and drinking.

The response to Wesley's preaching was at times overwhelming. On occasion, he preached to many hundreds of people at a meeting. And it has been estimated that in all he preached the message of salvation by grace through faith in more than 40,000 sermons. He is believed to have traveled some quarter-million miles—by boat, by foot, and by horseback.

Charles Wesley's Contribution to the Cause

Of the two Wesley brothers, John was the most influential and powerful preacher, but that is not to say that Charles Wesley wasn't a great evangelist and counselor in his own right. For the first 20 years after his conversion, Charles had his own ministry as a traveling evangelist who made his way all over England.

But as important as Charles Wesley's evangelism, preaching, and counseling were to the people of England, they were not the most important or memorable part of his legacy. Charles is now known for one thing: hymn writing. He was arguably the greatest hymn writer in the history of Christianity. He is known to have produced more than 7,000 poems and songs, many of which became classics that are sung in church worship services to this day.

Around the mid-point of the eighteenth century, Charles Wesley came to a point where he couldn't keep up the pace set by his brother. Charles married in 1749 and settled down in Bristol before moving to London in 1771. In London, Charles preached at the City Road Chapel and continued to write powerful hymns. John Wesley himself pointed to the importance of hymns and music to the Revival. More than one hundred of Charles Wesley's hymns still remain in the current *Methodist Hymn Book*.

Protestant Pearls

Call the Comforter by the terms you think best—Advocate, Helper, Paraclete, the word conveys the indefinable blessedness of his sympathy; an inward invisible kingdom that causes the saint to sing through every night of sorrow. The Holy Comforter represents the ineffable motherhood of God.

—Oswald Chambers (1874–1917)

Charles cut down on his preaching around 1750, but he never stopped writing hymns. For nearly every day of his 50 years as a Christian, Charles Wesley wrote verses of praise. The story is told about how Charles Wesley continued writing hymns, even on his deathbed, where he had to dictate a hymn because he was too weak to hold a pen.

The Rise of Wesley's Kind of "Methodism"

In putting together "Methodism," John Wesley never intended to start a new denomination. His goal was to care for the converts who came to the Christian faith through his preaching. He put it this way: "I determined by the grace of God not to strike one stroke in any place where I cannot follow the blow." In other words, John believed in following up with the new believers, and he set up a system to do just that.

Not long after he began preaching, John Wesley decided to begin taking the names and addresses of people who had come to the faith so that he could visit them later in their homes. From this came a society of Methodists, whose goals were to provide the care Wesley saw as needed for new converts.

Going Deeper

You're probably wondering if you've heard any of Charles Wesley's hymns. Well, if you haven't heard "And Can It Be That I Should Gain," then maybe you've heard "Rejoice, the Lord is King," or perhaps "Christ the Lord is Risen Today" or "O For a Thousand Tongues to Sing." And if you haven't heard any of those, there's no doubt that you've heard the classic Christmas hymn "Hark! The Herald Angels Sing."

Although he knew the importance of a strong clergy, John Wesley encouraged lay *people*— those with full-time jobs and most of the time with no real religious training—to become lay *preachers*. This approach gave people valuable experience, and many of them went on to become religious and civic leaders in their communities.

The Methodist movement grew rapidly. By the time John Wesley died in 1791, there were more than 76,000 Methodists. After his death, the Methodists formally separated from the Anglican Church and became their own "denomination." By 1801, the membership had grown to around 87,000 people.

Joining the Wesleys in the Methodist movement was George Whitefield.

The Early Life and Times of George Whitefield

George Whitefield was born on December 16, 1714, to parents who owned and ran the Bell Tavern in Gloucester, England. The Whitefields made a good living and provided well for their children, but as a bar-owning family in early-eighteenth-century England, they were often in the company of the worst kind of influences.

Whitefield's father died when he was two years old. His mother remarried, but her new husband wasn't able to provide for the family as they were used to. Still, George's mother was determined to get her son the best education possible, and in 1732 she sent seventeen-year-old George to Oxford, where he began his university-level studies at Pembroke College.

At Oxford, Whitefield began to think about his own spiritual life. He knew about Christ, but he knew something was missing within him. He realized he needed a change, and he joined the "Holy Club," which was led by John and Charles Wesley. This was the beginning of a long association between Whitefield and the Wesleys.

It was a radical way to live at that time, but none of the men in the Holy Club went as far with this life of spirituality and self-denial as Whitefield did. He deprived himself of all physical pleasures, believing that this was the best way to God. To him, it made sense to live that way. After all, before he joined the Holy Club, his life had been one of sin and the pursuit of pleasure.

But in March of 1735, something changed in Whitefield. As he studied the Bible, the light came on inside him, and he realized that he needed to have faith in the grace of God if he was to be genuinely "saved." His conversion experience was much like that of Martin Luther. It was not just a change in his behavior and practices, but a complete transformation of his thoughts, feelings, and purposes. Whitefield later wrote about it in his journals: "I found and felt in myself, that I was delivered from the burden that had so heavily oppressed me. The spirit of mourning was taken from me, and I knew what it was to rejoice in God my Savior."

> **Protestant Pearls**
>
> The Reformation which is brought about by a coercive power will be only outward and superficial; but that which is done by the face of God's Word will be inward and lasting.
>
> —George Whitefield (1714–1770), Calvinist evangelist

A New Purpose, a New Direction

As a boy, George Whitefield was something of a "ham." He had a very good memory and was a great speaker. He was even selected to make speeches for the town fathers in Gloucester. More than anything, Whitefield loved reading plays while imagining himself playing the parts. Whitefield wanted to be an actor when he grew up. He loved the idea of taking the stage in front of a crowd of people and performing for them. But after his conversion, he felt the call to do a different sort of presentation, while reading from a different "script": the Bible.

In 1736, Whitefield received his Bachelor of Arts degree and was ordained as an Anglican minister. He returned to Gloucester, where at the Crypt Church, the church of his youth, he preached the first of many thousands of sermons. From the very beginning, there was something special about the way the then-twenty-two-year-old Whitefield preached. He spoke with such conviction and fervor that at the conclusion of his first sermon, someone complained to the bishop of his Gloucester church that 15 people had gone mad hearing him. The bishop's response? "I hope their madness lasts until next Sunday."

Obviously, Whitefield's preaching was like nothing the people had heard. He preached with a kind of passion not seen before from the English clergy. He spoke with such emotion and power that he often wept as he delivered his message. When people heard Whitefield preach, they left assured of two things: his passionate love for God, and his love for those in the congregation.

His preaching combined with his obvious concern for people made Whitefield a busy man. After his first sermon, he was invited to preach in many churches in Bristol and London, and overflow crowds came to hear him. In a short time, Whitefield barely had time for himself, as people wanting spiritual counsel would show up where he was staying. It got to the point where people who passed him in the streets would go out of their way just to touch his clothes, thinking they would receive some special blessing.

It's the Message, Not the Method!

Whitefield found out quickly that it didn't matter where he preached, only what he preached. Whether it was from a pulpit, from under a tree at a park, from upon a stone wall, or on horseback, he preached with passion the message of the gospel.

It was in about 1738—just two years after he began preaching—that Whitefield first did something that became a hallmark of the Evangelical Revival of England. As he stepped to the pulpit to preach at a church in Bermondsey, he noticed that the sanctuary was packed with people eager to hear his message. That wasn't unusual for Whitefield, but what really bothered him was the 1,000-plus people outside who couldn't get in to hear him preach.

Although it was against English law to preach outside (except at public executions), in around 1739 Whitefield began his "open-air" preaching, and the results were "congregations" of thousands hearing him speak at once. He began this kind of preaching when the Anglican Church took steps to keep him from their pulpits.

Going Deeper

Open-air preaching is a method of preaching used by George Whitefield and later by John and Charles Wesley. This method arose for a couple of reasons. One is that many of the Anglican congregations in England wouldn't allow the leaders of the Methodists to preach from their pulpits. The other is the massive number of people who came to hear Whitefield and Wesley preach.

Whitefield's first experience with open-air preaching is said to have been to a group of coal miners in Kingswood, Bristol. They were hard-working, hard-fighting men with little hope for a better life. They were illiterate and vulgar, and they were treated as outcasts by most social classes in England. It would take great courage for a preacher—one in full clerical dress, no less—to stand before them. But Whitefield had that kind of courage, and it was his lack of fear before these men that won them over.

Whitefield preached to them from the gospel of Matthew. The miners were greatly moved by the message, and he was greatly moved by the response. In just a few days, thousands in the areas were converted. He later wrote of this experience,

> The first discovery of their being affected was to see the white gutters made by their tears which plentifully fell down their black cheeks. Hundreds and hundreds of them were soon brought under deep convictions, which, as the event proved happily ended in a sound and thorough conversion.

The open-air style of preaching caught on and became the standard of the Methodist Revival. John and Charles Wesley, who began preaching after Whitefield, took his advice and began preaching outdoors. For them, the results were only slightly less astounding.

The idea behind this kind of preaching was simple: It meant reaching people where they were. Instead of bringing people—sometimes reluctant people—inside a church to hear the message, Whitefield and the Wesleys took the message to the people—much the way the apostle Peter had on the day of Pentecost.

Before long, there was nothing anyone in the Anglican Church could do to stop this "new" movement!

You Can't Stop Him! You Can Only Hope to Contain Him!

The incident with the Bristol coal miners was one of many great stories of Whitefield's preaching. He continued to travel and to preach in the "open air" forum, and the results were great opposition from the established Anglican Church—not to mention conversions by the thousands!

Whitefield's preaching was very popular among all social and economic classes in England. The London aristocracy was as moved by his preaching as were the common laborers.

Whitefield didn't limit his activities to England, either. Between 1738 and 1770, he made seven journeys to the colonies to preach. He even preached aboard the ship on his way to America, and the result was many conversions to the Christian faith. In 1741, Whitefield made the first of several visits to Scotland.

His preaching in the colonies helped bring about the spiritual revival called the Great Awakening, a time when the churches in New England moved from sterility and coldness to a newfound zeal for God. During his overseas trips, he worked with many spiritual leaders, including Jonathan Edwards, the revival preacher. His other work in the colonies is said to have been pivotal in the founding of around 50 colleges and universities. Among his many supporters in the colonies was Benjamin Franklin, who remained a life-long friend.

The Calvinist Brand of Methodism

Following his 1741 visit to Scotland, Whitefield returned to England, where a movement sprang up around him. As was the case with the Wesleys, large numbers of people were converted through his preaching, and those people, most of whom considered themselves Anglicans, began meeting in local fellowships. Leaders arose within those groups, and some of them turned out to be very good preachers.

Going Deeper

Calvinist Methodism was the branch of Methodism established and espoused by the evangelist George Whitefield, a Calvinist who believed in the doctrine of predestination, which states that God alone is responsible for the "election" of those who will receive salvation and eternal life. This was the cause of the split between Whitefield and the Wesleys.

A similar movement began in Wales, and in 1743 Whitefield met with some leaders of that group. This conference resulted in the Calvinistic Methodist Association. This was the first of the Methodist associations. It would be a year and a half before Wesley started a similar association in England.

Whitefield later gave up his position of leadership in this association, first because he had planned to devote himself to service in his adopted land of America, and second because of opposition on the part of his good friend, John Wesley.

Several of the Calvinist Methodist leaders begged Whitefield to stay, but he refused and replied to them, "Let the name of Whitefield perish, but Christ be glorified. And let me be but the servant of all."

A Split in the Methodist Movement

Whitefield had a background in the Anglican Church, and he held to the Anglican beliefs of Calvinism, which held that a person's eternal destination was actually decreed from eternity by God. In short, God "elects" who will be saved and who will be lost. Wesley, on the other hand, despite the fact that he was also an ordained Anglican priest, was an

Arminian, so he believed that a person's eternal destination was rooted in the foreknowledge of God, meaning that God knew in advance how someone would respond to the gospel message. This position was more or less the "middle ground" between those who believed in election by God and those who held that man had free will when it came to salvation.

> ### Going Deeper
>
> Arminians (in the tradition of Arminius from the sixteenth century) believe in predestination to a point. They believe that God's election of those who would come to know him was based on his foreknowledge. In other words, he created some for salvation in that he knew beforehand who would accept the gospel of Christ and who would reject it. This contradicts the Calvinist view of predestination, which holds to the view that God decrees who will be saved and who will be lost.

John and Charles Wesley preached openly against the doctrine of predestination and other tenets of Calvinism, and that led to a split in the Methodist movement. During Whitefield's trip to New England in 1740-1741 that anti-predestination preaching of the Wesleys turned the people of England against him. He immediately began preaching in London, and he won back a congregation.

The Winding Down of Whitefield

Whitefield made his last trip to the American colonies in 1769. He never returned to England after that. On September 29, 1770, he prayed out loud, "Lord Jesus, I am weary in thy work, but not of thy work. If I have not yet finished my course, let me go and speak for thee once more in the fields, seal thy truth, and come home and die."

Whitefield had reason to be tired. From the age of 22, he had engaged in a lifestyle of non-stop travel and preaching. It has been estimated that during his career as an evangelist he delivered between 18,000 and 30,000 sermons. There wasn't enough time in the day for a normal man to do the things Whitefield did, and he solved that problem by rising at four every morning to pray and read the Bible, then getting to his work, which in addition to preaching—sometimes several times a day—included letter-writing and personal visits with seekers.

George Whitefield preached his last sermon on September 29, 1770, and he did it in his own semi-original style—in the open air at Exeter, Massachusetts. He died the following day in Newburyport, and was buried there.

Charles Wesley died on May 29, 1788 in London and was buried at the Marylebone Parish Church. His brother John passed on March 2, 1791, in London and was buried at the City Road Chapel.

Going Deeper

Though they differed in theology, Wesley and Whitefield maintained a close friendship until the death of Whitefield. Later, Charles and John Wesley wrote of the kindness and love Whitefield expressed to them, despite the results of the anti-predestination preaching. Despite their differences, Wesley had great respect for Whitefield. Once, when he was asked if he believed he would see Whitefield in heaven, he replied, "I fear not, for George will be so much nearer the throne of grace."

Among the three of them, John and Charles Wesley and George Whitefield left behind an incredible legacy of revival and reform within Christianity in England, in America, and in other parts of the world.

The Legacy of the Methodist Revival

John Wesley was influential in that he believed in putting some social action behind his message. He believed in caring for the poor and sick and for those in prison. He made sure that collections for the poor were taken up at Methodists services, and he worked at finding employment for those who were without work. He even started a fund to provide loans to those who wanted to start businesses.

Wesley wasn't just a religious reformer. He was a social reformer who based his ideas on the teachings of Christ and the apostles in the Bible. At his death, one publication praised John Wesley for his "infinite good to the lower classes of the people." It was through the work of Charles and John Wesley that "the ignorant were instructed, the wretched relieved, and the abandoned reclaimed."

You Can Look It Up

Abolitionism was a movement to make slavery illegal in Europe and in America. The Abolitionist movement was greatly influenced by the Methodist movements started by John and Charles Wesley and George Whitefield. The cause was picked up late in the eighteenth and nineteenth centuries by former slave trader John Newton and by William Wilberforce, a Christian member of the English Parliament.

John Wesley was also an advocate for prison reform and spoke out against the practice of slavery—in England and in America. In his *Thoughts on Slavery*, he helped blaze the trail for *abolitionism*. In a letter to Christian abolitionist William Wilberforce (1759–1833), Wesley referred to slavery as "that execrable villainy, which is the scandal of religion, of England, and of human nature." It was the influence of Wesley, as well as slave-trader-turned-abolitionist John Newton (1725–1807), that helped encourage Wilberforce toward his abolitionist activities in the England Parliament.

People You Should Know

John Newton (1725–1807) of England was a former captain of a slave ship who became a Christian, then the author of many great hymns, including one of the best-known and best-loved of all time, "Amazing Grace." Newton was involved in the Evangelical Revival, and was especially close to John Wesley. He greatly influenced William Wilberforce, the abolitionist.

Through their humanitarianism, the Wesleys and George Whitefield made a tremendous difference within their worlds. But their number one goal was always preaching the gospel.

In the end, the Methodist Revival was one of a series of historic revival/renewals that had its roots in the Protestant Reformation. And it was also the starting point for revivals in other parts of the world, including the American colonies.

The Least You Need to Know

- ◆ In the early 1800s, the spiritual, moral, and social conditions in England had deteriorated very badly.
- ◆ The Methodist Revival of England took place largely through the evangelism of John and Charles Wesley and George Whitefield.
- ◆ Methodism was not meant to develop into a new "denomination," but only to be used as system (or "method") of caring for new converts to Christianity.
- ◆ It was through the works of reformers/revivalists such as abolitionist William Wilberforce that many social changes were made.

Chapter 20

The Reformation: What It Left Us

In This Chapter

- ◆ The far-reaching effects of the Protestant Reformation
- ◆ The political, economic, and social aspects of the Reformation
- ◆ How the Reformation affected education, literature, the arts, science, and philosophy
- ◆ What the Reformation did—and is still doing—for religion in the Western world

Most historians mark the mid-1600s as the end of the Protestant and Catholic Reformations. But that wasn't the end of the legacy of the Reformation. Far from it.

The effects and after-effects of the Protestant Reformation didn't end with the Thirty Years' War or with the Peace of Westphalia. As it turns out, the Reformation would continue to influence and shape Western culture for the rest of the seventeenth century, then into the eighteenth, nineteenth, and twentieth centuries. In fact, if you know what you are looking for, you can see the profound effects of the Reformation in Western culture today.

In poll after poll, the world's most prestigious and learned historians list Martin Luther as one of the 5 or 10 most influential men in the history of the Western civilization. Furthermore, those same historians would also list the Reformation itself as one of the most important movements—or, more accurately, series of movements—in history. When you look at the events that took place following Martin Luther's posting of the 95 Theses on the door of the Wittenberg church, it's hard to argue that point. From that day forward, events unfolded at sometimes breakneck speed—first in Germany, then in the rest of Europe. Germany was never the same after that, and neither was the rest of Europe.

So What Was So Great About the Reformation?

As you have read through this book, you've seen that the Reformation wasn't some kind of "quick fix" for the religious problems of Middle Ages Europe. It was a painful time for the Christian religion, a time when all of Christendom was ripped in half. It was a time when men and women staked out their theological and religious positions and refused to move from them.

The nature of the conflict wasn't one where both sides were able or willing to settle their difference through civilized debate, either. There were many times when the Reformation looked more like a violent revolution. Following the outbreak of the Reformation in the late 1510s, there were terrible times of war and persecution on all sides of the Reformation struggle.

> **Protestant Pearls**
>
> My heaven is to please God and glorify him, and to give all to him, and to be wholly devoted to his glory; that is the heaven I long for.
>
> —David Brainerd (1718–1747), American evangelist to the native Americans

In hindsight, it's hard to look at that violence and understand how the Protestant Reformation could have much of a positive effect on our culture as a whole over the past three centuries. How can something good come out of a movement that tore Christianity in half? And how can there be a positive legacy out of a reformation that led to the deaths of millions? How can men kill and persecute one another over religion?

The violence associated with the Protestant Reformation is a tragedy, to be sure. But much good came out of the Reformation. When it was all said and done, when the wars and persecutions finally died down and armies stopped taking up arms, we are left with a movement that did tremendous good for the humanity that was to follow over the next four centuries.

In a very real sense, then, the Protestant Reformation can be seen as the birth pangs for a new and improved world.

The Good the Reformers Did—Intentionally AND Unintentionally

The Protestant Reformation was, first and foremost, a religious movement.

When Martin Luther issued his challenge for debate in Wittenberg, it was because he wanted to discuss some possible changes in the church he had served all his adult life. And when the other reformers—Zwingli, Calvin, Knox, Cranmer, and the rest—took their stands, it was because they wanted a better religious world around them. When the "radicals" from the Reformation arose—the Puritans and the different Anabaptist movements—it was because they believed there was something amiss in how the religious establishment of the day was doing things.

But the effects of the Protestant Reformation didn't stop with religion. The Reformation had far and deep reaching effects on European culture as a whole—and, consequently, on the culture of the New World.

Without a doubt, the Reformation has had profound effects on nearly every aspect of Western culture as a whole—either directly or indirectly. And while many of the important lasting social and political movements in the West during the past three centuries don't have their original roots in the Reformation, almost every aspect of our lives—political, economic, social, and, of course, religious—have been affected in one way or another by the Reformations of the sixteenth century.

Before we talk about the specific changes the Reformation made in the religious world of Europe—and how those changes would set the stage for the establishment of the church in other parts of the world—let's take a look at the effects it had on Europe, on the political, social, scientific, and artistic world as a whole.

Protestant Pearls

When I survey the wondrous cross on which the prince of glory died, my richest gain I count but lost and pour contempt on all my pride.

—Isaac Watts (1674–1748), Independent minister and hymn writer

Politics and the Religion of the Protestant Reformation

The Reformation of the sixteenth century did plenty to influence the development of political thought over the next four centuries.

Both Martin Luther and John Calvin had the personality and drive to successfully challenge the government and church authorities of the time. Their approaches were daring for the time, even revolutionary. But both of them, in their own ways, demonstrated great respect for the established governments, even to the point of holding that obedience to government authority was part of the true Christian faith.

Luther taught that the state (or the government) was like the church in that it was divinely established and for that reason, he believed that followers of Christ should honor the institution of government. There was one exception, according to Luther, and that was those situations where the rule of the government contradicted the rule of God as spelled out in the Bible, which he held to be the ultimate authority. Furthermore, he taught that the government ruler, who himself was divinely appointed, was answerable to God for how he ran his city, principality, or nation.

Calvin agreed with Luther that it was God who instituted the government, but he stressed more activism in government. Calvin believed that the government should be Christian in nature and responsible for furthering Christianity among the people. It was his belief that government should be responsible—in conjunction with the church—for discipline, proper doctrine, and worship. And, when it was necessary, the government should have a hand in dealing with heresy—by force when necessary.

When it came to the government's role in church affairs, Calvin wasn't too concerned about what form of government it was, although he believed that a monarchy (as in England) put too much power in the hands of one person and detracted from the rule of God. But he also believed that pure democracy moved too close to anarchy.

In some respects, Calvin's form of government in Geneva—although it was a theocracy—was a forerunner to the type of constitutional government established later on in the United States. That form of government assured that power would neither be concentrated in the hands of a very few, but that it would also not be run on the basis of a pure "majority rule."

Protestantism: One of the Roots of Democracy?

The church and civil governments suggested by the reformers, while they weren't adopted in full by any present or future state, greatly influenced government in Europe and in the New World.

Protestant Pearls

How many of these [arguing about religion] have turned their weapons against each other, and so not only wasted precious time, but hurt one another's spirits, weakened each other's hands, and so hindered the great work of their common Master?

—John Wesley (1709–1791)

It has even been argued that the Protestant Reformation was a sort of forerunner in its own right to the development of a democratic form of government. D. Hay Fleming put it this way in his book *The Reformation in Scotland*: "If democracy was the child of the Reformation, it was a child born in the extreme old age of its parent."

It probably isn't accurate to say that democracy was a direct result of the Reformation. But many historians assert that the Reformation was a contributing factor to the rise of democracy. Neither Martin Luther nor John Calvin espoused a purely democratic form of government, but there were seeds of democracy in the teachings of these reformers, especially Luther.

For example, it was Luther who stood before the authorities at the Edict of Wörms and refused—unless someone could point out in the Scriptures why he should—to recant of his teachings. It was also Luther who made the layperson important in the church by espousing what he called the "priesthood" of individual believers.

In asserting the priesthood of the individual believer, Luther helped make the Christian faith a religion anyone could practice—without the interference or input of a Catholic Church that saw itself as center of the spiritual life of all Christians. Luther held that there was one mediator between God and humans, and it was Jesus Christ. And for that reason, there was no need for the priest, at least in the Catholic sense of the word. One of the effects of the Protestant Reformation, it turns out, was that individual believers were free to think and pray and read the Bible for themselves.

The medieval and Reformation-era Catholic leadership saw that as a threat to the authority of the Catholic Church, which, as it turns out, it was. People were attracted to the Protestant form of Christianity, even if it wasn't Luther's form. And in time, that led to a "balance of power" between Protestantism and Catholicism. It's a balance that lasts to this day.

The Economics of the Reformation

The reformers of the sixteenth century had something to say about economics. That included issues such as interest for loans. Luther believed in hard work, but he also believed that the state should be what we might call a "safety net" by establishing a system of care for the poor and sick. He also believed strongly in publicly funded education, an idea that was widely embraced in Europe and later on in the United States.

Luther believed in absolute honesty in all economic transactions, and he hated greed on the part of business owners (mostly agricultural) of his day. He didn't believe, as some radicals did, in the abolition of private property, but he did believe in the government's authority to set fair prices for goods, based on the ability of laborers to pay for those goods.

Although Calvin was far from a pure *capitalist* (it has been suggested that his teachings actually slowed the development of capitalist states in Europe), his beliefs concerning economics influenced the Western world greatly. He believed it was the duty of the Christian to serve society through his work, and to do that in the framework of honoring and obeying God.

You Can Look It Up

Capitalism is the economic system in which the means of production are owned by private individuals and operated by those individuals for profit. Most of the reformers weren't **capitalist** in the true sense of the word, but they contributed much to what would later develop into the capitalist systems of the Western world.

The Reformation and Public Education

Under the leadership of several of the reformers, the Reformation played a huge part in the world of education. Part of that came from the emphasis—particularly on the part of men such as Calvin in Switzerland and Knox in Scotland—on the need for an educated clergy to lead their congregations.

In Germany, Martin Luther was ahead of his time as a huge proponent of a system of public education. The man who started the Protestant Reformation wanted to see publicly supported schools opened in every city, town, and village, and he wanted every German child to attend. Luther didn't want these schools to be merely centers for religious instruction—although he certainly wanted the children to know the fundamentals of the Christian faith. He wanted children to receive a broader education that included teachings on the culture of Germany and on classic literature. To that end, Philip Melanchthon, Luther's closest associate, worked with the authorities in Saxony to establish what we would today call "public" schools. He also wrote several widely used textbooks and had the idea of dividing the school children into classes (much as they are today).

Under the Protestant King Henry VIII, there were few if any developments in England when it came to public education. But Henry's successor, the Protestant Edward VI, whose reign ran from 1547–1553, is remembered for founding around 30 grammar schools. What started under Edward continued on after his reign ended, and by the end of the seventeenth century close to 500 new schools had been founded in England.

This emphasis on education made its way to the American colonies, where the Pilgrims aggressively pushed for publicly supported education. By the mid-1600s, public education was offered to all New England colony children.

The Reformation and Some Good Reading Material

One of the primary factors in the starting of the Protestant Reformation, and later the Catholic Reformation, was the new emphasis on literature. This emphasis was a part of the Renaissance, which started in Italy and made its way—in different forms—into most of the rest of Europe.

This emphasis on literature influenced the Reformation, and in turn the Reformation had great influence on literature. Martin Luther's German translation of the Bible was a milestone of literature in that language. The same can be said of John Calvin's *Institutes of the Christian Religion* for the French language. And the King James Bible remains not just a great work of translation, but a great work of literature that is to this day the best-selling book of all time. It is truly a literary classic, and it has influenced the speaking of the English language throughout the world.

Other lasting and influential Protestant literary works included William Tyndale's Bible, the *Book of Common Prayer*, and *Foxe's Book of Martyrs*. The Catholic Reformation also produced its share of influential literary works, including Ignatious of Loyola's *Spiritual Exercises*, which remains a classic and a greatly influential piece of Christian literature.

Some other great pieces of literature that were greatly influenced by the Reformation include John Bunyan's *Pilgrim's Progress* and John Milton's *Paradise Lost*.

Going Deeper

Foxe's Book of Martyrs, which was written by John Foxe (1516–1587), is a classic piece of Reformation-era Christian literature. The book is a collection of stories about martyrdoms in the history of Christianity. The book has been updated several times since Foxe's death in 1587. John Foxe was an English Protestant clergyman. He was born in Boston, Lincolnshire, and educated at the University of Oxford.

The Writings of History and of the Past

Could you imagine the kind of controversy and debate that would take place if some historical event the magnitude of the Protestant Reformation were to take place today? There was no CNN or *This Week* on which to debate the issues of the Reformation, but the debate raged on for decades.

One of the outcomes of that Reformation debate was an interest in church history, and because of that, the Reformation period left behind a rich legacy of writings on history, including that of the church up to that time. Much of the writings are fascinating, as they give their own "spin" on the events of the past and those of the present.

One of the best known of the church histories was compiled and published by a man named Matthäus Flacius (1520–1575) and six collaborators. It was called the *Magdeburg Centuries*. The work was done between 1559 and 1574. It consisted of 13 volumes, and each volume covered a century of church history, up to the year 1300. It was heavily biased toward Protestantism. It took a view of history as a struggle between good (God) and evil (the devil), and it referred to the pope as the Antichrist and the Roman Catholic Church his empire.

Going Deeper

The *Magdeburg Centuries* was the first comprehensive history of the church. It was published by Matthäus Flacius (1520–1575) and six collaborators between 1559 and 1574. It was a work of 13 volumes, and it covered the history of the church to the year 1300—one century per volume. It was one of the important historical works of the Reformation era.

Naturally, the Catholics had to respond to the *Magdeburg Centuries*, and that response was the *Ecclesiastical Annals*, by Caesar Baronius (1538–1607). Baronius's work was just as biased as Flacius's, and it was published in several editions between 1588 and 1607.

The first significant history of the Reformation from a Protestantism point of view was titled *Commentaries on the Religious and Political History of Charles V*. It was written (and written well) by a Lutheran by the name of Johannes Sleidan (1506–1556) and published in 1555. It handled the subject matter—the Reformation from its beginning in 1517 to the Peace of Augsburg of 1555—in an even-handed and mostly unbiased way.

There were many, many other historical writings from the Reformation period—too many to list here. But they left historians with a rich variety of material from which to study this vitally important time in Western history. Even that material that has a pro-Protestant or pro-Catholic bias (and there were plenty of both) has added something to the study of the Reformation period.

How Great Thou "Art"

The Reformation influenced the "fine arts"—architecture, sculpture, painting, and the like—probably even greater than it did literature.

In the 1500s, some of the most beautiful art and architecture came together in Rome and Venice. The work of Raphael and Michelangelo can still be seen at the Vatican Palace. The best artists of the time—Bramante and Michelangelo, to name two of the stars of what was going on artistically in Rome—got together to do the work on what was to be the greatest of all Christian churches, St. Peter's.

In Venice, artists such as Titian and Tintoretto dominated, both of them painters. It was during the second half of the Reformation that a style of art and architecture called *baroque* appeared on the scene. Tintoretto—also known as Jacobo Robusti—was among the first of the Italian masters to display baroque characteristics in his work. One of his most memorable works was *Presentation of the Virgin in the Temple*.

You Can Look It Up

Baroque is a style of art that developed in Europe in the sixteenth and seventeenth centuries. The word "baroque" was initially a negative. This style is characterized by its sense of movement, energy, and tension. In baroque art, there are strong contrasts of light and shadow. In the Reformation era, baroque art included images of spirituality. In the Catholic countries, it included scenes of religious ecstasies, martyrdoms, and miracles. It is divided into 21 chapters, each covering a place during a certain era.

The art scene in reformation-era Germany was different from that of Italy and other places. There were a lot of painters in Germany at that time, but no real masters. It was in Germany that Albrecht Dürer portrayed Christian themes and personalities in his paintings and woodcuts.

People You Should Know

Albrecht Dürer (1471–1528) was the most famous Reformation-era artist in Germany. He is known for his paintings, drawings, prints, and woodcuts, many of which depicted biblical and religious scenes. He is said to have greatly influenced the sixteenth-century artists in Germany and in the Low Countries. One of his most famous works was the woodcut *The Four Horsemen of the Apocalypse*.

Historians say that as far as art is concerned, the ideas and struggles of Protestantism were expressed best through painting. And the greatest of the "Protestant" painters—by that, we mean painters whose work were strong expressions of Protestantism—were Dutchmen based mainly in Harlem, Amsterdam, Delft, and Dordrecht. World famous masters such as Frans Hals, Solomon and Jacob van Ruysdael, Simon de Vlieger, and others.

The greatest of these Dutch Protestant painters was Rembrandt van Rijn (1606–1669), a Mennonite whose work covered biblical and historical themes. In his paintings, Rembrandt portrays Christ not as the mighty leader of men, but as a humble servant and preacher whose purpose in life was to meet the needs of those around him. His *Supper at Emmaus* (1648) is a great example.

It Has a Nice Sound, and You Can Worship God to It

It makes sense that the Reformation would greatly influence music. After all, Martin Luther himself said that music was God's greatest gift to mankind outside of the gospel message. Luther and his associates developed a congregational hymn. Luther also believed in making musical instruction part of the educational experience, and that helped spread his musical influence throughout Germany and beyond. Luther himself wrote several classic hymns, including the standard "A Mighty Fortress is Our God." He is also said to have written part of the German Mass.

The Lutheran tradition of music reached its high point with the works of classical composer Johann Sebastian Bach (1685–1750), who had as his goal writing music of praise, most of which he wrote for the Lutheran church. Bach wrote about 300 cantatas, many for specific seasons of the year, including the classic "Christmas Oratorio." Bach is still considered the greatest composer of all time for the organ.

The Reformation ushered in an era where songs—those that could be sung by the congregations—became a huge part of church services, and the demand for songs was met by a series of hymn writers. Our modern culture has been richly blessed through the works of many of the songwriters of the seventeenth and eighteenth centuries. Isaac Watts, who is called "the Father of English Hymns," wrote more than 600 hymns, and many of those are still being sung in churches today. For example, his "When I Survey the Wondrous Cross" is still a standard in Protestant circles. Watts authored *Hymns and Spiritual Songs*, which appeared in 1707 and became a best-seller. As we discussed in Chapter 19, "The Renewals and Revivals of Europe," John and Charles Wesley—particularly Charles— were great hymn writers. It was Charles who wrote literally thousands of hymns, many of which became classics, even in the "secular" world. In addition, John Newton, who prior to his conversion to Christianity was a slave ship captain, also gave our culture the beautiful classic "Amazing Grace," among other great hymns.

> **Protestant Pearls**
>
> Grace the free, undeserved goodness and favor of God to mankind.
>
> —Matthew Henry (1662–1714), Nonconformist Bible commentator

The Catholic Reformation also helped lead the church in Europe to a revival of hymns in the sixteenth and seventeenth centuries.

When Science Stopped Answering to the Church

When Martin Luther challenged the long-established authority of the Roman Catholic Church, he set an example that many would later follow. Among them were the scientists of the Reformation era and beyond. It was a whole new world for the mathematicians, astronomers, and physicists of Europe. No longer were they bound by the orthodoxy of the Catholic Church. Now, they could move ahead and do their work independently of Rome.

The results of this "revolution" have been far-reaching to this day.

One of the most important developments of this time was what is called the "Copernican Revolution." Nicholas Copernicus (1473–1543) was a German/ Polish mathematician and astronomer who lived during the Reformation, and what he was suggesting in his *Revolutions of the Heavenly Bodies* disturbed the Catholic power structure only slightly less than did the works of the reformers. In *Revolutions*, Copernicus posited that the earth and the rest of the planets revolved around the sun and that the moon revolved around the earth.

> **Going Deeper**
>
> *Religio Medici* ("Religion of a Doctor") was written by Sir Thomas Browne (1605– 1682) around 1635. It is a Reformation-era discourse in which the skepticism and scientific reasoning of the early 1600s are mixed with faith and revelation. Browne was a physician and essayist who was born in London, England. He studied at Winchester College, University of Oxford, and abroad at the Universities of Montpellier, Padua, and Leiden.

Copernicus wasn't at all accurate in his calculations, but the basis for his ideas were later picked up by men such as Italian Giordano Bruno (1548–1600), Dane Tycho Brahe (1546–1601), and German Johannes Kepler (1571–1630).

Galileo Galilei (1564–1642), the brilliant Italian scientist, later validated Copernicus's hypothesis when he gave further development to the telescope, which he used to more accurately observe the rotations of the solar system.

The new developments in astronomy were mirrored in other scientific fields of physics, chemistry, anatomy, medicine, biology, geology, and others. Here are just a few of the Reformation-era developments in science:

- In physics, Englishman William Gilbert (1540–1603) laid the foundation for the study and use of magnetism and electricity.

- In chemistry, Jean Baptiste van Helmont (1577–1644), a Flemish physician, researched the behavior of some gases and first recognized carbon dioxide.

- In anatomy, Leonardo da Vinci (1452–1510) made many discoveries about the human body through the dissection of more than 30 cadavers. Also, Fleming Andreas Vesalius (1514–1564) published the first modern book on anatomy, titled *The Structure of the Human Body*.

- In the field of medicine, Swiss physician Theophrastus Bombastus von Hohenheim (1493–1541) pioneered the use of various chemicals and drugs.

It can be argued that these and other discoveries would eventually have been made with or without the freeing effects of the Reformation. Still, there is no question that the Reformation—and the encouragement toward independence of thought that came with it—helped hasten these developments.

The Protestant Reformation and What It Did for Philosophy

The Protestant Reformation had a profound effect on some of the philosophers of the sixteenth century and beyond. During and after the Reformation, there was a different kind of philosopher than the ones whose writings and thoughts came to a new light during the Renaissance.

One of the philosophers was Frenchman Blaise Pascal (1623–1662), who was greatly influenced by the work of the Catholic Reformation. Pascal is responsible for what had come to be known as "Pascal's Wager," which states that the belief in God is a safe bet for the one who is concerned about the destination of his or her eternal soul. If the believer is wrong, he has lost nothing. But if the unbeliever is wrong, he has lost everything. Pascal—who achieved excellence as a mathematician, physicist, and inventor—is considered one of the great religious thinkers in Western history. He wrote that people could come to a personal knowledge of God through Jesus Christ through faith, and that the faith itself was a gift of God.

Englishman John Locke (1632–1704) wrote many great volumes on politics and religion, and in 1695, he published *The Reasonableness of Christianity*, which was a dominant theological writing of the time. In it, Locke stressed the simplicity of the Christian faith. He also wrote *Essay Concerning Human Understanding*, which took a philosophical approach to faith. Locke believed that the Christian faith was something that had to be personally experienced, and that part of that experience was observing the world around us, which, he said, pointed to the existence of a loving and all-powerful God.

In the seventeenth century, there arose a philosophy called "rationalism." This line of thought says that all things are judged by the reasoning of mankind. The rationalists weren't hostile to the idea of God. They just approached his existence in a more "rational" way, meaning that it was something that could and should be "proved." The greatest of the rationalists was Catholic René Descartes (1596–1650). Others included Baruch Spinonza (1532–1577), who was Jewish, and G. W. Leibniz (1646–1716), a German Protestant.

Protestant Pearls

He who has learned to pray has learned the greatest secret of a holy and happy life.
—William Law (1686–1761), Clergyman and writer

The Protestant Reformation helped along some of the philosophies that followed because it stressed individual thought and individual faith. Some of the philosophies that were influenced by the Reformation were "God-friendly," while others were hostile to the idea of God, at least the God of the reformers.

The Reformation's Bottom Line: Changes in Religion

There is no question that the Protestant Reformation had far-reaching effects in many areas of modern life—far more than a quick glance at twentieth-century culture might show. Even people who hold no religious orientation of their own have benefited greatly from the effects of the Reformation.

But the bottom line is the Protestant Reformation was more than anything a religious movement, and it had its greatest effect on the world of Christianity.

The Reformation, though it didn't accomplish what it did easily or cleanly, gave the Christian world something it had never before had: the freedom to worship and pursue God in the way each individual saw fit for him or herself without the interference of a huge, bureaucratic church capable of controlling and influencing every area of life.

One of the most obvious legacies of the Protestant Reformation in modern America is the number of different "sects" of the Christian faith. We call these different branches of Christianity "denominations." Prior to the Reformation, there was in Europe—aside from a few "radical" sects that sprang up from time to time—only one church, and it was the Roman Catholic Church.

Each of these denominations—from Baptist to Presbyterian, from Anglican to Lutheran, from Catholic to Methodist, not to mention the ones outside of what might be considered "mainstream"—have slightly different teachings, but all of them have one thing in common: They owe their existence, in part or in whole, to the Protestant Reformation. Not all of Europe embraced Martin Luther's brand of reform, called "Lutheranism." But all of Europe eventually *did* embrace some kind of religious reform, even if it was reform in the Catholic Church. It is for that reason that we now have the freedom and the opportunity to choose how and where to worship.

The Protestant Reformation and the Catholic counterpart did something to Christianity that had been needed for many centuries. These movements purified the Christian faith and how it was practiced. To the average Christian—the layman or laywoman—the most important effect of the Protestant Reformation was the revival of practical religion. By that, we mean a kind of religion that is personal, that can be practiced by the average man or woman without the help of some complex religious power structure.

That—as Martin Luther, Ulrich Zwingli, John Calvin, and John Knox would tell you today—is what the Protestant Reformation was all about in the first place.

Historians say that the Protestant Reformation ended sometime in the middle of the seventeenth century. But in a lot of ways, the Reformation has never really ended. The effects of the Protestant Reformation are so deep and far-reaching that in some ways the Reformation continues to this day.

The Least You Need to Know

- The period of the Protestant Reformation was a difficult one for Europeans, but many great things came out of the Reformation movements.
- The reformers in the Protestant movement were also social reformers in many ways.
- The period of the Protestant Reformation meant changes and innovations in education, literature, art, and the study of science.
- The Protestant Reformation had far-reaching and long-lasting effects on all of Western culture, but its greatest effects were religious ones.

Chapter 21

The Reformation in North America Before the American Revolution

In This Chapter

- The Colonies as missions for Reformed Church of England people
- How the New World changed the Puritan Churches and Pluralism to an "Evangelical culture"
- Puritanism and the Great Awakening
- The cooperation and separation of church and state before the founding of our country

English explorers poked around the edges of the New World, which people everywhere were starting to call "America," but ordinary believers of the re-formed religions hung back from actually moving there. Despite persecution, wars, and internal strife, the men and women who had embraced this fresh, reform faith stayed home. They preferred harassment from neighbors whom they knew to savages and diseases in a New World that they did not know. Celibate Roman Catholic clergy could travel the wilderness of New Spain and Quebec, but Protestant ministers had families to consider.

Why in the World Would Anyone Move to America?

In 1584, an English clergyman, Richard Hakluyt, lit interest in moving to America when he published *A Discourse on Western Planting*. He mentioned the "commodities that are like(ly) to grow to this Realm of England." He wanted men to explore North America—the "western continent—and use it for the "enlargement of the gospel of Christ." He reminded his boss, Queen Elizabeth, that "the princes of the Reformed Religion are chiefly bound to spread the Gospel." He flattered her when he said that Her Majesty was the "principal leader of the Reformed Religion."

Hakluyt wanted people to move to America to make money and to spread the gospel of the true faith at the same time. It would help Queen Elizabeth if she thought about how much it would mean financially and spiritually to plant her Church of England overseas in North America.

In the long view, this little document said some things that have proved very important for us: Go there to make money and to spread the Reformed Religion. England should be the main one to do this.

You Can Look It Up

In England, the king or queen owned any land explored by the citizens of the country. A company had to get a charter or franchise to set up business there. This **charter** would include business, social, religious, and legal restrictions and guidelines. Like any contract, it directed the one side to do something, while expecting a return of some sort.

Twenty years passed and nothing happened. In the early 1600s, businessmen with some extra cash started investing in companies legally "chartered" by the English government to send colonists to North America. The *charter* for one of these, the London Company, included the requirement for the company to spread the Christian religion to the savages—oh! while you're there, civilize them! The board of directors of this London Company included practicing, devout members of the Church of England, and into the charter they wrote that settlers would keep the faith of the Church of England.

But there was something else. This board of directors sympathized with "Puritanism," a reform within the Church of England that was starting to show up here and there.

What Is So Pure About Puritanism?

During the 1600s, Puritanism referred to just one strand along with many others that were changing the religion in England. Believers were spinning three main strands through the developing fabric of the Church of England.

One strand held out for hanging on to traditions, whatever remnants of the Roman practices that they could keep in England. This conservative wing still rejected obvious things that no Protestant at all would stand for, like the papacy and a celibate clergy.

At the other extreme, some reform-minded people wanted to make the Church of England really Protestant, really reformed. Some of the more extreme of these people coalesced into the Puritan faction, what we might call the "left wing," or "radical." For these, the English church would be the "pure" form of Christianity.

On the middle ground stood people who believed that the Church of England represented a unique role between the extremes of Roman Catholicism and the radical Reformation sweeping away so much all across Europe. For them, Anglicanism—the real church of England—meant being both Protestant and Catholic, and neither one. Whether there were worship services like the Catholics (high church) or worship services like the Protestants (low church), England could believe the best of both worlds.

The Heart of Puritanism

Puritans, who were the left wing, dreamed of purifying and reforming the Christian church in England by putting every aspect of life under the umbrella of the Bible. Believing in the Calvinist view of sin and predestination, they felt only the Bible life was right for them. Holding on to their membership in the Church of England, they believed that the only worthwhile life meant a Protestant one. They focused all living on God, convinced the God of Christians gave the Bible to humans to provide direction for the most detailed elements of secular life.

Puritans were not thinking of really separating church and state—at first. Puritanism wanted a civil community—a kind of common life, but not run by priests or ministers, not a true theocracy, not a throwback to Roman Catholicism and its Papal States. No, you need society's civil, secular rulers to make laws and pass judgments, but in obedience to God, by listening to their ministers and learning from Bible study. Religious ministers and leaders of the congregation preach and teach the Bible to all, but they do not make laws. Both religious and civil leaders join each other in obeying the one God and Lord of all.

Where did Puritans fit into the general Protestant picture? The Puritan religion rested on the same general Reformation principles as all the other Protestant religions focused on Calvinism. Puritans emphasized that fallen, sinful people can show they are God's elect by a conversion experience. Puritan believers admit their sinfulness and—this is very Puritan—they admit it happens by God's covenant of grace, rather than in or through any ritual of baptism, as Roman Catholics taught. Because human beings are so sinful, people need what the Puritans called the "covenant of grace," the choice by God to save us. In faith, a person responded to this covenant by acknowledging sinfulness and the need for God. In faith, a person then joins other "elect"—members of a congregation elected or chosen by God in a religious covenant, a congregation whose true and only leader is God.

Puritans of course emphasized the Bible. What you read there, they said over and over, applies to every and all aspects of life. Because both church and state worship the same God and read the same Bible, society gels or harmonizes into one big community of church and state operating in close harmony with each other.

Going Deeper

A covenant is a rich idea. It means a contract, or agreement, between or among parties, each of which benefits from its terms. A covenant structures personal bonds between people. In the Judeo-Christian tradition, covenant has a special meaning. Derived from ancient treaties between vassals and lords, the biblical covenant expresses personal relationships between God and his people. God initiates the biblical covenant—agreeing to self-imposed terms of love, salvation, and redemption on his part, while expecting acceptance on the human side. This acceptance is expressed by obedience to laws, intangible allegiance, and ritual reminders.

Finally, Puritans loved the idea of a "covenant." Puritans used this word to include all kinds of relationships between God, community and individuals. Devout people—that means Puritans—covenant with each other into "congregations," a term often associated with the Puritan religion. Sometimes called "covenantors" in their time and in history, what we used to call Puritans have now become "Congregationalists." That is a little too simple, but basically true.

Puritans saw themselves as the ultimate Protestants. You could not get any more Protestant, they were sure, than an English Puritan. Only for them is it true that God, through the Bible, is in charge of every aspect of human life, both personal and public.

Where Did the Puritans Come From?

This actual "sect" started to become a noticed group under Queen Elizabeth I. Before her time, England had endured a back-and-forth situation—Edward, a Protestant child-king, was followed by Mary, a Catholic queen who killed off many of her opposition. Seeing these events, a few dedicated Church of England people decided they wanted to purify the half-heartedness that was ruining everything.

In 1582, Robert Browne published *Reformation Without Tarrying for Any*. He meant: "Don't stop, let's keep the Reformation going until we finish the job, no matter who gets hurt." It was extreme for the time, but he expressed something that a number of other people felt. They just wanted to "finish the Reformation" in England by eliminating any and all vestiges of Roman Catholicism. It was these people who came to call themselves and were called "Puritans."

To Separate or Not to Separate, That Was the Question

Some Puritans did stay as members of the larger Church of England. People called the Puritans who considered themselves part of the Church of England "Non-Separatists." The true faith would always be for them the Church of England. You just fix what's wrong with it from within. These Puritans would want to stay in England, and practice their religion with ministers of the Church of England.

Other Puritans gave up on the Church of England and walked away. These "Separatists" kept all the Protestant elements of the Church of England, but eliminated what seemed particularly Roman Catholic, like sacraments, veneration of saints, and so on. These Separatists wanted to integrate the Calvinist elements of the Reformation—rather than the Lutheran ones—into the English ways and let the "Church of England" die away.

We Have to Keep the Roman Church from Spreading!

Puritans, whether Separatist or Non-Separatist, wanted to stop any expansion of the Roman Catholic infection. The New World was the battleground. Spain was spreading the Roman church into Central and South America. France, another Catholic enemy, was successfully expanding into Quebec.

It was just when the Puritans were starting that Haluyt wrote his influential paper. "We have to do something," the position paper for the Queen implied, "to keep England on top! We have to work better as merchants, as businessmen with the New World, and we Anglicans have to be the ones who will convert the savages to Christianity." Only a few years later, businessmen started companies to finance settlements in North America—where the Puritans were going to move.

What Made Them Go

Politics pushed the Puritans toward America. Elizabeth I, then James I, and then Charles I—each successive monarch seemed to inch religion a little farther backward toward Roman Catholicism. Elizabeth herself issued a specific law to halt Puritanism. In Elizabeth's Act Against Puritans of 1593, English leadership expressed their fear that the Puritan belief "denied, withstood, and impugned her majesty's power and authority in causes ecclesiastical." Then James I and Charles I, rulers who followed Elizabeth, acting as heads of the state religion, encouraged a centralized priestly leadership and a Church of England structure that was simply anti-Puritan. These rulers tolerated and even encouraged the old practices and rituals of Catholicism. Charles even had a Catholic wife! How dare he?

One other good reason to move to the New World grew out of the very nature of Puritanism. Puritans dreamed they could create a perfect society, a heaven on earth—some place where people who shared Puritan views could live peaceably and morally according to the Bible. As a matter of fact, Englishmen in general, including Puritans, very often thought England was special. They thought it enjoyed a singular position in God's world as a holy nation elected by God for the true faith. But Puritanism pushed that thinking even further. We Puritans—they believed—represent the true faith. Our lives define perfection—or at least the perfection possible in a Calvinist, sinful world. We need to go somewhere where we can live it out.

One other push to move came from the poverty in England. An economic depression in England made people poorer and put them out of work. If you needed money, you could sell your self and your services as an "indentured servant." You could work your debts off in the New World and slip out from under the risk of debtors' prison or other legal threats. This poverty was fostering rebellious thoughts and feelings against the establishment running England.

In the next century this attitude helped cause a civil war in England between Puritans and the Establishment.

Puritans Get to Virginia—What Now?

In 1607, the London Company sent some men to settle Virginia. The Rev. Robert Hunt, a clergyman with a Puritan outlook, held a communion service immediately on landing, and then conducted prayers twice daily and preached several sermons every Sunday based on the Bible.

Two years later, the London Company reorganized itself into the "Virginia Company of London." This time, in their rules, they made it plain. They would settle Virginia first, to baptize "a number of poore and miserable soules," secondly, to build up the public honor and safety of the king by making room for surplus population, and, third, to develop a business that would produce "commodities," like tobacco unavailable in England. Jamestown would be an extension of England, with a mere ocean in the way.

Here we find motives that would get many Puritans to the New World—to enlarge their religion, find room to live, and make money, a place where the rest of the world would leave them alone.

Then a very tough man, Sir Thomas Dale, came to Jamestown as governor. He "established" the religion of the new colony. He forced the settlers to attend morning and evening prayers every day, with severe penalties for absences. He made other strict laws, imposing the death penalty for such things as stealing grapes, killing chickens, and trading with Native Americans. Puritans meant it when they made laws. With him came another Puritan sympathizer, Alexander Whitaker, an educated man but a layman, who went out to convert the local Native Americans.

Going Deeper

Living at Jamestown was tough, no matter how religious you were. Starvation, fire, and disease killed many settlers. Although they wanted to start tobacco farming, they did not have good seeds. Although they wanted to convert the Native Americans, they would fight them off instead. You had to kidnap a Native American, like Pocahontas, Powhaten's daughter, and hold her hostage to keep them from attacking. (Later, of course, she would marry John Rolfe, one of the kidnappers.) In the winter of 1609–1610, 80 percent of the settlers died!

Jamestown was not making money for the company. The company decided to loosen its grip on details, and let the settlers have more say in their own lives. By 1619, when the company reorganized again, a new policy specified a local assembly to make rules for the colony.

This new assembly established the Church of England as the official religion of the colony. Other changes restructured the settlement to ensure that Puritanism would not dominate the community the way it would later in Massachusetts. The ruler-makers in Virginia would never involve the clergy, but would be a genuinely secular, elected government—flavored with Puritanism—that would handle the future of the Virginia colonists.

This same year brought the ship *Jesus* to Virginia with "twenty or so" indentured black men. The English, with their ingrained attitude of superiors and inferiors, and the Calvinistic mind-set of elect and damned, saw these new people as inferiors, as beings sent by God to be servants. These new field hands for Virginia and Massachusetts fit nicely into the worldview of Puritanism: The order of nature is the law of God. Society, for Englishmen, needs structure; this means civilized and civilizing Christians ruling over pagans and papists—the benighted people who would not or could not appreciate true Christian culture and religion.

Going Deeper

When African-American slaves started becoming "Christian" later, especially during the Great Awakening of the next century, the churches debated about what Christian freedom means. When "Negro Spirituals" began, the words often played on double meanings of freedom. It meant something religious to the white master and something else to slaves. After a slave revolt in 1725, based on the Bible, Christian conversion was sometimes associated with revolt by slaves. Secular law in the south had to explicitly decide that baptism did not free someone from slavery, only from sin.

The Land of Witch Trials and Scarlet Letters!

In New England, the Puritan colonists arrived with a difference. The New England settlements and the Virginia settlements both were officially glued into Church of England practices. Both Massachusetts and Virginia saw the king as ruler and head of their church, however "separatist" they might have felt. Both started with Puritan ingredients. Both felt threatened by their Catholic neighbors north in Canada and south in Florida and the Caribbean. But there were big differences in the two colonies, north and south.

Let's Follow the Pilgrims to Massachusetts

A congregation of Puritans left England in 1608. The Church of England was harassing them because they were Separatists; they wanted to be part of English culture, but not members of the Church of England. This group traveled to Leiden, Holland, where they lived as an English-speaking, closed-in little community. Twelve years passed. Time, the absence of English-speaking neighbors, and maybe sheer homesickness softened their determination to stay "separate" from the Church of England.

In Holland—this may be their strongest motive for moving again—the Puritans noticed their children were starting to lose their fervent Puritan way of life. Their leader, John Robinson, helped the community decide that some of them would exit Holland and some would stay. John Robinson himself stayed behind in Holland as minister to the larger number.

So it was, in 1620, that a little group of Puritans got a charter from the businessmen of the Virginia Company of London to aim for the New World. Starting from Holland, the *Mayflower* Puritans picked up fellow Separatists in England—more than the original passengers of the ship—and headed out to join the established Virginia colony. In November of that year, 37 Puritans, along with 65 others who had packed themselves into the tight little *Mayflower*, landed off-course at Cape Cod too late to sail south to Virginia.

To avoid friction between the religious groups and from the professionals whom they needed, the men decided to "covenant" among themselves to decide their future governance. They signed "The Mayflower Compact." This civil document grew out of the Puritan focus on covenanting, and proved to be a terrific model for self-government that stretches clearly into our own constitution. Its principal architect, Governor William Bradford, described its purpose: "we ... combine ... to submit to such government and governors as we should by common consent agree to make and choose." The signers pledge that they "covenant and combine (themselves) together into a civil body politic." Part of the reason they wrote this significant document lay in the legal fact that their patent or charter did not seem to include New England as a place to remain. They needed a legal, organizational justification for staying where they were.

That first winter, half of the pilgrims to Plymouth Rock died. The pilgrims had no pastor to minister to them. Elder William Brewster led worship services. They gathered twice on Sundays. They prayed and studied much, they were serious and devout. All by themselves.

Puritans as Separatists

When the London Company did send a clergyman four years later, in 1624, he proved to be an Anglican more interested in creating a rival colony than in serving the Puritan community with its Separatist ways. They sent him packing. Their first real Puritan pastor, Ralph Smith, arrived only in 1629.

Puritans back home in England were getting frustrated with the conditions there. Those who wanted to stay within the Church of England (the "Non-Separatists") could not achieve responsible positions in the Anglican hierarchy. Both as Bishop of London and then in 1633 as the Archbishop of Canterbury, William Laud saw Puritanism as a serious threat to the Church of England.

Some Non-Separatist businessmen gained control of one business and got a royal charter in 1629 for "The Governor and Company of the Massachusetts Bay in New England." John Winthrop, a devout Puritan layman, managed to establish a loophole in this charter, so that the headquarters need not stay in England. In 1630, along with his whole company, he sailed away to New England.

All up and down the coast of Massachusetts, Puritans now ushered in a remarkable Puritan world. Based squarely on the Bible, these idealists were attempting to create a kind of heaven on earth, a place where fallen, sinful mankind might achieve harmony with God and one another in a tightly woven and enforced social fabric. Civil and spiritual leaders worked together to ensure a uniform practice of their religion.

 **Going Deeper**

The Massachusetts Bay Colony was founded by the whole company with John Winthrop, and it was Non-Separatist. South of it on Boston Bay was the Plymouth Colony, the earlier one, founded by the Pilgrim Separatists who came on the *Mayflower*. For many years they stayed separate and somewhat hostile, but they eventually overlapped and the members formed Massachusetts Colony.

Because Puritans thought of themselves as "THE Protestants," they tried to come as close as possible to a perfect Biblical Christian community. In New England, outsiders might see differences between the Separatist-tending Plymouth colony and the Non-Separatist Bay colony, but they are not important now. The old country in the early- and mid-1600s treated all Puritans the same—badly. Puritans everywhere felt they were victims of what was happening back there in England, and it was ricocheting into their world, but they kept on trying hard to practice the positive part of church reform.

The Plantations Grow into a Big Plant

During the mid- and late-1600s, the New World of North America woke up to find crowds of people swarming to America. Floodgates had opened, and in came the torrents!

In New England, during the 1640s, about 20,000 Englishmen followed John Winthrop to Massachusetts Bay. People ran away from the Church of England, and Archbishop Laud, and Charles I. Church and state were hounding the Puritans out of their homeland, as the Church of England kept rolling the clock back toward Roman Catholic practices.

These people came converted. They came with families. They came to stay. They came determined to be free of Charles I and to practice pure-pure-pure Puritanism. That's why they came. Free, free at last!

Puritan Life

People around Boston Bay were about as happy a people as Puritans could be. People had money. Families were growing. You could usually enjoy two sermons every Sunday. Church membership let you vote for a representative to make laws for you. If you lived in town, you were usually safe from attack by Native Americans. If people did something wrong, they got punished, whether whipped, or hanged, or made to wear a scarlet letter for adultery. Actions had consequences.

On Martha's Vineyard nearby, Thomas Mayhem was preaching to Native Americans with some success. John Eliot, the minister to a Puritan congregation, translated the Bible into Algonquin Indian and even preached in that language. These ministries, we should note, were the exception; most settlers looked down on the "savages," afraid for their lives. English Puritans felt that God did not normally call non-European people to be among the elect. When trouble with Native Americans did flare, settlers just killed as many as they could and justified the massacres from the Bible where such massacres happened.

For a while there, though, the Puritans must have felt they were in heaven! Then came the disturbances.

Heaven Interrupted

One big problem bloomed from the very heart of Puritan ideas. To be a member of a Puritan congregation and the church, an adult Puritan had to experience conversion. As years passed in New England some of the baptized children of devout Puritans did not "convert." Like many Christians today, though, who have grown up in the tradition of their parents without joining the church, these young people wanted their own children baptized. A real problem!

The Puritans invented a "halfway" covenant that sounds much like our modern solution. A congregation could agree to baptize an infant even when the parents did not attend church, and the baby would have a "halfway" membership in the church. A special synod of ministers in 1662 said that this would work for the Puritan church. We shall see what happened to that compromise later.

Whoops, Here Come the Baptists!

A second problem troubled the waters in time—Baptists.

Baptists started in England a little later than the Puritans. When in 1612 some devout English Puritans—Separatists—encountered Mennonites and people called Anabaptists in Holland, they published a manifesto of what they believed.

Baptists felt themselves to be as Protestant, as true, and as fervent as other Puritans, but they became a group separate even from the Separatist wing of the Puritans. Certain that baptism meant adult baptism, not infant baptism, these people formed their new religion around that conviction. They were even more convinced than Puritans of the need for local churches to run their own lives, independent of any civil magistrates whatsoever. (You can see how well this will go over in Massachusetts!)

The pivotal Baptist in the New World, John Clarke, arrived in Rhode Island in 1639, but we need to update what was happening in Rhode Island before he got there.

A man named Roger Williams, a dyed-in-the-wool Separatist, hated the very idea of any established religion and therefore resisted the Holy Commonwealth of Massachusetts, a place which was almost the very definition of belonging to an established religion. In 1639, he was legally and religiously banished from the Puritans' Church of England in Massachusetts.

> **Going Deeper**
>
> The Puritans shaped their ideas by encounters with other religions in the Old World, sometimes hostile, sometimes friendly. Nonetheless, these encounters, especially in Holland, suggested the many changes that the American religions would undergo as they rubbed shoulders in the New World.

Williams escaped arrest by traveling first to some fellow Separatists in Plymouth Colony, and then staying with helpful Narragansett Indians. Finally, he reached what we now call Providence, Rhode Island, where he started a settlement open to religious refugees, people persecuted anywhere for their unorthodox beliefs. Quakers came, Baptists came, and so did Anne Hutchinson, the articulate critic of Boston Puritan preachers.

Roger Williams particularly welcomed Baptists, with their emphasis on adult baptism, and himself became a Baptist for a little while. He ended his long life, though, as a self-described Seeker—one who kept looking for the True Church which he could not find on earth. We remember this man fondly as a first—the first person to really tolerate religious differences.

Oops, and Here Come Other Protestants!

Another problem for the Puritans came in the shape of other Protestants from other parts of Europe.

The Dutch, for example, had grown significant as aggressive international businessmen because they built and maintained large fleets for fishing, navies, and commerce. Henry Hudson, an Englishman, had contracted for the Dutch when he explored the Hudson River in New York. A few years after the English made land at Plymouth Rock, Dutch Calvinists were building their own settlements on Manhattan Island and land nearby. By the early 1740s, like the English, ordained ministers were serving the Dutch and establishing a genuine "congregation" with all that that meant. Several decades later, Peter Stuyvesant arrived at Manhattan (New Amsterdam it was then) and started persecuting anybody not a strict Dutch Calvinist. English Puritans—who were Reformed Protestants—might pass as okay, but German Lutherans and Dutch Mennonites were not good enough—so the Dutchman persecuted them in the New Amsterdam colony.

Later on, in the mid-1600s, New Sweden appeared where we now see Wilmington, Delaware. A wealthy, dedicated Dutchman, William Usselinx, who had helped start New Amsterdam, joined Peter Minuit, the competent German who was no longer working for the Dutch, and together they persuaded Swedes to start a trading colony in the New World. Some Finns tagged along. These people professed Lutheranism and worshiped according to the Augsburg Confession. By 1650, three Lutheran churches graced the Delaware landscape—and their minister was working on the language of the Delaware Indians.

Pieces of a Jigsaw Puzzle

All up and down the Atlantic seaboard Protestant colonies were growing bigger and better, most of them supported, encouraged, or directed by their national church back home in Europe. Between the two English, more-or-less Puritan colonies farthest north around Boston and farthest south in Virginia—those two anchors of religious enforcement—the other Protestant settlements displayed a range of freedom of religion.

In the 1600s, Massachusetts Bay, now the biggest colony, did not tolerate at all any one or any idea different from theirs. The Puritans drove out as heretics two people who disagreed with the Puritans' total control of everything: Roger Williams (1635) and Anne Hutchinson (1637). In 1651, they whipped Obadiah Holmes, a visiting "Anabaptist"—the early term for a Baptist. Around 1660, they hanged several persistent Quakers.

Those hangings triggered a reaction in England. England forced the Puritans to stop putting to death people who practiced other religions. Some other things happened, too, to start moving the colonies towards religious tolerance and freedom.

In the late 1600s, a minister at the Old North Church in Boston, Increase Mather, took to task a preacher in western Massachusetts, Solomon Stoddard. Increase Mather, a famous man in Boston at the time, was overshadowed by his much more significant son, Cotton Mather. Increase, however, started the work of reflecting on Puritanism, on its foundations and its consequences.

Going Deeper

Solomon Stoddard broke ground by reasoning towards a variant of covenant theology. In his system, people "prepared themselves for" salvation. Very liberal by the standards of the time, Stoddardism suggested a kind of "Arminianism" that threatened strict Puritanism. He advocated "open communion" and a stronger control exercised over local churches. Stoddardism survived these attacks and began to influence others.

Cotton Mather

Cotton Mather became the colleague-past to his father, and supported the old ways, the "Old Calvinism," but he chose to also explore science and philosophy, reexamine the value of missionary work and research political thinking from "modern" men like John Locke and Isaac Newton.

He held respectful disputations with Stoddard. He broke ground by his efforts to integrate "enlightenment" thinking into Puritanism. In short, Cotton Mather updated the old Congregationalism to make it more sensible and more appealing to nonbelievers.

Along with Jonathan Edwards, the grandson of Solomon Stoddard, the writings of Cotton Mather influenced the minds and hearts of thoughtful people, laying frameworks that

Going Deeper

Arminianism suggested that the grace of God's covenant needed cooperation on the part of the human heart and will. Trying to remain faithful to its Calvinistic roots with the emphasis on God's ineffable majesty, this approach tried to include some "good works," in the sense of human action. Humans could not be completely passive.

would enable a later generation to revolt against their mother country and then create a nation of united states. It was their Protestant and updating-Protestantism ideas that led their readers toward the Revolutionary War and eventual union of the states.

Some colonies, like early New Haven, Connecticut, carbon-copied hard-line Massachusetts. Others like Rhode Island represented just the opposite—people defiant of Massachusetts's established way of life. That refugee from Massachusetts oppression, Roger Williams, in Providence, Rhode Island, for example did not approve of Quakers at all, but there Quakers stayed with no problem. Protestants who lived in New Amsterdam (New York), New Jersey, and Delaware were practicing their religions and secular policies independent of New England, while they themselves practiced intolerance toward many religions and some tolerance toward kindred religions.

Pennsylvania—The Colony with a Difference!

In the late 1600s, William Penn helped Quakers settle in his place, Pennsylvania. This new colony offered freedom of religion for anybody who believed in one God. The founding of Germantown, Pennsylvania, marked a decisive moment because it incorporated two religions—German Mennonites and Dutch Quakers—into one town! The Penn administration treated Native Americans fair and square.

Now Come the Presbyterians!

Francis Makemie, a Presbyterian Irishman educated in Scotland, preached for the Presbyterian religion throughout the colonies, and finally established the first real Presbyterian congregation in Maryland in 1684. A public trial in New York accusing him of preaching without a license publicized Presbyterians as defenders of freedom of religion. Not surprisingly, the first Presbytery started in Philadelphia, that haven of freedom of religion.

Presbyterians of Northern Ireland and Scotland also started what eventually would become that very American Protestant institution, the "camp meeting" or "*revival*." This practice would eventually find full blossom—and prove fruitful—in the Great Awakening. The revival style of preaching has marked American Protestantism to this day.

You Can Look It Up

How did the **"revival"** or "camp meeting" start? Presbyterians did not offer the Lord's Supper frequently. They preferred to set aside a few days a year for preaching, praying, confessing sins, and expressing the need for forgiveness. The gathered believers, now ready for the Lord's Supper, would walk up to large tables for a communal sharing of the bread and wine. Other religions started imitating this practice, irregularly until the Great Awakening.

The Pieces Start to Come Together

All the pieces were falling in place for the colonies to come together in a cooperative way politically and with a sense of religious tolerance for one another. One or the other Protestant majority ran each colony; the Church of England served as the established church in the most important ones.

Establishment included such things as ...

- the government paid ministers' salaries.
- the right to a political vote depended on church membership.
- the church educated children in "public" schools—while college education normally meant preparation for the ministry.
- that as a rule the civil government punished people who broke religious laws such as adultery, murder, and preaching a false religion.

Colonial men—not women—had some say-so in their own colonial government whether for religious matters or for civil affairs. England and the English language dominated the cultural landscape, even though America now had cities of immigrants from Germany, Holland, Sweden, and various other European sources.

Negatively, one flaw kept happening. It involved the not-so-good ministers who came to the New World—a situation that has clearly shaped American Protestantism. Although some saintly Protestant ministers stand out for their devotion, selflessness, industry, wisdom, leadership, and competence, all too often sponsoring countries did not provide good ministers to American settlers. The earliest settlers, despite immense emphasis on religious practices, too often got their leadership and preaching from untrained laymen. Because the ministry meant a licensed, paid position, unscrupulous men sometimes came forward, and abused the offices they held. As is always true, a few bad apples gave the whole situation an unsavory feel. What also happened was a desire to develop a better home-grown ministry.

Changes, Changes!

The Protestant population of North America grew amazingly fast. It reached half a million or so people by the early 1700s. International politics and war among European countries were gradually drawing all the Atlantic colonies into the English orbit. Local, non-English-speaking villages, small towns, and parts of towns, held on to their native European cultures and religions. In places like New Jersey, Pennsylvania, and Delaware, settlers from a variety of religious backgrounds did not try to force the main religion onto everyone or oppress people for having a religion different from theirs.

Finally, even Massachusetts had to practice some form of religious tolerance. After the 1660s when the Puritans there hanged the four Quakers, England and public pressure required the Puritan leaders to refrain from the death penalty for religious differences.

Going Deeper

When unusual smaller Christian sects started to grow out of the old reformed religions on American soil, they did not last long—but they suggested a phenomenon that has become much more common since then. The "Rogerenes," for example, a little sect-community in New London, Connecticut, flourished briefly in the late 1600s. Refusing to pay taxes, they adopted Saturday as the Sabbath, denied infant baptism, practiced faith healing, and urged pacifism. Sounds a lot like some religions today that have flowered from American sources but stay fairly independent of religious traditions and authority.

Evangelism—The Child of Puritanism

The fervor of Puritanism died with time, freedom of religion ripened, and something new appeared to replace the religious dream of a perfect Protestant world.

The Decline of Puritanism

First, what happened to Puritanism? The very emphasis that the Puritans and others placed on the local congregation destroyed the uniformity of the whole society. That "halfway covenant" of 1662 in Massachusetts changed the world as they knew it—by accident. Some local congregations just decided not to follow the rules. When that happened, the central Puritan leadership could no longer count on any congregation to adhere to the one true faith as they decreed it.

Witchcraft trials, religious tensions in England, financial successes of members, unexpected wars with the Native Americans—all of these factored into the psychological weakening of the central Puritan leadership and the decrease in their control. By 1691, a fresh royal charter for the Massachusetts Colony provided freedom of worship for all Protestants. (Of course, the Salem witch trials happened after that. Freedom of religion has its limits.)

The Rise of Religious Tolerance in America

Secondly, people began to deal with the situation of neighboring religions in America. These were not exactly new religions, but American colonists found creative ways to handle the familiar problems from within the Biblical, Protestant traditions.

The Carolinas in 1669 passed a law, "Fundamental Constitutions," offering religious free-dom, even though it also maintained public financial support for the Church of England. Congregationalists (community control of the church) and Presbyterians (synodal, or "church" control over churches) expressed their controversy publicly. This open-air discussion led people towards thinking more independently about social reorganization. These discussions would later help civil leaders understand a "federated" or "federal" form of government. Religious tolerance was simply becoming a fact, if not the norm, in most of the colonies by the early 1700s.

Another change occurred as foreign-speaking groups started learning English, and even very different communities started helping one another. One example: The German Justus Falckner, ordained under Swedish Lutheran auspices, became a pastor for a Dutch Lutheran Church in New York.

The Great Awakening

Starting around 1720 in America, people started to "wake up to God." There is no other way to describe it. This sensational stirring of American hearts has many names, but most writers call it The Great Awakening.

Going Deeper

A force that would seem to resist an emotional element in religion is the so-called Enlightenment. This movement of the seventeenth and eighteenth centuries emphasized human reason and history, rather than religion and revelation, as the way to solve human problems. The movement produced the mathematics and science so important in our modern lives, not to mention political and economic ideas that developed independent of the Bible. It also led to the excesses of the French Revolution and some intense hostility toward organized religion. Some "common sense" Scottish Enlightenment thinkers deeply influenced both the political and religious foundations for the new country.

There was no particular reason for the tidal wave of conversions that swept across the colonies. Church membership was increasing at the time, even though it was not staying in proportion to the population. The traditional Protestant churches were all doing all right. In Europe, the way of hard, cold, scientific logic we think of as the "Enlightenment" was traveling toward America, and you would think that this rationalism and sober thinking would stop an emotional awakening to religion—but it did not.

There was some need for awakening the churches. "Mainline" churches had lost the origi-nal intensity of the first settlers. That generation was gone. People, though, still wanted and expected more from their religion. Success and materialism were starting to make religion seemingly less necessary, and people knew that.

Some specific preachers prepared the way for the harvest of souls that would come. Theodorus Frelinghuysen, originally from Holland, and the Tennent family—William, the father and Gilbert, his son—and George Whitefield from England are the names of the main preachers, but many others unnamed by history participated as leaders of this movement. In particular, the early Baptists started using this form of preaching regularly.

When Theodorus Frelinghuysen, an educated Calvinist of the Dutch Reformed Church, arrived in New Jersey, he criticized the external, formalistic observance of Christianity he found there. He harped at his new parishioners for using religion to stay Dutch rather than to follow Christ. He wanted to use excommunication to straighten things out, and his efforts became public.

Near Philadelphia, a Presbyterian family, the Tennents, the father William and his eldest son, Gilbert, in particular, started preaching that people had to repent of a "presumptuous security" in the formalities of religion. Their style had the appearance of an attack on correct doctrine and formal religion; so, the older generation of Scottish Presbyterian ministers attacked them from the pulpit.

The congregations, however, who actually heard the Tennents responded with great gusto—weeping, cries of terror, having seizure-like fits—a very emotional scene. The Tennents, encouraged by such strong responses, began traveling outward to other congregations, and into the open air, developing and expanding the itinerant style of preaching that had characterized the lay preachers down through the years.

These preachers were lighting a fuse that led toward a great explosion.

In the early 1740s, George Whitefield, an English evangelist, came to America—like a forest fire! He had been close to the founders of Methodism, John and Charles Wesley, at Oxford, and with them developed a piety that was to reinvigorate English Protestantism.

This Anglican clergyman lit the hearts of the country people, reaching even into the pocket of that notorious skeptic and practical man, Benjamin Franklin. In his famous *Autobiography*, Franklin describes with some humor how he came to hear an open-air sermon of George Whitefield. Very skeptical at first, he gradually came to empty his pockets of money for the man.

Whitefield's emotional and effective preaching changed the heart of America. Based on the Bible, he called for a conversion to Jesus Christ as Savior. As he traveled from colony to colony, his preaching united the various peoples as word of his power leaped political and religious boundaries. He awakened the slumbering Christian churches to an enthusiasm and conversion experience that marked the colonists for years.

His preaching also proved divisive. Some reacted against his unorthodox use of emotion and his seeming carelessness about doctrine. In particular, the Presbyterian Church split apart. On the Old Side, traditional Presbyterians believed that preachers needed training, church approval, and orthodox Calvinism to answer the call to preach. The New Side emphasized the conversion experience. Eventually the two sides reconciled and found great strength in their unification and, by the eve of the Revolution, Presbyterians had grown into one of the major religions of the colonies.

The Baptists embraced the Great Awakening and gained many converts. Their closeness to the center in Philadelphia enabled them to draw on its inspiration to send missionaries north and south, holding meetings and forming church communities. In their understanding of Calvinism and in their piety, they became very similar to the New Side Presbyterians.

People You Should Know

In New England, Jonathan Edwards, a towering figure in American theology, history, and literature, arose to complement the work of Whitefield. Whitefield did the popular preaching; Edwards did the thinking and writing to inspire the Great Awakening.

A graduate of Yale, the sermons of Jonathan Edwards re-summoned the true spirit of Calvinism and predestination, and he supported his arguments with profound reflection and brilliant honesty. In 1742, right in the midst of the New England Awakening, Edwards preached and published his magnificent sermon "Sinners in the Hands of an Angry God," possibly the greatest American sermon a Calvinist ever preached. It employed powerful imagery yet showed careful concern for common sense and weak sinners.

As part of the Awakening, Jonathan Edwards wrote outstanding books to defend the practices of the Great Awakening because he foresaw the opposition rising against it. At Harvard, Yale, and other colleges originally designed to form Protestant preachers, the faculties were afraid that mere emotionalism would take the place of learning traditional doctrine.

On his second visit to New England, Harvard officially censured Whitefield. Ministers refused him their pulpit. For his part, because of his strict Calvinistic views, Jonathan Edwards eventually had to leave his parish and ended his days ministering to a congregation of whites and Native Americans.

Waking Up Sometimes Takes Time

In the southern colonies, the Great Awakening spanned a longer, slower, quieter time, although its effects were just as strong and long. In the middle and northern colonies, preachers had been preparing the way for Whitefield for years. In the south, this was not so. When Whitefield preached to great crowds, the readiness for sudden enthusiasm was just not there. The established Church of England there did not foster excitement.

Going Deeper

In her first published poem—a memorial to George Whitefield—Phyllis Wheatley, an emancipated slave in Boston, wrote about Whitefield:

"He freely offer'd to the
　　num'rous throng,
That on his lips with list'ning
　　pleasure hung...
'Take him, ye Africans, he
　　longs for you,
Impartial Saviour in his title
　　due;
Washed in the fountain of
　　redeeming blood,
You shall be sons and kings,
　　and Priests to God.'"

Nonetheless, deep roots of the awakened religion extended through the south. Enthusiastic religious groups of Presbyterians and Baptists started congregations. Slaves also responded to the interest shown to them by preachers willing to preach to anyone willing to listen. African Americans started forming their own congregations based on the itinerant preaching that was part of the Great Awakening. Their start in the Great Awakening gives us some insight into why African-American churches have continued to include participation by the congregation in the preaching.

The End of the Great Awakening

Publicly, the Great Awakening ended by 1743. When Whitefield visited New England in 1745, controversies and theological arguments had dissolved the fresh devotion and readiness for commitment. A few ranting fanatics also had gone over the top and poisoned the air.

Among the faithful, the Great Awakening has lasted in one form or another to this day. It appears in the revivals of many Protestant churches, it appears in the style of camp meetings, it appears in many Baptist and Evangelical services, it certainly appears in many African-American churches.

The Rising Star of Methodism

Methodism had been born at England's Oxford University in the family feeling that nurtured George Whitefield, but it arrived in America after the Great Awakening. The first thing these original Methodists did—in Virginia—was to develop an American version of the itinerant preaching instituted by Charles Wesley and emphasized by George Whitefield and the other preachers of the Great Awakening. The Methodist circuit rider has become part of American lore.

Protestants Preparing for the American Revolution

Between 1607, when that first preacher worked with the men of Jamestown, through the brilliant writings of Jonathan Edwards, and into the men—and women—who created the United States, reformed thinking was shaping the national character. The uniting country grew together, infused with a sense of human evil and with God's terrifying love. Both religiously and psychologically, the colonists absorbed and transmitted to their children a need for order and system from England. The organizational arguments between colonies, religions, and divisions of religion caused the temper of the citizens to be argumentative—but got people into the habit of listening to the other side.

The Puritan idealized a commonwealth in which citizens are guided by the Scriptural God and can reach perfection—but not ruled directly by church leaders. This ideal, with its hints of a thousand-year reign of Christianity, has stayed in the imagination of Americans. There has existed down through the years this vague sense that America is a land where the millennial reign of Christ just might be realized.

An ecclesiastical structure of independent congregations, with one group of people beside one another, all guided lightly from above by an assembly of elected officials—this pattern fits easily into the state, regional, and federal system that the constitution of the United States assumes, embodies, and balances. The argument and framework stood in place as the colonies approached the Revolution.

The changeover of fervent, primitive Puritanism to a more flexible congregationalism was wrought as idealism met the real world, the harsh physical environment, and the practical needs of living alongside other people. Competition with other points of view, success in business, the generation gap, the passage of time—it took all of these ordinary human developments to temper the Puritan dream into a different, more practical vision. Strict Puritanism as a mental plan also met the emotions of the Great Awakening, to form a tension between mind and heart, a creative tension which helped form a new nation.

The people of this country started with a vision of achieving "the good life" guided and aided by the "creator" (identified in the Declaration of Independence). This vision is part and parcel of pursuing life, liberty, and happiness as rights "unalienable" to all. This vision is not the same vision as the Puritans had, but it is a direct descendent of it.

The Great Awakening—in many ways a reenactment for Americans of what the Reformation meant to the Catholic Church—keeps inspiring Protestantism as an effort to go back to the start, to the sources. But it has become more than that. That first Great Awakening, and its successor, the Second Great Awakening around 1803, exist in America today like the low-grade radiation said to be evidence of the Big Bang. Its democratic tang at the time, its inclusion of African Americans, its vision of destiny, its preaching style—these are American. That national experience created a common feeling based on a dream that threads America together, giving the Protestant religion here a peculiarly American flavor distinct from all its different European origins. The Great Awakening crystallized the "Americanization" of Protestantism.

The Least You Need to Know

◆ Colonists influenced by a Puritan outlook founded both Jamestown and Massachusetts Colonies, and thereby set the tone for much that has happened in America since.

◆ Their original goals included a desire to spread Christianity, to make money, and to expand England. In Massachusetts, they also dreamed of setting up a kingdom of God on earth.

◆ Such a variety of other immigrants to America came to the middle colonies that religious tolerance began to become normal.

◆ The Great Awakening of the 1740s describes a widespread movement toward religious conversion among the colonists. Emotional and profound, this Awakening helped shape the culture of America and developed patterns that led to the Revolutionary War.

The Reformation During and After the American Revolution

In This Chapter

- ◆ The Great Awakening prepares the colonies for the Revolution
- ◆ Who moves the bishop?
- ◆ Going into Revolution—the churches and the Founding Fathers
- ◆ Coming out of Revolution—a disunited state of Protestantism
- ◆ The Second Great Awakening
- ◆ The Protestant work ethic in America

Before the American Revolution of the 1770s and 1780s, several religious events stirred people up. Some were happenings, like the Great Awakening. Others were quarrels, like how to appoint Church of England bishops. In any case, although they were essentially religious, they prepared people to make political changes in their world. They became, in essence, skirmishes before the war broke out that would mark the political break with England and the formation of the new country, the United States.

The Great Awakening—What It Meant Before the American Revolution

First among these events was the Great Awakening and its profound impact on the colonists. It divided loyalties between old and new, it created new organizations, it affected slavery and allegiances, it left behind a huge train of consequences for virtually every colonist, who was often forced to choose for it or against it.

The Great Awakening involved a psychological dimension as well as a religious one. Part of a long off-and-on religious tradition in the Judeo-Christian community, worship and preaching might inspire what we call ecstasies, trances, prophecy, and tongues. Members experience powerful and often lasting psychological effects during one of these religious gatherings. Afterwards, commonly, they feel "committed to Christ" and are aware that their perception of the world has changed towards a more religious outlook.

First of all, ordinary men and women felt a psychological break. They could feel psychologically able to break with the larger communities to which they belonged and in which they had grown up into adulthood. If Anglicans chose to listen to a Methodist preacher, they did so, and there were no serious consequences. If Congregationalists, or even Puritans, responded to an effective Baptist minister, so be it. Doctrine did not rule their minds and hearts so much as that original impetus, the conversion experience, the need to commit oneself to Christ.

Besides the individual cause-and-effect, there was the public debate. During and after the Great Awakening, well-known preachers and theologians debated with each other respectfully as well as disrespectfully—but openly! Readers and listeners could judge for themselves about the doctrines and the practices of a church because the two sides printed and preached their arguments out there for everyone to see. The Great Awakening permitted you to have an emotional revolution against your "parental" authorities and against religious ideas and convictions that had nurtured you as a child. Psychologically, therefore, it did not require so horrible a step to consider political revolution against the mother country politically. A bold act is always easier the second time.

Another Matter—Where Do Bishops Come From?

Another explicit controversy involved the appointment of leaders for American churches—in particular, *bishops* for the Church of England and its offspring, the Congregationalists, Presbyterians, and Baptists. This hot religious quarrel in the early 1760s fanned the flames of political revolution.

You Can Look It Up

The word **bishop** comes from the Greek word for "overseer." It referred to the financial, pragmatic strawboss, or superintendent, over groups of people, although it also included a religious dimension. In many Christian churches, bishops appoint, ordain, and supervise the ministers of their church. In some churches, they are called "superintendents." They also are usually part of a synod, assembly, conference, or convention that makes general rules for the church. Their authority often extends into civil society because they speak authoritatively for the church or denomination. Only rarely does a bishop deviate from the doctrines of his or her community, and then that helps define the community. Bishops represent order and hierarchy—a connection with the larger Christian community and tradition.

Back in England, Americans knew, bishops of the Church of England fulfilled civil as well as religious obligations for the government. Bishops, for example, ordinarily sat in the House of Lords. Common lay folk and many a Protestant minister were afraid that appointments from England might—would—mean the loss of liberties, the suppression of practices America cherished. Sure, churches needed better, more defined leadership because they were growing so big, but the real question was: Who would pick the men for the office of bishop?

The established Church of England in America wrestled with a real quandary. Along with many other related churches they saw that this issue was part of the bigger picture, the whole relationship with England. As a matter of fact, the violently hated *Stamp Act of 1765* got specifically intertwined with this controversy.

If the mother country could decide to tax colonists with no representation, they could also decide to send bishops whose job it would be to make any errant colonial religions toe the line. English bishops would indoctrinate loyalty. They would emphasize the virtues of obedience. They would bring their own people from England into positions of authority here.

No, No! the colonists said to that. Most traditional Church of England members— Episcopalian/Anglicans—supported getting Bishops appointed by London; but Congregational-Presbyterian held joint annual conferences in the late 1760s and early 1770s to publicly resist such appointments.

You Can Look It Up

The **Stamp Act of 1765** imposed taxes on the colonies by way of a costly stamp, as we pay on cigarettes. This tax began without any say-so from the colonies. It became the object of much heated debate about the abuse of America by the mother country, people arguing that such a flow of cash from America demonstrated the tyranny of the king. The rhetoric got stronger and moved towards arguments for independence.

Would a Catholic Bishop in Quebec Mean Tyranny in the Thirteen Colonies?

In 1763, France gave Quebec to England. The population of Quebec was Catholic. Almost 200 Catholic priests lived and ministered there. And they needed a Catholic bishop.

Delicate negotiations between the papacy, the British government in Quebec, and Quebec's senior Catholic clergymen brought the consecration of a bishop there in 1766. Now, this happened despite the official position of London that Canada would be "Anglicized" in religion as well as everything else. London was saying one thing and doing another. They were fostering a Romanism that they said they were going to destroy.

You can imagine the feelings of Protestant North Americans! Like adding gasoline to the grill.

So How Did the Churches Approach the Revolution?

Someone has said that when the American Revolution broke out, about a third of the people did not want to break with England, about a third resolved to be independent, and about a third didn't care or could not make up their minds. And maybe this final third was the "largest" third!

In some ways, this triple division described the approach of the Protestant Churches to the Revolution.

You would not expect the Church of England, especially in the American South, to advocate breaking with the mother country, but they did in fact. Much leadership of the Revolution came from Church members in Virginia, and as a matter of fact, two-thirds of the signers of the Declaration of Independence belonged to the Church of England. In the northern colonies, which felt ties with Massachusetts, on the contrary, the majority of the members of the Church of England were alienated from the Puritan influences around them and opposed the Revolution. They considered themselves much more a "part" of England.

Perhaps the difference was that, in the north, Puritans generally thought of themselves as already detached from the established church, and their departure from England had been a matter of persecution. When the chance came to sever the ties politically as well—well, what difference does it make? As a matter of fact, Church of England members who felt strong ties to England were often submerged in the tide of Puritanism. Closer ties with England would mean a stronger church for them, more status and independence in the community. In any event, a significant number of Loyalist Church of England members fled to the safety of Canada during the War, a place not in revolt, and there they stayed. Church of England membership declined dramatically in Massachusetts because of the war.

The Church of England lost the war, along with its mother country. It emerged from the war severely reduced in numbers and significance. To show their opposition to England, its members would switch to some other religion—a change made easier by the Great Awakening earlier in the century.

Puritans—actually by now the term Puritant meant Puritan descendants of the Calvinist or Reformed churches—generally supported the Revolution. Their basic attitude stressed a kind of independence of spirit that would resist tyranny. John Locke, the Calvinist English philosopher, had also adduced some principles which guided American minds toward revolution and a system of checks and balances.

The Methodist Opinion

The Methodists, just starting to claim the minds and hearts of Americans, had some of the same ambiguity.

As the Great Awakening was tapering off in the South just before the Revolution, the Methodists were finally starting to make great headway because of their enthusiastic style of preaching and their general approach to religion.

Methodists did have a problem. The founder of Methodism, John Wesley, came out against the Revolution. This choice of his to remain faithful to an America united with England affected the Methodists psychologically, forcing them to factor religion into their political decisions. The war also cut them off from their source of ordained English ministers. As usual, American ingenuity stepped in. The religion did the same as the settlers had done. It continued to grow because the members found lay missionaries to do the job of "real" ministers.

What About Other Religions—The non-English Colonial Religions?

The other religions operating in the colonies also found themselves either splitting into Loyalist and Patriot factions or taking stands that brought further complications. Loyalists professed loyalty to the crown. Patriots chose independence for their American homeland (patria). The movie *The Patriot* reflects some of the ambiguity and changing sides that happened during the Revolution.

Lutherans, under the Father of American Lutheranism, Henry Melchior Mühlenberg, a German pietist who had migrated to Charleston, felt divided. The Church of England had helped Lutherans escape persecution by Puritans and other Calvinist religions. Mühlenberg appreciated that the wing of protection spread over the newly arrived Lutherans, and so he became a loyalist. His sons, strong men and powerful preachers, however, went the other way, and eventually led the majority of Lutherans to support the Revolution. One of his sons was a general under George Washington, and another served significantly in the nascent government.

It should be noted that, once the Revolution was over, it became clear that Henry Mühlenberg's organization plans for local churches (which developed into greater local independence), his advocacy of "American" liturgies for Lutherans, and his general competence served as the solid foundation for American Lutheranism. Following his original work, it has become the fourth largest Protestant church in the United States. His careful notebooks have proved a treasure trove of history.

Going Deeper

Quakers, Moravians, and Mennonites were pacifists who came to this country. From their beginning in Europe, when their tradition focused on pacifism at a time of genuine religious wars, they have been misunderstood. Their quiet pietism, their preference of lifestyle over emphasis on doctrine, their simplified worship style—these have always inspired others and triggered hostilities.

Quakers, Mennonites, and other groups like them preached pacifist principles during the War in ways that upset both sides. To this day, the pacifist position is difficult to understand, and people outside this outlook tend to distrust and oppose any neutrality or pacifism as helpful to the other side. Opponents of these communities used bitter language, sometimes joined to military or mob action. People died—partly because of confusion. For example, the British drove a group of Ohio Indians, whom Moravian pacifists had converted, from their land. When they returned back home, a company of American militia slaughtered them.

Nonetheless, Quakers and their like opposed the Revolutionary War openly, and have continued to oppose war down through the centuries, including recent wars such as the Gulf War and the warfare involving Afghanistan. At that time, their resistance to war was seen as helping the other side, and they suffered persecution for their stance.

And How About Them Founding Fathers?

The religion of the Founding Fathers, Washington, Franklin, Adams, Jefferson, Madison—still today remains an issue. Multiple biographies about them have portrayed their religious outlooks. We can say a few things about them in general and a few things in particular.

Protestantism affected them. The general culture was Protestant. Protestant ideas and practices that affected them, included …

- The notion of local self-government with a republican idea of checks and balances in the practice of power.
- The dream of establishing an ideal community—looking ahead and trying to make the world a better place.
- A readiness to change, adapting and flexing principles to fit new situations, and listening to one's opponents to find a common ground.
- A willingness to break with the structure that had guided them since childhood.

All of the Founding Fathers, with their often very strong-minded wives, brought a sense of history, literature, and awareness of the future from a generally Protestant background.

People You Should Know

George Washington, the commander-in-chief of the Revolutionary Army and our first President, was a quiet, disciplined man, wealthy with slaves and a large plantation, who practiced his Church of England heritage as steadily, seriously, and observantly as he did everything else in his well-ordered life.

John Adams and his family were solidly Protestant Bible-readers; he once said that "the Bible contains more of my little philosophy than all the libraries I have seen."

Benjamin Franklin, publicly an agnostic with an earned reputation for womanizing, maintained a serious, respectful friendship with George Whitefield, the great preacher, all his life.

Thomas Jefferson, the most serious thinker among them, was labeled an atheist during a presidential race, but there were many charges, some of them true, some not. He wrote his book on Jesus to sort out his religious views, but did not publish the book, probably because he did not truly reach final conclusions.

George Washington, a church-going Church of England member, seemed unaware of the Great Awakening and showed little need to integrate his public life with religion, public or private. He went to church regularly in Alexandria. He kneeled in prayer at Valley Forge, according to the legend. He was sincerely religious and made reference to God. Nevertheless, Washington apparently did not closely connect any of his religious convictions with his political and military principles.

Other main leaders—John Adams, Benjamin Franklin, Thomas Jefferson—all displayed a somewhat distant relationship between church and state. They practiced what they preached about separation of church and state, each in his own way.

Their personal views on religion, on the Bible and the sinfulness of men, and on organizational issues reflect, but do not equal, the general Protestant attitudes of the time. These men all read their Bible and knew it well because of their education in colleges, but they interpreted what they read as humanitarian and cultural, as moral guidance and suggestions—rather than normative. Virtually all of them would have seen in Jesus a good, very good, man who had offered helpful observations. Thomas Jefferson, called an atheist by his opponents, did write a life of Jesus, unpublished in his lifetime. The book portrays Jesus as a good man, minus the miracles and divinity.

Nonetheless, the larger vistas of Protestant culture influenced what the Founding Fathers wrote and what they did. The popular emphasis on democracy and the value of the individual connected the colonists to Protestantism's fierce determination to resist autocracy and papal authority. Their desire for and creation of a system of checks and balances had some roots in the Calvinistic view of the sinfulness, failures, and mistakes of human nature. Their balancing of state and federal government connected to their skepticism about the natural goodness of people, as well as the discussions they experienced in the working out of congregational government. The decision to use layers of administration on federal, regional, and state levels reflected some of the arguments earlier in the century about the organization of churches.

Rationalists and children of the Enlightenment as they were, the Founding Fathers translated the Protestant impact on them into the documents and decisions they made to start and organize the new nation. In turn, their fundamentals have translated into generations of freedom and rights.

Post-Revolution Protestantism—A Special Religious Crisis

After the Revolution, just like the nation itself, the churches found themselves in pieces needing to be put back together. The churches sought some fresh, true way that would be faithful to each European heritage, but recognize and acknowledge the developments that were shaping their American environment.

In particular, most large bodies of believers had had ties to England. They felt part of a tradition involving cultural, personal, and religious connections to people in England. Particularly in the case of the Church of England, the members had to find some way to express their affinity with the England of their past as well as their vision of the future for themselves. The other major churches faced some of the same problem, though, and each needed some redefining to decide exactly where they stood in relation to the past.

The Church of England faced several storms. Some members had fled to Canada, others joined other religions, still others just drifted away. High- and low-church members, i.e., those who advocated more Roman style ritual (high) and those who advocated more "Protestant" style preaching (low), had had a chasm between them to begin with. Several meetings after the war helped the members to find one another personally and religiously, to restart a sense of community, to start exploring what their future would be, as well as to take up the legal needs left over by the ravages of war.

Prime among their objectives was the reestablishment, in America, of an American hierarchy with an American bishop and archbishops and all that implied. The clergy could not receive consecration from any English bishop, because English bishops had taken an oath of allegiance to their monarch that prevented consecrating American bishops.

The Americans selected Samuel Seabury, a prominent missionary-minded clergyman, and managed to get some Scottish bishops with apostolic succession to consecrate him as the first "Episcopal" bishop in 1784. Renamed now the "Protestant Episcopal" church, the (former) Church of England met in convention in 1785 with more emphasis on "low-church" practices and lay people.

By 1789 the Episcopal Church possessed bishops, a constitution, a bicameral house for decision making, a fully functioning body of canons (rules), and a revised Book of Common Prayer. It had become no longer the Church of England, with its contempt for all the "lesser" churches dotting the American landscape, but an American church, one among others. Episcopalian canons included respect for other Christian religions and denominations; it allowed "full and equal liberty" for other Christian churches to practice their customs and principles.

The Methodists ended the war still without any ordained clergy and therefore without sacraments for themselves. Methodists had been participating in Church of England services. Through complicated political and theological maneuvers, John Wesley, the original founder of Methodism, ordained Dr. Thomas Coke as superintendent—the equivalent to his position as "presbyter" in the Church of England. Wesley also wrote up material American Methodists could use in their services and preaching. When the Americans got these, they reminded Wesley of the need in America for "consent of the governed," but then, the American Methodists accepted virtually everything Wesley had produced, with some additions.

The reorganized Methodist Church started, for all practical purposes at Christmas, 1784, with Thomas Coke and Francis Asbury, a faithful American leader, as superintendents. The habit of evangelism in this church fostered church growth, and Methodism had grown to 57,000 members by 1790. Coke and Asbury took to calling themselves bishops, to the consternation of John Wesley.

The other Protestant churches had grown much more American and independent than these offshoots of the Church of England. Some of the smaller reformed churches, such as the Lutherans, needed to learn English and started switching their worship services over to conform to the world around them. They also needed to cut official ties with their sponsoring churches in Europe. Presbyterians used the occasion to work out their own views on organization, with careful efforts to allow latitude to the local presbyteries while maintaining an over-all structure for the church as a whole.

One other feature of the American world as it adjusted after the Revolution involves a basic change of direction. The culture of the colonies had flourished in an atmosphere basically religious, with competitive Protestant communities fighting for allegiance on the premise that every American believed in God. The number of Jews, Catholics, and Native Americans who practiced their religions was inconsequential at the time, and atheism did not exist.

After the Revolution, however, forms of deism, agnosticism, and even atheism emerged as from caves to tempt the American citizen. The Revolution spawned ideas about religion that involved not a "reformation" of Christianity, but a rejection of it. Colleges and pamphlets, former ministers, and political leaders talked about religion as something of the past. It would take reason and nature—without God—to lead people into a better world, they said. Notice that the dream of a better world—a Protestant basic—endured while the means to achieve that dream underwent change.

The Second Great Awakening

In the 1790s, Protestantism woke up again.

A need presented itself—these dangers of wild rationalism and the threat of *deism* and what deism led to, such as the French Revolution. Those Protestant religions that had emphasized piety and conversion over doctrine and structure had been working alongside rationalists to create a United States independent of the English structures and its dead doctrines. These same religions now turned against their former partners, the rationalists. They joined the Methodists and other "preaching" evangelical churches to inaugurate a Second Great Awakening in the country.

You Can Look It Up

Deism refers to a belief in God. Period. No real doctrines or rituals beyond that. A deist knows that a god has created the world, but he or she does not need revelation, authority, the Bible or mysticism. A deist needs only common sense, reason, and maturity to know the existence of God. Deists are often humanitarians. Deist writers of the seventeenth and eighteenth centuries describe a god who started the universe, but has taken no further part in its workings.

Before discussing that, we need to focus on that other feature which affected both the growth and the dynamism of Protestantism in the late eighteenth and early nineteenth centuries—the millennial vision for America. The English Puritans had dreamed that God had destined America for greatness. They came to this country as to a Promised Land, hoping to shape it into a realm of God, a perfect community.

Many Protestant pulpits thundered with that vision of progressive, dedicated men creating a New World. This New World might involve the Second Coming of Christ, or it might be some form of heaven on earth. The old Puritan dream would not stay dead.

Rationalism—a belief in human reason as moral guide and as the basis for truth—continued to grow for the next century, and existed in a variety of forms both as part of religions and as opposed to religion. As part of religion, it gave birth to Universalism and some forms of Transcendentalism; as opposed to religion, it gave birth to faculties and colleges which became hotbeds of anti-religious thought. As mentioned early, its broader cultural outlook, called the Enlightenment, had a strong influence on American thinking.

The nation as a whole re-embraced its Protestant heritage at the beginning of the nineteenth century in the Second Great Awakening. As the century began, only about 10 percent of Americans belonged to a church of any kind. Leaders had been reorganizing remnants and relics of the great numbers, the thought and piety which no longer existed.

Leaders of the Protestant Churches both welcomed and were wary of a rising tide of Revivalism as the century turned. They feared excesses and they feared doctrinal watering-down of the old Calvinistic principles. Nonetheless, they welcomed the resurgence of interest and involvement as preachers stirred people more and more with their enthusiasm.

Then the Second Great Awakening came—revivals swept through the country, this time tempered by leaders who felt able to control the excesses, and who bent rules in accepting shifting of doctrinal ground. Numerous converts flocked to the Methodists and Baptists who were familiar with the evangelistic style of preaching and could use it so effectively. The older Congregationalists and Presbyterians shared the rising tide of converts with Methodists and the new Universalists.

The frontier moving westward offered a challenge to the churches. A Plan of Union between Congregationalists and Presbyterians aimed at sharing resources to evangelize the West (beyond the Appalachian Mountains) backfired for the Congregationalists. As it worked out, the Congregationalists lost some of their own members and most of the new converts to the Presbyterians.

Nonetheless, the resources from this Plan enabled the Great Awakening to spread significantly into Ohio and other regions considered the frontier at the time—between the Appalachian Mountains and the Mississippi River. The Camp Meetings of this Second Great Awakening became an almost constant feature of the moving frontier as it spread beyond the Northwest Territory into the Great Plains. These revivals and camp meetings continued for decades, improving to some extent the moral tone there, although occasionally there were abuses of the emotionalism that arose in them, as again, we note in the literature of the time.

The mid-1900s saw the connection of East and West. Protestantism was the dominant religion throughout this time, although there started to arrive much more significant numbers of poor Catholics from Ireland, fleeing the "Potato Famine," and Chinese and other Asiatics arriving on the West Coast to work on railroads and in California fields. These two groups presaged the coming of the immense variety of religions we see today—Hindu and Orthodox Christian, Moslem and Sikh, Vietnamese Catholics and Korean Baptists. A look at the diversity in ordinary, mid-western cities shows us the expansion of this nineteenth-century development.

The winning of the West involved Protestantism and the effects of the Reformation—positively and negatively. It was not simply a matter that Protestant Europeans shared the European disdain for "savages" and stepped all over the cultures of the Native Americans they found in the West. Nor is it the positive effort of the preacher to reach into western outposts and influence American customs as they spread with the white man. It is both richer and more complicated than a few simple sound bites about Protestantism and the winning of the West. Let us focus on what seems the single most important element, the Protestant work ethic, which played a considerable role in the motivation to expand westward, as well as in the inventiveness and courage Americans displayed in the process.

The Protestant Work Ethic and the Spread of the United States

In the early 1900s, a German sociologist, Max Weber, connected the rise of capitalism with what he called the Protestant Ethic. His point? That Calvinist ideas about work fostered capitalism, if it did not in fact create it. Weber maintained that the Reformation in general changed how people approach the value and meaning of work. He meant any kind of work—manual labor, literary work, or just earning a living.

In the medieval world of Roman Catholicism, people worked, Weber said, for obedience rather than for profit. Your job—as smith, miller, or farmer—carried on the family tradition rather than permitting any individual achievement. Your career was to continue the work of your father. You submitted to the order of society, which put each person into a life-task that fit like a cog into the machinery of life.

The Reformation changed all that, Weber said.

Luther started the change. He maintained that God called people to work, to a career, to meaningful labor. Because God was the one doing the call—not society nor the church—all work involved the grace of God and therefore was substantially of equal value. In the Middle Ages, for example, people thought that contemplation and prayer—a monk's work—possessed more value that manual labor—a farmer's work.

Calvin took the meaning of work a step further. Successful work, he said, indicated election. Idleness, failure at work, lack of diligence—these marked people not predestined for heaven. Success in life implied success in heaven. God's blessing was for this world and the next.

Calvinist thinkers nurtured this basic idea into a huge structure of interrelated ideas. Some preachers encouraged men to leave their families to make money—to make as much money as they could. If you wanted to change your job to get ahead, that initiative shows that you are among God's chosen. If you succeed and make gobs of money, then you better reinvest it so that you can make even more money—that enthusiasm for profit marks you as one of God's chosen people.

Serious dedication to a job well done became a mark of a good Calvinist, and in turn of Puritans. Puritan society valued the hard worker, the devoted businessman, the careful farmer as one of the elect. All society could see that your goodness was entwined with your success and the probability that you would be in heaven when you died.

Other Calvinists wanted to balance these views with other Christian ambitions. They would preach and write that the faithful had to avoid greed and avarice. They tried to keep the pursuit of profit on a spiritual plane, and advocated generosity and sharing with others. They wanted to remind the faithful to be successful, but not at the cost of covetousness and thievery, of hardness of heart and, well, simple greed.

In America, in particular, this Protestant work ethic seems to have unfolded, in time, into an American secular habit, an almost absent-minded routine. In this country, the Puritan who came here first showed a strong feature of serious and steady work competence. Their approach to work inspired their own people, but it also stirred competition from outsiders, who noticed their success and wanted to imitate it.

Capitalism, Calvinism, and the American Way

Down through the centuries, capitalism and the Protestant Reformation outside of America have seemed to show a continuous linkage. Protestant countries of central and northern Europe, using capitalism, seem to have prospered financially in ways that Catholic and non-Christian countries around the Mediterranean have not. It is not our concern to discuss whether other factors have been at work here.

The fact is that, in America, a Protestant-based sense of work and associated pursuit of profit seems to have become a secular value running like a strong electric current affecting the American way of life. Whether specifically religious or in the guise of assumed habit, this dedication to work has marked the United States since the beginning.

Benjamin Franklin, an agnostic, demonstrates this work ethic in such books as his *Autobiography* and *Poor Richard's Almanac*. In those books, readers find constant reminders of the need to keep busy, to seize opportunities for advancement—and to defer pleasure. Thomas Jefferson, another nonreligious person, exemplified the Protestant work ethic by his constant busyness as politician, writer, scientist, plantation owner, traveler, horticulturist, etc. The sober, serious George Washington personified the attitude a little more quietly and steadily. Later Americans who were not particularly Christian, like Emerson, continued to extol the virtues of serious, competent work both by their lives and in their writings.

These worldly men—not really Protestant, barely Christian, sometimes nonreligious—learned to like work almost for its own sake from the sober Puritans whose work ethic had shaped society a hundred years earlier.

Hard-Working Protestant Americans

Up till the mid-1800s, most colonists and then citizens farmed the land, or they had jobs tied to farming or other basic needs. In these circumstances, the Protestant work ethic meant simply another part of ordinary living—doing a good job. From Jamestown on, Americans had been taming a wilderness, kept food on the table, and got the job done partly to help establish the kingdom of God on earth. The rhythm of American labor joined the rhythm of nature's God—work and recreation or leisure succeeded one another like waves of the sea. People harvested and planted, then rested in between. The Sabbath came as a day of earned rest, after six full days of labor.

Work, Work, Work—In a Factory?

Then people got richer and more secure. Factories started up in the United States. People turned from farming to capitalism and entrepreneurship, just as the Protestant work ethic was turning into a nonreligious habit. Historians have identified the first real industrial town as Lowell, Massachusetts, right at the heart of the old Puritan work ethic.

To make their work meaningful, these factory workers could not count on the traditional Protestant work ethic. For these workers, success on the job could hardly have anything to do with salvation. No matter how religious they were personally, factory workers could not believe that working on an early "assembly line" had much to do with God at all.

Workers no longer found meaning in their particular jobs, much less any successful manual labor. Factory work took away responsibility for finishing a task. Work meant just something you did to earn a living. What you did to earn a living, in turn, just could not merit the name of a calling, and certainly not a calling by God. Nor did people earn psychological rewards for producing a well-made product, as they had when work involved skill with tools in or near your home. There was little psychological reward in being a gear in the factory machine.

It is at this juncture that professionals start disagreeing about the meaning and value of work to Protestant America and the secularizing tendencies that have followed after the ebbing of its core religious reward system. Is there work which takes people from God by its very nature—demeaning, repetitive, mechanical jobs that poorly educated, or migrant, workers are enslaved to?

The work ethic of the past has certainly drifted into our information age, and it has given us the modern instances of the workaholic, the working mom, the two-job parents, the impatient baby boomers, the internet entrepreneurs and stockbrokers eager for immediate returns on their efforts. Writers disagree on the good and bad of our present work habits, except for a general agreement that they derive, in America, from the meaning of work the Calvinistic Puritans practiced.

Protestantism and Slavery

Calvinistic thinking predisposed Americans to think in terms of the elect and the damned. Once you started with a belief in the predestination of the elect, you begin seeking to discover what are the "signs" of election. Are you "saved"? Success is one sign of salvation, and implies God's blessing. Failure implies the opposite, and the very fact of slavery in particular would suggest damnation to a Puritan.

A person is enslaved, strict Calvinism would say, because that person is not chosen for election; does not have God's blessing. You can justify slavery from the Bible easily—the curse of Ham, or the acceptance of slavery in the Letter to Philemon. You can, of course, argue against slavery from the same Bible, using different texts.

This oversimplification suggests a general and pervasive way Protestants (and most Christians, as a matter of fact) viewed the slavery situation. Most American Christians, north and south, accepted slavery as part of the American way of life, and justified it from the Bible. Quakers and Mennonites, along with individual New England Protestants, however, fought the "peculiar institution" of slavery in every way they could. Abolitionists likewise were squarely based in the Christian heritage, with ministers voicing strong opposition to slavery. Abolitionism included Transcendentalists and other non-Christian voices.

Martin Marty, a leading Protestant theologian today, has noted one peculiarity in this matter. In a population that was frequently apathetic about church-going before the Civil War, most people—no matter how secular they thought they were—found it important to turn to the Bible and the clergy for explanations to make up their minds about the morality of slavery. In other words, while people did not "belong to a church," they read their Bible, and felt it important to base their moral decisions on their interpretation of what it said to them.

Before the Civil War, the slavery issue sliced the main Protestant churches in two. The Southern Baptist Convention, for example, formed in 1845, in Augusta, Georgia. This southern half of the church advocated slavery and justified it in either the curse of Ham in the book of Genesis, or suggested that being black was the "sign of Cain." The preachers also used the theology of predestination to justify what they felt to be God's truth—that success in life marked those predestined for heaven, while a lower economic status, such as slavery, implied the opposite.

Going Deeper

A slave Baptist church in the South started around 1773. Founded near Silver Bluff, South Carolina, it grew slowly. After the Great Awakening, the religious spirit that had been developing in the fields and slave huts developed into congregations. Eventually the movement grew into the National Baptist Convention by joining several independent African-American Baptist churches into a larger unity.

The Silver Bluff church started and was served by slaves. In doctrine and practice, it was simply straightforward Baptist. The only real difference lay in race. Around 1895, this church congregation and its allies in the National Baptist Convention assumed the role of preparing "African Americans for full participation in the life of American democracy."

The northern half of the churches opposed slavery. Sometimes this meant an implied abolitionism, but, remember, the federal government, especially after the Dred Scott Decision, forced citizens to consider slaves as property. Abolitionist were considered law-breakers, violators of the secular covenant, or understanding, in society that slavery was to be tolerated in the South and ignored by the North. To the churches, this situation forced real decisions of conscience.

In some cases, the African-American churches have turned into some of the largest Protestant churches! From very humble beginnings, associated with the first Great Awakening, blacks, both slaves and free, began forming congregations into which they integrated elements of their African heritage. Their membership in these churches came to mean much more in their lives than religion did to their white counterparts.

Going Deeper

The Dred Scott decision by the Supreme Court in 1857 reminds us of the faults of democratic government. A slave, Dred Scott, was taken by his mistress to Illinois, a free state, where he lived for seven years and married. In time, his slavemaster's family brought him back to Missouri, a slave state. He sued for his freedom. The Court decided 1) that slaves were property, not human, and not—ever—capable of citizenship, and 2) the Missouri Compromise limiting the expansion of slavery was invalid.

This decision polarized the country, making Northerners fear the federal legal system that would eventually permit slavery throughout the country and awakening Southerners to the dangers of independence and abolitionists. It led directly to the Civil War.

African-American churches, of course, have become significant factors in social change. It was in many instances the black Baptist churches that fostered the Civil Rights movements of the 1960s. Today, it is the black preacher who often speaks the mind of African

Americans, who initiates controversial social stands, who appears in the news on major issues of the day. Black Protestant churches have become the cutting edge of our social conscience. Sometimes they sponsor Quixotic causes, and sometimes they effect major differences. There is no question of their importance.

The White Protestant Churches After the Civil War

In time, after the Civil War, most white Protestant churches which had split over slavery rejoined. These reunifications have taken a long time, and deep feelings of difference and mistrust still run through the rejoined denominations. You will find instances where the very conservative branches of the major denominations still want to stress traditional doctrine in such a way that it affects social issues. The divisions might have been effected legally, but psychological and historical differences still remain.

The Least You Need to Know

- The Great Awakening entertwined with other events to prepare the country for the American Revolution.
- During the Revolutionary War, the country and its Protestant religions split into many parts. After the War, most of the divisions ended, and the churches were stronger than ever.
- The Founding Fathers were not religious, but they were very much influenced by the Protestant culture of the colonies.
- A Second Great Awakening occurred in the early 1800s.
- The Protestant work ethic has become part of the American culture, and still functions, but without its religious basis.
- Slavery divided the Protestant churches of the United States before the Civil War, and the effects of that division have lasted.
- As religions, the predominately black sectors of the main Protestant denominations are very influential in the political, religious, and cultural spheres of the United States.

Chapter 23

Protestantism Today

In This Chapter

- Protestantism today—as good as it gets
- The good that the reformed outlook can do for society—as well as some of the dangers
- How America and democracy have mixed the Protestant dream with nonreligious aims of success
- The future of Protestantism

Through the nineteenth and twentieth centuries, reformed Protestantism has become many things to many people. Pretty much, you can find whatever you are looking for. You can find magnificent evangelism and heroic missionary work. You can find venal televangelism and nasty fights within a single church about the views of the minister. You can criticize a denomination's lack of doctrinal consistency, and you can praise its immense commitment to social concerns. Protestantism today is as good as it gets, and as bad as possible.

As Good As It Gets

The Protestant world is thriving. In America, you see mainline churches evangelizing as never before, modifying the world around them. Conservative Christian denominations are having significant impact on politics, shaping the policies of the White House and influencing the culture of the country; similar public policies are at work on the left for civil rights. The black communities, especially the Baptists, often are the only voices you hear raised to express the injustices, the oppression, and the continued prejudice tearing at the fabric of society.

To some, this is exactly what Protestantism is about—shaping the social environment through Scriptural reminders of the Creator's love for justice and humankind. It is the role of reformed religion to guide our political community in the right way to go. It came as little surprise when, after the tragic events of September 11, 2001, American citizens spontaneously organized prayer gatherings whose American form seemed basically Reformation Protestant. The spontaneity of this turn to God suggests the undercurrent of religion still pulsing through the veins of American citizens, after all these years.

People You Should Know

The Rev. Billy Graham stands out for his huge influence on the American religious, political, and cultural scene. Billy Graham early on showed power as a preacher in the Youth for Christ movement after World War II. In 1949, a widely-publicized tent crusade in Los Angeles brought him to the attention of the whole country. Since then, he has effectively continued the work of George Whitefield by preaching and evangelizing not only to his own religious associates, but, like Whitefield, attracting members of other religions. His involvement with politics is well-known, but the downfall of his friend Richard Nixon, and subsequent revelations, have humbled him and helped him to evolve towards a highly respected position as a speaker listened to when he addresses issues of arms control, world peace, and religious tolerance.

In the global picture, Protestants are evangelizing effectively throughout the world, with clearly positive effects in places like Central and South America, Asia, and Africa. They have been at it, in most cases, for a century or more. Because of that length of time, missionaries approach their evangelizing more wisely, without the attitude that skin color implies a lesser culture—much less that the missionaries are confronting "savages." No longer does Protestantism simply equal "whiteness," as it did for so many centuries.

Missionaries—and martyrs—dot the landscape of the world as European and American Protestantism reaches out as never before to evangelize the rest of the world. Evangelization shows a healthy awareness of local culture. In the process, missionaries have learned to incorporate and adapt, and missionaries use sophisticated modern techniques to touch the lives of people they want to reach.

Protestant worship services generally seem to convey creativity, honesty and a healthy dose of *ecumenism*. Randomly attending a First Lutheran service in Bloomington, Illinois, or a Westminster Presbyterian service in Dayton, Ohio, you are met with warmth and friendliness by members and pastor alike. People welcome strangers. You find woven into the Sunday morning services arrangements for a religious education of children that is nicely suited to them. As a visitor, you find beauty in the choir and thoughtfulness in the sermon.

Less of an anecdote, the public world we hear and see fills our minds with Protestant music and news. Gospel and Christian music floods out into the entertainment world, and subcategories of religious music "climb the charts." Radio stations and TV channels focus on Christ; preachers like Billy Graham have reached millions with their message, not to mention the hundreds, if not thousands, of radio and TV ministers reaching out to unseen congregations. That reveals only a public and publicized observation. Much Sunday preaching seems to have returned to a Scriptural, i.e., Protestant, core.

> **You Can Look It Up**
>
> **Ecumenism** refers to the effort on the part of mainline Protestant churches as well as Roman Catholicism and Orthodox churches to find common ground, or a unity, or at least mutual acceptance. The success of ecumenical measures is often measured by the amount of "intercommunion" between or among the participating churches. Participants find many interrelated issues of history, faith, culture, and interpretations involved in ecumenical discussions.

Worship services themselves seem less structured by mechanical "traditions," less preacher-oriented, and more "Christian." Commonly, reflective Christians join the preacher for a discussion afterwards, or later in the week, about the topic of the sermon.

Although Protestants have for some time worked on what worship means, some scholars point to the Vatican changes in Catholic liturgy as spilling over into Protestant interest. These days, Protestants and Catholics often share the same Sunday lectionary of Bible readings, and this practice has enabled preachers to focus on Scripture and to share ecumenical worship.

Finally, writers note that the pervasive Protestantism that has spread through the Western world and is evangelizing elsewhere has come to seem more generally "Christian" and less "denominational." than what it was in the past. Protestant public discussions focus not on how to divide one Protestant doctrine from the other, as they have so often in history. No, Protestant preaching seems more positive, preaching Christ against materialism and paganism in our culture, against personal evil and failure as seen from a Judeo-Christian heritage.

The Negatives

Reformation Protestantism does have problems, genuine and deep ones. As is true of so many cultural and religious issues, these problems receive significant publicity and controversy in the United States.

The Loss of Members

No matter how vibrant the preaching, no matter how caring the members, no matter how involved the social committees, no matter how saintly the leadership, no matter how effective in public life a church is—membership in the churches is decreasing. In late 2001, the Presbynet internet site listed some statistics:

◆ Formal church membership shrank by 10 percent between the 1960s and 1990s.

◆ Half of America's churches have fewer than 75 members.

◆ These churches are dying at the rate of 50 every week in America.

The Division of Race

The racial issue continues to plague American Protestant churches. Dr. Martin Luther King Jr. once remarked that the greatest racial divide in this country happens at 11:00 on Sunday mornings. The race division is very obvious, not simply when you observe membership in the denominations, conventions, churches, and synod. There you find black versions of white churches virtually side by side in the same community.

> **Going Deeper**
>
> According to Garland Hunt in *The Mandate: A Call to Biblical Unity,* "American society is growing more integrated and racial groups work and play side-by-side more than ever before, yet hidden behind this facade of coexistence lies a history of turmoil, reflecting the reality that becoming integrated does not necessarily imply that racial groups have become reconciled."

The historical growth of the churches has caused the black and white churches to start separately and continue apart, as two opposing branches of the single tree. For the foreseeable future, we cannot seem to find a means to reverse this trend. Efforts are happening, initiated by African Americans as well as whites, but the larger picture maintains the separateness of the churches.

African-American churches and white churches have some significant differences, even within the same historical Protestant tradition. Styles of worship, the way fundamental beliefs are stated, the roles of the minister and church offices—these appear very differently in African-American Protestant churches than in their corresponding white congregations.

You can find integrated churches, outstanding congregations who work effectively and publicly. You can find well-publicized efforts to unite churches, to cross over with visits, common services, and common social efforts. But the very publication of these efforts often highlights their more general absence.

In a final outlook on the racial issue in the American churches, it could be said that there exist hopeful signs for the future, and genuine effort to solve the problem.

Political Clout As a Two-Edged Sword

The political clout of conservative Protestant churches in the United States cuts both ways—like a two-edged sword.

For some citizens and church members, the religious involvement by conservative Christian churches in the late twentieth century implies a mixing of church and state seen as un-healthy for the body politic. As in the case of the election of the Catholic John F. Kennedy, people in the street and in the pew fear a return to some forms of church control of the state.

A significant number of individuals and groups fear that a powerful religion influence in government might cause repressive influence on civil rights, civil liberties, and human cre-ativity. Law courts keep deciding about the placing of the Ten Commandments and nativity scenes on courthouse yards, about prayer before football games and at graduations, about biblical study groups using public schools, and similar issues where the "separation of church and state" is hotly argued and defined with increasing fineness.

Even as African-American churches foster civil rights, so their opposite numbers at times appear to de-foster them, with hints of old-time Protestant religion reestablishing a white majority that is much more cultural than religious.

Protestant leaders like Pat Robertson, the Rev. Al Sharpton, or Franklin Graham (Billy Graham's son and successor) receive publicity for preaching positions that sometimes appear extreme or harmful to ecumenism or evangelization. Perhaps that result remains meaningless to the preachers, but to many these pronouncements do not echo the major-ity of Protestants or their church in this country. The perception persists that the speaker is stating a secular point of view vaguely understood as a religious position or doctrine. Sometimes it is a matter of how the doctrine is presented.

The Divisions in Protestantism

The divisions in Protestantism also continue to be a scandal for many. For some, this divisiveness destroys the Biblical expectation of "one Lord, one faith, one baptism." Nonetheless, this divisiveness has pestered the Christian Church from its very beginning, as Jews and Christians debated their differences. Perhaps division as scandalous does not mean that it is an error or defect, but simply a condition.

An even greater concern related to this arises when false prophets are perceived as "Protestants"—leaders such as James Jones who engineered the self-destruction at Jonestown and David Koresh who led his Branch Davidians into such an untenable condition. Most people saw them as generic "Protestants," even though their sects were purely American creations, and not truly from the long tradition of the Reformation. The old traditions become tarred with bad publicity from similar-looking cults and sects. A charismatic leader or preacher may or may not be a true prophet.

A number of other issues bother Reformation Protestantism both in the United States and in the world.

One of these continues to be the role of women in the church. Can they take offices in the church, and which ones? The Bible has clearly identified males as public leaders of the early Christian church, but has included in certain ways significant women, including Mary, the mother of Jesus, the women who bore witness to the resurrection, and various individuals named in Acts and the letters of the New Testament. These days, following various cultural shifts, the Christian church is evaluating its complex stance on this matter.

Some Representative Protestants Today

As we look out at the world of Protestantism today, we see a mighty sea of religious folks, of immense diversity in belief, practices, involvement, creativity, sharing and structure. It is impossible to discuss them all. Impossible. Only by trying to examine a few threads can we get some idea of the whole cloth.

Lutherans Today

Before 1918, some 150 distinct Lutheran bodies dotted the American landscape. Lutherans today form a much smaller family of churches, based loosely on national origins, but also concerned with theology. In the United States two major groups—the Evangelical Lutheran Church of America (ELCA), and The Lutheran Church—Missouri Synod (LCMS) hold most of American Lutherans. In the rest of the world, the Lutherans have a wide variety of standings. In Denmark, for example, they are still the established church.

The Lutheran churches in America have embarked on a course of ecumenism. Besides joining with other Lutheran groups, the evangelical wing, in the late 1990s, has made agreements on full communion with the Presbyterian Church (USA), the United Church of Christ, and the Reformed Church in America, as well as the Episcopal church and the Moravian church.

Presbyterians

The Presbyterians comprise a complex grouping of about nine major organizations that claim to be Presbyterian. These include the Presbyterian Church in America (PCA), Presbyterian Church (USA), the Cumberland Presbyterian Church (which began with the Great Revival of 1800, the Second Great Awakening), The Presbyterian Reformed Church, New Covenant, etc. A number of recent churches have pressed for more involvement of gays, lesbians, and transgendered people (more Light Presbyterians).

The Presbyterians have long involved themselves in mission work in Asia, China (when they could), Japan, and Korea and with Asian immigrants in North America. Both North America and these Asian countries support many Presbyterian churches of long standing. It is difficult to get a handle on all the far-flung work of all the various Presbyterians missions, but they continue to do substantial missionary work throughout the world.

Christian Reformed

It is difficult to single out from the vast network and mosaic interweavings of churches what still remains of the great Calvinist, Arminian, and Presbyterian tradition.

Let's take one example, The Dutch Reformed Church. The Reformed Church in America was formed in the colonial period by trueblue Dutch reformed immigrants who clung to their Heidelberg Catechism down through the years. They resisted the approach of the Great Awakenings. They emphasized doctrine and sober worship; they maintained their own schools and Dutch culture as much as they could.

Eventually, they became the Christian Reformed Church (CRC), and in the process, grew more towards confronting the issues of modern America. They have had some major influences in Canada as well as publishing in Michigan, in particular, the William B. Eerdmans Publishing Company. It seems this particular church has managed a careful balance of holding on to cherished tradition in a quickly changing world.

The African-American Churches

The large Baptist and Methodist denominations of African Americans have a significant history. Out of slavery, they devised shrewd and effective means of education and self-improvement through the churches that they either joined or formed. The white reformed churches certainly did not integrate them. On the contrary, slaves might accompany the master's family to church, but commonly the slaves went to a separate part of the church, such as the balcony.

As often as not, slaves and former slaves learned to use the religious traditions permitted to them to get around oppression and white efforts to "keep them in their place." Negro

Spirituals are famous for their double meanings, using "freedom" and "Jordan" to refer as much to a spiritual hunger as for an application to their American condition.

They also used worship services to create and recreate forms of worship as expressions of a unique history and heritage. These modes of expression have been a means of preserving their own history of salvation as a parallel to church and Bible history. In turn, these have influenced other congregations as well as popular entertainment.

It is perhaps this history of using the church for "other ends" that has made the African-American versions of the reformed churches so involved, so effective and so determined in political matters. The Baptist ministers Dr. Martin Luther King Jr. and the Rev. Jesse Jackson exemplify this concentration of black ministers on social issues.

How Evangelicals and Fundamentalists Have Been Shaped by the Reformation

In the United States, the most public religions at the turn of the twenty-first century are the evangelical and fundamentalist ones. There seem to be two elements in this development: first leadership and then effectiveness in touching the minds and hearts of other Americans.

The Reverend Billy Graham stands clearly at the head of this development both because of his personal charisma and because he has orchestrated so well the Christians who have followed him. What is not well known is that he has linked himself to the Reformation, joining the Southern Baptist church and regularly worshiping with Presbyterians, two mainline churches with their roots in the sixteenth and seventeenth century.

Billy Graham, like other evangelists, has the savvy to use modern means of communication. Modern evangelists use radio networks, the internet, televangelism, schools like Oral Roberts University or Regent University to expand their ministry. These preachers have not abandoned old-fashioned revivals. They have clearly modernized, with sophistication, the methods of the American Great Awakenings. And they have concerned themselves with continuing their ministry of evangelization by instituting these schools and large foundations.

People You Should Know

Two of the most prominent modern theologians, Reinhold Niebuhr and his brother H. Richard Niebuhr, were ordained in the Evangelical and Reformed Church. Their thinking—far more liberal and social-minded than is common among both evangelicals and Reformed churches—has helped shape the religious world today. They retained old efforts to have the religious mind meet the civil government, but in ways they think would make secular power more responsive to the will of God. They articulated the fact that liberals as well as many conservatives still dream of perfecting God's world on earth.

Look carefully and you see that American politicians still nurture a dream of a society formed with Christian ideals and Christian social harmony—from a very Protestant root-edness many of them might deny. These leaders would achieve this dream with certain old economic and political motives transformed into a worldly, even materialistic, pursuit, unaware of the religious origins that started that pursuit in the first place.

Today, Protestantism, the Great Wellspring of the sixteenth century, continues to flow into American lives. It is part of the purpose of this *Complete Idiot's Guide* to show that the Protestant Reformation back then—five hundred years ago—has caused us to be the way we live today. Partly. The Reformation is not the whole story. Protestantism does not explain everything. It does, though, give us some self-knowledge, and that self-knowledge offers guidelines for our future as a country, as a culture—and, sometimes, as individuals.

In this book we have looked at many people and much history. We have seen how different leaders preached basic ideas. Then their followers tried to put those ideas into practice. These followers started calling themselves Lutherans and Calvinists.

Still other people took the currents that these ideas triggered in the community. They added more practices, motives and habits, they cultivated fresh corrections in the face of tribulations, they went in new directions necessary to adapt to changing times. All of this vast current developed then even further until they became this major change in the direction of the community that calls itself Christian.

Building a Big Thing—A Bridge or a Church

Building elements or wings of the Christian Church has resembled building a bridge.

You make plans. You see how others did it. You redraw your plans to correct mistakes. You put down the bases. You start upwards and reach out. The span starts to appear. You add some more strength and some more airy steel threads. More and more of the bridge appears and you can get to the other side. But it is not finished. Roadways and walkways and more strong pieces have to fit in. Along the way, you find flaws and fix them. You make mistakes and go back and do it right. If it is a huge bridge, people may die building it. If the project is done right, it proves to be a solid edifice that weather and time will not destroy.

The Reformation began as a call by honest, dedicated Christians wanting to examine afresh Christian commitment. Like all human endeavors—no matter how mixed with divine purpose—these original founders of Protestantism mixed personal motives with more public pursuits. Which is to say that from the distance of 500 years they appear as real people, not quite saints and not quite sinners—but both.

No matter their personal or public motives or success, they aimed to reform the way people lived their lives. But the bigger picture exceeded that aim, like a controlled fire that shifts into a great forest fire, or the way a baby always becomes more than the parents imagine.

The "original" Protestant leaders shared that one aim—to control their destiny, and to make other Christians aware that not the pope, but they themselves, were in charge of the future.

Evangelism

When Protestants evangelize, they succeed. When they fail to evangelize, and as they become more institutionalized—then something in Protestantism withers. Church history teaches this point. An obscure argument that erupted in the late 1850s between Methodists in northern New York defined the two directions that Protestantism is pulled—between religion as mere benevolence and religion as mere form. "What we (traditionalists) call religion they call fanaticism," B. T. Roberts wrote in 1856, "and what they denominate Christianity, we consider formalism." His group of "Old School Methodists" criticized the liberal direction of the church for substituting MERE good works for "repentance and faith in our Lord Jesus Christ." Some New School Methodists wanted to define the church simply as "benevolence" rather than "devotional." Mr. Roberts, on the contrary, wanted to define Methodism as Biblical, not just a "Wesleyan institution."

Protestantism tries to change the real world. As Pilgrims to Massachusetts or Presbyterians in China. As evangelists using technology or as workers under the Protestant ethic (seen in its religious form). Protestantism continues the dream of its founders—finding a world that is in a bad state and then reconnecting that "bad" or "sinful" state to a loving God's grace.

Going Deeper

Although Calvary Chapel is a modern ministry started in southern California, it speaks the language of traditional Calvinism. "Jesus, I know that I have sinned against You ... I am relying totally and only on You ... You are the only one who can save me ... show me how to live my life in a way that is right and pleasing to You." This ministry uses sophisticated electronic means to spread its message of the gospel. It emphasizes the King James Bible, and Bible study. It specifically confronts the historic debate between Calvinism and Arminianism, and attempts to get past it to the deeper truths of the Bible.

It is significant in our world that the fastest-growing elements of Protestantism are the Calvary Chapel, the Vineyard Christian Fellowship, and Hope Chapel. These congregations have generated more that 1,000 other congregations/communities. Why? Because, according to Charles Miller in Reinventing American Protestantism, they address felt issues of ordinary people—"how the sexes relate to each other, how to raise children in a violent society, and how to find love in a world that seems to value possessions over relationships." In other words, they are treating the experiences of daily life as the raw stuff for religious experience. Conservative they are, but they are open to repairing the defective cultural world they find. They require commitment to internal transformation rather than focusing on external change. But external change follows.

The Mixture of Religious Dream and Nonreligious Aims

This religious dream has become also a nonreligious one. Edges are blurred between Protestantism as a revolutionary mission to transform the world and a committed Americanism as a manifest destiny to "free," democratize, and uplift the rest of the (non-Western) world. Some modern thinkers suggest that the American dream and work ethic have simply replaced the religious view of the Western world. Religion is now irrelevant.

Protestantism's vision and version of Christianity did form a basis for America to think that its task is to fight for freedom and create democracies. Those American ideas did not come from thin air. On the other hand, the fact that slavery endured so long under the auspices of a "religious" South in the United States (with Biblical texts used to justify it) and that racism, an attenuated form of slavery, continues—this fact forms a constant reminder that the American Protestant vision arises from a limited, human point of view. The vision remains a flawed one needing constant prayer and constant returning to ever-deepening Christian sources for the whole picture. It needs prayerful people who experience Christ, who keep looking for God, who see past society and its deeply embedded traditions into the will of the father of Jesus.

Protestantism as a Source of Democracy—And the Future

In the Protestant dream, the leadership of priests, bishops, and popes stands diminished. Why? Because Protestantism has embedded individualism—with such beliefs as "private interpretation of Scripture"—into its whole interpretation of Christianity. Out of this dream has come the ambition to achieve some form of democracy for our world.

In Protestantism, the individual enjoys significantly more importance than in other Christian traditions. Individuality is opposed to a collective way of thinking, and in this tension, the Roman church and Orthodox branches of Christianity clearly tend towards "group think," towards a unity of thought, rather than a harmony of thinkers. This individualism is tested at times by Protestant preachers, charismatic leaders who claim the mantle of Protestantism, and yet lead their followers in an obedience exceeding that of popes. Preachers arise who may be unorthodox in suggesting their ideas, and time is needed to test whether they are harmonious with the Protestant tradition or not. Time tells whether they prove to be a John Wesley or a James Jones.

Nonetheless, Protestantism and democracy, at this time, seem intertwined. The religious element or dimension of democracy means religious people devote themselves to the community because of shared religious values—values that surpass what we see and feel and hear and touch. That religious basis requires renewal at times.

> **Protestant Pearls**
>
> "I accept this award today with an abiding faith in America and an audacious faith in the future of mankind. I refuse to accept the idea that the 'isness' of man's present nature makes him morally incapable of reaching up for the eternal 'oughtness' that forever confronts him. I refuse to accept the idea that man is mere flotsam and jetsam in the river of life unable to influence the unfolding of events which surround him."
>
> —Dr. Martin Luther King Jr., in his acceptance speech for the Nobel Peace Prize

What happens otherwise becomes a kind of "mobocracy," to use Thomas Jefferson's word. Anything goes. Majorities destroy minorities, instead of respecting them. Coalitions and gangs and committed cliques run everything. Think about the McCarthyism of the 1950s, the isolationism and anti-Semitism of the 1930s. These deviations from democracy echo the deviations from Christianity, as people convinced they are "right" attempt to create a better world for the rest of us.

The democratic American dream as a development of the Protestant aim to make the world a better place needs a constant "revival" of committed Christians to maintain its balance, its course, and its truth. As long as Christianity remains an ingredient of the democratic ideal, democracy keeps its self-correcting power; once it loses that ingredient, democracy loses its roots and becomes something else, something worse, like a cake without flour, a soup without water.

The Future of Protestantism

Protestants redefined the world as future. The "catholic" (or majority) Christian community had come to think of heaven as what happened after death when you went "into the sky," and therefore considered indulgences, canonized saints, images of saints, the grace of the sacraments, and so on as important. But the Protestants appeared and protested that we can make a difference in this world, that the kingdom of heaven is a dimension of earth, a "now" that we need to deal with because we are earthy, sinful flesh—and our world needs "now" an intrusion of the grace of God. This now means "I" am important—not with pride and independence, but with responsibility and commitment to Christ.

It is this confidence that our salvation is entirely God's doing from start to finish that enabled the reformers and later Protestants to achieve so much in this world because they were sure of the next. The results remain today and will surely impact our future for the good.

The Least You Need to Know

- Protestantism today is seen as flourishing and vibrant with life. It has overcome many of its historical flaws and is having a great impact on the world.

- Protestantism today is seen as dying, losing members and split by racial, political, and denominational issues.

- Protestants representative of the state of the Reformation today show a tendency towards ecumenical success, a tendency to ally or join with other communions toward a larger unity of Christian religion.

- Evangelism and fundamentalism are extremely involved with the American political scene, for better and worse.

- The future of Protestantism depends on maintaining the roots found in Martin Luther and the reformers of earlier days, especially the "this world" elements of faith, the need for constant evangelization, and the focus on the Bible. All three of these have created—and become entangled with—the American and democratic dream of shaping the future.

Martin Luther's 95 Theses

As you recall from the chapter, "It All Started Over Indulgences" Martin Luther nailed a summary of his initial thoughts regarding that and other subjects on the door of Wittenberg Cathedral in 1517. Following is the content in its entirety.

DISPUTATION OF DOCTOR MARTIN LUTHER ON THE POWER AND EFFICACY OF INDULGENCES OCTOBER 31, 1517

Out of love for the truth and the desire to bring it to light, the following propositions will be discussed at Wittenberg, under the presidency of the Reverend Father Martin Luther, Master of Arts and of Sacred Theology, and Lecturer in Ordinary on the same at that place. Wherefore he requests that those who are unable to be present and debate orally with us, may do so by letter. In the Name our Lord Jesus Christ. Amen.

1. Our Lord and Master Jesus Christ, when He said Poenitentiam agite, willed that the whole life of believers should be repentance.

2. This word cannot be understood to mean sacramental penance, i.e., confession and satisfaction, which is administered by the priests.

3. Yet it means not inward repentance only; nay, there is no inward repentance which does not outwardly work divers mortifications of the flesh.

4. The penalty [of sin], therefore, continues so long as hatred of self continues; for this is the true inward repentance, and continues until our entrance into the kingdom of heaven.

5. The pope does not intend to remit, and cannot remit any penalties other than those which he has imposed either by his own authority or by that of the Canons.

6. The pope cannot remit any guilt, except by declaring that it has been remitted by God and by assenting to God's remission; though, to be sure, he may grant remission in cases reserved to his judgment. If his right to grant remission in such cases were despised, the guilt would remain entirely unforgiven.

7. God remits guilt to no one whom He does not, at the same time, humble in all things and bring into subjection to His vicar, the priest.

8. The penitential canons are imposed only on the living, and, according to them, nothing should be imposed on the dying.

9. Therefore the Holy Spirit in the pope is kind to us, because in his decrees he always makes exception of the article of death and of necessity.

10. Ignorant and wicked are the doings of those priests who, in the case of the dying, reserve canonical penances for purgatory.

11. This changing of the canonical penalty to the penalty of purgatory is quite evidently one of the tares that were sown while the bishops slept.

12. In former times the canonical penalties were imposed not after, but before absolution, as tests of true contrition.

13. The dying are freed by death from all penalties; they are already dead to canonical rules, and have a right to be released from them.

14. The imperfect health [of soul], that is to say, the imperfect love, of the dying brings with it, of necessity, great fear; and the smaller the love, the greater is the fear.

15. This fear and horror is sufficient of itself alone (to say nothing of other things) to constitute the penalty of purgatory, since it is very near to the horror of despair.

16. Hell, purgatory, and heaven seem to differ as do despair, almost-despair, and the assurance of safety.

17. With souls in purgatory it seems necessary that horror should grow less and love increase.

18. It seems unproved, either by reason or Scripture, that they are outside the state of merit, that is to say, of increasing love.

19. Again, it seems unproved that they, or at least that all of them, are certain or assured of their own blessedness, though we may be quite certain of it.

20. Therefore by "full remission of all penalties" the pope means not actually "of all," but only of those imposed by himself.

21. Therefore those preachers of indulgences are in error, who say that by the pope's indulgences a man is freed from every penalty, and saved;

22. Whereas he remits to souls in purgatory no penalty which, according to the canons, they would have had to pay in this life.

23. If it is at all possible to grant to any one the remission of all penalties whatsoever, it is certain that this remission can be granted only to the most perfect, that is, to the very fewest.

24. It must needs be, therefore, that the greater part of the people are deceived by that indiscriminate and highsounding promise of release from penalty.

25. The power which the pope has, in a general way, over purgatory, is just like the power which any bishop or curate has, in a special way, within his own diocese or parish.

26. The pope does well when he grants remission to souls [in purgatory], not by the power of the keys (which he does not possess), but by way of intercession.

27. They preach only human doctrines who say that so soon as the penny jingles into the money-box, the soul flies out [of purgatory].

28. It is certain that when the penny jingles into the money-box, gain and avarice can be increased, but the result of the intercession of the Church is in the power of God alone.

29. Who knows whether all the souls in purgatory wish to be bought out of it, as in the legend of Sts. Severinus and Paschal.

30. No one is sure that his own contrition is sincere; much less that he has attained full remission.

31. Rare as is the man that is truly penitent, so rare is also the man who truly buys indulgences, i.e., such men are most rare.

32. They will be condemned eternally, together with their teachers, who believe themselves sure of their salvation because they have letters of pardon.

33. Men must be on their guard against those who say that the pope's pardons are that inestimable gift of God by which man is reconciled to Him;

34. For these "graces of pardon" concern only the penalties of sacramental satisfaction, and these are appointed by man.

35. They preach no Christian doctrine who teach that contrition is not necessary in those who intend to buy souls out of purgatory or to buy confessionalia.

36. Every truly repentant Christian has a right to full remission of penalty and guilt, even without letters of pardon.

37. Every true Christian, whether living or dead, has part in all the blessings of Christ and the Church; and this is granted him by God, even without letters of pardon.

38. Nevertheless, the remission and participation [in the blessings of the Church] which are granted by the pope are in no way to be despised, for they are, as I have said, the declaration of divine remission.

39. It is most difficult, even for the very keenest theologians, at one and the same time to commend to the people the abundance of pardons and [the need of] true contrition.

40. True contrition seeks and loves penalties, but liberal pardons only relax penalties and cause them to be hated, or at least, furnish an occasion [for hating them].

41. Apostolic pardons are to be preached with caution, lest the people may falsely think them preferable to other good works of love.

42. Christians are to be taught that the pope does not intend the buying of pardons to be compared in any way to works of mercy.

43. Christians are to be taught that he who gives to the poor or lends to the needy does a better work than buying pardons;

44. Because love grows by works of love, and man becomes better; but by pardons man does not grow better, only more free from penalty.

45. Christians are to be taught that he who sees a man in need, and passes him by, and gives [his money] for pardons, purchases not the indulgences of the pope, but the indignation of God.

46. Christians are to be taught that unless they have more than they need, they are bound to keep back what is necessary for their own families, and by no means to squander it on pardons.

47. Christians are to be taught that the buying of pardons is a matter of free will, and not of commandment.

48. Christians are to be taught that the pope, in granting pardons, needs, and therefore desires, their devout prayer for him more than the money they bring.

49. Christians are to be taught that the pope's pardons are useful, if they do not put their trust in them; but altogether harmful, if through them they lose their fear of God.

50. Christians are to be taught that if the pope knew the exactions of the pardon-preachers, he would rather that St. Peter's church should go to ashes, than that it should be built up with the skin, flesh and bones of his sheep.

51. Christians are to be taught that it would be the pope's wish, as it is his duty, to give of his own money to very many of those from whom certain hawkers of pardons cajole money, even though the church of St. Peter might have to be sold.

52. The assurance of salvation by letters of pardon is vain, even though the commissary, nay, even though the pope himself, were to stake his soul upon it.

53. They are enemies of Christ and of the pope, who bid the Word of God be altogether silent in some Churches, in order that pardons may be preached in others.

54. Injury is done the word of God when, in the same sermon, an equal or a longer time is spent on pardons than on this word.

55. It must be the intention of the pope that if pardons, which are a very small thing, are celebrated with one bell, with single processions and ceremonies, then the Gospel, which is the very greatest thing, should be preached with a hundred bells, a hundred processions, a hundred ceremonies.

56. The "treasures of the Church," out of which the pope grants indulgences, are not sufficiently named or known among the people of Christ.

57. That they are not temporal treasures is certainly evident, for many of the vendors do not pour out such treasures so easily, but only gather them.

58. Nor are they the merits of Christ and the Saints, for even without the pope, these always work grace for the inner man, and the cross, death, and hell for the outward man.

59. St. Lawrence said that the treasures of the Church were the Church's poor, but he spoke according to the usage of the word in his own time.

60. Without rashness we say that the keys of the Church, given by Christ's merit, are that treasure;

61. For it is clear that for the remission of penalties and of reserved cases, the power of the pope is of itself sufficient.

62. The true treasure of the Church is the Most Holy Gospel of the glory and the grace of God.

63. But this treasure is naturally most odious, for it makes the first to be last.

64. On the other hand, the treasure of indulgences is naturally most acceptable, for it makes the last to be first.

65. Therefore the treasures of the Gospel are nets with which they formerly were wont to fish for men of riches.

66. The treasures of the indulgences are nets with which they now fish for the riches of men.

67. The indulgences which the preachers cry as the "greatest graces" are known to be truly such, in so far as they promote gain.

68. Yet they are in truth the very smallest graces compared with the grace of God and the piety of the cross.

69. Bishops and curates are bound to admit the commissaries of apostolic pardons, with all reverence.

70. But still more are they bound to strain all their eyes and attend with all their ears, lest these men preach their own dreams instead of the commission of the pope.

71. He who speaks against the truth of apostolic pardons, let him be anathema and accursed!

72. But he who guards against the lust and license of the pardon-preachers, let him be blessed!

73. The pope justly thunders against those who, by any art, contrive the injury of the traffic in pardons.

74. But much more does he intend to thunder against those who use the pretext of pardons to contrive the injury of holy love and truth.

75. To think the papal pardons so great that they could absolve a man even if he had committed an impossible sin and violated the Mother of God—this is madness.

76. We say, on the contrary, that the papal pardons are not able to remove the very least of venial sins, so far as its guilt is concerned.

77. It is said that even St. Peter, if he were now pope, could not bestow greater graces; this is blasphemy against St. Peter and against the pope.

78. We say, on the contrary, that even the present pope, and any pope at all, has greater graces at his disposal; to wit, the Gospel, powers, gifts of healing, etc., as it is written in I Corinthians XII.

79. To say that the cross, emblazoned with the papal arms, which is set up [by the preachers of indulgences], is of equal worth with the cross of Christ, is blasphemy.

80. The bishops, curates and theologians who allow such talk to be spread among the people, will have an account to render.

81. This unbridled preaching of pardons makes it no easy matter, even for learned men, to rescue the reverence due to the pope from slander, or even from the shrewd questionings of the laity.

82. To wit: "Why does not the pope empty purgatory, for the sake of holy love and of the dire need of the souls that are there, if he redeems an infinite number of souls for the sake of miserable money with which to build a church? The former reasons would be most just; the latter is most trivial."

83. Again: "Why are mortuary and anniversary masses for the dead continued, and why does he not return or permit the withdrawal of the endowments founded on their behalf, since it is wrong to pray for the redeemed?"

84. Again: "What is this new piety of God and the pope, that for money they allow a man who is impious and their enemy to buy out of purgatory the pious soul of a friend of God, and do not rather, because of that pious and beloved soul's own need, free it for pure love's sake?"

85. Again: "Why are the penitential canons long since in actual fact and through disuse abrogated and dead, now satisfied by the granting of indulgences, as though they were still alive and in force?"

86. Again: "Why does not the pope, whose wealth is today greater than the riches of the richest, build just this one church of St. Peter with his own money, rather than with the money of poor believers?"

87. Again: "What is it that the pope remits, and what participation does he grant to those who, by perfect contrition, have a right to full remission and participation?"

88. Again: "What greater blessing could come to the Church than if the pope were to do a hundred times a day what he now does once, and bestow on every believer these remissions and participations?"

89. "Since the pope, by his pardons, seeks the salvation of souls rather than money, why does he suspend the indulgences and pardons granted heretofore, since these have equal efficacy?"

90. To repress these arguments and scruples of the laity by force alone, and not to resolve them by giving reasons, is to expose the Church and the pope to the ridicule of their enemies, and to make Christians unhappy.

91. If, therefore, pardons were preached according to the spirit and mind of the pope, all these doubts would be readily resolved; nay, they would not exist.

92. Away, then, with all those prophets who say to the people of Christ, "peace, peace," and there is no peace!

93. Blessed be all those prophets who say to the people of Christ, "cross, cross," and there is no cross!

94. Christians are to be exhorted that they be diligent in following Christ, their head, through penalties, deaths, and hell;

95. And thus be confident of entering into heaven rather through many tribulations, than through the assurance of peace.

Bibliography

Books

Boer, Harry R. *A Short History of the Early Church*. Grand Rapids, Michigan: William B. Eerdmans Publishing Company, 1976.

Dowley, Tim et. al. *Eerdmans' Handbook to the History of Christianity*. Grand Rapids, Michigan: WM. B. Eerdmans Publishing Company, 1977.

Gielow, Frederick John. *Popular Outline of Church History*. Cincinnati, Ohio: The Standard Publishing Company.

González, Justo L. *Church History, An Essential Guide*. Nashville: Abdington Press, 1996.

Grimm, Harold J. *The Reformation Era 1500–1650*. London: The Macmillan Company, Collier-Macmillan Ltd, 1970.

Hurlbut, Jesse Lyman. *The Story of the Christian Church*. Grand Rapids, Michigan: Zondervan Publishing House.

Stevenson, William. *The Story of the Reformation*. Richmond, Virginia: John Knox Press, 1959.

Todd, John M. *Reformation*. Garden City, New York: Doubleday & Company, Inc., 1971.

Treadgold, Donald W. *A History of Christianity*. Belmont, Massachusetts: Nordland Publishing Company, 1979.

Vos, Howard Frederic. *An Introduction to Church History*. Chicago, Illinois: Moody Press, 1984.

Walker, Williston. *Ten Epochs of Church History: The Reformation*. New York: Charles Scribner's Sons, 1901.

Walton, Robert C. *Chronological and Background Charts*. Grand Rapids, Michigan: Academie Books, Zondervan Publishing House, 1986.

Woodbridge, John D. *Great Leaders of the Christian Church*. Chicago: Moody Press, 1988.

Internet Resources

www.Encarta.msn.com

www.inlink.com

www.gty.org

www.reformation.org

www.geocities.com

http://mars.wnec.edu/~grempel/courses/wc2/lectures/luther.html

http://www.mb-soft.com/believe/text/lutheran.htm

http://www.acronet.net/~robokopp/bio/luthrbio.html

http://history.hanover.edu/early/prot.html

http://www.mun.ca/rels/hrollmann/reform/reform.html

http://www.newgenevacenter.org

http://www.mcauley.acu.edu.au/~yuri/ecc/mod3.html

http://www.elizabethi.org/elizabethanchurch/background.htm

http://www.harrisroxas.com/qha/

http://anabaptists.org/history/

http://www.clas.ufl.edu/users/gthursby/mys/whoswho.htm

http://history.hanover.edu/early/massacre.htm

http://www.studylight.org/his/ad/fbm/

http://ic.net/~erasmus/RAZ247.HTM

http://www.encyclopedia.com

http://www.historylearningsite.co.uk/thirty_years_war.htm

http://www.strategos.demon.co.uk/tywhome/index.htm

http://www.newadvent.org

Index

A

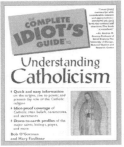

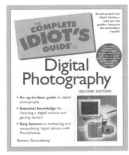
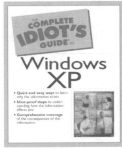